PORTFOLIO

WALL STREET VERSU

Gary Weiss is the author of *Born to Steal: When the Mafia Hit Wall Street.* He is an award-winning investigative journalist known for writing hard-hitting cover stories during his many years at *Business Week* on subjects from microcap fraud to manipulation of Treasury securities by Salomon Brothers. Weiss is a founding member of Project Klebnikov, a global media alliance investigating the July 2004 murder of Paul Klebnikov, editor in chief of the Russian edition of *Forbes* magazine, and other subjects. He lives in New York City.

WALL STREET

VERSUS

AMERICA

A MUCKRAKING LOOK AT THE THIEVES,
FAKERS, AND CHARLATANS WHO ARE
RIPPING YOU OFF

GARY WEISS

PORTFOLIO

For Anjali, with love

PORTFOLIO
Published by the Penguin Group
Penguin Group (USA) Inc., 375 Hudson Street, New York, New York 10014, U.S.A.
Penguin Group (Canada), 90 Eglinton Avenue East, Suite 700, Toronto, Ontario, Canada M4P 2Y3
(a division of Pearson Penguin Canada Inc.)
Penguin Books Ltd, 80 Strand, London WC2R 0RL, England
Penguin Ireland, 25 St Stephen's Green, Dublin 2, Ireland (a division of Penguin Books Ltd)
Penguin Group (Australia), 250 Camberwell Road, Camberwell, Victoria 3124, Australia
(a division of Pearson Australia Group Pty Ltd)
Penguin Books India Pvt Ltd, 11 Community Centre, Panchsheel Park, New Delhi – 110 017, India
Penguin Group (NZ), 67 Apollo Drive, Mairangi Bay, Auckland 1311, New Zealand
(a division of Pearson New Zealand Ltd)
Penguin Books (South Africa) (Pty) Ltd, 24 Sturdee Avenue, Rosebank, Johannesburg 2196, South Africa

Penguin Books Ltd, Registered Offices:
80 Strand, London WC2R 0RL, England

First published in the United States of America by Portfolio, a member of Penguin Group (USA) Inc. 2006
This paperback edition published 2007

1 3 5 7 9 10 8 6 4 2

THE LIBRARY OF CONGRESS HAS CATALOGED THE HARDCOVER EDITION AS FOLLOWS:

Weiss, Gary (Gary R.)
Wall Street versus America : the rampant greed and dishonesty that imperil your investments / Gary Weiss.
p.   cm.
Includes index.
ISBN 1-59184-094-5 (hc.)
ISBN 978-1-59184-163-0 (pbk.)
1. Securities fraud—United States. 2. Securities industry—United States. 3. New York Stock Exchange.
I. Title.
HV6769.W43 2006
364.16'3—dc22
2005055230

Printed in the United States of America
Set in Adobe Garamond
Designed by Elke Sigal

ACKNOWLEDGMENTS

T his book is in many respects a product of my two decades covering Wall Street, mostly at *Business Week* magazine. One of my colleagues once referred to what I have just described as providing a "front-row seat" to the pageantry of financial history. I am not so sure about that. Financial journalists occupy the bleachers, and sometimes we are in the restroom when the really good stuff is going on. Fortunately I had two fine bosses who were unsurpassed at grabbing journalists by the lapels and forcing us to cover the real stories—not just the ones that were on the agenda set by the powers of Wall Street. They guided coverage of finance and economics at *BW* with distinction for three decades, and their absence was felt for a long time thereafter.

I refer, of course, to Seymour Zucker, senior editor for finance and economics, and William Wolman, the chief economist. Both men are truly giants of journalism, and their willingness to challenge the conventional wisdom gave *BW* its edge for many years. Their retirement in 2001 was sorely regretted by anyone who cared about hard-hitting, tough journalism. Bill and Seymour were implacable foes of stodgy thinking, and fearless advocates for investigative reporting and negative stories in the face of what was, at times, formidable internal opposition. They provided courage, imagination, and backbone when it was most needed. When I resigned from *Business Week* in May 2004 to write this book, my decision to leave was not anywhere near as difficult a choice as it would have been a few years earlier, when these two men were overseeing our Wall Street coverage. This book is theirs as much as it is mine—though I must hasten to point out that neither of these gents read the manuscript, and I am sure they would give me an argument on some of it. Still, they must bear the burden of having taught me whatever I know about the Street.

Among the colleagues whom I left behind in the fast-changing masthead of *Business Week,* special thanks go to Mara DerHovanesian, Jeff Laderman, Tony Bianco, Emily Thornton, and . . . you know, I think I've gotten enough people in trouble.

It was only after I left *BW* in 2004 that I came to appreciate how much the McGraw-Hill Companies, which owns *BW,* cares for the welfare of its people even after they have moved on to other pursuits. My heartfelt thanks go to Kenneth M. Vittor, general counsel; Robert Pritchard; and, of course, the terrific Cal Mathis. My thanks also go to Devereux Chatillon and Robert Gifford.

At Portfolio, Adrian Zackheim believed in this project passionately from the beginning, and his guidance and wisdom kept it on track. Bernadette Malone was an enthusiastic and skillful editor of my raw and muddled prose. My thanks also to Gary Mailman of Herrick, Feinstein LLP and to copy editor Randee Marullo.

As always, Mort Janklow proved that he is an agent's agent, protecting my interests tirelessly and providing wise counsel in many areas.

Last but not least, my gratitude goes to my sources and friends, many on Wall Street, who, I hope, will still be speaking to me after this book is published. Apart from the ones named in this book, such as the courageous Rand Groves, the great Harry Strunk, and the fearless Floyd Schneider, they shall remain forever and, I am sure, gratefully anonymous.

CONTENTS

INTRODUCTION

THE BATTLE OF TRENTON

On August 20, 2004, a man by the name of Rand Groves walked into the Mercer County Courthouse in Trenton, New Jersey, on a task that just about any knowledgeable person would view as utterly futile. The legal system can produce miracles like Clarence Gideon, whose handwritten petition to the U.S. Supreme Court guaranteed the right to counsel for future generations. It can establish social policy, save lives, and send corporate executives to prison. It can restrain presidents and resolve age-old grievances. But there are certain things the legal system cannot do. Rand Groves was asking for too much.

The title of his lawsuit said it all: *Rand Groves v. Merrill Lynch Pierce Fenner & Smith Inc. and Llewellyn G. Ross and National Association of Securities Dealers Inc.* One man against the most powerful brokerage firm in the world and the primary regulatory organization for all of Wall Street. It was absurd, and not just because he didn't have a lawyer. Rand Groves was trying to get an American court in the year 2004 to reverse an unjust decision of a securities industry arbitration panel.

Such a thing could not be allowed to happen. It would be against all the principles of modern securities law.

In a 1987 United States Supreme Court ruling, *Shearson/American Express Inc. v. McMahon*, it became the law of the land that nothing that might come between a broker and his client would ever again be adjudicated by a judge and jury, as is theoretically guaranteed by the Seventh Amendment to the United States Constitution. The standard "arbitration clauses" in account documents, which most customers signed without even reading, took precedence over the Constitution. The *Shearson* ruling held that even cases of the most serious kind, alleging securities fraud, had to be batted out in closed-door arbitration proceedings.

Once that principle was established, it became a kind of holy thing to Wall Street and the two regulatory agencies that operate arbitration systems, the NASD and the New York Stock Exchange. Whenever anyone has sought to tamper with the arbitration system without the consent of Wall Street, as was recently attempted by the California state legislature, the Street has closed ranks and fought back with the unflinching support of the government agency that oversees the securities industry, the Securities and Exchange Commission.

Rand Groves was unlikely fodder for such a confrontation. He was a marketing consultant, fifty-two years old, an erect six-footer with graying sandy hair, a neat mustache, and steel-rimmed glasses. He had a wife, three children approaching college age, and a house in Princeton Junction, New Jersey. He had a night-school MBA and once worked for a major advertising agency.

Groves was the embodiment of a social phenomenon that goes by several names. The media calls it the Investor Class. George W. Bush calls the Rand Groveses of this country an Ownership Society. It is a slogan that resonates with the natural yearnings that people have nowadays for empowerment and control of their own financial destiny, their own retirement savings and healthcare costs, free of the heavy hand of government.

Groves used to feel that way. In fact, he still did as he cleared the metal detectors, checked his cell phone and took the elevator to the courtroom. It's hard to let go of fantasies.

In 1999, Groves performed marketing work for a couple of companies, both of which granted him a generous allotment of stock options. These were Internet companies, so the underlying stocks were worth a great deal of money by late 1999, $5 million or so, all on paper and carrying various kinds of restrictions and mumbo jumbo that Groves didn't entirely understand. His primary concern was that his entire financial well-being was tied up in two volatile Internet stocks. So he did what people do in such situations, which was to seek expert guidance to help him manage this theoretical onslaught of paper wealth.

Firms of standing and prestige stood ready to lend a hand, their offices friendly and welcoming. There was Goldman Sachs, the prestigious investment bank whose former CEO was now a senator from New Jersey. There was Morgan Stanley, whose name conjured up images of unimaginable, robber-baron-era wealth. In years to come its gently comical ménage à trois TV commercials would portray a firm whose brokers were so "unusually devoted to your dreams," so obsessively focused and involved "one client a time," that they became a kind of marital third wheel, cheering on the kids at football games and making vacation-home plans while gazing longingly at the receding tide.

One firm was already anchored in Groves's mind—the "King of the Brokers." Merrill Lynch's reputation was beyond reproach. Its treatment by the media was respectful, deferential. Its handling of the media was distant, correct. An invitation to its annual press dinner, at the Securities Industry Association annual meeting in Boca Raton, was highly coveted—a sign of status and acceptance by Wall Street's premier brokerage.

Merrill's public image, despite occasional but not disproportionate lumps during the analyst scandal of the new millennium, was essentially unblemished. Its advertising in the late 1990s was lofty in tone and content, establishing Merrill as a valued friend and advisor. Merrill took the position that people need to run their lives like a business, and that Merrill stood ready to provide expert assistance.

To Groves, these ads spoke directly to the heart. Every word resonated. Merrill employed "consultants," not brokers. They were there to "help," not sell. "They weren't in the brokerage business, they were in the wealth management business," Groves later recalled. One Merrill ad that sung out to him was published as an insert in the *New York Times Magazine* of April 25, 1999. "Your Life, Incorporated," it began. "Corporations like to refer to themselves as 'families.' Shouldn't it be the other way around?" The ad went on for several pages to describe its seven hundred analysts in twenty-six countries, "all linked to one account. Yours." It said that a Merrill Lynch FC, or Financial Consultant, is an "advocate in your corner, helping you create opportunities in every department of your financial life."

The last page contained a simple pledge: "We hold ourselves accountable for making suitable recommendations based upon your goals, risk preference and time horizon."

It was a long text ad, of the kind that companies reserved only for their smartest, most select, high-end customers. It was flattering, it pushed the right buttons, and it worked.

Groves was a marketing professional. He knew all about the "hidden persuaders," as the ad-biz critic and commentator Vance Packard called them when the mysterious power of advertising was being explored, like the nucleus of the atom, back in the fifties and sixties. Groves knew the hypnotic spell of advertising slogans . . . *Ban Takes the Worry out of Being Close* . . . *Silvikrin Puts the "Ooh" in Shampoo* . . . *Us Tarryton Smokers Would Rather Fight Than*

Switch . . . as they are drummed into our heads year after year. He knew Packard's writings and he was savvy to hype and image-management. Yet the Merrill ads had had their intended effect long before a handwritten note arrived in the mail from Llewellyn G. Ross, a Financial Consultant in the Private Client Group of Merrill's office in Lawrenceville, New Jersey, just outside Princeton.

Ross was dapper, gray without being grandfatherly, a Princeton man in his sixties. He was always impeccably dressed, and reminded Groves of the post–*Mission: Impossible* Peter Graves, serious and debonair. Ross was the head of a small marketing company before he joined Merrill. The two men had worked together briefly several years before. And now here he was, a financial expert, a late-career change that put him on the cutting edge. Groves was impressed. He did find it a little odd that a man with a marketing background was now an expert Financial Consultant, but he suppressed his doubts. Ross was with Merrill, and Merrill knew what it was doing. Groves opened his account in November 1999.

All of the above is pretty much agreed to by all the parties concerned (except that Merrill claims that Groves contacted Ross and not vice versa). From here on things get disputatious and sullen and prickly, which is not surprising considering that litigation ensued. What nobody denies is that Groves wound up losing his nest egg, though how that happened—whether the fault was Merrill's or Groves's or the unseen hand of the market or the malevolent karma of generations past—remains in dispute.

As Groves tells the story, Ross did not generate the expert advice that he had expected. A "financial plan," for which Groves paid $250, turned out to be boilerplate that didn't deal with his primary conundrum, which was that all his wealth was concentrated in two Internet stocks. In the first months of 2000 Internet stocks were not doing very well. The Internet bubble was ending, but that was not known at the time. There had been brief dips and corrections in the past, including a particularly ferocious one in late 1998, and in early 2000 there was no way of knowing for sure what was going on. The decline in Internet stocks seemed to many people to be a "blip," a "correction," a "buying opportunity," and not the rapids just upriver from the Horseshoe Falls.

Luckily, help was at hand. Ross, either at his own initiative or at Groves's urging—depending upon whose story you believe—consulted the best mind available on such matters. Merrill's in-house expert on all things Internet-related, the famed analyst Henry Blodget, was contacted for an opinion. What he actually said is in dispute. Blodget either indicated to Groves, through Ross, that Groves's main holding was unlikely to fall below ten dollars, or he offered no opinion, depending upon whose story you believe.

What no one disputes is that the blip turned into a belch that turned into outright, prolonged retching throughout 2000 and into the following year. By the end of 2000, Groves was transformed from a paper millionaire to a paper thousandaire with $53,000 in his account. By mid-2001 he was a hundredaire and then a nothingaire. It was all over. His paper windfall was gone, but not the tax bill it generated. Groves was broke.

In April 2002, Groves hired an attorney and filed a claim against Ross and Merrill, using the only remedy permitted by a standard clause in the account agreement that he had signed in 1999—an arbitration panel organized by NASD Dispute Resolution, Inc. His claim contended that Ross was inexperienced and not properly supervised, had failed to provide proper investment advice, and was therefore responsible for the disaster that ensued. He asked for $4.2 million in damages. Merrill and Ross, through their attorneys, denied all the allegations.

If one despises lawyers as so many people do, and is upset with the trend of what George W. Bush describes as "junk lawsuits," the Wall Street system of re-solving customer complaints is a dream. There are no junk lawsuits. In fact, as a result of the *Shearson* decision and several others, there are no lawsuits. Instead there is a dispute-disposal mechanism very much unique to Wall Street. Ordi-narily, arbitration involves bringing a quarrel to a neutral forum, such as the American Arbitration Association. Wall Street likes to keep things within the family. Its form of arbitration differs from ordinary arbitrations in small ways and large, none of which was apparent to Groves at the outset (not that it would have mattered if they had been apparent, as there wasn't a thing he could have done about it).

As in ordinary arbitrations, papers are exchanged, and they are much sim-pler and freer of the legalese and Latin expressions and attestations and other lawyer-speak nonsense that is so prevalent in courts today. Advocates of arbi-tration are particularly enthused about that, as well as that there are no costly pretrial depositions, in which both parties take down testimony from each other in advance of trial. This is done to assist in the calm and orderly weighing of the evidence, without surprise to either party. Groves felt that no surprises were likely in his case. It seemed pretty clear-cut to him. He liked the arbitration process—its simplicity, its no-nonsense approach to things.

Arbitration has the salutary effect of being an educational process for the laypeople who are caught up in it, and Groves was no exception. He learned some things he didn't know before.

For example, he learned that the Merrill Lynch "Private Client Group," which conjures up images of "private bankers" snifting brandy at the Club, was actually a name Merrill slapped on *all* its brokers. Wall Street firms rarely used the words *broker* and *stockbroker* anymore. They had long abandoned those terms in favor of the more soothing, more professional "financial consultant" or "financial advisor." By the late 1990s, the "B-word" (and, of course, the official term, "registered representative") was rarely to be found outside of legal papers and regulatory filings.

In replying to the allegations, Merrill Lynch tended to drift a bit from its advertising and portrayed Groves as an individual who didn't need much help at all from Merrill. As a matter of fact, anyone reading its reply might have gotten the impression that Merrill was a kind of deep-discount brokerage that just executed trades for customers who were in full command of all the finer points of investing. The firm pointed out that Groves's account was nondiscretionary, meaning that Groves called the shots, not his broker. Merrill's reply went on to say that Ross on several crucial occasions recommended that Groves sell his holdings before the roof fell in. That was quite the opposite of Groves's position, so it would be necessary for the arbitrators to listen carefully to the parties, weigh the evidence, and decide which of them—Groves or Ross—was telling the truth.

Groves read the legal paperwork with a growing anger. The denials, and the deviations from the truth as he had experienced it, annoyed him. So did the effort to skirt responsibility. As he saw it, he had relied on Ross and Merrill in very much the way a patient relies on his physician to care for his health. He would explain that to the arbitrators and they would understand, when the time came for the hearing. They would believe him.

After a leisurely procession of still more paperwork and routine delays, two years went by. A standard delay, similar to what Groves might have experienced in a New Jersey court, if not a bit longer. (The Securities Industry Association maintains that arbitration is "generally much swifter and more efficient than court proceedings," but plaintiff attorneys tend to dissent from that sentiment.) It was now early 2004, and Groves was feeling increasingly desperate. His entire financial destiny, the one he wanted to control, was tied up in all the wealth that had vanished in 2000 and 2001. The arbitration hearing was his only hope. He had every reason to expect that this was not a faint hope, if he happened to read the literature that the NASD generously provides litigants, lawyers, and pretty much anyone else even remotely interested.

According to the NASD, investors were winning "53% to 61% of their cases." This statistical encouragement evaporated when one considered that any award, even arbitrarily slashed in half or by two-thirds or nine-tenths, was considered a win for statistical purposes. Groves didn't know that. All he knew was that he was finally getting his day in "court." It wasn't a court, but that just seemed to be a minor detail.

The arbitration sessions, which took place during January and February 2004, were much more comfortable than a comparable court trial. Instead of a stuffy courthouse, they were held in the pleasant surroundings of the Crowne Plaza hotel in downtown Philadelphia. As is common in arbitrations, there was a lengthy hiatus between sessions, with three weeks separating the second and third day of hearings. Three arbitrators presided—one representing the securities industry and two members of the public. The latter's numerical domination of the panel is required by NASD procedures designed to ensure the public's confidence in the fairness of the arbitration process.

Arbitrator selection is where the Wall Street system really distinguishes— perhaps a better word might be *differentiates*—itself from both the court system and other forms of arbitration. In an ordinary court trial some pesky investor lawyer or judge would probably see to it that nobody with a Wall Street background comes within a hundred feet of the jury room. Or, more likely, the trial would be settled out of court because brokerages don't like having disputes resolved by juries of ordinary people who aren't smart enough to understand the nuances and peculiarities of the way the Street does business.

That potentially thorny problem does not exist in arbitrations run by the NASD or NYSE. Since one of the three arbitrators is always a person who knows Wall Street backward and forward, the panel is less likely to be swayed by sympathy or pro-investor prejudice, or get all weepy and idealistic and go off half-cocked like Henry Fonda in *Twelve Angry Men.*

In the case of *Groves v. Merrill,* the industry representative—the smart person who'd be sure that the rest of the panel had the right facts—was a very nice lady who was a branch manager from UBS Paine Webber. Groves remembered that UBS was deeply involved in the Wall Street research scandals—the epicenter of which was none other than Henry Blodget, the man who either advised Groves or did not (depending upon whose story you believe). Blodget had been splattered over the media for emails that differed in embarrassing ways from his public comments on Internet stocks.

Groves felt that the presence of this UBS lady constituted a conflict of interest. Tough. The UBS lady was on the panel whether he liked it or not. In a NASD arbitration, the parties pick panel members from lists compiled by the NASD. If both parties can't agree, the NASD picks the panel. The parties didn't agree, so the NASD picked the panel and the UBS lady was one of its picks, and that was that.

Think of how interesting litigation would be if all civil disputes were handled this way. Imagine taking a chiropractor to court for crushing your vertebrae into jelly, and a chiropractor *must* be on the jury. The rest of the jury consists of people selected by the American Chiropractic Association. Instead of a jury of six or twelve people, all fussing and arguing, this panel is a modern and streamlined three people, which for the sake of efficiency also doubles as the judge. To add closure to the matter (which any psychologist would tell you is desirable), its findings are as final as the Nuremberg Tribunals—except when they go against the Street, in which instances the cases are frequently dragged through the inefficient court system that securities firms abhor. To preserve the privacy of all concerned—or, if one is of a cynical bent, to make it harder for investor lawyers to build future cases—the proceedings are as firmly closed to the public as a prison tribunal at Guantánamo. Spectators, including the media, are forbidden. Except for the final decision, all the papers that go flying back and forth between the parties are kept under lock and key, and are more definitively exempt from public disclosure than personnel files of the CIA.

The chiropractor-juror in our hypothetical case may be a passionate believer in ridding the profession of people who turn vertebrae into jelly. Or maybe he's more concerned that malpractice premiums are increased by big-jury verdicts. Then, using his superior knowledge of the spine-crack and neck-twist and all the other arts of the adjustable couch, he knows just what to say to carry the day with his two other jurors in reaching their etched-in-granite decision.

The NASD and NYSE and SIA and every brokerage firm in the world would want me to underline at this point, so I will do so right now, that in Wall Street arbitrations, two of the three arbitrators are always members of the public. There you go—I've underlined it. Ordinary guys and gals like you and me, people off the street. Right? Well, not exactly. "Public arbitrators" are hardly rounded up at random at the Greyhound station. They're much nicer than that, much smarter. They're the kind of people you find on the boards of Gold Coast co-ops or waiting to tee off at golf clubs in Locust Valley. They tend to be older people, white-buck-shoe people, businesspeople, Caucasian people. You know, the kind of people who might remind you of the post–*Mission: Impossible* Peter Graves.

In the Groves arbitration, one of the two "public" members was just some ordinary guy you'd find walking down the street who happened to have worked for seven years as general counsel of an investment bank. That was a long time ago, back in the 1980s, so it was permitted by the rules. If this were a jury, he'd have been tossed out without so much as a second thought. As Groves was soon to discover, this was not an American courtroom, with all its untidiness, messiness—and ironclad rules of fairness.

Groves v. Merrill was a routine case. Both sides politely jousted. And then—the note.

Not long before the hearing, Groves's lawyer and Merrill provided the arbitrators with loose-leaf binders containing copies of relevant documentation. There it was. Ross had, very fortunately it seems, written a note to himself on his personal notepad stationery, dated February 17, 2000. It said as follows: "Called Rand Groves. Left message concerning NBCi, stock in a downtrend." NBCi was one of the Internet stocks that Groves owned, and which was about to go over the Horseshoe Falls.

This note substantiated Ross's position, which Groves denied, that he had warned Groves that the stock was looking mighty weak. There it was, in his legible handwriting on Merrill Lynch stationery, with an address in Princeton right on top. In a case that turned on the credibility of the parties, it was dynamite.

There was only one problem: Ross wasn't in Princeton in February 2000. He was in Lawrenceville. He moved to Princeton three months later. He couldn't have written a note on Princeton stationery in February 2000.

For the rest of his life, Groves will be able to recall with crystal clarity how his lawyer nailed Ross like E. G. Marshall in an old *Defenders* episode. It stands out in his mind how his lawyer went through his brokerage statements one after the other, had him read the address on each, and then the coup de grâce: The lawyer asked Ross if he wrote the note after he learned of the claim, and not in February 2000. The response, as recalled by Groves and his lawyer: Ross saying the magic, credibility-destroying word *yes*. The proceedings then adjourned for three weeks, and at the next session Ross denied that he had created the document after he had learned of the claim, and said he did not remember when it was written. But the damage had been done, as far as Groves and his lawyer were concerned.

The arbitration panel made its decision on March 4, 2004. On the following day, Martha Stewart was found guilty in the glitziest of the Wall Street scandal cases that Groves had been reading about. Tampering with evidence had been her downfall—changing a phone log to omit a warning about a stock declining. Obstruction of justice, they were calling it. Doing something wrong is bad enough, but lying about it always compounds the error. That's how things are in the American system of jurisprudence. It seemed to Groves that Ross had done something worse than altering a phone log. His broker had manufactured evidence as far as he was concerned, and that would destroy his credibility just as it had Martha's. If this were a court trial, fabricated evidence would be a killer. Case over.

The arbitration decision was communicated to him while the Martha news was blaring on the cable news channels. The ruling was a model of simplicity and economy of phrasing. True, it did not deal with Ross's testimony, or his alleged manufacturing of evidence, but it didn't deal with Groves's testimony either. As a matter of fact, it didn't deal with anybody's testimony. As a matter of fact, it didn't deal with anything. The unanimous decision of the arbitration panel in Case No. 02-02253 was not so much a decision as it was the kind of "drop dead" response you get when you dispute your cell-phone bill. This was the panel's ruling:

"Claimant's claims are denied in their entirety."

That was that.

No, actually that wasn't that. The NASD also sent Groves a bill for an Initial Filing Fee ($600), an Adjournment Fee ($1,200), and Forum Fees ($6,000), a total of $7,800. He had already paid $1,800, so he owed $6,000. In all, he would have to fork over about $7,500 more than he would have had to pay in court fees if this had been an ordinary lawsuit. (Oh, I almost forgot to mention, arbitration is "economical for investors," according to the Securities Industry Association.)

Groves was stunned, and when the disbelief wore off, he had questions to which no answers were readily available. Why didn't the arbitrators say anything about the manufactured evidence? Why didn't that destroy Ross's case? Why didn't Groves win? Or, more to the point, why didn't Ross lose?

There was no decision, so there was no answer to these questions—not then, not ever.

Groves immediately talked with his lawyer about an appeal. His lawyer was adamant on the subject, and so were the twenty or so securities lawyers he found through the Internet and the phone book. All said pretty much the same thing: "One said to me, 'Is it raining outside? You have a better chance of being struck by lightning than winning this case.' Another said I had a better chance of winning the lottery."

Groves learned that arbitration decisions are infuriatingly uninformative because they are supposed to be infuriatingly uninformative. The aim is to provide no basis for a court to pick apart a decision. He learned that arbitration decisions cannot be overturned just because the verdict is against the "weight of the evidence," or some other standard that courts apply. He learned that arbitrations are absolutely, positively not subject to appeal under pretty much any circumstances. The legal standard is stiff. The federal Arbitration Act requires the courts to enforce arbitration agreements rigorously. The arbitrators have to be either crazy or corrupt. Or, as one federal appellate court pointed out, the proceedings must have been a "mockery or sham" or been conducted "illegally or by corrupt arbitrators." A merely stupid, unfair, or unjust decision is—well, it's just fine, when rendered by an arbitration panel. Arbitrations can also be tossed out if litigants climb a common law Mount Everest called "manifest disregard" of the facts and law—sort of a nice way of saying "a crazy decision." But attacking the judgment on that or any grounds is kind of tough (actually, pretty near impossible) when the arbitrators don't provide their reasons, as happened in Groves's case.

Groves immediately ran into a problem as he went about meeting his formidable burden of proof. A tape recorder had been whirling during the entire arbitration hearing. A total of fourteen tapes were made. He asked for the tape that contained Ross's testimony. Thirteen were fine. One was blank on both sides.

Guess which one.

Something musta happened. Maybe one of the arbitrators goofed, said the NASD. Why? Beats me. Beats the NASD. Beats Merrill Lynch. More than anything, it beats Groves. As a matter of fact, it beats him to a pulp.

The silver lining, Groves reasoned after recovering from the shock, was that the failure to record a crucial part of the proceedings might be considered a serious irregularity—serious enough to provide grounds for a court to reverse the decision. Again, the lawyers he consulted were unencouraging. Legal clinics, usually after some initial interest, reacted similarly. Groves was learning that arbitration was a specialized field of law, securities arbitration was a subspecialty of that specialty, and investor appeals of securities arbitration cases were a subspecialty of a subspecialty of a specialty, and about as rewarding to most lawyers as removing a cake pan from a hot oven with their teeth.

I met Groves as he was wrestling with this horror. I had just written a story for *Business Week* on the Wall Street arbitration system, and he was hoping for publicity that might shake loose a lawyer willing to take his case. I thought it might be a decent story, but it was a tough sell.

At *Business Week,* the relevant concept was "bore." As in size, magnitude, explosive power. This was a term I had begun hearing in 2002, but similar concepts have long been employed throughout financial journalism. Enron, which *Business Week* glorified in a 2001 cover story and thrashed later that year, was "large bore." Tyco, which *Business Week* glorified in a 2001 cover story and thrashed the following year, was "large bore." The latest news from the New York Stock Exchange, down to the last detail of its dispute with Dick Grasso and the most esoteric complexities of its internal structure and competitive challenges, was "large bore," in the sense of being weighty enough to be part of the established agenda of financial journalism—which was pretty much what the editors of *Business Week* read about every morning over breakfast, preparatory to their nine-thirty meeting, in the *Wall Street Journal* and the *New York Times*.

Anything that those two very fine publications did not regularly cover was "small bore." As a matter of fact, even such grave and recurring investor issues as fraud involving microcap stocks—which still savaged thousands of investors every year, and which had once been large bore—had shrunk down to small bore by 2004. Rand Groves could not shed light on Enron or WorldCom or Arthur Andersen or market structure or any of the other large-bore issues that preoccupied *BW* and the rest of the financial press in 2004. He was just a little guy with a big problem, so he was small bore. A story on his plight would be laughed out of any meeting of *BW* editors. My editor passed on it.

Groves was batting a thousand. Everybody was failing him.

He had only a short time to appeal, if he was going to appeal. Not that, as he saw things, he had much of a choice. He was broke and without a job, he had no savings, and all his wealth had been tied up in those two Internet stocks. He didn't even know where to file the papers. He lived in New Jersey, but the arbitration was in Pennsylvania. Groves went to libraries to find the right legal forms, read some law books, decided to go with New Jersey, specifically the Superior Court of Mercer County, Civil Division, which is located in Trenton. He filed his lawsuit with the clerk on June 4, 2004, and named both the NASD and Merrill Lynch as defendants. He asked for the arbitration decision to be overturned, and for the court to order a new hearing before a different panel. Merrill promptly moved to have the whole thing tossed out of court.

Groves had to fight the motion without a lawyer. His efforts to find one who was willing to accept the case on a contingency basis—paid only if he won—had come to naught. His parallel effort to obtain publicity had gotten some results, however. A weekly business publication called *NJBIZ* had run a lengthy piece on his plight. It was a good article, a fair article, an accurate article, and such an affront to the honor of a Wall Street firm was not to go unanswered. Merrill Lynch spokesman Mark Herr immediately wrote an outraged letter to the editor that was published two weeks later.

Merrill had no problem with anything specific in the story, but had a real problem with the story being published at all. Since the travails of customers of large brokerage firms fell into the small-bore category employed by *Business Week* and other trendsetters of financial journalism, the *NJBIZ* piece was the kind of outlier that really gets Wall Street PR people mad. It was almost as if Merrill had been a fly on the wall of my meeting with my editor, and was annoyed that such good judgment was not universal and that this pipsqueak little business publication wasn't as intelligent and discerning as larger and more sophisticated media outlets that followed the established financial news agenda. "It is astonishing that you would allow Groves the soapbox you did," the Merrill letter complained. While it asserted that Groves made "false claims," and repeated Merrill's contention that Groves was shifting blame to his "financial advisor" for his own misjudgments, that is about as far as it went in disputing anything in the piece. As far as Merrill was concerned, his claim was the height of effrontery. Indeed, Merrill seemed to feel that it was a victim of injustice by having to put up with a pest like Groves crying foul. "It is hard to imagine anyone less entitled to a do-over," said Herr.* After all, "Rand had his day in court and lost."

Well, actually that is what Groves was trying to get—a hearing in an actual U.S. courtroom—and Merrill at the moment was working hard to get it kicked out of court. Merrill's motion to dismiss the case was terse and confident, though lacking the moral outrage of the letter to *NJBIZ*. As in the letter, the brief did not have much to say about that smoking-gun note, the one showing that its broker may not have been brutally honest at all times. In a footnote, reflecting Merrill's view that the whole thing was a big yawn, the firm's lawyers said that "neither Merrill Lynch nor Mr. Ross concedes" Groves's account of what was said when the tape recorder wasn't working. The NASD's answer said that it "lacks knowledge and information sufficient to form a belief" on the subject, and "leaves plaintiff to his proofs." (The latter, incidentally, was standard legal boilerplate and not an attempt to be sarcastic.)†

A few weeks before the case was called, the NASD asked for the hearing to be postponed. Firms often ask for delays in Wall Street arbitrations, sometimes

---

* Merrill's response to repeated requests for comment is described in the Epilogue. Ross said he was unable to comment because of company policy.
† Merrill later clarified its position in a legal filing, conceding that the "smoking gun" note was written after its ostensible filing date of February 17, 2000. However, Merrill maintained that, at the session that wasn't taped, Ross denied that the note had been written after he learned about the claim.

for legit reasons and sometimes to wear down the opposing party, and they are usually granted. But this wasn't a Wall Street arbitration. Judge Mitchel E. Ostrer said no, and the case went on as scheduled.

So there he was, that sweaty day in August 2004, in the Mercer County courthouse. Groves was aware of the painful irony that he was in the midst of the glories of our Revolutionary past. Across the street, at the site of what was now a Lutheran Church, George Washington met with his generals in the home of Alexander Douglass on the evening of January 2, 1777. A tarnish-green plaque attested to the fact that there, on that date, Washington decided on a perilous maneuver. One week before, Washington had crossed the Delaware to the north of the town and seized Trenton from the Hessians. The First Battle of Trenton was won. But the British had regrouped and were driving south. Right across the street, Washington had embarked on a plan of action.

Groves waited in the cold of Christmas every year to watch the reenactment of Washington crossing the Delaware and marching on Trenton—usually to be disappointed, because it was almost always called off because of bad weather or rough waters. He believed in the sappy stuff that every American schoolkid is taught—or, at least, was taught in the early 1960s, when Groves went to school—about the fundamental principles of liberty and fairness and the decency of our civil justice system. So he didn't mind being a *pro se* plaintiff, facing lawyers from the firm of Stradley Ronon Stevens & Young LLP, representing Merrill Lynch and Ross, and Drinker Biddle & Reath LLP, representing the NASD.

Had this been an arbitration hearing, a guy like Groves facing off against the two leading powers of Wall Street would have been a can of Gaines dog food, chopped up and put on a plate before a hungry Rottweiler. But this wasn't an arbitration hearing. Judge Ostrer rejected Merrill's effort to toss the case out of court.

The judge's decision—as detailed and clear as the arbitration ruling was brief and opaque—was a heartening example of the judicial system working to protect the meek against the mighty. It gave Groves every benefit of the doubt, bending over backward to help him, pointing out the inapplicability of cases cited by Merrill very much as a high-priced lawyer for Groves would have done. But it was narrowly worded. The decision made clear that to win Groves would have a heavy burden of proof. He would have to prove that the tape was intentionally erased and that, as a result, testimony wasn't considered and Groves didn't get a fair hearing.

So there he was—victorious but only for the moment, winning an interlocutory decision that was like overrunning one foxhole with the rest of Pork

Chop Hill looming above. Except that in this case even a final victory didn't mean pushing the enemy over the Yalu, because the most Groves could hope for was that his case would be sent back to arbitration for another appealable-only-if-crazy decision.

A U.S. citizen was fighting for his right to due process of law, a right he had learned back in grade school was guaranteed by the U.S. Constitution. It was crazy. What made it crazy was that in the eyes of the law, it was not even a close question. Merrill Lynch was in the right.

Groves was also right, not legally, but in the realm of the kind of gnawing feeling that settles in the gut when something really bad is happening to a person and not a goddamn thing can be done about it.

It was crazy, but it was also predestined.

Years of conditioning, media hype, advertising, image-building, and scandal-suppression by Merrill and other titans of the securities industry have produced a generation of Americans who sign papers they don't read, and buy investment products they don't understand from brokers whose backgrounds they don't bother to research. They deal with brokerage firms and mutual funds and hedge funds and investment vehicles of all kinds that are hyped by the media and treated with deference by the regulators that are supposed to be keeping watch over it all. When they get into a dispute with the Street, they are caught in a system that is Dickensian without the cute English accents.

As Rand Groves and thousands of other people have learned, investors in trouble have no friends. Not Eliot Spitzer, the media phenom who chose his targets carefully—the Wall Street arbitration system being one of many glaring omissions—as he briefly breezed through Wall Street. They didn't have a friend in Arthur J. Levitt Jr., the SEC chairman during the Clinton administration. Levitt presided over the worst abuses to descend upon Wall Street since the 1920s. He failed miserably at dealing with the problems that he did not ignore entirely, but he did a couple of things better than just about any recent SEC chairman in history—give speeches, and court the press. As early as 1997, Levitt was already being hoisted on a pedestal as "one of the most powerful and effective SEC chairmen in memory," one who had cleaned up the OTC markets and rogue brokers—when in fact thievery was running rampant, unimpeded by Artie's SEC.*

The canonization of Arthur Levitt is just one example of the blunders the press makes, again and again, whenever Wall Street or its regulators are

* See footnote, page 168.

involved. Artie swept us off our feet. We all loved him. We still do. Who wouldn't? He looked like the rich, childless uncle we all wish we could have had. But the 1990s were on Artie's watch, and he blew it, big time, in just about every way you can imagine. One lasting legacy of Artie's SEC is something one of his top aides, a guy named Barry Barbash, did in 1997. That's when Enron got the exemption from the Investment Company Act that it needed in order to structure its operations in South America and Europe in a way that would conceal them from investors and shift debt off Enron's books. (A little detail Artie left out of his book. Remember that one? He should have called it *Take On the Street—I Sure As Hell Didn't.*)

At the conclusion of his term he was proclaimed as "The Investor's Champion"—quite literally; this was the title of a profile of Levitt that made the cover of *Business Week* in late 2000. A good example of the Levitt approach can be found in his immensely hyped fight with the accounting industry. As "The Investor's Champion" piece put it, "powerful auditor-consultants are the targets of Arthur Levitt's crusade." When the smoke cleared, it was a victory—for the powerful auditor-consultants. The central tenet of his reform plan, a ban on firms offering consulting services to audit clients, went out the window, replaced by a meaningless disclosure requirement. Under Levitt, his predecessors, and successors, the SEC devoted substantial portions of its limited energy and resources to wheel spinning, media spinning, and bureaucratic trivia, while completely ignoring, or acknowledging and then ignoring, such basic investor concerns as the grotesquely unfair securities arbitration system.

Whatever you may think of the media's coverage of Iraq or the government generally—well, toss it out the window when it comes to Wall Street and its regulators. The media are on board, very much a part of the team, albeit with a proregulation, inside-Beltway tilt. You might have read about how the business community got mad at all the "SEC activism" under Levitt's successor, William H. Donaldson, so that President Bush was moved to appoint a conservative, probusiness Republican named Christopher Cox to replace Donaldson. Wasn't Cox a bad guy and Donaldson and Levitt good guys (or the reverse, depending upon your political orientation)?

The answer is "none of the above." It didn't matter whether Cox was openly pro–Wall Street, as was Levitt's successor, Harvey Pitt, or talked a good game and did nothing in the Levitt tradition, or proposed meaningless reforms that crumbled upon closer examination, as was Donaldson's practice. When it comes to protecting your interests, each of these approaches is equally ineffective. As you read this book, try to put aside your political leanings. Leave your political baggage at the door. Keep in mind that when it comes to Wall Street, Democrats and Republicans, liberals and conservatives, have joined hands. The New York Stock Exchange's biggest defenders include the liberal New York congressional delegation, and both the left and the right have their advocates and friends within the hedge fund community. Together, putting aside all differences, the left and the right have seen to it that very little of what the SEC and the other regulators do has impact on you—except, when warranted, negatively.

You're not going to read about partisan politics in this book, because it doesn't matter, and you won't read about Enron in this book either. (My little bash-Barbash anecdote is about all I have to say on the subject.) That's not because Enron is history but because it is the kind of history that is not going to repeat itself. The WorldCom scandal, the father-son pillaging of Adelphia Communications, the Arthur Andersen accounting fiasco, the lying Internet analysts—they're all yesterday's problems. Enron will never rip off another investor. You can use Tyco's financial statements to paper the walls of an operating theater—they're that clean. John and Timothy Rigas, the father-and-son team that stole and lied at Adelphia, have been punished so decisively that I'm sure they'll be model citizens until the earth is shoveled over their coffins.

Scandals like those at Adelphia and Tyco can't hurt you. They're one-shot deals—"scores," as the crooks put it. It's the long-running sagas, the scandals of yesteryear that have a way of recurring, that should trouble you. They become today's scandals, and tomorrow's.

Another thing you won't be reading about much in this book is the solution that Congress whipped up to answer the corporate crime frenzy in 2002, the law known as Sarbanes-Oxley. You won't be reading about that law because it is simply a nonstarter when it comes to tackling the problems we'll be exploring in this book. "Sox" gives corporate officers some forms to fill out, some "independent directors" to hire who won't make a difference, and a requirement to beef up their "internal controls" that won't affect corporate behavior one bit. It is a lot of bureaucratic wheel spinning that is justifiably criticized by American corporations. It's like the nice mahogany coffin you buy your Aunt Martha because you didn't treat her right when she was alive. A nice gesture, but meaningless.

Nor am I going to waste your time by talking about things that hurt the Street but don't help or hurt you one bit, such as class-action lawsuits. I'll leave it to lawyers to tackle that open sore in the legal system, which has never meant a thing to investors and merely enriches a few wealthy attorneys. As you'll be seeing toward the end of this book, one prominent class-action lawyer is actually fighting *against* investor interests, by taking up the cudgels of a campaign against a phony nonscandal called naked short-selling. One of the criticisms of Cox was that he pushed a law that made it harder for investors to pursue class-action suits. Not true. The law made it harder for *lawyers* to pursue those suits. Investors are just bystanders. You shouldn't care about class-action suits one way or the other—but neither should you waste any tears over Wall Street having to fight them.

You won't be reading much about nuisances or irrelevancies, but you will be reading a lot about regulation. This is a subject that makes a lot of people's eyes glaze over, and that is why it needs attention. It is much too important to ignore.

The system of Wall Street self-policing known as "self-regulation" doesn't protect the public from Wall Street. It protects Wall Street from you. That is its job. You might even say that serving the Street is the self-regulatory system's role in the economic paradigm, if you adhere to what is known in the academic world as Capture Theory. That is a kind of unified field theory of how the government interacts with business, and it is widely (though not universally) embraced by economists and academicians. It holds that securities regulation, and other forms of governmental intervention in business, has been co-opted, or "captured," by the very people and institutions it is designed to regulate.

You don't have to believe in Capture Theory if you want to understand Wall Street, but it helps.

The self-regulatory system's shortcomings will be one of the recurrent motifs of this book, not because the SEC, the NASD, the stock markets, and their employees are in any way bad or corrupt or malevolent, but because preserving the status quo is their institutional role in the paradigm—a role regulators execute under Republican and Democratic administrations alike. Thus you'll find that I respectfully dissent from some of my colleagues who have painted a more upbeat picture of the Street's regulators, the SEC in particular, and Wall Street in general. Media coverage is mentioned a lot in this book because the financial press is not just an observer on the Street but a player—an essential participant. Often we "participate" by not participating—ignoring issues we should be covering—or by writing stories that are just plain dumb.

Speaking of which, on some issues that I've addressed in articles and commentaries over the years, readers with particularly good memories will note that I've changed my opinion somewhat. One area in which my thinking has evolved over the years relates to the solution to what you'll be reading about in this book. It is not more government, more regulation, more bureaucrats breathing down the necks of the markets. It is not more lawsuits, except for damages you have personally suffered. Neither is it the panacea of free markets advocated by some, not if "free markets" are defined by Wall Street.

The answer to the market's woes is you.

That's not just a figure of speech. You'll see in this book that the solution is *literally* you—your investment choices, your actions, and, above all, all the things that you shouldn't do.

Don't expect the business and financial press to help you by pointing out the real issues and by holding regulators to account. (See? I'm back to the press again, and it's only been four paragraphs.) Sure, the press exposed some of the major Wall Street calamities of recent years. However, the media was a conduit for the relentless hype that made those calamities possible—and are making future calamities possible by timidity and puffery, and by failing to expose regulatory fakery. We just haven't learned our lesson. Even after the major corporate blowups of 2001 and 2002, the media's love of hype—its predilection for "puff pieces" glorifying Wall Street and Corporate America—continued unchecked. By 2003 the press was churning out puff pieces as if nothing had happened, and would blithely do so in the years ahead. "Too many crooks in business, too many failed earnings reports, and too many investigations are taking their toll," said one commentator, who went on to observe in November 2003 that "editors and writers who spent the last two years apologizing for rogue companies they earlier canonized—and for CEOs who turned their firms into personal piggy banks—are now selling the next boom."

I'm not taking this from a rant in *Mother Jones* or the *Village Voice,* by the way. What you're seeing here is the verdict of *Across the Board,* a limited-circulation journal for the corporate elite. That's right. We in the media have become so sugary that even the intended beneficiaries are getting a toothache. Referring to a spectacularly wrong-headed *Fortune* puff piece on the soon-to-be ailing Krispy Kreme, *Across the Board* noted, "Credible advertising agencies wouldn't dare serve us that much saturated goo. But who needs expensive advertising when some reporters will provide it for free?"

By 2005 it was business as usual. *New York Times* media columnist David Carr observed in May 2005, in an article exploring the woes afflicting business publications, that "skeptical readers now reserve special distrust for the business press, which blew air into faux companies and created princes out of people who turned out to be frogs, and felonious ones at that." Carr was talking about the three major business magazines, but he could also have been talking about all of the major conduits for financial news, including the cable news channels, newspapers and wire services, financial columnists, and the obsequious Wall Street trade press.

It's not getting better. Bottom-line pressures make financial journalism even less willing, and able, to devote the resources needed to root out Wall Street's ills. Fear of libel suits continues to discourage hard-hitting reporting. So does the proregulation mentality that afflicts many journalists otherwise skeptical about government. What a lot of us ignore is that in many instances regulation just isn't the solution. All too often we find ourselves advancing the position that as long as regulations are passed, and they look nice, all will be well. That's the only possible explanation I can come up with for the really miserable coverage of Wall Street regulators.

When he was SEC chairman, Bill Donaldson—a "Rockefeller Republican," as the press admiringly called him when he quit in June 2005—milked the media's love affair with regulation almost as effectively as did the Democrat Levitt. When Donaldson irritated business lobbyists and sided with Democratic SEC commissioners who favored some of Donaldson's regulatory initiatives— well, that was that for the media. A hot-and-heavy romance ensued. Soon stories emerged that Donaldson was "warring with business interests" and "Republican commissioners"—the same kind of hagiography that infected the media during the Levitt era. The fact that some of the regulations Donaldson's SEC churned out ranged from weak to counterproductive—the hedge fund and mutual fund governance rules are examples of the latter—didn't matter because the media didn't notice. By the time he left his job, Donaldson was being rhapsodized almost as much as the ineffectual Levitt had been five years earlier.

Part of the problem is an unquestioning proregulation mindset that—to cite one obvious example—ignores whether it really matters if mutual fund board members are "independent" or not. What you're also seeing is a reflexive worship of money and power. This mindset became endemic in the 1990s, when the first hedge fund "Superinvestors" came on the scene, and many of us in the media wrote stories during that era that unduly glamorized some of the biggest players.

The media's love affair with power and money is scrupulously apolitical. The financial media are equal opportunity deifiers, putting the left-leaning mogul George Soros on a pedestal, downplaying his missteps, with just as much devotion as they do to his far more numerous conservative brethren. The common denominator is not ideology but color—Intaglio Green, the color of the cloth-pulp concoction that is Wall Street's only moral compass, only purpose and allegiance. Intaglio Green knows no ideology, no political party, no religion or race.

Wall Street's yen for your wallet afflicts with equal rapacity Republican and Democrat, liberal and conservative, Arab and Jew, anti- and proabortion, rich and middle class, and even a lot of people who think they're too poor to care. It doesn't matter if you view yourself as an investor or not. It doesn't matter whether you love or hate Wall Street or whether you own any stocks or bonds or money market funds. Chances are, Wall Street is a part of your life whether you like it or not, even if you keep your money in a passbook savings account or a tin box in the backyard.

Maybe you don't vote or pay taxes. Maybe you just don't care. If so, Wall Street loves you for that. Wall Street *doesn't want you to care.*

You can't turn back the clock to the days when only the rich were "in the market," and you wouldn't want to. In 1962, the Federal Reserve found that only about one-fifth of middle-class people, the Rand Groveses of that era (households with a net worth of $5,000 to $25,000, or about $30,000 to $150,000 today), were owners of stock. The figure for people who had a net worth of more than $100,000 (about $600,000 today) was 79 percent. Those people owned 90 percent of the shares in American companies.

According to the most recent figures, which are from 2002, the picture has changed dramatically. Counting stock held by mutual funds, about half of all households own stock. Mutual funds, pension funds, 401(k) plans, and so on, consisting mostly of your money held in trust, have long since become the biggest players on the Street.

So you own the Street and you own Corporate America, in theory. That gives you enormous power, in theory. The reason all this power is theoretical, the reason you're not exercising it, is that you don't know you have that power. You also have no choice.

You have a relationship with Wall Street whether you like it or not—and it's not working out.

CHAPTER ONE

MR. GRASSO'S NEIGHBORHOOD

This book is, in a sense, a tour of Wall Street. Most tours of Wall Street begin at the intersection of Wall and Broad streets, and this tour is no exception.

There it is, beyond the illegal barricades that keep taxpayers and terrorists alike from a public street and public sidewalk, right beyond the courteous gents with helmets and machine guns where tourists used to line up for the now invitation-only visitors' gallery. Our tour begins at that symbol of all that is holy and bizarre and wretched about American capitalism. It is where Wall Street wraps itself, sometimes literally, in the American flag. It is such a patriotic location that it is easy to get confused and think that George Washington took his oath of office on the trading floor and not at Federal Hall across the street.

The New York Stock Exchange is emblematic of many things, some of them very interesting, some very dull, and some ironic. In the latter category, what could surpass that day in April 2005 when fifteen traders were arrested by the feds for alleged felonies in this building on the *same day* the same U.S. Attorney's office was rounding up some Islamic loonies for allegedly plotting to blow it up? One can almost imagine the defense that might be offered: "We were just trying to fight willful violations of the 1933 Securities Act and associated stock exchange regulations, O cursed infidel!"

The NYSE represents all the obnoxious aspects of Wall Street, but let's be clear on something at the start: *The actual activity that takes place in this building, the buying and selling of stocks, is of no consequence to you whatsoever.* I mean "no consequence" and "whatsoever" in every sense of those words. You shouldn't care how stocks are traded if you buy stocks. In fact, you shouldn't buy stocks. Period.

Let's take those concepts one at a time:

1. The precise manner in which stocks are bought and sold, whether that happens on a trading floor or trading ceiling or electronically or via hand signals or through open outcry or mumbled curses—none of that matters, not to you. Forget all the voluminous coverage in the press. Bypass the stories about whether the NYSE will merge or dissolve or flake away like a bad paint job. Don't pay any attention to whether the NYSE trading floor will survive or be turned into a shopping mall. It shouldn't matter to you even if you spend all your days buying and selling stocks—in which case there is an excellent chance that you are either a professional stock trader who cashes out his positions at the end of each day or a damn fool amateur who is trying to beat the market based on what they tell you on CNBC.

2. This entire building, from the fake Greco-something pillars in front to the hunting scenes on the men's room wall, represents a big, fat lie— which is that what happens in this building can make you rich by your buying "good stocks." It can't, not in any systematic, logical, or predictable way. And if it could, it wouldn't. Sure, you can and should invest in stocks, and take as high an exposure to the stock market as your financial circumstances allow. But picking stocks is for suckers.

Make-money-on-Wall-Street books are right up there with weight-loss plans and find-your-mate-in-ninety-days books as instructions for voyagers into cloud-cuckoo land. The markets are so rude and chaotic, so absurdly and consistently surprising, that some traders occasionally dredge up chaos theory, used to predict such arbitrary phenomena as the weather and the movement of raindrops, and try to apply it to the ups and downs of the market. Professional investors are notorious for failing to beat the market, and amateurs are worse. Not that it matters, of course. People never tire of wanting to get rich or thin, or sexy without being rich or thin. Much of Wall Street is built on catering to that fantasy (the rich part, that is).

You can reasonably expect to do as well as the market. As you'll be seeing in the chapters on money managers, index funds and ETFs (Exchange-traded funds—stocks that replicate the indexes) are your only sane choices in U.S. equities. Sure, doing your own research and picking stocks is more fun than just putting your money in an index fund, but it has been proven to be an expensive pastime.

Wall Street firms don't want you to know this, but the general rule is that so-called small investors stink as investors and stink as stock pickers. The studies that have been conducted on occasion—and there aren't many of them; this is one area of research the Street is *not* interested in funding—all pretty much say the same thing. Probably the most dramatic is a landmark study of 66,000 households, conducted in 2000, which found that between 1991 and 1996, households earned an average return of 16.4 percent, underperforming the market by 1.5 percentage points. The more people traded, the worse they did, with active traders showing an average return of 11.4 percent.

If you think that ordinary folks have dramatically improved as investors since the early 1990s, look at the more recent study by the consulting firm of Watson Wyatt Worldwide. The firm found that self-managed 401(k) plans achieved an annual return of 6.86 percent between 1990 and 2002, while professionally managed plans realized 7.42 percent. The kind of underperformance described by Watson Wyatt can drain a $100,000 portfolio of $88,000 over a thirty-year period, if you are chump enough to think you can consistently pick stocks that can beat the stock indexes.

Evidently amateur stock investors tended to keep a lot of cash and fixed-income stuff in their 401(k) plans, which was fine in horrible years such as 2002 but lousy in years like 1995. In that year, the S&P 500 rose 37.6 percent, while amateur investors' 401(k) plans lagged a full 20 percentage points behind. Pension funds did only slightly better, 19.5 percent. All that "do-it-yourself investing" stuff that you've been hearing preached by everyone from Peter Lynch to the aptly named Motley Fool Web site to the financial press—including the contrite author of this book, who cowrote an article for *BW* in 1993 called "You Can Do It"—just doesn't pan out.

In the same year as my forgettable *BW* article, the S&P 500 had a total return of 10 percent. Amateur investors who did their own research and picked their own stocks and asset allocations realized a 7.9 percent rate of return, according to the Watson Wyatt study, while active managers did only a hair better.

That brings me to Dick Grasso. He got rich—$140 million rich—the Wall Street way. He didn't get rich by picking stocks, as that is for suckers and Dick Grasso was no sucker. He didn't do anything particularly intelligent or clever. He didn't invent a new "financial product" that anyone can remember, and neither was he particularly innovative.

You may find it disagreeable that he made so much money, and you may find it distressing that he did so. You may have bought this book because you wanted further support for your feelings in the matter. Well, I am sorry to disappoint you. Dick Grasso was fairly paid, and I can prove it.

Grasso and his colleagues, predecessors, and successors* earned their paychecks by keeping alive, and thriving, an institution that by all rights should have been dead and interred in a marble crypt a long time ago.

To say that the New York Stock Exchange is alive is something of an overstatement. It is actually undead, the Dracula of Corporate America, which makes its living by clinging, leechlike, to a securities industry that is sick and tired of it, but has no practical alternative because all the trading—the "liquidity"—is there. Every spouse in a bad marriage can understand the situation. Can't live with it, can't live without it.

Mind you, there is a significant difference between being undead, as is the NYSE, and being half-dead or comatose or even obsolete. A hideous thing you've probably forgotten still exists, the American Stock Exchange, periodically arises from a stupor to stagger around a few blocks away from the NYSE (across the street from a cemetery, which figures). Nobody ever pays it very much attention anymore. In May 2005 its president resigned for some reason, and that barely made the papers, buried way back. Even in its best days the Amex was known as "the Curb," and it is hard for an institution named after the gutter to fall very far.

Originally the Amex was owned by its members, just like the NYSE. As it stumbled from blunder to blunder it was acquired with much fanfare by the NASD. It continued to stumble and trip and stagger, so it was sold back to its members, but it didn't matter anymore because the Amex was in a kind of semicomatose state. Any other business in America would have long since declared bankruptcy—actual bankruptcy, as opposed to the moral bankruptcy that has long afflicted this very creepy, much-investigated, poorly managed, and horrifically regulated little stock exchange.

At last look the Amex listed options and some microcap stocks, and had a lovely building that would probably be more valuable to the New York City economy if it were subjected to the kind of "adaptive reuse" that turned the old police headquarters on Centre Street into condominiums. Real estate agents put the value of the building at about $70 million, which means it could easily be worth more than the actual Amex business, even if you throw in the barbershop

---

* One NYSE factotum, copresident Robert G. Britz, walked away with a lottery player's fantasy—a million bucks a year *for life*—when he retired in 2005 at the ripe old age of fifty-five.

on the first floor. As James J. Angel, a finance prof at Georgetown University, told *Business Week,* "Amex as an institution lost its reason for being long ago. The real question is whether it should start liquidating the assets and put them to better use." Which makes sense, except when you realize that this is not just any old business. This is a stock exchange, so the "free market" applies only when it is not inconvenient.

In contrast to the Amex—well, there really is no comparison. The very words *New York Stock Exchange* make you want to sit up straight and brush the crumbs off your lap. It oozes class and reputation. It has a brand identification that Dracula himself would find difficult to beat, even after that lousy Broadway show. The Grasso mess didn't change its public image all that much. And if you think about how he served the NYSE—well, you really have to marvel at what a great job he did.

What made Grasso so valuable to the exchange was not that he managed the NYSE so well but that he managed to maintain the regulatory and political environment, whose ethos is more Stalinist than Calvinist, that protects the NYSE's franchise from encroachment. In a strictly free-market environment, the NYSE would have become a slightly larger version of the Amex years ago, openly ridiculed as it wheezed along. Grasso ensured that the free market impinged on the NYSE only as much as the NYSE wanted to be impinged on. His pride and joy was a "trade-through rule" that required big institutions to direct their stock trades to the NYSE whether they liked it or not.

Basically, Grasso was paid a lot of money to ensure that the NYSE did a lousy job, and to ensure that the big firms traded there whether they liked it or not.

Think that's easy? Try it some time. Work in your basement every night to come up with a worse mousetrap. Not a better mousetrap, but a mousetrap that lets the mice wriggle away and is inferior to cheaper mousetraps you can pick up at Wal-Mart. Then try selling that mousetrap on street corners and see if you can achieve market dominance *without anyone believing it does a better job.*

If you can pull that off, you have replicated the business model of the New York Stock Exchange.

The evidence for this achievement, this worse mousetrap, can be found in several million pages of studies and research (about half of which—the ones paid for by the NYSE—describe the NYSE as terrific, and the other half—the ones paid for by its competitors—describe it as lousy).

First some definitions are in order.

The floor of the exchange is not just a colorful backdrop for broadcasts by the cable news channels, or a place for the after-hours parties that Grasso used to keep the press in tow (until he became a piñata, at which time the towline was cut). No, its primary function is to be a market—a place where stocks are sold just as your grocer sells meat or canned goods. Instead of men in blood-splattered white smocks, you have traders in blood-splattered . . . no, make that clean, well-tailored blue jackets and hand-tied bow ties.

There are two types of brokers on the floor of the exchange—floor brokers and specialists. The specialists are sort of like the men behind the counter who take your order for hamburger or prime rib. They specialize in trading certain stocks—hence the title "specialist." Unlike the man who sells you meat, and who is pretty well free to gouge whomever he wants, specialists have a legal obligation to see to it that the prices are accurate and fair—a "fair and orderly market," as it says in the regulations.

Since you are not permitted to go onto the floor of the stock exchange to place your order, the exchange has a bunch of fellows called floor brokers, who are the only ones allowed to take your order to the specialist.

I have oversimplified things here, but that is the gist of the situation. Now, not all stocks trade on the NYSE by a long shot. Thousands of stocks trade elsewhere—a few hundred on the half-dead Amex, thousands on the Nasdaq Stock Market, and then a few thousand more on the Pink Sheets, wherein are listed the microcap runts of the litter. Nasdaq is a computer network. No specialists, no floor brokers, no trading floor. Most stock markets nowadays, from Tokyo to London, are like that—all electronic.

In other words, as in the old wisecrack, NYSE floor traders can be replaced by a computer—literally. What they do requires very bright people, much as it would take a very bright person in the seventeenth century to perform calculations that a utility in your Palm Pilot can perform in a nanosecond.

The NYSE maintains that its trading floor does a better job of trading stocks than would a computer network of stock dealers. In a way, the NYSE *has* to say that. That's because the people who own the exchange are its members, also known as seat holders, and those are the same people you see down on the floor on CNBC, walking around purposefully and throwing bits of paper on the floor. The ones who don't own their seats lease them from retirees in Florida who used to do that walking-around and paper-throwing when they were younger.

The NYSE floor also serves a valuable public relations function. You can't interview the push buttons of a self-service elevator, but my friends in the cable news channels can interview the few remaining elevator operators when they do a story about elevators, and they can interview their counterparts, the floor brokers and specialists at the New York Stock Exchange, whenever they want a sound bite on the markets. In fact, Nasdaq, which really *is* a computer network, was so jealous of all those interviews and photo ops that it established a "market site" on Times Square to give the cable-news talking heads a place to talk.

The NYSE and its defenders (such as every New York City elected official going back to Peter Stuyvesant) say that having people throwing papers around on a trading floor contributes measurably to the smooth flow of the markets generally, thereby justifying the existence of the specialist system and the existence of the exchange and the existence of the big building at Wall and Broad with the columns in front, and all salaries and benefits and pensions paid therein. The stock exchange, and the specialists themselves, of course, tend to portray specialists as the firefighters of finance, rushing into unrewarding trades when others are fleeing in the opposite direction. They are there for you—to "put you [brokerages] and your customers first," as the Specialist Association put it in a handout circulated in the industry a few years ago.

The job of all those specialists on the exchange floor—their legal obligation, in fact—would seem to be extraordinarily high-minded to the point of masochism, if done properly. They have a duty to buy and sell stocks against the flow of the market, such as buying when the market is crashing, when other traders are cashing out and cutting their losses, putting their capital at risk just for the sake of seeing a smile curl on the lips of people they have never met.

The NYSE's various factotums insist that this is not a fatuous pipe dream but an actual, glorious reality. They point to several million pages of studies and reports, while the NYSE's opponents point to several million pages of studies and reports.

However, there's one number that really tells the story.

Everything the specialists do is counted and measured pretty minutely, including the extent to which they buy when stocks are going down and sell when stocks are going up. The term for that is the stabilization rate. This is a big, fat, important number. NYSE rules require that specialists go against the grain 75 percent of the time. If they don't do a good job stabilizing prices, specialists can get their stocks yanked away from them.

Well, here's what the NYSE's own numbers say: In the sixties and seventies, the stabilization rate was 90 percent or better, sometimes as high as 95 percent. In the eighties it got worse. In the 1990s it got lousy. By the mid-1990s the stabilization rate was scraping by at 75 percent, and in 2004 it climbed a bit but was still 80 percent, a lot worse than it was three decades earlier.

What these numbers mean is that over time, NYSE has managed to pull off a steady, quantifiable degradation of its supposed market-soothing function.

These specialists aren't dummies. Have you ever heard of *anybody* on Wall Street trading stocks not because they want to make a buck but because they want to serve a noble purpose? When pros engage in short-term trading, the aim is to go with the flow and buy when stocks are rising and sell when stocks are declining. Buying when stocks are declining (or selling when they climb) is known as fighting the tape, and it is a risky thing to do when your time frame is a few minutes. Unless, of course, you know that a short-term downtrend is about to reverse. Only two kinds of people in the world have access to such red-hot market information—psychics in carnival acts and people who work on the floor of the stock exchange. They know the trades that are coming in from all over the world.

Still, 80 percent is a big number. Nice of them, isn't it? Well, maybe not so nice, and not so stupid.* It so happens that a fellow named Marios A. Panayides, now a professor at the University of Utah, carefully studied the way specialists buy and sell stocks, and over the past couple of years he has been publishing papers containing his findings. One of the findings of his studies—which I should point out was not financed by any of the NYSE's competitors—received absolutely zero attention despite all the hubbub over the NYSE, even though it cuts to the heart of the NYSE's role in the markets. It's what he describes as a "forecasting factor influencing [specialist] transactions."

Marios found that in 1990—the freshest data he could get—62 percent of specialist transactions that are stabilizing (buying when prices are going down and selling when prices are going up) "happen when the prices are about to change direction. The opposite holds for destabilizing transactions." Assuming that number is about the same today, it would mean that when specialists stabilize the market, they do so because they know they'll be able to make a buck. He found "strong evidence that the Specialist is in fact able to differentiate between when the market prices are moving in the same direction or changing trends." And when they are buying with the market, they usually know the market is going to continue in the right direction.

Marios's conclusion, after years of poring over NYSE data, is that the specialists don't make money when they abide by the NYSE rules and do stuff such as provide price continuity—no sudden increases or decreases in share

---

* It would also be nice if the NYSE updated that vital number more often than *once a year*—particularly since far more esoteric numbers are available monthly, weekly, or even daily.

prices—and stabilization. They make money only when they can get away with *not* doing all that good stuff. Thus the specialists are being asked to act against the grain of the free-market system, which gives traders not just the right but the obligation to maximize their profits. It's unnatural—an inherently dysfunctional system that is an open invitation to abuse.

In light of the interesting data Marios has collected, you can understand why scandals keep happening at the NYSE. It's just as a muffler dealer on Jerome Avenue in the Bronx once explained to me many years ago, when one of his friends (my uncle) was initiating me into the mysteries of the auto-repair business. Overcharging customers was the only way to make a living in a very tough, competitive, low-margin business.

If Dick Grasso had been paid $140 million to defend a useful, rational institution, it would have been a squalid form of self-overpayment. Being paid that sum to defend and keep alive an obsolete, inherently irrational institution that hasn't always treated its customers very nicely—that isn't at all squalid. It is the quintessential American success story as adapted by the postmillennium Wall Street: the man with the malfunctioning, but more politically powerful, mousetrap.

It is also the work of a fundamentally honest man. Such work requires the kind of dedication that comes only from a true believer.

I came to a full appreciation of Dick Grasso's honesty and dedication one lovely summer evening when we met for dinner. The date was June 30, 2003. I am sure that Grasso, as a product of the New York City public school system, was aware of the meaning of that day. For every New York City schoolkid in the fifties and sixties, June 30 was Graduation Day. It was the day kids received their report cards, still written in blue-black ink on acid-free white paper, describing their academic performance and behavior and containing comments such as "Gary is a lovely boy!" or "Gary needs to work harder to achieve his potential." Grasso was about to graduate from the NYSE, and he surely must have known that his report card was being written every day, and that he was getting really lousy grades from people like me. For years he had been everywhere in the media, a little bald man with comical talent of an outer-borough variety that brought to mind Larry "Bud" Melman of the pre-CBS *Late Night with David Letterman*. Coverage that had once been all kissy and loving was now turning nasty and almost spiteful.

You might have gotten the general impression, if you followed the gleeful coverage of Grasso's travails, that the press was pursuing an almost personal vendetta against the NYSE and its once-lovable bald leader. And you would be onto something. That's because all those years it had only *seemed* as if the press had been the NYSE's biggest fans. In fact, the press was utterly terrified of the NYSE. Such had been the state of affairs since at least the 1980s, when the exchange's PR apparatus was known for being—well, maybe just a bit nasty toward members of the media. I'll leave it at that.

Over time, attitudes mellowed on both sides. Personnel changed. Tempers cooled. Still, it is fair to say that well into the Grasso era, the NYSE was still roundly despised by a great many people whose employers bought ink by the barrel. Relations did not improve when the NYSE devoted a section of its Web site to press goof-ups. It was used as a bludgeon to bawl out such hotbeds of left-wing extremism as the *Wall Street Journal* and the *New York Post*. Such unauthorized use of the First Amendment was not to go unavenged.

When Grasso stumbled, the media pounced, and loved it, and kept on pouncing. I did my pounce when the pay scandal broke in mid-2003, and *Business Week* put me to the task of writing a profile of Grasso. I requested an interview, and the exchange responded in typical, heartwarming fashion by having its chief flack at the time call the editor in chief at the time, Steve Shepard.

Grasso insisted, through his flack, that Shepard or some other grown-up accompany me to the interview. That struck me as inept. If I were being interviewed by a potentially hostile publication, I would insist on limiting the number of questioners. It was also ill-advised from another standpoint. Did he really want to get my editor in chief personally invested in this story? His other requirement was even more peculiar. Grasso insisted that the interview be conducted in a restaurant, and over dinner. If the interview were to be on Grasso's home turf, in mid-workday, he would be in control of the environment and could limit the length of any questioning. He could be trapped with me for hours. It was like having a first date in a hot-air balloon slowly drifting to the Azores. It made absolutely no sense for a man who was trying to avoid being, pardon the expression, screwed by the media.

Another shock came on the day of the interview, which took place at a mediocre but pricey establishment in an out-of-the-way part of midtown, me with an editor other than Shepard and Grasso with the flack. As a rule, no CEO under attack would ever consent to the recording of a leisurely, relaxed interview. The danger is that the interview could then be shoved down his throat, verbatim, in an article. However, Grasso had no objection to the interview being recorded.

The best explanation I can come up with is that Grasso did not feel that he had anything to hide, and wanted to tell the truth. Maybe he also wanted me to see him up close, near enough to see the polish glisten off his shaved head, hear his organs process his low-carbohydrate food, and become infected by his charm. If that was his objective, he succeeded. Up close, Grasso is charming and unflappable. I had just been interviewing members of his family, a former high school teacher, and old school chums to get insights that might make him writhe a little, but I did not have any luck that night. He was impervious, deadpan.

Grasso was perfectly straightforward. He had nothing that he perceived as requiring concealment. At one point he looked me straight in the eye and told me how he pretty much hand-picked his board of directors, much as you might put your wife or golfing buddy on the "board" of the Subchapter S corporation you set up to shelter income from stamp collecting. He said he had an annual "audience"—the papal terminology went over my head at the time—with the board's nomination committee, and gave them a list of people whom he wanted on the board. They went ahead and picked the members from that list, and never went to the trouble of coming up with names on their own. He said that he believed that this method of picking the board was completely "independent," and actually a better method than was generally used by companies to pick their boards of directors.

He also insisted that he had no influence on his pay, and that the only thing he ever said, after receiving his annual pay package, was "Thank you." He also has been quoted as saying that he has responded "I'm blessed" when given his paychecks. Dick Grasso was indeed blessed, and so was the NYSE. Both had ample reason for gratitude and many people to thank, especially in Washington.

The NYSE is more than just an obsolete marketplace, party space, terrorist target, and generous paymaster. It is a regulator. When it comes to regulating, the NYSE is the trendsetter for the rest of Wall Street. It sets the standard that the Street has been striving to meet, if not exceed, for many years.

CHAPTER TWO

HOW TO BE A WALL STREET PROPHET

I t's easy to predict Wall Street. Not the stock market. *Wall Street.*

Sure, you may have a sense of where the stock market is heading in the next ten seconds or maybe the next ten minutes, if you have access to the right databases and analytics and if you devote your life to watching the index futures-cash spread. The problem is, even if you figure out how to arbitrage the futures and cash indexes, you can't exploit them. The commissions will eat you alive.

Sure, with a little work you can find stocks whose prices are being goosed into the stratosphere, but you can't profit from that. The SEC, caving in to a handful of scam artists, loudmouths, and crackpots, recently passed a rule that prevents even the pros from betting against crummy, manipulated stocks. We'll be delving into that sorry bit of nonsense later in this book.

You can certainly hand over your hard-earned money to one of the thousands of market seers, newsletters, financial publications, and seminars, all aimed at helping you predict the stock market and individual stock prices. However, you stand to gain as much benefit doing that as you would by folding your money into paper boats and sailing them down the Niagara River.

Microcap stocks take that predictability principle to its logical conclusion by offering a guarantee. They are a sure thing. They are *always* a center of fraud. They were. They are. They always will be. This market's stoic adherence to the crooked borrows from the Cheyenne, for whom the past, the present, and the future are intertwined into a single, continuous entity. Just as the Native American warriors of old would cry, "It is a good day to die," you must have the same attitude of stoic acceptance when buying a microcap stock. "It is a good day to be ripped off!" Let that be your battle cry.

Yet while there are plenty of newsletters, analyst reports, unsolicited emails, and Web sites that helpfully assist in the perpetration of microcap fraud, using names such as "The Next Big Winners," you'd be hard-pressed to find many with names such as "The Next Big Scandal." That's because fortunes are made on Wall Street by catering to your greed. Not a penny is to be made protecting you from Wall Street's greed. That's *your* job.

The reason for this is fundamental to Wall Street. You might say that Wall Street is like a cozy blue-collar neighborhood or a small town where people are hospitable, if not exactly friendly, to outsiders. In the eyes of the law, Wall Street is not Dodge City, as it is often portrayed in the media, but rather a tree-shaded side street in Mayberry, one that Opie might have used on the way to the fishing hole.

In Mayberry, the doors are always unlocked. People trust one another. The entire system of Wall Street policing is based upon this kind of small-town neighborliness and confidence—not your confidence in Wall Street, but the confidence that Wall Street has in its regulators, and vice versa.

In this very special world, the New York Stock Exchange is a very special place. If the SEC is the easygoing Andy Taylor in the regulatory Mayberry, the NYSE is the goofy, goggle-eyed Barney Fife. Not the man you'd want to charge into a crack house. But there are no crack houses in Mayberry, only nice people who occasionally get involved in wacky situations.

Mayberry is a self-policing little town, where neighbors watch out for neighbors. Wall Street is self-policing too. Perhaps you have heard the term "self-regulatory organization," or SRO. That is what the NYSE is supposed to be. Let's focus on that for a moment. This expression and acronym are used in the media so much that it is easy to be lulled into a sense of numbness. Since the word *regulatory* is in there, it is widely assumed that something regulatory is actually involved, in the sense of, perhaps, the voltage regulators that used to actually regulate voltage in old Chevys.

If that is what you think, you have made a fundamental mistake. Remember that this is Mayberry, where people trust one another and where there is no real policing going on—just a couple of good old boys with badges.

Organizationally, the SROs and their government overlords are arrayed in a kind of pyramid. At the top is a U.S. government agency, the SEC, along with a few other governmental bodies that oversee the options and commodities markets, banks, and other financial conduits. Below them, on the second tier, are the NYSE, NASD, and various stock markets, and commodities, futures, and options markets. And then we come to the bottom segment. "The most critical element in the self-regulatory system" is what it is called by no less an authority than the standard, lawyer-thumbed text on the subject, *Wall Street Polices Itself*, by David P. McCaffrey and David W. Hart, published in 1998 by the very distinguished and serious Oxford University Press.

Let's see if you can guess that all-important third layer of the pyramid from the following four choices:

A. State regulators, as exemplified in recent years by the much-acclaimed New York State Attorney General Eliot Spitzer
B. Federal prosecutors and the FBI
C. Nobody—the bottom of the pyramid is hollow
D. Wall Street

If you guessed "A," you made an understandable error, but failed to take the long view. New York attorneys general and nosy state regulators may come—but they invariably go. Besides, acclaimed and praiseworthy as he surely is, for some reason Eliot has rarely used his inherent powers to bring criminal charges against Wall Street transgressors. So he has not left as much of a mark as would seem warranted by the press coverage. During the period we are blessed by their presence, Eliot and other such interlopers are viewed by Wall Street and the pyramid as a recurrent affliction. They are to be tolerated until they lose interest or run for higher office.

"B" is also wrong. The feds are another recurrent disease, albeit a particularly nasty one because—unlike Eliot Spitzer—they can be counted on to toss people in the jug. Rudy Giuliani periodically incarcerated Wall Streeters during the overblown insider-trading scandals of the 1980s. A decade later, the FBI and prosecutors briefly stepped in as *de facto* regulators when the NASD and the SEC did nothing about rampant criminality among microcap brokerages. As I will be describing later, the microcap market has now shifted back to its accustomed status of being universally ignored.

"C" is a trick answer. Anything quite so straightforward as "no regulation at all" would simply not live up to the deceptiveness required to preserve the status quo while providing the illusion of action. That was the problem, incidentally, with Harvey Pitt, the Wall Street lawyer who took time off from defending Wall Street as a private attorney so that he could defend Wall Street as George W. Bush's first head of the SEC. Harvey was a very proud, very undisguised Street partisan, who made it plain from the beginning that giving tough speeches and furrowing eyebrows was not for him. An Artie Levitt approach, tough-talking but nonregulating, was not for him. He was going to give *nice* speeches while doing nothing. That would never do.

The correct answer, "D," is the one you might have thought was the distracter, to snare those of you who didn't study for this quiz. Brokerage firms are the first line of defense against excesses committed by brokerage firms. Every brokerage firm, every peddler of stocks and mutual funds and options and futures—you name it—is a little self-regulatory operation of its own. All of them, without exception. Even the tiny outfits that sell microcap stocks, where you might find gangsters toting guns—they are all self-regulatory operations, with "compliance" officers who are supposed to see that brokers who bought their licenses abide by the securities laws.

Just as the Wall Street version of meting out justice can be easily applied to other forms of disputes, this self-regulation concept can also be easily applied to every commercial endeavor. If you are a tenant, the first line of defense against excesses committed by your landlord could be a "housing-law compliance officer" in your landlord's company. That dumpy restaurant that gave you a dose of food poisoning—well, surely a "compliance chef" in the kitchen would take you to the hospital. If the doctor there cuts off your leg instead of pumping your stomach, the hospital's "medical compliance" officer would be your protector. And so on and so forth.

If you're a broker, you can't cut off a customer's leg, but you can cheat him. You can break the law. When that happens, the self-regulatory system swings into inaction.

My favorite saga of self-regulation—it's really nonregulation, but let's not get hung up on semantics—involves the NYSE. What's nice about this story is that it is so clear-cut in its murkiness and in the serene flow of its double-talk and hypocrisy, and is laid out in reams upon reams of court papers. It is a tale that more or less concluded in August 2004. It began in a happier era, when we were all so much more prosperous and optimistic.

The year was 1998, and visitors still lined up outside the NYSE building to wait their turn for the gallery elevators. On the floor, brokers were happily trading away. There were the specialists, who had a job that is, as I described, theoretically masochistic. And then there were the floor brokers, who had what has got to be one of the most frustrating jobs in the world.

Imagine a job at a rather shady racetrack in which you work as a courier, and you get to convey the results of the eight daily races *before the horses have even left the starting gate.* Now, wouldn't you feel just a bit tempted to put in a bet yourself, or to slip a few bucks to a pal to do that for you and split the winnings? Floor brokers have the job of going to the specialist booths and executing trades, without making a buck for themselves on all that inside info they get just because they work on the exchange floor. They know when big, market-moving orders are about to take place—really hot inside information.

Weakness is part of the human condition. A *tiny number* of floor brokers succumbed to temptation. A *very small and unrepresentative number* of brokers did that, the NYSE has long since emphasized, and would probably want me to emphasize, so I have done so.

The shocking news broke on February 25, 1998. "Big Board Floor Brokers Charged in Illegal Profits" said a front-page article the following day in the *New York Times*. It was big news. Confidences had been violated. Bonds of trust, upon which the entire self-regulatory system depends, had been allegedly tossed away by eight floor brokers. Instead of just carrying out their frustrating jobs, acting as couriers toting orders around the floor, they had actually made a few bucks by trading for their own profit, which they shared with customers. Bad! Wrong! Mary Jo White, the U.S. Attorney for Manhattan, a small woman with cropped hair and a stern and implacable demeanor, was righteously indignant. In a statement, handed out to the press early on February 25, she pointed out:

> When Congress passed the Securities Act of 1934 it determined that floor brokers who engaged in proprietary trading on national securities exchanges had a significant—and fundamentally unfair— informational and trading advantage over their customers and other market participants. Congress prohibited proprietary trading by floor brokers because it determined that allowing floor brokers to exploit this advantage would undermine public confidence in the integrity of the securities markets.

That last point justified all the indignation. You'll read words like "public confidence in the integrity of the securities market" whenever Wall Street does something bad. If members of the public feel that nasty stuff is happening, they may think that Wall Street is just a rigged game and stop buying stocks. Now, that's actually not a bad idea at all, as we've seen. But let's put that aside and agree with her for the moment, just to be nice.

Mary Jo White did not have the last word on February 25. Dick Grasso, now three years into his term as chairman, assured the public that the NYSE, working with the federal government, had the malefactors cornered like rats:

Our enforcement [and] market surveillance divisions have aggressively worked hand-in-hand with the U.S. Attorney's office on this investigation. Any activity by a NYSE member or member firm that violates federal securities law or NYSE rules simply will not be tolerated. This has long been paramount as we preserve the integrity of our marketplace.

This is truly an example of what can be accomplished when the federal prosecutor, the federal regulatory authorities and self-regulatory organizations work in cooperation toward a common goal.

Inspiring, isn't it—all that "aggressively working hand-in-hand"? (They say you can always tell an Assistant U.S. Attorney or NYSE enforcement guy by the scratches on his palms, from all that aggressive hand-in-hand working.) In an interview the following morning on CNBC's *Business Day*, an SEC enforcement official named Henry Klehm portrayed the NYSE floor in stark terms— as a kind of Old West open range, where right and wrong stood out in stark contrast to each other in the clean, thin air of the high desert. "These rules are very clear as a matter of the federal securities law and as a matter of the New York Stock Exchange rules," said Klehm.

The legal process began to churn immediately. Contrary to the prevailing view that the criminal justice system coddles defendants, it is actually a fearsome thing to behold when viewed from the criminal perspective. Guilty pleas began, superseding indictments were handed up, court rulings were issued, and pretty soon the whole thing lumbered heavily out of the public view. Scandals are like that. They begin with a great thunderclap of attention, but then the ponderous machinery of justice takes over. Unlike the swift and fair adjudication that Rand Groves and other brokerage customers encounter when they file claims against brokers, the judicial machinery in criminal cases is ponderous and wordy, producing a great many filings and documents.

The court files bulged, and continued to fatten through 1998 into 1999 and 2000, as the public yawned and stretched and assumed that matters were well in hand. The World Trade Center fell and the court file was still fattening. New scandals arose, nudging aside old, obsolete scandals. The floor-broker cases drifted off the front pages and onto the back pages, and then faded away. As public attention drifted elsewhere, the secrets of the entire Wall Street policing system were being revealed in court files for everyone to see, in the public-records room on the third floor of the new federal courthouse on Pearl Street overlooking Chinatown. While journalists and public officials were scratching their heads trying to figure out what was wrong with Corporate America and Wall Street, anyone could have found out the answers right there at the courthouse—and then gone out for some great dim sum.

The reason all these insights were still there, available for all to see in the public-records room, was that one of the floor brokers wouldn't cop a plea. Usually, faced with the possibility of a life-ruining prison term under the inflexible sentencing guidelines, defendants in such situations don't engage in hair-splitting legal circumlocutions. They cut a plea bargain, do their time, and move on. However, a floor broker named John R. D'Alessio wouldn't play along. He pleaded not guilty and actually had the gall to sue the NYSE.

D'Alessio and his lawyer, a feisty one-man practitioner named Dominic Amorosa, made allegations that were self-serving and seemed wild and hard to swallow, even if they didn't concern an institution of such formidable reputation as the NYSE. D'Alessio asserted that he was prosecuted, and in the process saw his career go down the toilet, for doing things that were not unambiguously wrong as alleged by Klehm, but were sanctioned and tolerated. D'Alessio's NYSE was a sleazy, morally ambiguous world, a good deal more David Mamet than John Ford. His NYSE trading floor was so slippery that you'd think they'd have to wear cleats, all nine hundred specialists, traders, clerks, and cable-TV talking heads.

There was some media coverage of all this, as other floor brokers came forward to claim that they were being singled out for punishment for conduct that was tolerated by Grasso and other NYSE managers. I wrote one lengthy piece on D'Alessio et al. in early 1999, and TheStreet.com covered the story doggedly. Still, none of the stories got much traction. Even when the NYSE was put through the ringer in 2003, after which it was under new leadership and supposedly reforming, D'Alessio's very troubling allegations were completely forgotten. When *Fortune* lambasted Grasso in a ten-thousand-word profile in October 2004, the magazine didn't even mention the floor-broker cases at all.

D'Alessio's allegations didn't even help D'Alessio all that much. The criminal case against him was dropped by the U.S. Attorney's office, but apart from that he lost every step of the way. His suit against the exchange was dismissed. His hopeless battle finally came to an end in August 2004. (Or, to be more precise, when his appeal of the federal court ruling dismissing his appeal of the SEC action rejecting his appeal of an NYSE disciplinary action was rejected by the Second Circuit Court of Appeals.)

D'Alessio's allegations against the exchange would be tossed on the dung heap of history were it not for something that emerges when you look at all those mountains and mountains of court papers: D'Alessio was telling the truth. His case is so well documented that it is hard to come to any other conclusion. The August 2004 appellate court ruling in his case, and a similar case involving other floor brokers represented by Amorosa, paint a troubling picture of the NYSE's oversight of the trading floor. Indeed, when you read these decisions, you really wonder whether the feds went after the wrong guys in 1998.

That SEC enforcement guy who gave the morning-after interview on CNBC, Henry Klehm, was right, though not in the way that he intended. Klehm and Mary Jo White might believe that the law prevented floor brokers from trading for their own profit. The law may very well have the clarity of a Norman Rockwell painting. But a very different reality existed on the floor of the exchange, in much the same way as real estate salesmen really do have to follow all the niceties of consumer protection laws, but things break down a little when Mitch and Murray are putting on the squeeze and the Glengarry leads are going only to closers.

Just as muffler mechanics had to overcharge customers if they wanted to make a living on Jerome Avenue in the 1970s Bronx, floor brokers had to cut corners as well if they wanted to make a living on Wall Street. You really can't blame them. They were caught in an inherently illogical, deeply corrupt system of which exchange bosses were perfectly aware. They even had a name for it—it was variously known as "flipping" or "trading for eighths"—and it was the very same kind of trading that resulted in indictments in 1998. Beginning in "at least" 1991, according to a subsequent SEC action, flipping was going on unimpeded on the exchange floor.

D'Alessio alleged, and the exchange denied, that almost half of all floor brokers, 230 of them, were engaged in such trading. The exchange's denials seem a little pathetic when you go through the court filings. So does Dick Grasso's statement to the media in February 1998.

It's hard to believe that the NYSE was doggedly pursuing crooked floor brokers when it was fully aware of what they were doing, and had no problem with it. In fact, on March 4, 1993, the NYSE established an Advisory Committee on Intra-Day Trading Practices, and its mission was to "review, and, as appropriate, make recommendations regarding" all this flipping stuff. The aim was to determine whether such trading "interferes with public participation in the agency-auction market and is a practice that is detrimental to the best interests of the Exchange." The committee eventually issued a report on these intraday practices and recommended that they be restricted.

Were they restricted? Nope.

They were not only not restricted but—well, they were kinda okay. When he sued the NYSE to overturn its sanctions against him, D'Alessio was able to include some damaging quotes from the already lengthy public record to bolster his version of events. He quoted SEC testimony from Edward Kwalwasser, who was head of the NYSE's regulatory mechanisms throughout the 1990s. Kwalwasser had been asked if it would have been a violation of the law, back in the 1990s, for a floor broker to share in profits from trading on the floor. His response was that it was okay, as long as the account was not in the broker's name. Grasso also made that point in his letter to the SEC, quoted at some length in D'Alessio's lawsuit. Kwalwasser's SEC testimony later that year was quoted, also at length, in a December 1999 ruling on the floor-broker cases issued by Judge Jed S. Rakoff.

So basically the NYSE's position in the 1990s was that Mary Jo White was wrong. Title 15, U.S.C. Section 78 (k) (a) (1) was wrong. Title 16, CFR, Section 240.11 (a-1) was wrong. NYSE Rule 352 (c) was wrong. The latter said that floor brokers couldn't "directly or indirectly take or receive or agree to take or receive a share in the profits" from trading.

What apparently trumped all this black-letter law was a kind of "let boys be boys" attitude among the NYSE leadership. As another NYSE official later told the SEC, the belief among NYSE officials in the 1990s was that floor brokers getting a share of the profits was "appropriate." "The law? We're the law!" was the NYSE's position on floor brokers skimming off profits—until the indictments came down, and then it was bad.

Official verdicts on the NYSE's sheer gall were almost British in their understatement, as they sought to avoid being publicly nasty with this august institution. After all, you can't get teed off at a flag-draped institution upon which the investing public's confidence supposedly hinges. Judge Rakoff, a former criminal defense lawyer, reached into his thesaurus and said that the NYSE's various excuses for profiteering by floor brokers were "anemic." Other rulings, by the courts and the SEC, called the NYSE's "interpretation" of the floor-trading laws "restrictive." None came out and said in plain English that the NYSE let floor brokers break the law by trading for their own profit, and that its excuses were a crock.

The chairman and CEO of the NYSE when all this was going on, by the way, was none other than the old Bush family friend and subsequent SEC chairman, William H. Donaldson. The buck stopped with him. He knew all about this flipping stuff, if he bothered to read some pieces of paper that flitted across his desk from time to time. As an appellate court ruling observed, Donaldson as

NYSE chairman had "received communications related to the practice of 'flip-ping.'" Again, a very legalistic and precise way of saying "He knew what in hell was going on."

Now, there are certainly worse things in the world than floor brokers squeezing out a few bucks the way they did in the early 1990s. The illegal trad-ing on the floor of the exchange was kid stuff compared to the widespread ripoffs in the Nasdaq market at the time, which ranged from price fixing to massive microcrap thievery. So with all that worse stuff to ignore, this being Mayberry, you can bet that Arthur Levitt's SEC wasn't going to get all riled up about the town drunk. The bonds of fatherly tolerance and affection just leap off the pages of Administrative Proceeding File No. 3-9925, *In the Matter of New York Stock Exchange Inc.,* by which the SEC gave the NYSE a firm slap on the fanny about a year and a half after the indictments were handed up. In stern, sanctimonious regulator-speak, Artie's SEC found that "the NYSE, with-out reasonable justification or excuse, failed to enforce compliance with" the var-ious rules and statutes that are "aimed at preventing independent floor brokers . . . from exploiting their advantageous position on the NYSE floor for personal gain to the detriment of the investing public."

You have to admire the SEC's sense of irony and understatement. Actually the NYSE hadn't just failed to enforce compliance with the laws. You might construe, from all the legal documents piled up in that courthouse, that the NYSE had given the floor brokers a big thumbs-up, allowing them to do stuff for which a few of them were later indicted.

The bottom line was that the SEC, which as pinnacle of the self-regulatory pyramid is supposed to supervise the NYSE, had failed to enforce compliance by the NYSE in its failure to enforce compliance by the floor bro-kers. So it was inevitable that the NYSE would get a pass. The SEC wasn't about to give the exchange a bat on the skull when it might bounce back and bop Artie Levitt on the nose. The NYSE was ordered to design programs and implement systems and file an affidavit after twenty-four months and have an independent committee of its board of directors draft a comprehensive man-ual and appoint a consultant. You can bet that all those "independent" direc-tors did a great job doing that, just as great a job as they did overseeing Grasso's compensation.

The NYSE probably could have negotiated this kind of cozy, let's-all-be-pals agreement if it had used one of the ambulance chasers who advertise on the subway that rumbles down Broad Street, but instead it hired the best Wall Street lawyer it could find. His name was Harvey Pitt, and a short while later he climbed to the top of the self-regulatory pyramid and became head of the SEC until he was laughed out of office.

Even the terminally shame-deprived Levitt, who can spin the most laughable cop-out into an investor victory, found this whole NYSE wrist-slapping episode to be so lame that he didn't bring himself to mentioning it in *Take On the Street*. That's the book in which he says that the NYSE "operates at times more like a country club than a quasi-public utility." He ought to know. When Artie was SEC chairman, he used to moonlight as the groundskeeper.

So there you have the self-regulatory system in inaction. A few flunkies indicted, a wrist-slap, and the status quo was preserved. You will note that Grasso played his role to the hilt in that statement on the day the indictment came out, in which he did an excellent job of preserving the illusion of regulation. He issued a tough statement that made it seem as if the NYSE were right there at the front of the posse, hunting down crooked floor brokers. In fact, the SEC said in its 1999 wrist-slap of the NYSE that the probe was initiated by federal prosecutors, and that the NYSE "learned of the scheme from [federal prosecutors] in 1997." The exchange had no choice but to tag along, albeit aggressively and hand in hand.

There is an epilogue to this story of the "where are they now?" variety. We know what happened to Grasso. After he turned the piggy-bank NYSE upside down, he went back home to Locust Valley, applied for food stamps, and hired a flack. Ed Kwalwasser, the chief of regulation, decided to retire in early 2004. He had done a splendid job and would be difficult to replace. It was a touchy business. Since the NYSE is owned by all those people on the trading floor, finding a chief regulator is like hiring a maid who has the job of going through your check stubs whenever she feels like it. Kwalwasser was a real fine old gal—the Wall Street version of Andy Taylor's Aunt Bee. He'd frown and fuss but everyone knew that his heart was in the right place. You could see the love in everything he did, whether it was figuring out a way to let floor brokers break the law, or seeing to it that all those rules and regulations and surveillance mechanisms kept the New York Stock Exchange frozen in time like Petra. He was more a curator than a regulator, or maid.

When Kwalwasser retired in early 2004, the NYSE embarked on a worldwide hunt for a replacement. A search firm gathered résumés from anyone who had ever so much as *read* a regulation—that's how thorough the search was. The résumés were piled knee-deep in a football stadium, teams of highly paid specialists combed through them, and who did they pick of the six billion people who were under consideration? Well, this wide net happened to snare the one person who would make the specialists and floor brokers all warm and cozy. His name was Richard G. Ketchum, and he was president of the NASD when Nasdaq traders were fixing stock prices and systematically screwing investors. At the time the NASD settled Justice Department and SEC charges, it became known that the NASD was aware of Nasdaq price fixing as far back as 1990, but did nothing. Yep, all that was going on while Ketchum was in charge, and he was the guy who fended off Artie Levitt's SEC and the Justice Department, and told the world that everything the brokers did was okay. He was possibly the only person in creation who could play the role of Aunt Bee as convincingly as Kwalwasser.

Think back to the heartwarming story of Kwalwasser and Ketchum whenever you read that some scandal means Wall Street is going to the woodshed. Doesn't happen, folks, not in Mayberry. The media, institutional investors, and Congress couldn't have gotten madder at the NYSE than they did after Grasso bled the place. By the time Ketchum got the NYSE job, all was forgiven and forgotten. Pretty much nobody noticed that Ketchum had done such an outstanding job for the membership of the NASD. Pretty much nobody remembered about the floor brokers and the flipping and all that stuff.

In any case, the SEC has had a lot on its plate, issues of a great deal more importance than floor brokers breaking a few silly laws and the NYSE letting them do it. There is the ongoing controversy surrounding Wall Street analysts, for example, in which not a stone has been left unturned.

Well, maybe just one stone—actually, it's more like a boulder.

CHAPTER THREE

THE BEST ANALYSTS MONEY CAN BUY

I f you're like a lot of people, you rely on the Web site Yahoo! Finance for an up-to-the-minute summary of market news. And well you should. There it is, all neatly lined up: "Today's Markets," "Stock Research," "Financial News," and other useful categories on one side of the page. One of the most useful features is something called "Popular Stories"—recent articles from news agencies and press-release wire services, posted because they were most frequently accessed by users. If you accessed the Yahoo! Finance site at midday on January 19, 2005, you would have seen that ConocoPhillips was applying for a new liquid-natural-gas terminal. Below was word that John M. Dutton & Associates, a Wall Street research firm, had upgraded the shares of Ampex Corporation to "strong buy." Below that, you'd have read that Pfizer stock was surging because of strong drug sales.

The Dutton report, which you could have accessed by clicking on the hyperlink, looked very much like the announcement of a typical analyst report. Down at the bottom, under "About John M. Dutton," you would have found that "Dutton & Associates is one of the largest independent investment research firms in the U.S." Then you'd have read that "its 29 senior analysts are primarily CFAs"—that is, chartered financial analysts, with certificates on the wall attesting to that—and that it covered 85 companies. And then, if you'd bothered to read down to the very bottom, this is what you would have seen:

> The cost of enrollment in our one-year continuing research program is US $33,000 prepaid for 4 Research Reports, typically published quarterly, and requisite Research Notes. The Firm does not

accept any equity compensation. We received $33,000 from the Company for 4 quarterly Research Reports with coverage commencing on 12/02/2004.

Yes, Wall Street research can be yours. All you have to do is pay for it.

The reason this is necessary is clear enough. Spending on research at the largest Wall Street firms declined by 40 percent between 2000 and 2004, according to a study of the subject by Sanford C. Bernstein & Co. Another survey showed 29 percent of companies complaining about reduced research coverage of their firms, as Wall Street firms have slashed their research divisions. That's known as sell-side research, as the purpose (which investors learned all too well in the Internet bubble) is to sell stocks to the public. At the same time, there was a growth in independent research firms, what is known on the Street as buy-side research, financed by large institutional investors—firms like Bernstein, Value Line, Argus Research, and other outfits that mainly focus on large and midsize companies. That has left in the lurch little public companies, which have trouble attracting research coverage, buy side or sell side or any side, in the best of times.

So they're paying for it. Straightforward enough, I guess, except when you think a bit about what that means—and particularly if you dwell a bit on uncomfortable phrases like "conflict of interest," and discomfiting words like *tout* and *shill*. Those are hard concepts to overcome. So when the Nasdaq Stock Market joined with Reuters in June 2005 to create something called Independent Research Network, which will provide analyst coverage to companies for $100,000 a year, the immediate reaction was skeptical. Phrases like "conflict of interest" and "how's that different from advertising" filled the scant coverage, which was a little remarkable because it was—well, *scant*. After all, hadn't two very prestigious organizations, one of which was a stock market, just endorsed a rather dubious way of providing research for investors?

Still, there are two sides to every story. Research firms that take money from companies have a spokesman, a tireless advocate. Let's meet him. He's a nice guy and—who knows?—maybe he'll convince you. He says that paid research is in your best interests.

To reach this man, it is necessary to go to Rego Park, a neighborhood of the New York City borough of Queens. There, in the basement office of a plain brick house, can be found a soft-spoken gent in his mid-sixties by the name of Gayle Essary.

Gayle, who hails from Texas and has had a varied career, is the putative savior of the great silent majority of American publicly traded companies—the 60 percent that don't enjoy the benefits of coverage by Wall Street research. It doesn't matter if your company is in the black or bleeding white. You don't even need a product, but just an idea for one—that makes you "development stage." You can have a bankruptcy lawyer on late-night standby at the courthouse. Your company can be such a disaster area that you are blaming the all-purpose bogeyman—short-sellers who bet against your stock—for your misfortunes. It doesn't matter. Enhanced Visibility and Shareholder Empowerment are just a phone call away. Be sure to have your credit card or checkbook ready.

Gayle is an interesting story in his own right. He is one of Wall Street's most glowing and unqualified successes—a really remarkable tale, even if you don't much care for what he does for a living. He is a man of many talents and occupations. He is a journalist of sorts, owner of a conduit for press releases and snippets of financial news that he calls FinancialWire. He is founder of a group called the CEO Council, which lobbies whomever will listen against the evils of naked short-selling and other supposed small-business concerns. Gayle is a would-be wheeler-dealer, having played a central role in the last IPO of the old millennium, though that was a source of endless aggravation, as bold ventures often are.

Above all he was one of the first visionaries to grasp the potential of the Internet in propagating information about the stocks that would benefit most from the propagation—the thinly traded, sometimes dreadful, but always popular microcap stocks. He began with an Internet stock-promotion mailing list. Over the years, his mind creatively turning, he saw his opportunities and he took them. Today he is believed to be the leading practitioner of paid research, through a company he founded that has gone through various names but is, for the moment, called Investrend Communications, Inc. The company boasts, or, to put it more precisely, Gayle boasts, that it has a stable of 70 analysts on contract and "research coverage" on some 170 companies. Actually determining just which companies are covered by Investrend is not a simple matter, because its Web site lists a lot of companies that have long since said *sayonara* as well as companies just tangentially mentioned, or briefly profiled for no apparent reason. Even if you factor in the padding, Gayle is definitely among the largest players in the field—and definitely the most outspoken in the ever-expanding universe of paid research.

Let's begin by defining the bad guys—nonpaid Wall Street research. Most of us wouldn't ordinarily say "nonpaid," as that is usually a given, but let's do that just this once for the sake of clarity. Nonpaid research is conducted by Wall Street investment banks, brokerage firms, and small non-brokerage-affiliated research firms. One of their common characteristics is that this research is usually costly for investors to purchase, or is distributed only to brokerage customers and the media. Paid research is usually as free as the wind.

A lot of Wall Street research is pretty good, but overall it has, of course, taken on an aroma of scandal that the Street has worked hard to counteract. You probably know how the whole field of research has been terribly torn by opprobrium, mainly as a result of the high-tech boom and bust and the IPO scandals. One would really have to work very hard to make Street research look good, considering its general reputation for bias and overoptimism. As a matter of fact, the general unreliability of Wall Street research has been studied and quantified so minutely that one can say very precisely how bad it really has been. For that we have to thank three leading Wall Street watchers in academia—Brad M. Barber of the University of California at Davis, Reuven Lehavy of the University of Michigan, and Brett Trueman from UCLA—who had their computers rip through the performance of analyst stock picks between 1996 and 2003.

Barber, Lehavy, and Trueman found that the stock picks of nonbrokerage research firms (not including company-paid research) outperformed investment-bank-analyst stock picks at an annualized rate of 8.1 percentage points. That's a lot. They credit this differential to a "reluctance to downgrade stocks whose performance dimmed during the early 2000s bear market."

That, in a nutshell, is the problem with Wall Street analysts. They are overoptimistic, they are basically engaged in dressed-up stock pushing—in other words, they just generally stink. During Artie Levitt's term at the SEC, the big accomplishment was something called Regulation FD, which did absolutely nothing to reduce the amount of misinformation that analysts and companies spread, but was aimed at seeing to it that everybody got the same crap at the same time.

So that's what passes for Wall Street research, and that's what passes for the self-regulatory pyramid's regulation of Wall Street research. Pretty lousy, isn't it? Can't get much worse, you would think. Well, hold that thought.

Paid research firms don't seem very different from nonpaid firms if you don't look at them very closely. They have boutique-sounding names like Taglich Brothers, J.M. Dutton (who we just met on the Yahoo! Web site), Blue-Fire Research, Fieldstone Research, and Equity Research Services. Their reports are superficially quite similar to what you find in Wall Street research. Put a Morgan Stanley research report next to a Dutton research report and you'll see the same jargon, the same target prices and buy or sell recommendations. You'll also find analysts who tend to have "CFA" after their names, meaning that they got their certificate from the CFA Institute—a perfectly respectable institution that, as a matter of fact, might want to think hard about letting paid analysts call themselves CFAs. Paid-firm analysts, CFAs or not, tend to be less experienced than brokerage analysts, however.

So there you have it—two types of research. Yet brokerage research has seen its reputation go into a free fall, while paid research hasn't. That's because in order for your reputation to go into a free fall, you have got to have a halfway decent reputation to begin with. Paid research does not. In fact, one not-unreasonable way of viewing company-commissioned stock research is that its very *existence* is a scandal, and that the self-regulatory pyramid has been lax in not wiping it off the face of the earth.

This is where Gayle Essary comes in. He is about to change all that. Being an organizing kind of guy, he has lassoed the ten largest players of company-paid-research-land into a FIRST Research Consortium. Its motto is "Putting Investors *FIRST*." The acronym stands for Financial Independent Research Standards Task Consortium. A little acronym-cheating there. Perhaps a better *T* could have resulted from more concentrated thinking. (Troubadours?) The Forest Hills post office box and phone number of the consortium are the same as Gayle's, and his guiding hand is apparent from other inimitable touches, such as the lofty, uplifting, "shareholder empowerment" theme of its various pronouncements and correspondence.

Gayle has an uphill but certainly not insurmountable battle ahead of him. The pot of gold lamentably—for Gayle & Co.—*not* at the end of the rainbow is the $432 million that the major investment banks are required to spend on independent research, under the terms of the global settlement hammered out by the banks with Eliot Spitzer in April 2003. Each of the major investment banks is required to hire three independent research firms, and distribute their output to consumers. That is supposed to be Standard & Poor's or Argus or Sanford Bernstein or some other dull mainstay of the Wall Street establishment. Paid firms were excluded from the settlement, but the SEC has shown some flexibility on the subject. In October 2005, it ruled that banks, under certain circumstances, could distribute paid research without violating the settlement. A welcome step, even though settlement moneys still couldn't go to paid research.

No doubt about it: In their battle for respectability, Gayle and his friends have an ally in our self-regulatory system. The entire concept of companies paying for regulation has not been a front-burner issue for the pyramid, and, most of the time, isn't even on the stove. There is something called Section 17B of the Securities Act of 1933, which requires that these paid firms tell the rest of us that they are being paid by the companies. As long as they comply with that (and even if they don't, actually) everything will be just fine.

As a result of this regulation-by-inertia, what you have is a frontier in which the cowboys, Indians, trappers, and gunslingers are free to do pretty much what they want. Gayle, the unelected leader of the paid-research crowd, is truly the man of the hour. He sets the standards. He chastises transgressors. Above all, he fights hard to deal with what might be called the "R factor." *R* as in reputation. *R* as in respectability.

That is the elephant in Gayle's basement. There is a line, a thin and some would say nonexistent line, between company-paid stock research by reputable firms and touting by slimy stock promoters whose "research" sings the praises of crumb-bum stocks. It is an area that has been ignored for years by the SEC under all of its various leaders, and all the rest of the broad expanse of the pyramid. The subject hasn't interested state regulators or Eliot Spitzer either. The man he enjoyed humiliating for several years in a row, Bill Donaldson, felt no particular need to get out in front on this issue, not even to make a splash and get a happy-talk story written about him.

It could be that the subject makes Donaldson uncomfortable. Before coming to the SEC, back when he was just another retired rich guy, he served on the board of a little company, EasyLink Services, which paid for research as a way of reeling in investors. In April 2005 the SEC, with Donaldson conspicuously recused, slapped its wrist for some accounting improprieties that improperly boosted its revenues. The SEC said EasyLink "was able to tout in press releases" that "the company met or exceeded analysts' revenue expectations"—saying that advertising revenues in one quarter were up 47 percent, when they "had actually declined 32.8 percent." Way to go, EasyLink Audit Committee member Bill Donaldson!

As you can see, some companies are in dire need of upbeat analyst coverage. In general, regulators have tended to mention paid research only in passing, when dealing with boiler rooms and stock promoters that pump and dump crummy stocks like EasyLink. As telephone cold-calling banks have fallen out of favor in this country (overseas is another matter), the Internet has taken over, and Internet stock scamsters rely on nice-looking "analyst reports" that are tailor-made for the occasion. Gayle and other paid-research people go to great lengths to distance themselves from that end of the business.

The Street itself, as represented by the two major analyst and investor-relations associations, hasn't much to say on the subject. The analyst community's only effort to grapple with paid research has been a terse, caveat-filled, ultra-cautious few paragraphs of "best practice guidelines" for stock research overall. These were proposed for comment in March 2004 by the Association for Investment Management and Research, which later changed its name to the CFA Institute, and the National Investor Relations Institute, a trade group of the people who write annual reports and such. The AIMR/NIRI guidelines said as follows: "Issuer-paid research is fraught with potential conflicts. Depending upon how the research is written and distributed, investors can be misled into believing that issuer-funded research appears to be from an independent source, when, in reality, it is solicited and paid for by the subject company."

Note the disdain, the sneering tone. It was grudging, it was cautious, and it was a little insulting. Note too how AIMR/NIRI pretty explicitly took the position that what paid-research firms produce is not independent. It must have really galled the folks in the paid-research biz, as "independent" is almost literally their middle name. Imagine how miserable they must have felt.

Well, here is how Gayle played it on the Investrend.com Web site, on a Web page entitled "Endorsements": AIMR and NIRI, he said, "recognizing the growing disparity between the public company 'haves' and 'have nots,' are institutionalizing the practice of paid-for independent research that meets high standards of practice in yet another industry quake in what already has been termed 'The Year of Independent Research.'"

When I first read this, I doubled back to see if Gayle was referring to the same grudging, picky document that I had read. Actually, AIMR and NIRI had only halfheartedly and conditionally accepted paid research—but what the heck, why put too fine a point on the thing? After all, anything resembling ratification of the rent-an-analyst community was music to the ears of the paid-research folks. "This is truly a momentous announcement," Gayle quoted himself as saying in the undated statement. The tough language remained in the final AIMR/NIRI document, published in December 2004, and was actually strengthened a little, but Gayle's joy was undiminished.

I suppose Gayle had reason to be happy. After all, AIMR and NIRI could have simply recommended that paid research be banned. It would not have been a bad idea. In fact, to put it another way, it would have been a good idea. Instead, it was almost as if mainstream analysts wanted the whole thing to go away. But paid research is like that pesky ex-spouse who keeps sending you Valentine's Day cards. It isn't going away. In fact, it is taking the apartment next door. To Gayle and his colleagues, respectability is just one press release away.

Gayle is the antithesis of the nonpaid research crowd in pretty much every way possible. He has no MBA. He has never worked for Wall Street. He is a self-made man, more the kind of individual one might find in a 1920s shoeshine-boy-to-mogul narrative of Wall Street than the yuppified recent era. He started out working for small publications in Texas, moved into marketing, and then, in the late 1960s, was infected by the virus of politics. By the end of the 1960s he was in Washington as head of a political consulting firm called the Institute of Motivational Sciences.

That makes sense. Politics, now a tedious and spirit-destroying enterprise, was alive and zippy back in the 1960s, while Wall Street had all the appeal of a sticky waxed floor. Gayle ran the institute from a town house on Capitol Hill, and had clients that included Democrat Tom Dodd, father of Chris Dodd, and the Republican Missouri senator and future UN ambassador John Danforth.

Not being the complacent and settle-down type, Gayle tired of the political scene during the 1970s and moved to California to try his hand as a publishing magnate. He did his publishing-magnating with a publication called *Dental Lab World*. Other ventures followed that took him to New York—and destiny.

Gayle's march on Wall Street is quite a story. He told me about it in his basement headquarters, with his thirtyish son Todd working nearby and his cat snoozing on the sofa upstairs. It was a scene of modest middle-class respectability and not conspicuous prosperity. Still, what Gayle has done is impressive, particularly when you consider that he was able to make a decent living on the investment end of Wall Street without knowing very much about investing. Unlike Dick Grasso, he built a better mousetrap, though exactly what can be considered the mice chewing at the bait are, in this instance, open to debate.

Gayle stumbled into stocks, the way many of us stumbled into stocks in the early 1990s. The difference is that when you or I stumble into something, we continue to stumble (or at least I do). Gayle immediately found his niche. He is that kind of guy—a niche-finding guy. He began by day trading— actually a subspecialty known at the time as "Dorfman trading." Back then a stock market columnist named Dan Dorfman made a daily appearance on CNBC, and almost every day he said something that moved the markets. Dan would speak, Gayle would buy, watch the stock go up, and then sell. "After a while I timed it out so that I knew that seven minutes after I bought was the time to sell. It would go crazy for seven minutes and then people would start taking profits." It was an early demonstration of how easily stocks could move in price. The quality of the information, which in Dan's case varied widely, was of no consequence. What mattered was that people *believed*.

A new form of information transmogrification was on the horizon, and Gayle stumbled into it. If trading was his drug, Prodigy, the online service, was his enabler. He began running a message board on Prodigy devoted to day trading, and when he tired of that he decided to start his own email group. Day trading wasn't out, but small-cap stocks were definitely in. They were so far in that thousands of investors were being fleeced every day. It was 1995, carefree 1995. The Investor's Champion, Artie Levitt, headed the SEC, and the Internet was viewed in the regulatory community as a kind of nuisance that could be dealt with through the concentrated application of lip service, and was paid almost no attention at all. As the regulators dozed, Gayle established an email list called the Waaco Kid, and that was the beginning of the then-fiftysomething Gayle's new career as a small-cap stocks guy.

The name was appropriate. This was a frontier, after all—and the nearest sheriff was three days' ride away. It was also a, well, *wacky* frontier.

Gayle quickly recognized the genius of the Internet as a populist, all-encompassing, low-cost method of information exchange, as well as a potential source of spare cash. Every list member, who had to pay ten dollars a month for the privilege, would have the right to post stock tips on the list. It was democracy in action, albeit a kind of grimy, Wall Street–style democracy. In fact, in their own little way, the Waaco Kid members could do what the big boys like Dorfman were doing—move the market. Members of the list could generally be counted on to buy the list's stocks, and then they would go up. It was an excellent example of what might be called the Greater Moron Theory of Investing. No matter how odiferous a stock may be, it can always be sold to a moron at a higher price. It helped that this was 1995, the Chinese Year of the Moron.

Looking back during his basement chat with me a decade later, Gayle recalled the Waaco Kid as a kind of online investment club that eschewed stock pumping and decorously minded its p's and q's. He said, "We kept the picks just to the community" because, gosh darn it, it was the right thing to do. "Today people don't seem to care about this, but we thought it would be wrong to submit this out to the general public" when the group was buying a stock, he said with the benefit of years of hindsight. After Gayle turned over reins to someone else, the Waaco Kid issued press releases proclaiming its picks in 1997. "The legendary Waaco Kid, as usual, made the outrageous seem normal over the 4th of July with his suggestion that we give the Boston Harbor back to the British," said one Waaco Kid press release in July 1997, again displaying the Kid's gift for understatement, by way of introducing its latest stock picks.

Even at this early moment in its history, the Internet was acting as a kind of echo chamber without which the Waaco Kid, and other stock-pushing outfits of the era, would have been hard-pressed to find their Greater Morons. Since Gayle's stocks were strictly for trading and not for investment, the risk—if you stayed in the stocks too long—was that you would be the Final Moron. If so, you might wind up being the proud owner of Innovacom, "Stock of the Year" for 1997, and thus be in a position to enjoy the thrills and chills of its bankruptcy in 2001. Or another high-adrenaline stock, HealthTech International, which the Waaco Kid highlighted in March 1995, after which it climbed from $3 to $4 in one day. A month later it was back down to $2.50.* Or you might have wound up with a real toilet splasher called Genesis International Financial, which Waaco Kid members had once hyped as the most "undervalued stock in America." Its shares became subjected to de-acceleration g-forces even before various alleged nastiness persuaded Artie Levitt's SEC to halt trading in the stock in 1997. Eight years later it was trading at one-hundredth of a cent per share. You can say it remained undervalued, in the sense that it was probably worth less than the scrap value of all the papers it had to file with the SEC during its miserable existence.

The Genesis International Financial disaster was a black eye for the Waaco Kid. But the Kid survived, as did Gayle. By then he was keeping his distance from the Waaco Kid. He had other fish to fry by 1997. Gayle had sniffed out a niche. The Waaco Kid had made him a Wall Street guy as well as a small-cap guy. He quit his job consulting for a financial publisher in 1996 and decided to go into business for himself, this time as a promoter of all those small-cap stocks that he had been pushing on the Waaco Kid, all the Innovacoms and Genesis International Financial and HealthTechs and all the promising biotechs like NeoTherapeutics, an emerging pharmaceutical company in 1997 that was still emerging eight years later under another name and at a fraction of the share price.

All these companies needed to get their stories out to the public, for the benefit of the shareholders. There was clearly a market here. Sure, there were stock touters out there—sleazy newsletters that very often accepted shares or stock-purchase warrants in return for touting the stocks, usually in newsletters. Gayle was against that. His enterprise had to be ethical, had to empower shareholders. He would eschew payment in stock and require payment in cash in advance—in theory, at least, imposing a lead shield before the green kryptonite of inherent conflict that comes from having a company pay for research. He

---

* The Waaco Kid really moseyed into the briar patch on this one. Louis Pasciuto, Mob stock peddler extraordinaire and the subject of my book *Born to Steal,* later told me that he was paid cash to peddle that stock to suckers throughout the land. Several Mob figures were charged with manipulating shares of the stock.

began to compare himself to the bond-rating agencies, such as Standard & Poor's and Moody's, which charge companies and local governments to rate their debt (albeit not to issue purchase recommendations; Gayle, though not the agencies, views that as a distinction without a difference).

Gayle was now a genuine, bona fide research guy, an independent-research advocate. No tout he. Would a tout be allowed to sponsor forums for small-cap companies at the New York Society of Securities Analysts (a staid organization that hosts corporate presentations for analysts)? Hell no! The perennially undervalued Genesis International Financial was one notable early forum client. It was a brilliant move, associating himself with the drowsy, establishmentarian NYSSA. Gayle gave his new paid-research venture the sonorous name Investors Research Institute, which made it seem less like a stock-promotion outfit than an operating theater in which investors were dissected and analyzed. He called it an "organization of individual investors," which made it sound even better, even though that was a somewhat imprecise description of his enterprise.

The IRI did good things for ordinary folks, such as announcing in June 1999 that "113 public companies have now pledged to adhere to higher standards of 'accessibility,' 'scrutiny' and 'disclosure,' acquiring the right to display the organization's 'Seal of Best Practices in Investor Relations.'" Fourteen of these companies had automatically earned their seal by enrolling in the "unique" "Public Analysis & Review (PAR) program, which assigns an independent analyst to regularly follow and report on companies with little or no coverage." True, this was not the world's most exclusive club. It says farther down in the release that "anyone may enroll a public company in the PAR program," at a cost he didn't feel moved to disclose at the time, and thereby earn that seal, maybe without even knowing it.

With this bit of promotion, the likes of which would have shamed a street necktie hawker in 1930s New York, the dingy field of paid research was getting a new lease on life, with nice-sounding words slapped on like a fresh coat of shellac. The timing was outstanding—the beginning of a bear market that caused Street research departments to reduce tremendously the number of companies they covered. By 2004, according to First Call, 60 percent of companies were not covered by Wall Street research. Surprisingly large numbers were paying for the privilege, to Gayle and others. According to a 2002 survey by NIRI, 10 percent of all companies surveyed paid for equity research, with more than one-fifth of all microcap companies using paid research. Only 12 of the 378 companies surveyed said they would never consider paying for research.

These are substantial—and, viewed from a different perspective—dismaying numbers. They show that, with Gayle as its voluble spokesman and advocate, company-paid research, like online dating and weblogs, has achieved respectability in what had once been a fringe endeavor utilized by losers. Horror-show companies always have to pay for stock research, much as a fat man of eighty-five with bad skin would have to pay for sex (unless he is a retired rich guy). But as those numbers indicate, not all the companies that pay for research are repulsive, fat, or otherwise unappealing.

Some of them are decent, clean-cut but bland, geeky companies that aren't in industries the Street cares for very much, or don't have the corporate version of social skills. They just find it hard to put on a clean necktie, go out there in the meat market, and sell themselves to Wall Street. Or perhaps they are the misfits of Corporate America, the inhabitants of the Over the Counter Bulletin Board. These are companies so tiny or insolvent or just so damn scary that they don't qualify for listing on any stock exchange or market, not even the crippled and stinky little Amex.

Paid research costs money—but look what you get. Gayle charges $39,840 a year for something he calls Wall Street Coverage. That is the Modified American Plan of paid research. You get a report of twenty-four to thirty-six pages, a quarterly research update, and research notes as needed. You get a stock rating and a target valuation. You also get "all components of Investrend Research Coverage Platforms," which means "announcement of coverage and initial report via Investrend Research Syndicate, FinancialWire™ & Global Press release, AnalystBroadcast™ (including separate announcement of webcast distribution via Investrend Research Syndicate, FinancialWire™ & Global Press Release)." And that's not all, folks. You also get a "permanent InvestorPower™ Page on Investrend Website" and, last but not least, for the entire term of coverage *plus six months* you get "news following via FinancialWire™ & FirstAlert network."

Whew! That's a lot. Now, if you want to pay less than that, you can go for Institutional Coverage—a somewhat inappropriate name, given institutional investors' aversion to stocks that haven't attracted bona fide analyst coverage. It costs $29,800 a year (12 percent discount for twenty-four months) and gets you an eight-page report and everything else you get in Wall Street Coverage. Shave $10,000 off that price and you're in the bargain basement already. You get a rating only "if appropriate" (which kind of implies that folks who pay more get a rating whether or not it's appropriate). You don't get any target valuation, thereby depriving potential investors of the fantasy that comes from thinking that an independent analyst believes the stock is worth such-and-such. Real cheapskates can go for a Criterion report—"One-time, 6-8 page 'expanded view' report by credentialed independent analyst *(with Rating, if appropriate)*"— and total pikers can head for the bottom of the barrel, the Focus report, which merely bestows a "one-time, 4-6 page 'snapshot' by credentialed independent analyst *(no Rating or Target Valuation)*." That costs you $4,950.

As time went on, Gayle built up a clientele of small, not necessarily good but usually gutsy little companies involved in all kinds of interesting if not profitable little businesses. There was Retractable Technologies, a maker of hypodermic needles out in Texas somewhere that struggled relentlessly against the big boys of the pharmaceutical business. There was International Monetary Systems, Ltd., described in a research report as "a provider of financial intelligence programs" (it runs an exchange that lets companies barter goods and services with each other, in case simply buying stuff is not to their liking). And then there was a gaming company called Starnet Communications. A hell of a company.

Starnet was one of Gayle's most illustrious and best-known clients. It was one of those ethical 113 companies that proudly could emboss the Seal of Best Practices on whatever they wished. On March 8, 1999, Starnet enrolled in the PAR, and was awarded a "buy" rating by none other than John M. Dutton, a PAR analyst at the time who later went on to run a paid-research outfit of his very own. Now, not even the best analyst can predict the future. It is certainly no reflection on Gayle or John that in August of that year, more than a hundred local cops and Royal Canadian Mounted Police raided Starnet's offices in Vancouver, arresting six company officials and charging them with illegal gambling and distributing pornography. The pornography charges were later dropped, but the gambling charges were serious stuff, gambling not being allowed in Vancouver. The stock declined 70 percent in one day.

Hey, stuff happens. Was John discouraged? Certainly not. Would he abandon Starnet? Not this guy. If this were a Wall Street nonpaid research firm, he'd have turned tail and run. Instead, John slapped a "temporarily avoid" rating on the stock, a unique rating that implied what happened next—off came the rating. Two months later he assigned Starnet a "strong speculative buy" rating. "We expect the Company can address the remaining legal issues," said Gayle's man on the Starnet beat. Throughout 2000, unsigned research updates tersely recorded the company racking up red ink and accepting its CEO's resignation, and noted that the RCMP held on to $7 million in company funds pending resolution of those criminal charges. The rating was never dropped, as best as

I can tell from the Web site, except that at some point the "strong" came off. Also at some point along the way Starnet dropped Investrend (and not vice versa, as a cowardly Street analyst would have done). Even so, for years afterward a "speculative buy" rating for Starnet (under its new name, World Gaming Plc) could be found on the Investrend Web site. Nowhere on the site was it mentioned that in August 2001, the company pleaded guilty to gambling charges and was fined $6 million. A January 2003 FinancialWire item called the Vancouver raid "a political fracas."

In September 2004, after pretty much everyone else had forgotten about the company, the SEC rushed to the scene, sort of like firemen in some old Keystone comedy rushing to a house after it had already burned to the ground. They took a hard look at the smoldering ruins that were charred to ashes seven years earlier, and slapped Starnet's former executives (though not the company itself) with cease-and-desist orders alleging all kinds of bad things—such as sale of unregistered securities, fraud, false financial statements, and so on—that had been going on while all that "research" was skipping out over the Internet. In July 2005, an SEC judge handed down an eighty-four-page ruling imposing fines and bars from the industry and generally banging everybody's heads together.

This is no knock on Investrend/PAR/IRI or Gayle or John. Stuff happens. But when a company's officials are arrested by the Mounties, doesn't that raise a red flag? What does a company have to do to be dropped by Investrend?

Well, it helps if the company is going to do the dropping.

By the summer of 2004, Investrend was pushing ahead full throttle. The IRI had just kind of faded away by then, and the PAR had long since vanished from the company's press releases. Dutton had left to set up his own firm, which became a promoter of, among other stocks, Bill Donaldson's favorite microcap, EasyLink Services. Gayle would regularly rail against ethical transgressions by his competitors, and late in 2004 Gayle had an opportunity to show just how upstanding he was. He was clearly not going to let another Starnet pull any fast ones.

One of his clients, Retractable Technologies, was growing restless. All that paid research, at $28,000 a year and higher, wasn't allowing its shareholders to dump their shares at a reasonably elevated price, even though Investrend had been rating Retractable a "strong buy" from the moment it began coverage in September 2001. "Stock is substantially undervalued relative to competitors," said the first report. Unsigned updates said much the same thing throughout 2002, 2003, and 2004. In October 2004, this era of good feeling ended. All of a sudden Investrend didn't like Retractable Technologies anymore. As Gayle tells it, it was a matter of principle, a matter of shareholder protection. Retractable stopped talking to his analyst.

Now, that is bad. That is worse than a company being convicted of a crime or its execs being tossed in the can. Literally. After all, Starnet never lost its rating for tangling with the Mounties. But Starnet did not attack the sanctity of the analyst-company-shareholder relationship, something that would irreparably hurt what Gayle never tires of saying is his *only client,* the shareholder.

On October 11, 2004, Investrend issued a report withdrawing its "strong buy" rating and target share price. It was the kind of fearless research to which any Wall Street analyst could point with pride: "A previous report (and previous analyst) on RVP rated the Company Strong Buy with a target valuation of $11 per share," said analyst Ryan C. Fuhrman. "The current analyst can neither refute nor support this rating due to an inability to speak with the Company and due to a current lack of visibility regarding future operations as a result of the below detailed developments. As such, the current rating has been revised downward to 3/No Rating."

Retractable fired back two weeks later by issuing a press release attacking Investrend for inaccuracies—and by pointing out a little detail omitted from the October 11 report. The company said in an October 22, 2004, statement that "Retractable notified Investrend president Gayle Essary of its decision to terminate the relationship in a letter dated August 13, 2004." It seems that nasty analyst report came out two months *after* Retractable fired Investrend. The October 11 Investrend report doesn't say that.

Gayle was not taking any of that lying down. He responded by lowering the rating again, on the grounds that the analyst hadn't said anything inaccurate and that Retractable was being inaccurate for saying that, and that shareholders shouldn't be misled in that fashion. Then Retractable filed a routine Form 8-K with the SEC containing its press release. "Looks like the company isn't going to let the matter die," Gayle emailed me the night that happened, ". . . what we call in Texas waking sleeping dogs."

So went the Battle of Retractable Needle Junction. It sputtered on for a little while like that. Clearly Retractable viewed the Investrend analysts as hired hands who could be told to take a hike like any other hired hand, and didn't buy any of that hooey about Investrend "representing the shareholders" or its analysts being "independent." As CFO Douglas Cowan put it in the October 22 press release, "We simply felt after more than three years of using the service that neither the company nor its shareholders had realized any benefit from it." You'd think that letting shareholders know what was going on would be benefit enough. You'd think that—if paid research were the real thing, and not dressed-up stock touting.

Regulators could put an end to all this phony-baloney posturing and play-acting malarkey by simply slapping an "86" on paid research. Or they could let the paid-research purveyors ply their questionable trade, but require that they say on the front page of each "research report," in boldface, **THE COMPANY PAID $XX,XXX FOR THIS REPORT.** That would go a long way to take the stink out of paid research.

Meanwhile, it would be awfully nice if the SEC would enforce the rules that are on the books right now. That shouldn't be too difficult. For one thing, most of the stuff cranked out by the rent-an-analyst shops is published on the Internet. They don't have to do very much legal spadework because there is only one rule (apart from the laws against fraud) that applies specifically to paid research—Rule 17b of the Securities Act of 1933. That's the one requiring disclosure of sums that companies pay to be analyzed. However, Rule 17b isn't worth anything unless it is enforced—with zero tolerance for violations.

In September 2004, years after these outfits started springing up all over the place, the SEC took action against a major rent-an-analyst mill. That was the first time it seems to have been done so against a major player in this rapidly growing field. The pinnacle of our self-regulatory pyramid found that Taglich Brothers, a leading vendor of paid research that also operates a brokerage, allegedly disregarded Rule 17b, systematically and "willfully," over a two-year period. The firm would put on its reports that it was being paid, but wouldn't say how much—which is, after all, the whole point of Rule 17b. You've got to tell investors how much you are paid to tout stock. It's really not that complicated.

The SEC had a golden opportunity to tell the paid-research crowd that it was all over them like a cheap suit, and that it would brook no further nonsense. Instead, Taglich was censured, ordered not to violate the rule in the future, and socked, very gently, with a $50,000 civil penalty. That for a firm which charges dozens of companies $20,000 a year for "research coverage." Taglich exemplified the problem with paid research—it looks like the real thing but really isn't. The SEC, unfortunately, reacted by imposing a penalty that looked like the real thing but really wasn't. Instead of giving Taglich a good thrashing with a tire iron, it flayed the firm with a wet soba noodle.

The SEC did not even get the satisfaction of hearing Taglich rend its garments and tearfully admit guilt. It neither admitted nor denied the charges, as part of a settlement with the SEC in which it agreed to the "sanctions" imposed.

This is standard SEC practice in settlements, by the way. A transgressor is allowed to say "I am not going to do X, Y, and Z ever again, so help me, but I'm not going to say if I just did X, Y, or Z."

The SEC, fresh from its triumph over Taglich, tucked away its soba noodles in a Ziploc bag, and hauled them out again a day before Inauguration Day. On January 19, 2005, the same day that Dutton & Associates made the Yahoo! Finance site, the SEC announced its second regulatory action in history against a major purveyor of paid research—John M. Dutton. According to the SEC, Dutton had been told quite some time before that he was not following that pesky Rule 17b. Yet darn it, he just kept on forgetting about the only rule specifically applying to his business. Back in July 2002, the SEC staff notified Dutton, "through counsel, that the general disclaimers used by Dutton in published research reports were insufficient and violated Section 17(b) of the Securities Act." Dutton didn't clearly disclose that the companies were paying for the reports. Despite the warning, Dutton allegedly continued violating Rule 17b through the end of 2002. Good news, though. After six months of thinking it over, Dutton changed its ways in 2003, and had complied with the rule since then.

Still, the SEC had to act. After all, it had been ignored. So, after the usual "let's sit around for two years and think about it" delay, the SEC and Dutton worked out a deal. Without admitting or denying the allegations, Dutton agreed to the sanctions ordered. From now to the end of time, Dutton would "cease and desist from committing or causing any violation or future violation of Section 17(b) of the Securities Act." That was that. No other penalties, not even the fifty-buck fine you get for parking in front of the SEC building in downtown DC (providing you are not booted or towed). Two days later, the SEC imposed a $25,000 penalty on the firm, which is less than one of those eighty-five companies pays for one year of coverage. There were no further penalties imposed on Dutton personally.

Now, don't get the wrong idea. If you think that the SEC wasn't on top of all this, you are very much mistaken. Bill Donaldson was personally involved, though he'd probably like you not to know that he was personally involved. If you looked at the list of companies that Dutton forgot to disclose were paying him, you would find EasyLink—the little tech company that Donaldson had the honor of serving as a director before he moved to the SEC.

The Taglich and Dutton settlements received little attention, despite the latter's uncomfortable association with the SEC chairman. Ditto for a soba-noodle slap on paid-report mill BlueFire Resarch ($50,000 penalty; no admission of guilt) in July 2005. That was not surprising, as SEC soba-noodle slaps happen all the time, and too many other events were taking place that diverted attention from this major league case of regulatory nonfeasance. A particularly vacuous presidential campaign had come and gone, meaningless "market structure" and dumb hedge fund reforms were under way, and, above all, the SEC was playing catch-up with Spitzer on the mutual fund extravaganza and a variety of scandals that were monopolizing everyone's attention.

After the Bush victory, word began to circulate that Bill Donaldson's job was in jeopardy. Business lobbyists were urging the president to get rid of him before completion of his term in 2006. He was just too tough.

Despite all the backbiting, Donaldson managed to keep his focus on the important things, such as small companies of the kind that he used to proudly serve as a diligent board member and audit-committee watchdog. So it was no real surprise that he received some help in that regard from Gayle's CEO Council.

On March 7, 2005, Donaldson announced the creation of the SEC Advisory Committee on Smaller Public Companies, established "to examine the impact of the Sarbanes-Oxley Act and other aspects of the federal securities laws on smaller companies." One of the charter members of this prestigious advisory panel was Investrend's director of corporate relations, the operator of a small New Jersey investment firm named James A. "Drew" Connolly III. The SEC announcement observed that "Mr. Connolly was a founding member of the CEO Council, an organization of executives of smaller public companies." Connolly's job on the SEC committee would be to "represent smaller over the counter companies and professionals who work with them, as well as investors in these companies."

Had anyone at the SEC bothered to look, they might have been able to locate a list, which was available for a time on the Internet, that identified some of the founding members of the CEO Council. Right there they could have found some familiar names that might have made them feel right at home.

There was Gabor S. Acs, CEO of a firm called Penny King Holdings, an alleged penny-stock huckster who had just been sanctioned by the SEC and socked with $643,962.81 in penalties and disgorgements for making false statements in press releases and on Web sites.

There was Ed Loessi, CEO of a firm called Build the Board, whose name was on a March 1998 list of brokers posted on the Web by a transnational boiler room called International Asset Management. Ed told me in an email that he was surprised he was on that list, because he just "stuck around" there for a couple of months. He left, he said, after he realized his job would involve pushing OTC stocks on people throughout Asia and his license was never transferred there. (Well . . . he says he was there in August 1997 and the list was posted in May 1998, but what the hell—the important thing is he was doing *absolutely nothing* for two or whatever months as he stuck around.)

And then there was the true star of the CEO Council inaugural list: Jonathan Lebed, who received some small measure of prominence in late 2000 as being one of the few fifteen-year-olds to ever be prosecuted by the SEC for securities fraud.

We'll be picking up again with Jonathan in a later chapter. For the time being, though, let's just leave Jonathan right there—a CEO, proudly on the roster of the CEO Council, right there with the Penny King and the totally innocent ex-IAM-broker-in-1997-or-1998, Ed Loessi. It's a good image to have in the back of your mind as you read this book, particularly the next chapter.

CHAPTER FOUR

DIALING THE GLOBE FOR DOLLARS

In 1997, word began to creep into the back pages of Irish newspapers that something sinister had been happening to a lot of hardworking farmers and merchants in the west of Ireland. People there were getting calls from very reputable-sounding firms that were, or said they were, in places like Barcelona and the United States and Switzerland.

This was the era of George Soros and the irresistible allure of global investing. Ireland had a small, dull little stock market of its own, with dull little companies in dull industries like cement and shipping and zzzzzzzzzzz . . . It was enough to put an investor to sleep! These people on the phone, who had very nice British or Australian accents, were giving Irish people the opportunity to reap gains from the U.S. market they were reading about at the time. High tech! Telecommunications! Motorcycles! Varrooom!!!!

What these hapless souls didn't realize was that the people calling them were doing the reaping—and that they were the harvest. The firms at the other end of the phone line had impressive-sounding names, and everything seemed legitimate. After all, cold-calling was, and is, an accepted technique by established stockbrokers. Who knew? Not the good people of west Ireland, even though these brokers were a bit overoptimistic in their sales pitches, even by what the Brits call stock-hawking standards.

It's not hard to see why the west of Ireland was targeted by overseas boiler rooms. Anyone who has ever been to rural Ireland can give you the reason. It comes back to a question that people often ask themselves when they go to places like Donegal, Tralee, Kerry, Dingle, and other such places: "Have you ever met such friendly, honest, delightful people?"

No, you haven't met such lovely people, people who would give you the shirts off their backs—and neither have stock scamsters, for that matter. They like people with those characteristics. They'll rip the shirts off their backs, if not offered. Big, dirty cities with cynical, suspicious people are poor prospects for telephone cold-callers. Green, lush places with moss on the stones (a sign of clean air, or so they say) are natural targets for scamsters. Rural people are trusting, or at least more likely to be trusting than big-city dwellers. They are honest, and as such they expect other people to be honest. That is a mistake when you get a call from someone trying to sell you stock.

The shares that were being pushed on the good people of western Ireland were run-of-the mill microcaps. They had names like DW Filters, Global Connect Direct, Titan Motorcycles, Arc Communications, Ultimistic, and Arc Technology. All were tiny U.S. stocks and most traded on the OTC Bulletin Board, the cesspool of the U.S. markets, the last refuge of stocks too small and dreary to trade anywhere else. The good people of Ireland who bought those stocks were getting a lesson in thievery from one of the stock-pushing world's perennial favorites—the offshore boiler room.

People across the world are enjoying the thrill of flushing their life savings down the toilet—and it is more often than not an American toilet.

The offshore stock-pushing wave that began in the mid-1990s in Ireland and western Europe, and spread like mad cow disease through the rest of the English-speaking world, is the latest incarnation of a Wall Street institution known as the pump-and-dump stock scam. If you pay any attention at all to financial news, you have probably heard word wafting over gently from Washington and the media that pump-and-dump scams are a thing of the past and that regulators have everything tightly under wraps.

In fact, they are alive and well and more dangerous than ever, and one of the things that make them far more lethal than previously is the public perception that stock scamsters are confined to wood-paneled boardrooms, where they engage in multibillion-dollar thievery of the Enron variety but have vanished from the more straightforward pastime of lying about a stock. The folly of that thinking was demonstrated in the early 1990s, when penny-stock scams dipped below the regulatory gunsights and regulators were saying publicly that they were on the wane. In fact, they were about to spring up again in a different guise, bigger and uglier than ever, as "chop houses," selling crummy microcap stocks and dodging regulators yet again.

This latest incarnation of the chop houses takes full advantage of regulatory ennui. It's tough enough to nudge the self-regulatory pyramid into action when American investors are being hurt. Overseas investors? Out of sight, out of mind—and out of the regulatory field of interest completely. The problem with that mindset is that the same people who gorge themselves on overseas wallets are not sated. They're only whetting their appetites—for you.

Here's a statistic that demonstrates the success of this form of stock scamming: According to the Australian Securities Commission, citizens of that country, which has fewer people than reside in the state of Texas, were ripped off by $400 million in the early part of the millennium by offshore stock pushers peddling American stocks. And that, the Aussies point out, is just a rough and conservative estimate. The overall figure worldwide is hard to calculate, but is believed by the Australian regulators to run into the billions of dollars. More than two hundred offshore stock pushers are listed on the Web sites of the Australian and New Zealand securities regulators. Though only a few of those firms are actually situated in the United States, American stocks are invariably involved and American stock-promotion firms, run by the same crooks who are always finding new ways to victimize you, profit from every one of the hundreds of U.S. stocks sold overseas.

In theory, at least, regulators recognize the scope of the problem. The SEC Web site is bubbling over with concern. But the U.S. response has been far from robust. The SEC, after sitting on its hands for about a half dozen years, brought its first case in recent years against an offshore stock scamster in 2002. By 2005 it had brought a grand total of three cases against offshore boiler rooms. The scorecard for Eliot Spitzer? Zip.

Overseas prosecutors have brought a smattering of criminal cases against the offshore boiler rooms. Thailand, Laos, Britain, Spain, France, and Australia are among the countries that have sicced the cops on offshore stock scamsters. But their efforts have been uncoordinated and ineffective. It's just too lucrative to be wiped out, particularly when U.S. authorities have been dozing through the whole thing, thereby allowing crummy U.S. stocks to become roving badwill ambassadors for this great democracy.

Besides, the economics are irresistible.

Offshore boiler rooms are a kind of outsourcing, but with a twist. Instead of hiring people in places like Bangalore to operate phone banks that *take* calls from American customers and *solve* problems for them, these overseas stock promoters operate phone banks—"boiler rooms"—in places like Bangkok to *make* calls, generally to non-American customers, to sell American stocks and *create* problems for them.

The key concept at work here is overabundance. At the customer service and technical-support phone banks in India, it is an overabundance of low-paid bright people. At the transnational boiler rooms, what you have is an overabundance of investor greed and a bumper crop of stocks that can be bought for pennies and sold for big bucks to the aforementioned greedy investors.

The effect of both forms of outsourcing is the same: As a result of the miracle of cross-border telephony, the profitability of the enterprise sponsoring the phone bank is strengthened, be it AOL, Dell, or the people who satisfy unreasonable investor expectations by pushing lousy U.S. stocks. The world is made "flat" for crooks, as Thomas Friedman might say.

The boiler-room business model has been a mainstay of Wall Street larceny for decades. The concept is simple: Stocks in shaky companies, obtained at little or no cost, are sold to investors at huge profits. In the 1980s and 1990s, boiler rooms ripped off Americans for gobs of money, perhaps $10 billion a year at their height in the mid-1990s. Their names occupy a special place in Wall Street history, penny-stock houses like First Jersey and Blinder Robinson in the 1980s, and their 1990s successors Hanover Sterling, A.R. Baron, and so on. There were dozens of them.

Domestic boiler rooms began to be replaced by the Internet in the late 1990s. But overseas boiler rooms have never slackened at all. In the 1980s, when the bull market in the United States was just starting to gear up, boiler rooms were operated in Amsterdam under the supervision of Irving Kott—definitely a name to keep in mind if you're keeping a stock-scamster box score. This Canadian fraudmeister moved to Europe after being nabbed in a mining-stock scam in Ontario. His name still pops up today, making this hardy troubadour a roving ambassador of Wall Street bad will. After paying a $4 million fine in Amsterdam in 1990 and moving back to these shores, Irving went right back into business, bless his greedy little heart, and has been tangling with regulators and law enforcement ever since.

Another early Vasco da Gama in reverse was a man whose name should reflexively send your hand to your wallet. His name was Thomas F. Quinn, and he is usually referred to in the media as a disbarred lawyer because that is one of the kindest things you can say about him. In the 1980s, at about the same time as Irving was establishing his boiler room amid the hippies and canals of Amsterdam, Tommy Quinn was in France, eating well and setting up a network of boiler rooms throughout Europe. He returned to the United States in the 1990s.

Quinn is also a kind of must-mention fellow for anyone writing a book about securities fraud, mainly because he has done so much of it and suffered so little as a result. He is relevant to this book chiefly in one sense: as an example of how simply marvelous it is to be sued!

I know, most of us don't like being sued. It is so . . . *rude*. All those accusations and nastiness and wherefores and forthwiths. A lawsuit is a kind of controlled, legalized form of rudeness, society's way of channeling aggression. Wall Street generally dislikes lawsuits, and, as Rand Groves and others so situated have experienced, the legitimate, established Street firms go to great lengths not to be sued, when you are the suer.

However, individuals who are not legitimate have a different perspective on the lawsuit than you or I. Quinn was one such person. As a disbarred lawyer, he had been subjected to a good deal more rudeness than the majority of ordinary people. In the 1980s, as federal prosecutors aimed their grand juries at insider traders, Mike Milken and other, better-publicized transgressors, the self-regulatory pyramid's weapon of choice against the Tommy Quinns and other penny-stock hucksters was the rude, annoying, but totally harmless lawsuit.

The SEC obtained a court order freezing and seizing Quinn's assets for some stock-fraud schemes he hatched in the United States. The SEC's effort to squeeze bucks out of the rock that was Tommy Quinn made the federal docket sheets long enough to stretch to China—without showing commensurate success. Tommy moved on to other things, including an association with rogue financier Martin Frankel. He had lost the lawsuits, but won the war.

In the mid-1990s, while the SEC was still chasing down Tommy Quinn's assets and just starting to get wind of the boiler-room menace in the United States, the scamsters were two steps ahead of them. That was when they made their move into the west of Ireland, and also branched out elsewhere in Europe and in East Asia.

The stocks they sold to the people of Europe and the Pacific Rim were in scuzzy little companies. Most would be a distant, foul memory within a few years. But they were, it must be emphasized, almost always legitimate, real companies, with actual or planned operations and even a smattering of revenues. They were certainly not the fictional outfits that the public usually associates with stock scams.

That perception was, in fact, a serious problem for the investors in Ireland and elsewhere who were sucked in to these scams, and would continue to plague investors as the offshore stock pushers spread throughout the world in the years ahead. It would have been much better from the victim perspective if the firms *weren't* legitimate.

Some years later, in a revealing study of boiler-room techniques commissioned by the Australian Securities Commission, researchers found that the legitimacy of touted companies was actually a major advantage from the crook perspective. The fact that these stocks existed "conferred legitimacy upon the broker," the Australian researchers said.

Also typical of offshore scams was that the stock peddlers—using a technique perfected by U.S. boiler rooms in the 1990s—spent time jawing with their customers. These were not quick-hit, scripted sales pitches. The brokers patiently answered investor questions and sent them brochures and written materials, just as legitimate firms did. True, claims in the brochures were fake and even the addresses of the firms were also, at times, fictitious. But the victims found out long after it was too late.

For the Irish in 1995 and 1996, what happened was a fairly typical pump-and-dump boiler-room scam, very much the same kind of thing that was going on in the States at the time. Some hapless Irish investors were sold shares in Applied Technology at about six dollars a share in 1995, and by the following year those shares were selling for about a penny. Applied, a legitimate company like the rest of its ilk, was engaged in "object oriented software development," but the only object that interested the stock pushers was known as the "wallet." The firm that sold Applied Technology to the Irish had the nice-sounding name of Unified Capital Group, was situated in Geneva, and conveniently vanished after walking away with a good chunk of the savings of western Ireland.

Other investors put their money with an alleged U.S. brokerage firm called Abbott Financial Services. That happened to be the name of several legitimate firms, which was probably why the scamsters used it. Its brochure showed an address in Seattle and a phone number, neither of which were its actual address or phone number when the Irish Embassy tried to track down the firm for a panicky investor.

That was a typical scenario that was to be repeated time and again in the years to come, right up to the present day. The boiler rooms fanned out to the Philippines, Laos, Bangkok, Portugal, Spain, and Switzerland, as well as the good old U.S.A. By 2000, investors were targeted in Japan, England, western Europe, Australia, and New Zealand. (India has been resistant to this form of reverse outsourcing, or so people there tell me.) Australia and New Zealand securities administrators fought back by listing the names of alleged scamsters on their Web sites, with Australia listing its first eighty-two unlicensed cold-calling firms in 2000. New listings were still being added in 2005. No surprise here. The supply of crappy American stocks is inexhaustible.

Hundreds of U.S. stocks are being peddled overseas, and in many instances buying these stocks is, if you can imagine, even worse than buying them in the U.S. Buying stocks from an offshore boiler room is very often a bit like stuffing your money into a Roach Motel. Often, stocks pushed overseas have to be held for a year before they are sold—which is an eternity when you are holding a piece-of-dung stock. That's because there is actually a class of shares that are designed to be stuffed into Roach Motels, exclusively for non-U.S. investors, under something called Regulation S of the securities laws.

Regulation S has been around since 1990, and abuses of this particularly odious section of the securities laws have been lamented in the media ever since. Most of the weeping and hand wringing that you may have seen involves *abuses* of Regulation S. But the problem is not that Regulation S is abused, but that it *exists*. As the overseas boiler rooms are demonstrating every day, Regulation S is America's gift to the stock scamsters of the world. It couldn't have been more beautifully drafted, from the crook standpoint, if the crooks themselves had dreamed it up. Like most daffy ideas that come out of Washington generally, this one had good intentions—to give companies, particularly the scrawnier ones, a way of tapping the overseas capital markets that might not otherwise give them the time of day.

Regulation S shares (they can also be bonds, actually) are unregistered securities and can be sold at any price the stock promoters conjure up out of thin air. Shares issued under Regulation S must be sold exclusively outside the United States. As originally envisioned by the geniuses who thought up this idea, the shares had to be held for forty days before they could legally be sold in the United States. So some bright scamsters would set up phony offshore accounts to buy Regulation S stock at a cheap price, wait the requisite forty days, and sell the shares at inflated prices back in the United States. To fix that anomaly, the holding period was extended to a year in 1998, during Artie Levitt's tenure at the SEC. Good old Artie—he knew just what to do. One scam ebbed away, another was nurtured. The Roach Motels were open for business.

A one-year holding period fixes one of the major problems facing stock scamsters. One of the things the scamsters hate the most is customers selling stock while they are hard at work in their boiler rooms, peddling shares. Selling depresses share prices, and you don't want prices to go down at the same time your cold-callers are selling them. A flood of shares on the market makes it impossible for them to control, or "box," the market in a particular cruddy stock. So crooked U.S. brokers have frequently refused to take orders from customers who wanted to sell their stocks, or allowed them to dump their shares only when a buyer could be found. Or—sort of like a dealer in gray-goods audio equipment—allowed the sales to be unloaded only in exchange for other lousy stocks. Such tactics are flagrantly illegal, and were often cited in the criminal cases against the boiler rooms in the late 1990s. Regulation S resolves that issue.

Regulation S stocks aren't used in every offshore stock scam, but in enough to make one wonder why the feds don't simply get rid of the thing entirely. After all, the markets managed to exist perfectly well in the pre–Regulation S years before 1990. From the boiler-room perspective, Regulation S makes a great crime into pretty much a perfect crime.

You might think that all these offshore boiler rooms got people mad and that people must have been thrown in jail, and that these outfits were shut down. You would be right. It has happened a couple of times—and it hasn't made a damn bit of difference.

One of the firms that was selling shares to Irish investors, the Lisbon affiliate of a Swiss-based firm called Paramount Securities, was raided by the Portuguese police in 1997. A British national who headed the local office was convicted of various charges, and the Swiss parent was shuttered by banking authorities. It was just what you'd see on an old episode of *Dragnet*. Bad guy arrested. Justice done.

The only problem was that the Irish investors were still saddled with stocks that weren't worth very much. And the scamsters were not deterred. While it was true that one of their people was nabbed, that was a fluke—and they knew it. Nor were they deterred when Thai authorities raided boiler rooms, all peddling Regulation S stocks, operated by three outfits—the Brinton Group, Benson Dupont, and Sigama Capital. That happened in July 2001. Even though the Thais put on a convincing Joe Friday act, arresting eighty-five cold-callers, deporting them, and eventually convicting the seven ringleaders, the result was the same. The boiler rooms continued to chug along throughout the globe—in Thailand and other places—as if nothing had happened. (It might have helped just a little that the seven were convicted on reduced charges, received suspended sentences, and cut loose.)

What did the United States do while all this was going on? Nothing. Not one single, solitary thing was done throughout the 1990s, into the 2000s, until 2002, when the SEC sued an operator of overseas boiler rooms called the Millennium Group. A different bunch of people were sued in 2003, and another bunch in late 2004—once a year. Not bad. In a hundred years or so, each of the hundred or so members of the offshore boiler-room community will have a lawsuit of its very own.

The 2003 case was the most interesting for a number of reasons. The suit was filed in October of that year against twenty-one defendants, led by a young fellow named David M. Wolfson. Whatever you might think of the SEC case against Wolfson & Co.—bold and ambitious or too little, too late—the documents in the case provide the first close-in look at how the overseas scamsters work. It is a pretty remarkable case in several ways.

For one thing, there is the timing. This scheme allegedly involved boiler rooms in Bangkok that were set up in October 2002, a year *after* the Bangkok boiler rooms were raided. Also remarkable is how open and brazen this alleged scam was, beginning with the defendant. Wolfson, who is from Salt Lake City, was twenty-three years old when the scheme was hatched. What's interesting is not his age but his family background. His father was Allen Z. Wolfson, a career stock swindler with convictions stretching back two decades. He was one of the principal defendants in a massive case, one that received widespread publicity, which was brought against dozens of Mob-linked stock swindlers in June 2000. The elder Wolfson was supposedly involved in the offshore scam his son ran, by helping to set up one of the companies peddled overseas. All that organizing and peddling took place after Allen Wolfson was arrested, and while his June 2000 case was working its way through court. He was convicted, after trial, in early 2004.

Did David Wolfson turn away from the alleged pursuit of an allegedly less-than-honest dollar just because Dad was targeted by the feds? I should say not. In fact, the SEC complaint indicates that he wasn't deterred by the fact that *he* was targeted by the feds. In 2002, David Wolfson was named, along with his father, in an SEC enforcement action related to yet another pump-and-dump scheme. But a lawsuit from the SEC just rolled right off his back. SEC documents make it stunningly clear that David did little to conceal his role in the scheme. He was president of the stock-promotion firm that put the whole deal together. His name wasn't on any of the companies that issued the stocks, but one of them, Stem Genetics (the one Dad helped set up), had the same address as a suite of offices where David openly ran several other companies.

By the way, be sure to stick the word *allegedly* into every sentence of the preceding paragraph. In the eyes of the law, David Wolfson is neither guilty nor innocent, but in a kind of twilight zone in which both are possible. He hasn't admitted a darn thing, but he hasn't denied anything either. He just isn't saying.

Shortly before Christmas of 2004, David settled the SEC charges that were brought against him in the offshore boiler-room suit in 2003 and the unrelated stock-scam suit in 2002. He neither admitted nor denied liability. He consented to $3 million in civil penalties for both cases. And, perhaps most important of all, he promised never to do it again.

Well, he may keep his promise. More surprising things have happened in the world. True, the charges that David was able to buy his way out of were about as nasty as the ones that were brought against his pa's dozens of boiler-room and mobster buddies in June 2000. If the younger Wolfson and the rest of them did all the things they are accused of doing, why not go all the way—and press criminal charges? The SEC failed when it sued Tommy Quinn. It didn't put a dent in the scamming that he committed, and it wasn't even able to squeeze a dime from him. Yet here they go again, suing, and settling, and not even getting an admission of guilt—a gut-wrenching, confession-is-good-for-the-soul admission, "I did it."

The boiler rooms still going strong in Europe and Asia haven't been even the slightest bit deterred by all this regulatory huffing and puffing. They've done the math, which is dramatically in their favor. The boiler room involved in the Wolfson case received 70 percent of the money that was poured into this scheme from investors around the world, and the other 30 percent was divided among the issuers and the stock promoter, Wolfson in this instance.

A tax-free skim of 70 percent of the take—more than 80 percent if you factor in the stock promoter—is enough to risk a spell in jail. Or to put it more precisely, the risk of getting away with it.

Of course, plenty of Wall Street crooks aren't getting away with it. Their problem is not that they committed a crime, but that they committed the *wrong* crime.

CHAPTER FIVE

THE GHOST OF MUTUAL FUNDS PAST

Charles Joseph Kerns Sr. is the kind of guy a lot of people in south Florida would like to sock right in the mouth. He is, by all accounts, a crook of many talents, a grifter who steals as casually as you and I brush our teeth in the morning. He is in his mid-sixties, a square-headed man with a bad toupee who steals with a practiced finesse, and steals from just about everybody who has made the mistake of crossing his path. "This was the worthless check written by Charles J. Kerns as earnest money for my house." That's the caption to a photo of a five-thousand-dollar rubber check that appears on charleskerns.com, which one of his victims designed as a less-than-loving tribute to Charles J. Kerns Sr. In the early part of the millennium, Kerns found a new method of accumulating victims. He took the path of many career criminals and joined the brokerage business, via a firm in Boca Raton called Geek Securities.

In several cases that churned their way through the federal courts of Miami during 2004, Kerns and the operators of Geek Securities were convicted of various crimes and sentenced to prison terms of varying severity. For Kerns it was a throw-away-the-key twenty-seven years. The charges in the Geek Securities cases were the usual Boca-brokerage sliminess. There was sale of unregistered securities, a stock-loan scam—and also something really bad. "THIRTY-SIX COUNT INDICTMENT CHARGES MUTUAL FUND MARKET TIMING AND LATE TRADING SCHEME" was the title of a press release that was issued by the Office of the U.S. Attorney for the Southern District of Florida on June 24, 2004.

Kerns and his co-thieves, the owners of Geek Securities, were playing an essential role in the regulatory process. They were serving very admirably as clay ducks in the latest Wall Street shooting match, the Mutual Fund Late Trading Scandal. Kerns himself didn't do any of that late-trading stuff. That wasn't his style. He was an old-fashioned worthless-paper-pusher. But he had fallen in with some bad company. As the Miami federal prosecutor pointed out in a press release, these were "the first federal court criminal convictions for mutual fund 'market timing' and 'late trading' in the nation."

Selling unregistered securities and otherwise ripping off investors in a straightforward fashion—in the sense of actually taking their money—won't get most regulators and law-enforcement people out of bed nowadays. But if you get caught up in the Mutual Fund Scandal—well, you had better put your bondsman on speed-dial and feed the goldfish before leaving the house every morning. Getting hooked up with a bunch of mutual fund late traders was the biggest mistake of Charles J. Kerns's miserable life. He should have gone down to Little Havana and hooked up with methamphetamine dealers instead.

So far in this book our self-regulatory pyramid has been in a state of repose, calmly snoozing away while investors are ripped off. But now you get a chance to see our regulators aroused, motivated, and in motion. The Mutual Fund Scandals, encompassing late trading, market timing, and allied forms of misconduct, are an area of endeavor about which our regulators have been as busy as a turkey farm in November, axes flying. Unless you've been orbiting Venus for most of the past few years, you probably know that there is such a thing as the Mutual Fund Scandals, and you probably know that they are bad, based on all that has appeared in the media and the sheer volume of publicized bloviating on the subject. Even so, you may not be too certain as to the exact nature of the scandalous conduct in these particular scandals, whether your fund was involved, and what if anything you should do about it. You've probably noticed that the term *late trading* has been tossed around a lot, and since people are being thrown in the clink for it, you might reasonably assume that it is pretty awful.

It is probably just as well if you haven't paid close attention and don't know what all this Mutual Fund Scandals stuff is all about. Because when you sit down and take a close look at this crusade *du jour* of the self-regulatory pyramid, you are likely to get mad. And you won't be mad for reasons that the self-regulatory pyramid wants you to be mad.

Let's go back to D-Day in what the *Wall Street Journal* described as the launching of a "new front in allegations of financial-market abuses," September 3, 2003. New York Attorney General Eliot Spitzer charged "that a hedge-fund manager arranged with several prominent mutual-fund companies to improperly trade their fund shares—some after the market's close—reaping tens of millions of dollars in profits at the expense of individual investors." So said the front page of the *Journal* the following day, and the front pages of the nation's newspapers were similarly alive with this new species of Wall Street greed.

It was startling for several reasons. A scandal in, say, the hedge fund industry would be far less jarring. Hedge funds, which are supposed to be private partnerships for the wealthy,* are mysterious—if you want to reach for an inappropriate adjective, as people often do when dealing with money, you might even say "sexy." You expect adventurous and "sexy" areas of the financial business, such as investment banking in the eighties, to have occasional scandals. But mutual funds are about as sexy as your maiden aunt, the one with the parakeet. They have carefully nurtured a reputation for blandness and scrupulous hygiene amid the general filth and cursedness of Wall Street. The fund industry, hewing closely to the wisdom of Hillel the Elder—"If I am not for myself, who will be for me?"—was always the first to admit that it had this reputation, and that it was well deserved.

Fund managers and their trade association, the Investment Company Institute, worked hard to ensure that word of their reputation echoed through the hills and valleys of the fund-buying heartland. After all, what's the point of a great reputation if nobody knows about it? If you praise a mutual fund executive in the middle of the forest and nobody hears you, is he really praised? Fund-industry executives, mindful of this age-old metaphysical dilemma, worked hard to ensure that the world knew about their reputation by making speeches and generating essays about their great reputation, and then issuing press releases pointing out what they had pointed out in speeches and essays.

The worse the news from the rest of the financial world, the more grotesque the scandals, the greater the swelling in the fund industry's pride. In October 2002, ICI chairman Paul G. Haaga Jr. made the following bold observation that was transmitted throughout the world: "The mutual fund industry's reputation is its most important asset. Strict regulation and the industry's adherence to the highest possible voluntary standards have helped us avoid major scandals." It was, he said, a "stellar record."

By 2003, when corporate scandals that were mere polyps in 2001 and 2002 rose up out of the earth and roared like creatures in a bad science fiction movie, the fund industry was serene. As in the late 1980s, when insider trading and junk bond scandals were alienating the population, the mutual fund industry

---

* They're actually quite a bit more than that, as we'll be seeing in Chapter 9.

was an island of goodness and decency. Mutual funds were once more dodging the raindrops of the storm, Mother Teresas with toll-free numbers.

In an address to the ICI's annual Mutual Fund and Investment Management Conference, held on March 31, 2003, in suitably clean and lush Palm Desert, California, ICI president Matthew P. Fink counted off the ways in which the fund industry was selflessly, without a thought to its own welfare, serving the investors of America. In a recitation that brought to mind the repetitious rhythms of the *Amidah* of Jewish liturgy and other prayers familiar to the faithful of all religions, Fink *davened* again and again,

"We are serving shareholders well because . . ."

"We are serving shareholders well because . . ."

Chief among his exhortations to the Higher Power (whatever media were in attendance) was this one:

"We are serving shareholders well because *the interests of those who manage mutual funds are so well aligned with the interests of those who invest in mutual funds.*" Amen.

This was not the usual self-congratulatory bullshit you find in any conference in any industry, in which the well-heeled periodically gather to give thanks, to administer to the spirit, to sanctify the mission that provides the livelihood and pays the green fees. This was more the kind of mass self-hypnosis that you'd see in Kim Jong Il's North Korea—a relentless immersion in propaganda that was effective and believed by all, including the ones who were supposed to know better. The mutual fund industry was so virtuous in the eyes of the media that the Strong mutual fund group (later pilloried in the fund scandal) and the ICI both sponsored journalism awards for years and no one in the press blinked an eye.*

No brokerage could have gotten away with putting its name on a journalism award. Mutual funds were different. Every financial journalist knew that mutual funds were virtuous, scandal-free, *boring*. "The mutual fund industry has avoided the abusive practices that betrayed investors in other parts of the marketplace," said Fink in his keynote address out there in Palm Desert.

Even after D-Day, the press rarely deviated from that line—that the industry's record was clean, an unparalleled record of trust that had just been abruptly fouled, as if by a passing car driving through a mud puddle. *Business Week* expressed the zeitgeist in December 2003, saying in an article entitled "Breach of Trust" that the fund industry was, in effect, a victim of overzealous

---

* One of the nonblinkers was the author, a recipient of both awards.

sales practices prompted by the bear market. "In 2000, the onset of the most vicious bear market since the Great Depression set the stage for the worst abuses by the mutual fund industry," said the article. "Many fund companies began resorting to shady practices" because they were "squeezed by competition for dwindling investor dollars." (An interesting excuse, by the way. In your business, does a competitive squeeze send you out to the 7-Eleven with a ski mask and a .357 Magnum?) Congress, the magazine said, was browbeaten by cunning fund lobbyists into keeping its distance from an industry that had a "60-year record of serving small investors (marred by only a few minor scandals)."

That was all over now, or such was the judgment of the media and the conventional wisdom. The regulators were on the case, and were competing with one another to knock fund-industry heads together. Bill Donaldson swiftly rose to the occasion, proposing various rules and saying the right things. The SEC began to sue, in competition with Spitzer, who raised the stakes a notch by convening a grand jury and actually indicting people instead of just suing them as he usually did. Prosecutors throughout the country took up the challenge. A kind of sweepstakes began for the greatest number of mutual fund late-trader scalps.

Regulators were reacting to genuine feelings of shock that swept over the country when the Mutual Fund Scandals commenced. Dick Grasso had just been shown to have pillaged the pride and joy of American capitalism, and he would be dead meat by the fall of 2003. Then came new-sounding allegations of improprieties in the supposedly squeaky-clean fund industry. How tragic it would have been, this fall from grace—if it really had been a fall, and if there really had been much grace to begin with.

Amid all the hubbub, some fundamental facts concerning mutual funds had been overlooked—such as the factual basis, or lack thereof, for that glorious reputation. As is often the case in a fast-moving news event, the media found itself parroting pap such as "sixty-year scandal-free record."

In fact, the mutual fund business did not have a clean history, and for most of its existence it did not even have a reputation for having a clean history. What it had was a reputation for having a reputation for having a clean history.

The mutual fund industry was (and is) in the same awkward position as Ebenezer Scrooge on Christmas Eve, haunted by the Ghost of Mutual Funds Past, Present, and Future. It's an industry with a dreary, smarmy history dating back to the period just after the First World War. The earliest fundlike outfits, which were similar to today's closed-end funds, were established in Boston in 1924. Since their origins go back so far, it's actually not a sixty-year record of anything, but rather an eighty-year record of . . . what?

Let's see what their reputation was in 1982, their actual almost-sixty-year point in selflessly serving the American public. In that year, in a book entitled *Regulation by Prosecution: The Securities and Exchange Commission vs. Corporate America,* a former SEC commissioner named Roberta S. Karmel commented on the reputation of the mutual fund industry. At the time, deregulatory fever was sweeping the nation, and the glory of free markets was returning to center stage in Washington. Here was Karmel's take on possible fund deregulation:

"Significant reform of investment company regulation, by either Congress or the SEC, will be difficult," she said. "The public has *historically feared and distrusted the fund industry,* and with some good reason. The Investment Company Act [of 1940] and its various amendments were passed in response to perceived abuses." (Emphasis added.)

So here we have an outspoken advocate of deregulation saying in 1982, when the fund industry really had a sixty-year record, that mutual funds not only had a lousy reputation but a lousy reputation "for good reason." And why? What's this stuff about "perceived abuses"? Why were they perceived so vividly that Congress had to pass a bunch of laws in response?

What Karmel was talking about, this perception problem that beset the fund industry for three-quarters of its existence, involved stuff that was *a lot worse* than the stuff that is at the center of the Mutual Fund Scandals.

That phrase she used for the title of her book, "regulation by prosecution," certainly applies to the mutual fund industry in its recent scandal. The fund industry, though heavily regulated, has not been regulated in a way that has kept fund managers from turning into slightly better-groomed versions of the sun-kissed grifters at Geek Securities. What makes the whole thing even messier is this: The fund abuses that affect you the most are not the ones that have been getting the headlines. All this late-trading stuff you've been reading about is about as old as the fund industry itself, and was allowed to fester because the fund industry *wanted* it to fester.

Let's take a close look at those phrases you keep hearing, *late trading* and *market timing.* They make it sound as if someone has a hand in the till.

It's a mighty big till, after all. At last count, some $8.2 *trillion* was held by the eight thousand or so mutual funds in the United States. That counts the whole gamut—funds holding stocks, bonds, and money market funds. Even if you narrow that down to stock funds, that brings the number down to a measly $4.4 trillion. A lot of mischief can happen when you are dealing with that kind of money, particularly when it is your money and you aren't around to watch it.

As you'll be seeing in the next chapters, there certainly is a whole lot of mischief going on in the fund business. However, the very worst abuses haven't made the cut. Sorry, but the stuff that really hurts you failed to make it through the tryouts and never were placed on the official roster of the Mutual Fund Scandals—that is to say, not as enshrined by the media and officially constituted by Spitzer, the SEC, and the rest of the self-regulatory pyramid.

Whenever someone talks about a scandal sweeping over Wall Street, there are questions you need to ask: "Who gets hurt?" and "How?" You then need to haul out a copy of *Les Misérables*. Okay, the Cliffs Notes will do.

You need to be skeptical when regulators stop acting like amiable high school substitute teachers and start imitating Inspector Javert. You want Inspector Javert pursuing Landru, not Jean Valjean. You want prosecutors, ambitious state attorneys general, and the SEC to use their limited resources against the people who are out to rob you. When I say "rob," I am invoking Sunday School morality, not the finer points of the securities laws. Concepts like "lie," "cheat," "bribe," "overcharge," and "steal."

Unless you can persuade the self-regulatory pyramid and law enforcement to get their priorities straight, you'll be cursed by what I call the Reverse Rationality Theorem of Wall Street Crime and Punishment:

Just because something is terrible doesn't mean that it will be punished, and just because something is being punished doesn't mean that it is terrible.

The Mutual Fund Scandal is the best example you can find of the Reverse Rationality Theorem of Wall Street Crime and Punishment in full bloom of sheer stupidity.

The clay ducks in the fund-scandal penny arcade, be they Geek Securities or Putnam or Strong or Janus, are not being fined or yelled at or arrested because of any of the Sunday School concepts noted above. A fund scandal is not comparable to an accounting scandal, either the ones that result in indictments or the ones that result in an SEC wrist slap or a financial-statement fix-it called a restatement. When you read "accounting irregularities," what you are really reading is "they lied." That's the thing about the Dick Grasso scandal that should bug you. He didn't lie or steal. He followed the rules and looked both ways before he crossed the street as he turned that building into a piggy bank. Calling a CEO being overpaid, however piggishly, a "scandal" distorts the term. Grasso's arbitration system was a scandal. Grasso's paycheck was not.

The Mutual Fund Scandal did not involve lying, cheating, or stealing. It involved trading. It wasn't a good thing, and the people involved should definitely have been caught and penalized. However, don't believe for a second that this was a terrible thing that arose all of a sudden and required the self-regulatory pyramid to drop everything and turn its attention to it. A perfectly accurate way of defining the conduct that everybody is upset about is "how the funds have done business since Adam and Eve shacked up at Eden Community College."

The relevant, naughty practices at issue have two names—late trading and market timing—but they both involve the same kind of thing, which is buying fund shares at stale prices. That's it, as far as scandalous conduct is concerned. One of those things, market timing, isn't necessarily illegal.

As told by the media, the first day of the Mutual Fund Scandal was September 3, 2003. But that's not true. I can't tell you when Day One took place because that's wedged somewhere in the distant mists of time, at the dawn of the mutual fund industry in the days when Harold Lloyd was the number one movie star. Today's Mutual Fund Scandal is just another name for a trading method that was a legitimate practice in the fund business for almost *five decades,* from the early 1920s until 1968, and which remained commonplace right up to the fund-scandal D-Day. For all those years, traders took advantage of flaws in the way fund shares were priced. Evidently the fund industry has never figured out a way of pricing fund shares without *you* being screwed.

That's right, folks. Over the past eighty years, the mutual fund business hasn't gotten the kinks straightened out about how to charge for their wares, even though the timing issue has been an invitation to mischief. You might think that maybe the fund industry wanted the mischief to continue, or didn't care one way or the other. You'd be right.

Here's the "problem":

When you buy into a U.S. mutual fund today, shares are priced at four P.M. New York time, when the markets close. But that's not how it was in the old days. Prior to 1968, funds engaged in what was known then as "backward pricing," which meant that you bought shares *today* at prices set at the close of trading *yesterday.*

When you bought shares in a fund in the old days, the price was automatically "stale." Backward pricing made the paperwork easier for the fund companies, at shareholder expense, while at the same time giving a bunch of fortunate people an opportunity to print money. These unnamed lucky cusses—"unnamed" because so few of them were caught doing it—made nice, riskless profits if they happened to work for the funds or were big customers of the funds or had pals at the fund companies.

If the market advanced nicely on a Tuesday, all you had to do was buy into the fund on the cheap late that day, when you knew the market (and your fund) would end the day with a nice advance over Monday's prices. Then on Wednesday you'd sell at Tuesday's prices to lock in your gain. Easy!

Ordinary people couldn't do that, because in those days the sales "loads"—sales charges, sometimes exceeding 8.5 percent—would have chewed away at any such trading. "Insiders and favored customers, however, often could purchase fund shares without paying sales loads," said a 1992 SEC history of the fund industry.

Such hijinks beset the fund industry during the carefree, modestly regulated 1920s and 1930s. In 1940, six years after erection of the self-regulatory pyramid, Congress finally got around to regulating the fund industry by passing the Investment Company Act of 1940. This was designed to fix all the problems that beset funds. And boy, were there problems. Trading on stale prices was just one of them. An SEC study of the fund industry, ordered by Congress in 1935, found that the mutual funds of the time were an absolute mess:

> [Before passage of the Investment Company Act of 1940] to an alarming extent investment companies had been operated in the interests of their managers and to the detriment of investors. A high incidence of recklessness and improvidence was also noted. Insiders often viewed investment companies as sources of capital for business ventures of their own and as captive markets for unsalable securities that they, the insiders, wished to convert into cash. Controlling persons frequently took unfair advantage of the companies in other ways, often using broad exculpatory clauses to insulate them from liability for their wrongdoing.
>
> Outright larceny and embezzlement were not uncommon. Managers were able to buy investment company shares for less than net asset value, thus enriching themselves at the shareholders' expense. In addition, reports to shareholders were often misleading and deceptive. Controlling positions in investment companies—represented by special classes of stock or by advisory contracts—were bought and sold without the consent, or even the knowledge, of public shareholders. Basic investment policies were changed without shareholder approval. The advisory contracts themselves were often long term and either noncancellable or cancellable only upon the payment of a substantial penalty by the company. Sales loads were as high as 20 percent. Management fees charged in connection with contractual plans sometimes bore no relationship to any actual managerial services.

Whew! Sounds like something from the Old Testament, maybe the part where the children of Israel make a Golden Calf, and Charlton Heston throws the tablets at them. Licentiousness! Debauchery! Congress certainly had its hands full. Still, it would be simple enough to tackle stale pricing and what regulators gently called the "riskless" trading that it encouraged. All they had to do was price shares at the closing prices on the day they were bought—what is known as "forward pricing."

That would have been a simple solution, which is probably why it didn't happen. The SEC's 1992 history of the fund industry describes what happened next: "The Commission could have cured riskless trading [that is, late trading] by requiring forward pricing. The industry, however, vigorously resisted."

So that was that. Instead, as a "compromise," the 1940 act included a rule requiring all customers to be charged the same sales load. That made it verboten for funds to be sold to some customers without loads and other customers with loads. That might have solved the problem, and probably seemed like a good idea at the time. However, many funds stopped charging loads over the years, and some funds just looked the other way and didn't charge loads to favored customers. Either way, traders could take advantage of stale prices.

A former SEC fund regulator named Karl C. Smeltzer, looking back on the era in an oral history for the SEC Historical Society that he dictated in 2004, noted that well into the 1960s it was "possible for sophisticated investors and professional traders to purchase mutual fund shares in a rising market at the last, previously determined, net asset value." Karl called this a "system, unintended by regulators, which could result in the dilution of the shares of buy and hold investors already in a fund." In other words, what you had going on here was a Mutual Fund Scandal, albeit without all the *Sturm und Drang* and embarrassing headlines.

Karl recounted that he and his colleagues, all conscientious career civil servants, put their heads together. "A group of us involved in the regulation of mutual funds urged the Commission to meet the above problem by adopting what we called the forward pricing of shares." Well, better late than never. The SEC adopted forward pricing in October 1968. That ought to fix it.

To enforce the new forward-pricing system, mutual fund examiners like Karl would randomly check time-stamping of orders to see to it that the prices were determined at the "next determined net asset value." That should have eliminated the entire problem of stale price trading—in theory. In practice, pals of the traders at the fund companies changed the date on the time-stamping machines. "Of course, improper, intentional back time-stamping could occur, and it can be even more difficult to detect today with orders recorded by electronic systems," said Karl.

Wait a second. If a fund is priced at four P.M., when the market closes, what could possibly be the point of buying a fund after four P.M. and backdate stamping the trade so that it seemed to be before four P.M.?

The reason is that a good deal of market-moving news takes place after four. That's late trading, and it is definitely illegal. But something very similar isn't illegal. Overseas mutual funds are priced along with domestic funds at four o'clock New York time, but are based on share prices when the overseas markets close—fourteen hours earlier, in the case of Japan. A lot can happen in fourteen hours to affect the price of Japanese stocks. So overseas fund prices often become stale while people are snoring in Japan.

If you buy shares in Japanese funds on a day when stuff happens in the United States to boost the Japanese funds, and sell the following day at elevated prices to make a riskless profit, what you have done is called "market timing." You will note, by the way, that this phrase is a misnomer. More accurate would be "stale-price trading." Though it's legal, it hurts long-term investors, and to do it in any volume, you have got to have a pal at the fund who will relax rules that restrict the amount of in-and-out trading that customers can do. That's how the fund companies get in hot water, because stuff like that can violate the law.

Fred Alger Management, a very prestigious firm, ripped its reputation to shreds by allowing late trading. That's a shame, when you think about it. If the public knew the crummy history of the fund industry on the subject of stale-price trading, there wouldn't have been all that much disappointment.

Looking back in the midst of the Mutual Fund Spitzerama, Karl Smeltzer expressed surprise that the media hadn't noticed that late trading was a problem that had been the subject of hand wringing so many years before. He noted that trading on stale prices was "a problem which was supposed to have been resolved by [the 1968 rule change]. I have seen no references to that in recent financial news or publications on the matter."

Oh, well. Just another lost opportunity in the 1960s (imagine if we had all bought into Berkshire Hathaway?). Still, you would think that somebody might have noticed when stale-price trading reared its head during the intervening three and a half decades.

Such as October 28, 1997. On that day, the Asian markets took a nosedive. By the end of trading in New York, while Asians were just starting to wake up, the U.S. market recovered. That was expected to make the Asian markets recover as well. Sure enough, if you bought an Asian fund at the stale, low price, you could turn around and sell at a quick, riskless profit the following day. Yep, just as Grandpappy might have done back in the 1930s, if you chose the right parents. This was legal, but not very nice, market timing.

Let's turn to Barry Barbash of Enron-exemption fame to see what happened next. He was head of the SEC's Investment Management division under Arthur Levitt. Barbash decided to address the problem in the Levitt manner, which was to give a speech. On December 4, 1997, he addressed the 1997 ICI Securities Law Procedures Conference in Washington. The theme of the speech was nostalgia.

"In the face of the impending millennium," said Barbash, "much of America these days seems to be looking backward." Teenagers were wearing bell-bottoms again. It was really something. Continuing to stroll down memory lane, well into his speech Barbash came to the point. He reminded his audience of fund hacks and lawyers that "during the Wonder Years of the 1960s, the Commission took one of its most decisive actions ever in regulating mutual funds"—Rule 22c-1, which abolished backward pricing.

Barbash went on to gently remind his listeners that backward pricing "encouraged questionable sales and trading practices in fund shares." In 1981 the SEC had encouraged—but did not, God forbid, require—funds to price shares at "fair market value" when fresh prices were not available. Some Asian funds did that. Some didn't. Therefore, some traders who hoped to make a quick killing on the Asian markets on October 28 were disappointed. The SOBs used fresh prices! Didn't let them turn a profit at the expense of other shareholders. So they complained—how's this for chutzpah—to the SEC!

The SEC responded by launching an examination of the affected funds. "Our review was completed last week and many of our findings are noteworthy," Barbash told the fund officials. "A striking finding of our recent exams, particularly in view of the Commission's policy goals in adopting Rule 22c-1, was the extent to which fund investors in October appear to have speculated in the shares of funds investing in Asian securities." He was clearly shocked—shocked!—that this had taken place. "We need to undertake a broader and more comprehensive analysis of fund pricing issues," said Barbash.

At this point the SEC swung into action. An SEC lawyer wrote a long and very polite letter to the chief counsel of the ICI, Craig S. Tyle, on December 9, 1999. Douglas Scheidt, chief counsel of the SEC's Investment Management division, politely pointed out that it would be very, very nice if the funds would think seriously about using fair value pricing.

Fund boards, he said, had a "good faith obligation" to see that fund prices were fair—not that there was any heavy lifting involved. "A board," he said, "would need to have comparatively little involvement in the valuation process in order to satisfy its good faith obligation." Scheidt concluded with a threat: "We will consider whether to provide additional guidance on pricing issues in the future. We would appreciate your sharing this letter with your members." The threat of still more correspondence from an SEC lawyer is, of course, usually enough to bring even the most recalcitrant malefactor to heel.

You can just imagine the kind of shock waves that this letter set off in the fund industry: There may be more letters! Oh, no! Oddly, the fund industry proved resilient to this heavy-handed bullying. (Perhaps they didn't believe there would be more letters? We can only guess.) So the SEC made good on its earlier threat, and wrote a letter. In April 2001, Scheidt wrote Tyle again. This time, Scheidt hauled out a big gun—he used **boldface**.

"The Failure to Determine the Fair Value of Portfolio Securities Following Significant Events May Result in Dilution," said Scheidt.

The boldface did not work. The fund industry didn't do anything, and neither did the SEC, under either Harvey Pitt or Bill Donaldson. Trading on stale prices continued, was examined periodically in academic studies that nobody noticed, and continued to fester. According to studies at Stanford University, trading on stale prices (market timing) had resulted in losses to long-term investors of $4 billion a year, while trading at night and back stamping of orders (late trading) had resulted in losses of $400 million. Those $4 billion/$400 million annual losses were achieved by, as the Scheidt letter indicated, "diluting" the value of fund shares.

That is not a lot of gobbledygook—it is a very real diminution in the value of fund shares, caused by all the trading I've described. But let's not go nuts about this, folks. It is bad—and backdating orders is rotten stuff—but it is not the kind of stealing that happens when some broker calls you and lies to you about a stock. It is not the kind of thing that happens when you buy shares in a company that has been fibbing in its financial statements, driving up share prices to boost the value of executive stock options. It is not, in other words, stealing. It's the kind of thing that might have caused a stern letter to be sent to your parents, but you wouldn't have been drummed out of Sunday School. Even so, when the Mutual Fund Scandals exploded on the financial scene, it seemed to be the worst thing that you could do with your clothes on. It wasn't.

You couldn't blame Spitzer—he needed an issue, and that was his issue. He needed something he could use to embarrass Bill Donaldson. He succeeded. True, he could have used an issue that was of more importance to investors, but his heart was in the right place. Besides, there's no question that he preserved investor confidence in the fund industry, and investor confidence in the fund industry is important—to the fund industry. If you don't have confidence in the fund industry, you won't give them your money.

That's the fun part of running a mutual fund, by the way. Taking your money.

CHAPTER SIX

HAPPINESS IS A WARM FUND MANAGER

Any mental-health professional worth his salt will tell you that striving for excellence is a really lousy idea. It's about the worst possible thing for your peace of mind. That theme has been hammered at time and again by psychotherapists in numerous studies, as researchers advance the fight against mood disorders. In his seminal work, *Feeling Good: The New Mood Therapy,* the noted psychiatrist Dr. David D. Burns observed that "the harder you strive for perfection, the worse your disappointment will become because it's only an abstraction, a concept that doesn't fit reality." His advice: "Dare to be average!" This sensible repudiation of perfectionism and mediocrity-phobia has been a path to contentment for thousands of people—including untold numbers of happy, well-adjusted mutual fund portfolio managers.

Mutual funds dare to be average. In fact, they dare to be lousy. They have long since ceased striving for anything resembling perfection when it comes to managing your money. They must be happy about it, because they have been bastions of mediocrity since the backward-pricing, embezzlement, and customer-screwing days of the Roaring Twenties.

You've probably heard that funds are a terrific place to keep your money over the long term. Bull market and bear, the long-term investor is the tortoise that beats the hare. It's appealing. It even rhymes. It makes a lot of sense until you realize how mediocre fund managers truly are. If you had shares in an equity mutual fund on January 1, 1984, just as the bull market was taking off, and held on to it until December 31, 2003, the chances are better than 90 percent that your fund failed even to match the performance of the Standard &

Poor's 500 stock index. Now, if that's not a repudiation of perfectionism and all the *agita* that comes with it, I don't know what is.

I say "better than 90 percent" because that number includes only the funds that survived for the entire twenty years. The real doggies, the ones that choked on their own saliva, are excluded. And that could be a lot of funds, particularly when you're talking long-term. One study found that of 361 funds that were alive and well and taking your money in 1976, seventeen years later 72 had been merged out of existence, usually because of crummy performance, and 37 were lured into station wagons by men in raincoats and wound up on milk cartons. They just vanished—with "no indication of what happened to them." So 90 percent is an underestimate of the chances that your mutual fund sucked wind.

Contrary to the prevailing wisdom of personal-finance journalism, buying into an actively managed mutual fund is not a "prudent" and "sound" exercise in "portfolio diversification." It is actually a "dumb" and "asinine" exercise in "paying people to do a lousy job of managing your money." You pay them handsomely to be mediocre, and you even pay for the ads in which they proclaim, and you pay for the flacks and data vendors who sucker the media to co-proclaim, that they do not stink but actually do an outstanding job in managing $8 trillion and counting of your money.

The real Mutual Fund Scandal is not *trading,* late or otherwise, but *happiness.* Fund managers are happy people with high self-esteem who draw fat salaries and bonuses for jobs that could literally be performed by *nobody*—an unmanaged index fund that mechanically invests in the S&P 500 or some other index. Fund companies cheerfully overcharge you for inflated fees and expenses, trade too much, pay through the nose in commissions, and overpay their pals in the brokerage industry in return for office space, research, and other perks, with you footing the bill. They are not neurotic or hesitant as they overcharge you. They do not cut back on their fees out of a self-destructive sense of shame or for a dysfunctional reason such as "doing a crummy job." Fund managers are blessed with healthy psyches. They confidently charge you fees that they don't deserve whether they are making or losing money, and they have job security that would make a postman envious.

If you do a sloppy job painting someone's house or designing a company's Web site, you'll be tossed out on your ass. But if you are hired by a fund-management company to manage money—in the dipsy-doodle language of Wall Street they call this an "advisory" contract even though they're not "advising" but running things—you are as snug as a nephew on the CEO's payroll. Above all, you are happy because mediocrity is embedded in the DNA of the fund business. People expect it. It is not a shameful thing. It is treated not as an infirmity but rather as a trait, like being left-handed.

I'd like to put a price tag on what I've just described, but I hesitate to do so, not because such figures are hard to come by but because you won't believe me. What you have to keep in mind is that the amount of bucks involved is a special species of humongous. Even after you comb out the $1.9 trillion in money market funds and the $600 billion in index funds, that still leaves $5.6 trillion of your money they're playing with. That counts bond funds, which also have been found to underperform their indexes. We're talking fifty-six hundred billion dollars.

Imagine a city the size of Kalamazoo where everyone has Dick Grasso's bank account—that's the kind of bucks we're talking about here. So when you read that, for example, $10 billion of your money is siphoned off each year to lure in other suckers—a U.S. government-certified scam called 12b-1—you have to remember that this is just a fly speck on the rhinoceros rump of the fund industry.

This is all easily quantifiable. These aren't rough estimates that some economist or "expert" has dreamed up. In the official Mutual Fund Scandals, with the golden-oldie scam of late trading at center stage, it's hard to figure out how much investors were hurt. Fund assets were hurt, but indirectly. Thus the amount late traders supposedly glommed off the Putnam fund group was calculated at $10 million in mid-2004. Then a consultant recalculated the figure in early 2005, and it was suddenly $100 million.

The real Mutual Fund Scandals are straightforward. No complicated formulas or consultants are required to determine how much people have been skinned. Nor is there any esoteric trading scheme that requires paragraph upon paragraph of explanation. The real scandals involve Sunday School morality and simple concepts, such as "taking." The money is there, so they take. You would too, if you had a few trillion bucks in your hands. You might even take more than they do, though you wouldn't have to.

Another trait of the real Mutual Fund Scandals is that they are not the kind of things that can be cured by regulation—and most definitely not by the anemic, almost goofy regulations that Bill Donaldson made such a show of proposing at the SEC, and which got the U.S. Chamber of Commerce so upset. This is one of those situations in which doing things that get people angry in Corporate America doesn't necessarily mean that you are being the slightest bit pro-investor or pro-consumer. As we'll be exploring in the next chapter, the SEC's approach to mutual fund regulation, in the post–Spitzer-rammed-it-down-their-throats era, has been downright silly. But even if the ideas were sensible, they wouldn't do very much good anyway.

They can cut down entire forests to print volumes of the Federal Register with regulations that get the U.S. Chamber of Commerce mad enough to sue, and that would still not get at the heart of the problem—which is that people let themselves be skinned by mutual funds. You're the cow they are milking, and nobody is forcing you to let them yank your teats. The answer isn't a new law or regulation, and it isn't Eliot Spitzer or Eliot Ness or even Robert Stack in the role of Eliot Ness. The answer is the one I mentioned at the beginning of the book: you. You need to know how the fund industry works, and what it does with your money, and then you have to decide what to do about it.

The real Mutual Fund Scandal, as opposed to the one that has laid siege to the headlines, involves the fundamental issue of fund performance—the real numbers versus the touted numbers and the ratings that you see everywhere. That is the elephant in the room, and involves uncomfortable facts that the fund industry and media don't want you to know. In this chapter I'll take that elephant by the tusks and parade it in front of you, and in the next chapter I'll describe the rest of the real Mutual Fund Scandal—assuming you're not so disgusted by then that you want to just skip it. Maybe you'll want to cash out entirely, or maybe you'll want to keep investing in actively managed funds even though the odds are stacked against you. Hey, it's your money. There are a lot worse things you can do with your bucks than giving them to even a mediocre mutual fund—such as, for example, giving them to a mediocre hedge fund. If supporting the lifestyle of a mediocre fund manager is your favorite charity, who am I to stop you? If not, read on.

As you may have noticed if you subscribe to the financial press, mutual fund reviews and scorecards appear every three months in the media. The ones that appear in January, describing the previous year, are always big sellers, and are usually packed fat with advertising from the fund industry. That's understandable, since just about everyone owns a mutual fund, either individually or through IRAs or 401(k) plans. The purpose of these regular doses of mutual fund propaganda is to pump you up and get you into a buying mood. You have plenty of choices. There were 4,551 equity funds, 2,040 bond funds, and 510 hybrid funds, investing in both stocks and bonds, as of year-end 2004.

In early 2005, the annual fund reports were upbeat. The market had just risen 11 percent during the previous year, as measured by the S&P 500, but

2004 had been uneven. The conventional wisdom is that such years are stock picker's markets, in which "savvy stock selection" carries the day. The January 2005 reports showed that mutual funds had indeed done a pretty good job of picking stocks. *The Wall Street Journal, Barron's,* the *New York Times,* and personal finance writers throughout the country all ran stories driving home that point, as did widely followed fund-watching outfits such as Lipper and Morningstar, saying that the average fund had beaten the S&P.

"An indulgent dessert can sometimes brighten the memory of an otherwise mediocre meal. So it was last year in the markets, when a sweet fourth-quarter rally gave owners of stock mutual funds plenty to rave about." That was how *Barron's* began the lead story of its *Mutual Funds Quarterly* on January 10, 2005. The title was "Sunny Returns."

According to the *Barron's* assessment of the previous year's tidings, the sunshine was particularly intense among small-stock funds. That made sense. This was a stock picker's year, and small-cap stocks are an area in which intensive research is said to pay off. "Right in the sweet spot of the market trend were small-cap value funds, which benefited from favoring cheaper and smaller shares over blue chips," said the weekly. That category of funds, the article continued, "was up 20.9% last year, and its five-year annualized return sits at a gleaming 16.2%, versus small losses over that period for the broader market." A couple of pages later, a chart showed that "small-cap growth" funds were up 10.7 percent during the year, and that "small-cap core" funds were up a much nicer 18.4 percent. So it was generally a terrific year for small-cap fund investors, when compared to the S&P 500 index, which *Barron's* used as a benchmark, or point of reference.

You might think, after reading the *Barron's* piece and similar annual fund-review stories, that the 90 percent number quoted earlier was from some crackpot with an ax to grind. After all, *Barron's* is the most sophisticated investment publication in general circulation, and its various statistical sections and articles have a wide following among investment professionals as well as serious amateurs. Any fool could see that funds beat the indexes hands down in 2004. It was a "stock picker's market" and the returns were "sunny." So said *Barron's* and so said the rest of the media.

Actually, fund returns seemed sunny only if you hadn't been outside very much. Another set of statistics came out a week or so later from the number crunchers at Standard & Poor's, and these told a different story. You might have surmised from the media coverage that fund managers were a neurotic bunch of perfectionists, striving for excellence and succeeding. The S&P study, however, indicated that fund managers were hewing closely to the principles of good mental health by striving to be average.

S&P found that most actively managed mutual funds—excluding funds that just mechanically replicate stock indexes—actually had done a *mediocre* job in 2004. The S&P Composite 1500, a broad market index, outperformed 51.4 percent of actively managed domestic general-equity funds. The S&P 500, which is the most widely followed large-cap index, outperformed 61.6 percent of actively managed large-cap funds in 2004, while the S&P MidCap 400 outperformed 61.8 percent of actively managed mid-cap funds. Here was the real kick in the rump—those performance numbers that you read in the business press were skewed in favor of the fund industry. It seems that large-cap growth funds were the only diversified equity funds to beat the market in 2004, and eight of the nine fund investment styles tracked by S&P actually had average 2004 returns that *underperformed* the market.

As for those small-cap funds that supposedly performed so sun-shinily throughout 2004—well, there were a couple of things that *Barron's,* along with the media in general, forgot to tell you in their quarterly mutual fund lovefest. They said that small-cap funds did a wonderful job, but that assessment was just a bit off base. They actually did a *horrible* job—I mean fall-on-your face, kick-in-the-ass, humiliatingly lousy.

Sure, the small-cap funds beat the market—if by "market" you mean the S&P, which didn't do as well as small-cap stocks generally. If you compare apples to apples—small-cap funds to small-cap indexes—what you find is that actively managed small-cap funds actually underperformed the market averages for that category of stocks.

In an absolute sense, as opposed to the "comparison to whichever benchmarks we choose" sense preferred by money managers, small-cap value funds did very nicely in 2004. It was certainly a better idea (assuming you were a comic-book superhero who could foresee the future) to put your money in a small-cap fund at the start of the year. But that's because small-cap funds were carried along like kayaks in white water, not because their managers were good oarsmen.

During 2004, the S&P/Barra 600 Small Cap Value Index was up 23.3 percent. The average comparable fund *underperformed* the index—by four percentage points, according to S&P, or two points according to the *Barron's* data source. As a matter of fact, these figures don't show the full breadth and scope of the crumminess of small-cap fund managers in 2004. During that year, 85 percent of actively managed small-cap funds were beaten by the S&P/Barra index.

The figure for small-cap value funds was almost as bad, 77 percent, and for small-cap growth funds it was a tongue-swallowing 94 percent. S&P also found that most funds were also beaten by the indexes over three and five years as well.

Now, I don't mean to beat up on *Barron's,* actually one of the better financial-news outlets. Its coverage was fairly typical of the fund stories that you find throughout the media. To be fair, I also have to point out that S&P is not an entirely disinterested party. It makes big bucks off its indexes, charging fees when they are used for index funds, futures contracts, options, and exchange-traded funds (ETFs) that are based on the S&P 500 and other S&P indexes. To balance that out a bit, it also makes money from the mutual fund craze by operating a fund-rating business. Its corporate compadre *Business Week,* also owned by McGraw-Hill, takes in serious bucks in mutual fund advertising, and also, like most of the press, ignored the S&P findings. But let's disregard all that for a second. Let's assume these S&P numbers are bogus and throw them in the garbage. Let's see what other researchers have to say.

Academic researchers have been studying mutual fund performance for a long time and they have plenty to say—most of it none-too-flattering. Studies have proven consistently since the 1970s that mutual funds do not beat the market. Those studies were of only academic interest in the days when there were limited index fund alternatives for investors. But today they are required reading for every investor, now that anybody can buy into one of the dozens of index funds or exchange-traded funds—stocks that track the indexes, such as the "Spiders" and "Diamonds," modeled on the S&P 500 and Dow Jones industrial average, respectively.

Today those indexers are widely available, yet the academic and scholarly studies that prove the consistent superiority of index funds get only grudging attention from the media. One came out in the same month in which the media was engaged in its quarterly mutual fund kissing competition. A scholarly publication called *The Financial Review* published a paper by a professor of finance at Princeton University named Burton G. Malkiel, describing in meticulous detail how poorly mutual funds have stacked up against the indexes over the years.

Malkiel's figures made the S&P numbers seem understated by comparison. He found that in 2003, 73 percent of actively managed funds failed to beat the S&P 500. The failure rate was just as bad over the long term—72 percent over three years, 63 percent over five years, 86 percent over ten years, and (this is the source of that number cited earlier) 90 percent over twenty years. The very oldest and most long-lasting funds were generally losers.

These numbers seem all the more distressing when you realize that Malkiel is not some crank, but is one of the most esteemed financial authorities alive. His book *A Random Walk Down Wall Street* is the bible of a financial school of thought called the Efficient Market Hypothesis. The EMH is one of the most widely respected theories of modern finance. Now that the growth of index funds and ETFs makes it easy for every investor to put its principles to work, the EMH is something that everybody needs to know. Apply its principles and you can never be ripped off in the stock market again. That's because you will never buy an individual stock again.

With *Random Walk* as its Big Book, the EMH functions as a kind of 12-step program for stock addicts. Malkiel doesn't quite phrase it this way, but his book and its underlying theory very much address the American public's addiction to the purchase of individual stocks. Step one is familiar to every alcoholic and overeater and smoker and procrastinator: *We admitted that we were powerless over stocks, and our lives have become unmanageable.**

The EMH teaches that you can't beat the market. You are powerless to predict stock prices. Don't "pick up" (buy stocks)! Stay out of taverns (brokerage offices)! Your Higher Power is the market. The market will go up, and it will go down. When it does well, and it will over time, you will too. You can do no better. Be happy with that. Don't be greedy.

The EMH originated back in the mid-sixties. Eugene Fama, Malkiel, and other early proponents of the theory are real investor heroes. That's not only because application of the EMH saves investors from subpar returns and investment ripoffs, but because it has spurred research that has produced a good deal of very valuable data. The EMH says, in essence, that no matter how much you might knock Wall Street, the stock markets themselves are blessed with a certain purity. Stock prices reflect all publicly available information.

There are, of course, plenty of inflated share prices and frauds out there, and scores of stock promoters, newsletter writers, and so on who spout all kinds of drivel about stocks. That doesn't mean the EMH is wrong. The EMH teaches that shares reflect all available information—not that the available information is true. But try to exploit those market inefficiencies and the odds are stacked against you.

The EMH is, as its name indicates, a hypothesis—a theory. You can choose to believe it or not, as you wish. Wall Street (which in this context includes the entire money-management industry) is firmly in the not-believing camp. That's

---

* Paul B. Farrell actually went through the whole twelve steps in the MarketWatch Web site on April 24, 2005. I'm not sure I agree with all of them, but he's on the right track. Amen, brother!

because the more investors adhere to the EMH, the fewer profits the Street gets at your expense. The Street views the EMH and its proponents the way you might feel about a war-veteran uncle who nods off after telling an after-dinner story about Nam. You can't really contradict him, as it wouldn't be very polite, so you just ignore him. No reason to get hepped up about the EMH. It isn't widely known among the people who count—the millions upon millions of people who buy individual stocks and actively managed funds.

What makes the EMH heresy for Wall Street is that Malkiel and other advocates of efficient markets have found, and demonstrated quite often, that entire segments of Wall Street have no basis for existing. "Savvy" stock pickers, the EMH people say, are just lucky. Smart analysts are lucky. Smart fund managers are lucky. Trading is a waste of money. These are not wacko theories. There is data in support of them—lots and lots and lots of data. If people acted on all that data, it would mean that all the "ace money managers" who you read about in the papers, the ones with the "terrific track records," all the *Institutional Investor*-certified analysts and hedge fund gurus and guys riding around on motorcycles looking for investment ideas—the whole bunch of them would be replaced by computer chips at index funds. Stock market newsletters would go out of business or be reduced to ranking the various varieties of index funds, and dozens of stock-pushing Web sites would vanish overnight. Entire industries would shut down, and one of them would be the mutual fund industry.

All this explains why your broker would rather his clients be Marxists who like to gamble than free-market capitalists who embrace the Efficient Market Hypothesis. That goes double for the mutual fund industry.

The numbers are pretty dramatic, when you consider how much money is poured down the drain in fees paid to people to actively manage your money. Let's go back to that $5.6 trillion figure I mentioned earlier. Multiply that figure by 1 percent. That is the amount of money that the mutual fund industry takes out of that figure in expenses. It's a little less for bond funds and a bit more for stock funds, but it averages out to about that number. That figure is an underestimate because it doesn't take into account commissions and "advisory" fees, as we will be seeing in the next chapter. But let's use that number as a conservative estimate.

One percent of $5.6 trillion is $56 billion. That is what you pay fund managers to pick stocks and bonds and manage all those mutual funds. If all that money were to be invested in index funds instead, that 1 percent number would shrink way, way down to 0.2 percent. Multiply 0.8 percent times $56 billion and you come up with $44.8 billion. That's how much you're paying the fund industry *every year* to do a lousy job.

Not all that money goes directly into the septic tank, of course. A lot of it goes tearing back through the economy, just as a good deal of the money used to purchase methamphetamine in Camden, New Jersey, is used to buy beer, video games, and other mainstays of the local Camden, New Jersey, economy. So I'm not going to say it is all a waste. That is for you to decide. The only question that you need to ask yourself, the next time you get a bonus or some other sudden money, is whether you want to roll the dice on the next hot fund manager, or surrender to the Higher Power of the stock market and put your bucks into an index fund or ETF.

Fortunately for the Street, the EMH hasn't proven to be much of an albatross because there are always plenty of "hot fund managers" and "investment gurus" able to prove—until they stumble—that they have beaten that EMH thing into the ground. And when the laws of probability catch up with them and they do stumble—well, memories are short. The three hedge fund superstars of the 1990s—George Soros, Julian Robertson, and Michael Steinhardt—were forced to shut down (or, in the case of Soros, reorganize) after making serious investment and trading blunders. All provided subpar returns for any investors who were able to buy into their funds when they were being hyped the most. At the time of his funds' descent into the Valley of Fatigue in early 2000, Robertson was blaming an "irrational" market for his failure. That was true. Markets are random, irrational, and inexplicable—that is what the EMH is all about.* Yet well into the new millennium, these living proofs of the EMH were still being touted as market seers by the financial press. In December 2002, Robertson predicted that "in the next year or two, we're coming into a very long-term problem"—and the market promptly rebounded, gaining 29 percent in 2003 and 11 percent in 2004. Irrational!

Mutual funds don't spawn overhyped "legends" as much as the hedge fund industry does. Instead they have a caste system of the kind that was outlawed in India when it broke away from England in 1947, but which still exists in accordance with religious principles considered no less holy than the ones used to rate mutual funds. The Brahmans of the mutual fund subcontinent are the five-star funds, while the Scheduled Castes, the untouchables who are shunned and prohibited from using the same wells and public bathing facilities as the higher-

---

* Though it's not what hedge funds are all about—if you fall for the hype. As *Barron's* observed at the time, "Hedge funds, it bears recalling, are supposed to make money in both up and down markets. That's why investors agree to pay the general partner a generous 20% fee on any trading profits."

caste funds, are one-stars. They live in a shantytown at the outskirts of the village. Even writing about them makes my fingers dirty, so I will have to perform an ablution after I finish this paragraph.

A number of very reputable and highly prestigious organizations provide fund caste ratings. *Business Week* has participated in the fund industry caste system for many years, using data supplied by Morningstar, Inc. So has *Barron's*, whose data are supplied by Lipper. These are both reputable firms that make good-faith attempts to determine whether a fund will do well. They do so by examining the funds' past performance.

The only problem in examining past performance is that, as the funds themselves are legally obliged to tell you, "past performance is no guarantee of future results." That exact language can be found strewn around all the fund advertising and fund Web sites, and is used so often that people tend to ignore it, the way they ignore warning labels on cigarette packs. Both warning labels are required by law because they're true. Cigarettes cause cancer, and buying a fund because it performed well last year is stupid. Today's low-caste fund, even one of the untouchables, might well rise out of the misery of its existence and ascend to a higher caste tomorrow. This is democratic, I suppose, but it also makes the whole fund caste system kind of silly.

The good professor Malkiel concluded in his recent study that "while highly starred *Michelin Guide* restaurants guarantee the diner an excellent meal, four, and five star Morningstar ratings do not provide mutual fund investors with above-average returns." So use the metaphor of your choice—a caste system with surprising upward mobility, an unreliable Michelin guide, or perhaps a movie critic with poor taste. All add up to the same thing—fund ratings aren't reliable. According to fund data going back to 1992, the funds rated highest by Morningstar consistently underperformed the Wilshire 5000 stock index, and by a wide margin.

Even Warren Buffett, one of the most oft-quoted advocates of so-called "value investing"—buying shares that are supposedly undervalued by the market—turns out to be a closet efficient-markets guy in his own right. He had this to say in his 1996 annual report: "Most investors, both institutional and individual, will find that the best way to own common stocks (shares) is through an index fund that charges minimal fees. Those following this path are sure to beat the net results (after fees and expenses) of the great majority of investment professionals." Not the kind of thing you find in those dozens of books that tell you how to invest "the Warren Buffett way." Seems that Warren wants you to invest "the Burt Malkiel way."

But, hey, this is a free country. You don't have to believe that the mutual fund industry is built on a lie, and that its primary economic purpose is to siphon off money from your account to fund a mammoth corporate welfare project. You can just give them your money and hope for the best. Hope for good performance. Hope that your fund manager has lost his copy of *Feeling Good*.

CHAPTER SEVEN

MUTUAL FUNDS AREN'T BULLIES

Mutual fund managers strive for perfection, worrying themselves sick and making themselves miserable in two vital realms of their existence:

1. **Taking**
   and
2. **Selling**

When it comes to taking your money, and selling you more stuff so they can take even more of your money, mutual funds are innovative and imaginative in ways that you'll never see when it comes to managing your investments. The fund industry's mastery of the Art of the Take makes the late-trading scandal that has obsessed regulators seem petty or even a little comical by comparison, a bit like Inspector Clouseau ticketing a car for double-parking while its occupants are robbing a bank. Like Inspector Clouseau, the fund industry has mangled the English language. Mutual funds have long embraced the credo most eloquently expressed by Clifford Odets—in a movie about people taking money—that "man was blessed with the gift of speech to conceal his thoughts."

Take that word you keep hearing—*fees*. Back when late trading (that is, the decades-old practice of stale-price trading) was rediscovered and given full-dress scandal treatment by Eliot Spitzer in September 2003, critics of the fund industry fastened their gaze for several months on fees. They noted that the fund industry was cursed with excessive fees and sometimes even hidden fees. In December 2003, Eliot Spitzer forced Alliance Capital, which had been caught up in that late-trading thing, to cut its fees by $350 million. Other firms—Strong Capital Management, Janus, MFS, Invesco—were also accused of late trading and forced to cut their fees. There was some squawking, as late trading had nothing on earth to do with fees, but the protests were subdued. After all, it was natural to presume that all this fee-attacking would come to an end, so better not make a fuss. Sure enough, it was all scaled down during 2004, and the self-regulatory pyramid and Spitzer pretty much wound up their fee-cutting assault in late 2005. The whole thing had dropped out of the headlines by then, but the word *fee* kind of hung in the air for a while, and the media coverage indicated that there was a "fee issue" out there somewhere, and that it was being pursued and dealt with by the SEC, albeit with prodding by Spitzer and other state attorneys general.

When regulators, the media, and the fund industry talk about fees, they are referring to the 1 percent and more of actively managed mutual fund assets that are removed each year to pay for the cost of running the funds. It's a bit like a corporate expense account with no limits except whatever are imposed by the fund manager's own sense of ethics and fair play. In other words, no limits at all.

Now, let's stop for a second and think about what I've just described. Isn't all this stuff terrible? Shouldn't the regulators take action? Shouldn't it all be stopped, and now?

No.

Like Dick Grasso at the New York Stock Exchange, the fund industry is doing precisely what you are letting it do. In this instance, you function more or less in the role of the famously semicomatose NYSE board of directors. Grasso did not break any law, nor did he violate any ethical principle of which I am aware. No Sunday School, no Hebrew school, no Islamic madrassa or Hindu temple, teaches that it is improper to be paid what people are willing to pay you. Spitzer may have found some principle buried in the fine print of the New York State Consolidated Statutes, but that doesn't give his politically motivated assault on Grasso even the slightest bit of moral justification.

Just as the NYSE paid Grasso what he wanted, you are paying the fund industry exactly what it wants. You are more powerful than Spitzer and the SEC combined. Only you can do the equivalent of sending Grasso back to his hovel in Locust Valley. Only you can *withdraw assets from mutual fund companies*.

If you've decided to stick with actively managed funds despite all the good reasons not to, it's your job to deal with this whole fee mess. Don't pass the buck to the SEC and the other regulators. However, you have to understand the nomenclature of fees, expenses, and such. Getting a handle on the dialect involved, what I call Mutualingo, is absolutely mandatory for those of you not willing to work the Steps to which I alluded in the last chapter.

Let's start this process of self-enlightenment by examining one phrase you may have seen tossed around now and then:

Mutualingo	English Language Equivalent
Soft dollars	*Kickbacks*

Etymology: Money used by mutual funds to overpay brokerages for commissions come straight out of your pocket—and aren't even included in the expense ratio that is used to measure fund fees. In return for the commissions they pass on to you, the funds get office space and research they can use to pick stocks that underperform the market. The offices purchased with these dollars are usually cozy and invariably contain "soft"-cushioned furniture. Hence the phrase "soft dollars."

As you can see, the fund industry has introduced a colorful, interesting way of expressing the concept of "kickback," which is so plain and so, well, *tacky* when expressed in English. Such is the richness Mutualingo brings to our national discourse as it accomplishes its higher purpose, which is obfuscation and portfolio depletion.

Understanding how funds separate you from your money also requires you to brush up on your arithmetic. It is very hard to escape mathematics when one is examining mutual fund taking. But it is not ordinary arithmetic, more like the "fuzzy math" and "voodoo economics" that have enriched our political discourse. How much of your money are they taking? Has that amount gone up or down over the years? The answers to questions such as these depend upon who you are asking—the mutual fund industry, as represented by the Investment Company Institute, or anyone else.

The ICI backs up its answers with facts, cold hard facts, as detailed in scholarly studies it has generously underwritten and which happen to back it up 100 percent. The ICI can show you all kinds of statistics based on numbers to which it has subjected all kinds of statistical bells, whistles, and body-crevice groping. I can boil down the ICI's well-crafted, carefully rehearsed boilerplate replies into this sentence: "Fund fees are reasonable and have been going down for many years, so everything is fine and don't worry and don't regulate us and go away and leave us alone."

Logic is on the ICI's side. The fund industry has grown quite dramatically in recent years. Equity funds, which are by far the industry's most profitable segment, climbed from $44 billion in assets in 1980 to $4.4 trillion at the end of 2004. That's a *hundredfold* increase. Industries that gain in heft can undercut their competition, force vendors to cut prices, and reduce prices for consumers. That is why you can walk into a Wal-Mart and pick up a pair of flip-flops that cost $1.88. The retailer's economic power, its muscling of suppliers to cut prices, has resulted in charges that Wal-Mart is big, bad, and mean—the "Bully of Bentonville," as a book by my ex-*BW* colleague, Tony Bianco, puts it.

Well, rest assured about this much, folks: Mutual funds are absolutely, positively not bullies. This megaindustry, so massive as to make Wal-Mart look like a lemonade stand by comparison, doesn't gang up and kick sand in the faces of puny fund managers and fund "advisory" firms, forcing them to cut prices so that they can charge you less. Not these guys. They're nice!

Hey, it's not just the fund industry that is being nice. You are too, by letting them get away with charging you high fees. You're paying too much for cruddy performance not because the fund industry is an ogre—not on this issue, Spitzer notwithstanding—but because *you don't care*. It all has to do with economies of scale—the same ones that let you buy flip-flops for $1.88. Mutual funds don't believe in economies of scale. It's contrary to their slogan, which goes something like this: "We buy in bulk, and don't pass the savings on to you."

Now that funds are a multitrillion-dollar business, the resultant economies of scale suggest that they must be less costly to run per investor. If a fund has a hundred stocks in its portfolio, it shouldn't matter whether each portfolio holding consists of a hundred shares, a thousand shares, or a million shares. Larger portfolios and larger client lists will mean higher operating costs—but not *proportionally* higher. Ten times the number of shares in a portfolio shouldn't mean ten times the number of portfolio managers. These are, after all, stocks, not schoolchildren in a town with a stiff class-size restriction. Or, as one of those pesky non-ICI-compensated academic researchers once put it, "Given the industry's explosive growth, one would expect that fund expenses on average would have plummeted."

They should have plummeted. But they haven't. As a matter of fact, they are actually *higher* than they were when the fund industry was far smaller than it is today. In September 2004, Morningstar released some figures on the expense ratios of the diversified equity funds in its database. Those are numbers that give a rough measure of the cost of running a fund in proportion to its net assets. As is usual with interesting studies that don't make the fund industry look very good, this wasn't exactly splattered over the headlines—the only pickup I could find was in one of the better finance Web sites, MSN Money.

Morningstar—anything but a captive of the index-fund industry or efficient-market types—examined expense ratios from the 1990s right up through 2003. Stock funds' asset sizes wavered a little bit during that period, peaking in 1999, declining through 2002 as the markets declined, and then regaining its strength and acumen in 2004. But that expense ratio fund-skimming number took a course of its very own. The expense ratio number climbed from 1.33 percent in 1990 to 1.41 percent at its peak in 1999, at a time when you'd have thought that all that "explosive growth" would have sent fund expenses way down. The ratio increased still more through 2002, when fund assets declined. Then 2003 came around, the fund industry was healthier, asset sizes climbed—and so did fees, way up to 1.51 percent of assets, an all-time high. Morningstar tells me the 2004 number held steady at 1.50 percent.

By the way, these numbers actually understated the situation somewhat, because they included the growing number of index funds, which tend to have far lower costs than actively managed funds. Even the ICI, despite its protestations to the contrary, has generated statistics showing the average cost of operating a fund had increased sharply over the years—gaining from 0.77 percent in 1980 to 0.88 percent in 2003.

Funds haven't defied the laws of economics. They have ignored them. Or, to put it another way, *you* have ignored them. You don't pay attention to fund fees, so they are not a factor in your decision-making in buying a fund, and funds haven't the slightest reason to cut fees to attract your business. You care about fund performance, not fund fees. The free market, which is busily at work here, obliges by socking you with fees that are unnecessarily high.

Now, that's not to say funds don't compete for your business. Of course they do. The fund industry boasts about that. In that revival-meeting speech in Palm Desert mentioned a couple of chapters ago, Matthew Fink of the ICI chanted in his repetitious little riff that the fund industry is competing "vigorously and fairly with one another and with other financial services and products."

There is a lot of truth to that. However, fund-industry execs know that people don't shop for a fund the way they shop for kitty litter or floor wax. Folks buy their funds because they think that they can get rich, beat the market, and spend their golden years lying on the beach on St. Maarten sipping melon pelicans and rubbing Bain de Soleil on the spouse. They know that most people don't know efficient markets from Adam and still are suckered by the delusion that you can pick a fund that will make you rich. They know that most people under the age of sixty cut their teeth on Mutualingo. That's why the investigative arm of Congress, the Government Accountability Office, observed in one of its several studies of fund fees that "mutual funds do not usually compete directly on the basis of their fees." Other researchers who have studied the issue, notably John P. Freeman and Stewart L. Brown in their landmark 2001 study of the fund biz, reached the same conclusion—and noted that mutual funds are consistently more costly to investors than pension funds, which cater to a more savvy, price-conscious clientele and which do in fact try to undersell one another. As they put it, "price competition is largely nonexistent in the fund industry."

Now, you might not care about any of this. You might wonder why the small fractions mentioned earlier are worth bothering about or shopping for, or worth a GAO investigation. I suppose that you might not feel right about begrudging your fund manager a point or two off your portfolio.

Well, go ahead. Begrudge.

Those little fractional expense ratio numbers don't mean a damn thing only if you're an in-and-out trader, like one of Charlie Kerns's pals at Geek Securities. Fund skimming matters if you are a long-term investor, one of those "buy and forget" customers who are the supposed subject of the fund industry's loyalty. The numbers work out like this, according to a GAO analysis: Over a twenty-year period a $10,000 investment in a fund earning 8 percent annually, with a 1 percent expense ratio, would be worth $38,122. With a 2 percent expense ratio the portfolio shrinks to $31,117—almost exactly $7,000 out of your pocket.

Now, at the risk of getting stuffy about this, I think I should identify at this point the rain that is supposed to fall on the parade whenever fund managers get their mitts on your money. It is an inconvenient, difficult-to-enforce theoretical concept called fiduciary duty. While you owe it to yourself to get the heck out of a fund that soaks you for mediocre returns, theoretically the fund management is supposed to feel a little guilty that it is soaking you and mumble to its collective self, "Gee whiz, maybe I shouldn't do this, me being a fiduciary and all . . ."

The ICI actually has been quite eloquent on the subject:

> Because mutual fund directors are looking out for shareholders' interests, the law holds them to a very high standard. Directors must exercise the care that a reasonably prudent person would take with his or her own business. They are expected to exercise sound business judgment, approve policies and procedures to ensure the fund's compliance with the federal securities laws, and undertake oversight

and review of the performance of the fund's operations as well as the operations of the fund's service providers (with respect to the services they provide to the fund).

That should make you feel all warm and fuzzy inside, if it wasn't a crock. Staffers of the U.S. Senate Governmental Affairs Committee looked into this whole fiduciary thing in 2004, and found that no mutual fund board had ever been held accountable for breaching its fiduciary duty to customers. That could mean that mutual fund boards have a spotless record, in which case the preceding few chapters would make excellent notepads, as they would be blank.

Actually it only seems as absurd as that until you realize the fund industry has been able to do such a great job because it *doesn't have to do a great job*. The Senate committee staffers found that the Investment Company Act actually imposes a weaker standard on fund directors than you find in the already flabby state laws. What this means is that fund boards haven't much incentive to give you a break when it comes to siphoning off your money in fees, face no real repercussions, and aren't expected to act very strongly in your interests because the law doesn't require it. Or, to put it more succinctly, funds can screw you and nobody will notice or care, and they'll get away with it.

The result is a reverse of that old expression "A rising tide lifts all boats." In this case, you have a sinking ethical tide making the entire fund industry stink to high heaven. It's not just the rascals who have been dragged into the mutual fund morass but also the Clean Genes of the industry.

Speaking of rascals—and I use that term with affection—it was no great surprise when word emerged in early 2005 that Bear Stearns & Co. was under investigation by the SEC for alleged involvement in that late-trading mess. You expect that kind of rambunctiousness from Bear, whose very name has a wild and woolly, defecation-in-the-woods quality to it. Bear became known through the years as the Eddie Haskell of Wall Street, always trying to figure out new ways of getting the Beaver to pull a fast one on Ward Cleaver. They used to handle back-office duties for A.R. Baron and the other leading lights of the 1990s boiler rooms, and it emerged in legal proceedings that they had a ringside seat to large-scale thievery, but just kept their traps shut and did their job. That gave a charming, continental, IG Farben quality to their Eddie Haskell routine—not that they were ever found guilty of doing anything underhanded, God forbid. The law insulates Wall Street firms from wrongdoing when they handle trades for other firms, even when the other firms are run by hoodlums. And besides, they were only following orders.

If Bear Stearns is the troublemaking Eddie Haskell of Wall Street, for reasons I'll be exploring further in Chapter 13, the American Funds Distributors fund group is the industrious Beaver who does his homework before supper and cleans his room without being asked. It would almost have been newsworthy if Bear *wasn't* involved in the fund scandal. But when the American Funds group was swept up in the fund morass—now, that was a surprise. In February 2005, at about the same time Bear was getting its name dragged through the woods without anyone much caring, the NASD filed charges against American Funds. Flags went half-staff throughout Los Angeles, where this very quiet and well-reputed fund group had its headquarters. The group, third largest in the nation, with 25 million customers and $450 billion under sound and paternal management, was almost as pure and sanctified in the media as the driven snow or even the Vanguard Group, the massive index-fund behemoth that has gained near-universal adoration because of its low-cost structure (Wal-Mart should have it so good). The American Funds group was founded in 1929 and has kept pretty much to the straight and narrow ever since. Sort of.

One inkling that all might not be so clean and tidy at American Funds came in June 2004. A gent by the name of John C. Carter, who lived in San Dimas, California, put some comments on the SEC Web site concerning his beef against Smith Barney, which he had accused in an arbitration case of not properly handling his retirement accounts. According to Carter, Smith Barney had a strange fixation on the funds of one, and only one, fund group—the Clean Gene, early-homework-doing, room-cleaning, well-reputed American Funds group. Carter said as follows: "We believe that our broker recommended only American Funds based on a commission that she would receive from the Capital Group parent company."*

It should be noted that Mr. Carter was not a realistic man. In fact, he appeared to be almost Utopian in his worldview, judging from his suggestion that "it would be very helpful to unsuspecting small investors if the SEC would require brokers working on commission, to have the word Sales in their titles such as Sales Advisor or Commissioned Sales Broker. Vague titles such as VP Investments or Senior Advisor only mislead the individual investor." Even if you disregard such fantasies, you have to admit that Mr. Carter's complaint was disturbing. It indicated pretty clearly that the American Funds group

---

* A company called Capital Research and Management Co. was truly the Ward Cleaver of this particular fund family, dispensing sage advice. In addition to being the corporate father, it was also the "investment advisor" that managed the funds. "Investment advisor," by the way, is Mutualingo for "the people hired to run the fund, and who always keep their jobs even if they suck eggs year after year."

wasn't doing all that great a job at its fiduciary duty. That impression was substantiated somewhat eight months later, on February 16, 2005, when the NASD filed its complaint against American Funds.

The NASD said that American Funds "entered into yearly sponsorship arrangements with approximately 50 NASD member firms that were the top sellers of American Funds." It said that "as part of these sponsorship arrangements [American Funds] arranged for approximately $100 million of brokerage commissions generated by American Funds portfolio trades to be directed to these top-selling retailers of American Funds to reward past sales and to encourage future sales."

Doesn't that seem to be just a bit of a conflict of interest for those "approximately 50" unnamed NASD member firms? As for the American Funds group—well, if there's any truth at all to these allegations, I'd say that just a touch of the Bear Stearns–Eddie Haskell quality, that same charming all-American mischievous desire to skin the investor, had rubbed off on the nerds at American Funds.

The NASD did not identify the "approximately 50" brokerages (they could have gotten a precise count, don't you think?) that enjoyed these sponsorship arrangements. But the Carter beef would seem to indicate that Smith Barney—a fun-loving bunch of fellows fond of wine, women, and more women, according to various lawsuits over the years—was one of those anonymous "approximately 50." "We have since discovered," Carter told the SEC, "that Smith Barney receives additional compensation from Capital Group as a top, if not the top, sales generating organization. This conflict of interest cannot be in the best interests of the small investor who, in good faith, may have entrusted their life savings to such a broker."

Mr. Carter was being entirely unfair to Smith Barney and American Funds. He may not have known it, but pretty much every major brokerage firm on Wall Street also sops its bread in mutual fund gravy. That has been an open secret for years, but the first firm to actually get a "tsk-tsk" from regulators on that issue was Morgan Stanley. In November 2003, Morgan settled with the SEC and NASD for not telling its customers about revenue-sharing arrangements—Morgan used the pretty phrase "Partners Program"—that it neither admitted nor denied having with sixteen fund companies, including American Funds. Morgan wound up paying $50 million, which is about what it spends on metal polish for the executive silverware. Still, it's not the money— or, in this case, the chump change—that was the problem. It was the hurt, the sense of betrayal. After all, we're talking about family here! Evidently all those "financial advisors" in the "unusually devoted to your dreams" TV commercials had a deep, dark secret while attending football games, lying on the beach, and being part of the family.

Taking payments for selling funds of favored fund companies is not a no-no in itself—at least, not according to the moral compass of the self-regulatory pyramid, the mutual fund industry, and the financial press, none of which have ever come out and explicitly condemned the practice. From the standpoint of Sunday School morality, or the workaday ethics of any industry other than Wall Street, it would be something else entirely. As a conservative Republican senator from Illinois, Peter G. Fitzgerald, put it, "If a publicly traded corporation, not a mutual fund, went to brokerage houses and said: We will give you a dollar for every share of our stock that you sell, that would be an outrageous fraud on the public." As a matter of fact, he pointed out, "In Chicago they call that a kickback."

The regulatory response to that is, "Kickback, shmickback." Revenue-sharing* kickback arrangements emerge on the radar screen only when the feds encounter a Cool Hand Luke brokerage or mutual fund. They'll reach for a whip only when they can say, "What we have here is a failure to communicate."

Let no man say that Smith Barney was guilty of a failure to communicate in its dealing with Mr. Carter's account—that is, not lately. In March 2005, the Citigroup subsidiary settled SEC and NASD charges that it had failed to communicate properly all that revenue-sharing stuff with customers in 2002 and 2003. The firm managed to keep in the SEC's and NASD's good graces since then by communicating—telling all the folks about its kickbacks. In June 2004 and again in June 2005, the firm disclosed on its Web site that "for each fund family we offer, we seek to collect a mutual fund support fee, or what has come to be called a revenue-sharing payment. These revenue-sharing payments are in addition to the sales charges, annual service fees (referred to as '12b-1 fees'), applicable redemption fees and deferred sales charges, and other fees and expenses disclosed in a fund's prospectus fee table." All this revenue sharing comes to $2 billion a year for the fund industry as a whole, according to the SEC.

Though the ICI likes to point out that since the payments come from the supposedly independent advisors, investors aren't directly socked for the fees, what that ignores is that, as an otherwise vapid SEC study has pointed out, the kickbacks are factored into the cost of hiring all those brilliant people to run

---

* More Mutualingo. This sounds more like that Nixon-era program of giving federal money to the states than what it is— *kickbacks*.

the funds. (If they weren't, the fund companies and their various affiliates and advisory companies would not be profitable—and that would never do.)

Smith Barney listed two classes of funds that engaged in those fee-sharing arrangements—a list of 42 funds on the left and 29 on the right in 2004, and 37 on the left and 25 on the right in 2005. The longer list consisted of the funds that received "access to our branch offices and Financial Consultants for marketing and other promotional efforts." In other words, what is known as shelf space at your local A & P. These were listed because of, "among other things, their product offerings and demand among our Financial Consultants and clients"—as if these funds were actually bought and not rammed down their clients' throats. The list on the right didn't get branch access.

The funds on the longer list were popular—and how. According to Smith Barney, they accounted for 96.2 percent of mutual fund sales in 2003 and 94.4 percent in 2004. It's quite a list. It was such a distinguished list that I thought it might be nice to duplicate the 2005 list here for you. According to Smith Barney, this list is rank-ordered, with the biggest-paying firms on top:

Smith Barney	*ING*
American Funds	*Nuveen*
Franklin Templeton	*Salomon Brothers*
Lord Abbett	*Scudder*
AllianceBernstein	*Seligman*
PIMCO	*Hartford*
Oppenheimer	*Mainstay*
Van Kampen	*Columbia*
AIM	*IDEX*
MFS	*Dreyfus*
Putnam	*Goldman Sachs*
Calamos	*Delaware*
Davis	*SunAmerica*
Fidelity Advisor	*First Eagle*
Eaton Vance	*BlackRock*
Pioneer	*JPMorgan*
Federated	*Legg Mason*
John Hancock	*Nations*
Evergreen	

Just a few trillion bucks under management here. The other group listed by Smith Barney, the twenty-five fund groups that were not so popular, were not broken out in 2005, but in 2004 they accounted for another 2.3 percent of sales. In 2003 (there was no aggregate number given for 2004), 99.2 percent of mutual fund sales by Smith Barney consisted of funds that paid extra for the privilege.

Funds don't have to compete when they're paying kickbacks. Rampant revenue-sharing kickback arrangements pretty much turn this whole issue of price competition into the joke that it truly is. The whole purpose of paying kickbacks is to *avoid* price competition.

So, back to our original question: Are you going to surrender to the Higher Power of the stock market and put your money in index funds, or are you going to give your money to actively managed funds that pay to be sold to you?

Before you mull that over, it might be worthwhile to pause for a moment and consider the phenomenon that you have just witnessed.

Over the past few years, various Wall Street firms and mutual fund groups have found themselves having to be shamed, and to pay small penalties for various offenses concerning both the Mutual Fund Scandals and all manner of other Wall Street unpleasantness. Many, if not most, could have spared themselves all the pain and humiliation if they had just put a few words in the appropriate document or on their Web sites—just as Smith Barney in the preceding pages—or in one of their mailings that nobody reads, so as to satisfy their quasi-confessional disclosure obligations.

It doesn't matter one bit that nobody reads that stuff. Fund disclosures, like corporate filings generally, are a kind of self-absolving confession. Once set down on paper, any nastiness is considered disclosed to the whole wide world. That's usually sufficient to fend off any accusations involving fraud or overcharges. No concealment, voilà! No fraud.

Imagine what a great world it would be if you could pull off that kind of thing yourself. Just write down on a piece of paper that you aren't particularly competent or honest, leave it somewhere in your supervisor's office, and it will keep you from being fired for incompetence or dishonesty. Or put it in a blog nobody reads. You'll have just tapped into the secret to a full and happy life, filled with mediocrity and riches, Wall Street–style.

One of the things mutual funds are not happy to disclose, in those statements you never read, is how much they pay in commissions for all the buying and selling of the stocks and bonds in their portfolios. This number is not reflected in the expense ratio that is commonly used to quantify mutual fees. Commissions are not something mutual fund companies like to talk about. That's because when it comes to trading, fund companies are the Wall Street equivalent of an oil baroness or Third World dictator's wife on a shopping spree in Paris. Imelda Marcos stocked her closets with shoes; your mutual fund stocks your portfolio with trades.

The more a fund trades, the higher its portfolio turnover rate. If you are one of the tiny sliver of fund customers who actually read all those boring mutual fund mailings, you'll find this term—"portfolio turnover rate." A 50 percent turnover rate means that half the assets of the fund changes hands over a particular period of time. It's not unusual for funds to have annual turnover rates of 100 percent or higher. But what does that mean for you? This brings us to the last Mutualingo concept we'll be studying in this chapter:

Mutualingo	**English Language Equivalent**
Portfolio turnover rate	*Stupidity quotient*

The problem with all of this love of trading is (1) the more they trade the more it costs, and they pass on the commissions to you; and (2) they are lousy traders. Trading is not only costly, it is stupid. The more they trade, the worse they perform.

That should really come as no great surprise, when you take into consideration that 90 percent of mutual funds don't beat the market over the long term. But this is more than just a good surmise. There is actually some reasonably good data on the subject. In 2001, a trio of researchers from three universities, John M. R. Chalmers, Roger M. Edelen, and Gregory B. Kadlec, produced a study on the costs and effectiveness of mutual fund trading. The Chalmers-Edelen-Kadlec team picked 132 funds at random, examined their trading data, ran the numbers through the usual statistical Mixmaster, and found "a strong negative relation between fund returns and trading expenses." (The assumption being that if they were good traders, and not just doing it for fun, it would have a positive impact on performance.) As a matter of fact, the researchers said, "we cannot reject the hypothesis that every dollar spent on trading expenses results in a dollar reduction in fund value." Money down the toilet! Yessir, your actively managed mutual fund in action.

Other studies have shown that it's not just trading dollars that are wasted, but every buck spent on running mutual fund portfolios, from commissions to manager salaries to the cost of the urinal mints in the men's room. Researchers have proven time and again that the cost of running a mutual fund portfolio is not justified. It is a waste of money more often than not. Chalmers-Edelen-Kadlec also found that funds "have incentives to churn their portfolios even when no value maximizing trades are found." Fund-compensation arrangements, they observed, don't penalize fund managers who trade incompetently or wastefully—still more evidence that this whole "fiduciary duty" concept is just a lot of kidding around by the fund industry.

At this point you may be wondering about all the fund watchdogs you've been reading about—the regulators and government officials who actually do seem to penalize fund managers and fund companies, and do indeed appear to take seriously this fiduciary stuff. They are on the case, and are working hard, or so the media has reported.

When an SEC factotum named Paul F. Roye announced in February 2005 that he was stepping down as chief of investment company regulation, the financial press used the opportunity to review all that Roye and the SEC had been doing on mutual funds, and the general consensus was that the regulators had been doing a lot, and were going to do a lot more. The MarketWatch Web site expressed the zeitgeist best as it described the kind of tough hombre needed to fill Roye's shoes: "Wanted: Tough, change-minded public servant to take over as the nation's top mutual-fund regulator. Must be able to handle controversy and heated challenges."

Change-minded? You bet. The SEC is proposing, and adopting, a bunch of changes. Let's see what they are.

CHAPTER EIGHT

MUTUAL FUND PAYBACK TIME—NOT

The pinnacle of our self-regulatory pyramid, the Securities and Exchange Commission, is not as imperious as its lofty position implies. When it regulates—and regulate it does, believe you me—it does so democratically. Longstanding procedures, common to all regulatory agencies, have bestowed upon the SEC an almost Athenian style of democracy. The SEC's chief method of regulation is known as the rulemaking process, and you can rest assured that the SEC is more than happy to let you participate in that process, if you so choose.

When John C. Carter of San Dimas, California, expressed displeasure about the payments Smith Barney received for pushing American Distributors funds, he was playing an essential role in the aforementioned process. So were many other individuals who, like Carter, had either written letters to the SEC or sent in their views via the Internet. Literally thousands of people were venting, pleading, persuading, and generally yammering on what to do about brokerages being paid to push mutual funds.

The SEC comment period on pending rules is a gateway through which anyone can enter. It is as accessible as an Internet bulletin board or even one of those "town meetings" that the Investor's Champion, Artie Levitt, used to convene when he wanted to get investor input before knuckling under to the Street or doing nothing. Anyone can toss in a comment, and you can bet that the SEC will be listening hard. That is its job. To listen to what people have to say, and to act. Well, to listen, at any rate.

When it comes to what actually emerges from the rulemaking process, it is probably safe to assume that the fund industry has more influence than, say, some guy with a Hotmail account and an opinion about mutual funds. A guy with an opinion about mutual funds does not hire law firms to lobby Congress and the SEC, does not have the opportunity to engage in cozy chitchats with SEC officials, and does not represent an industry whose law firms provide employment to SEC officials after they stop being SEC officials. Another reason this is a safe assumption is that the SEC hasn't written a single regulation that would seriously upset the status quo of the mutual fund industry. It has backed off from the few proposed regulations that have made the fund industry slightly uncomfortable. The end result of all this inaction and backing off is that the SEC hasn't moved even one millimeter toward correcting any of the fund industry's abuses—which underlines why reforming the fund industry is up to you.

This is not to say that the SEC hasn't moved. After the fund scandals were splattered all over the headlines in September 2003, regulators swarmed purposefully, like honeybees on a leftover Sno-Kone. More than a dozen regulations were proposed. That's a lot of activity. A lot of "changes," as the financial press puts it. As the regulatory agenda lengthened, media attention waned and regulators were able to face down their most feared enemy—an aroused public. The fund scandal, the subject of an almost hysterical media frenzy in late 2003, gradually drifted out of the public consciousness, smothered in an ooze of busywork and, as MarketWatch correctly observed, "heated challenges."

One of the first rules concerning the fund industry to come out of the SEC after the scandal outbreak was the one that drew the comment from Mr. Carter. It addressed revenue sharing and several other subjects. The proposal was published for public comment on January 29, 2004. The title of SEC Release Nos. 33-8358, 34-49148, IC-26341; File No. S7-06-04 conveys the clarity of vision that is the hallmark of the SEC: "Confirmation Requirements and Point of Sale Disclosure Requirements for Transactions in Certain Mutual Funds and Other Securities, and Other Confirmation Requirement Amendments, and Amendments to the Registration Form for Mutual Funds."

When this rule was proposed, it was widely hailed as an example of the SEC's speedy and vigorous response to the fund scandals. It had been only a couple of months since Spitzer and the SEC had taken enforcement action against brokers taking payments from funds. The regulation had every indication of being "fast, fast, fast relief," just as in the old Excedrin commercial.

SEC Release Nos. 33-8358, 34-49148, IC-26341; File No. S7-06-04 was not a by-product of hurried thinking or slapdash rulemaking. The pinnacle of our self-regulatory pyramid had been giving the subject a lot of thought for quite some time, without disturbing its repose by actually doing anything.

One key aspect of the SEC's thought-collection process was a study that the agency staff had conducted, and which had been thoroughly digested by all layers of the SEC bureaucracy as it hummed purposefully in late 2003. This well-researched piece of work found a pervasive practice—"selection of brokers to execute fund portfolio transactions on the basis of their sales of fund shares"—except that instead of calling such things revenue sharing or kickbacks, the name the study used was "reciprocal brokerage arrangements." These were no good, said the study. Such payments "tend to have undesirable effects on mutual funds and their shareholders," as did soft dollars, which the SEC also called by another name in this study. "The use of the funds' brokerage commissions as extra compensation to retail sellers of fund shares primarily benefits the [mutual fund] adviser-underwriters rather than the funds and their shareholders," said the study. It went on to say that these payments led to excessive trading of fund shares, and encouraged fund managers to direct their trades to markets that were not giving them the best prices for portfolio transactions. Add in the academic studies proving that fund managers stink as traders, and you have a system in which fund managers had a *special financial incentive to do a lousy job.*

Overall, the SEC study was good and thorough. Just about everything that emerged concerning fund kickbacks from 2003 onward was right there, in the study. The anticompetitive effects were there. The general sleaze was there, described in some detail. Quite a good read by bureaucratic standards. Definitely worth some time studying, digesting.

It's not unreasonable to expect that it would take the SEC a while to absorb the study—say, a couple of months, or a couple of years. The more time the better, right? So the SEC took the study and began reading it very carefully, for . . . oh, about thirty-seven years. That is how long it took for the SEC to turn its attention to fund kickbacks to brokerages after they were detailed in *Public Policy Implications of Investment Company Growth,* which the SEC sent over to the House Committee on Interstate and Foreign Commerce on December 2, 1966.

You know how it is in the weeks before Christmas. Vacation schedules. Uncle Leo flying in from Cleveland, buying the Christmas tree, that sort of thing. Stuff slips your mind. Before you know it thirty-seven years have gone by and it seems like a day.

One SEC official who came strolling by while *Public Policy Implications* was being chewed over by worms was a man who hated these revenue-sharing arrangements—*really* despised them. That was, of course, the Investor's Champion, Artie Levitt. We know how much Artie hated revenue sharing because he harshly condemned it in a 2002 book that was modestly illustrated with his picture on the cover.

Since Artie headed the SEC during the entire Clinton administration, all eight years of it, and since he was the Investor's Champion, you might expect that in all that time he must have swooped down on revenue sharing like a peregrine falcon and clawed it to pieces. Artie certainly knew about that 1966 SEC study—or he could have fished it out of the basement or the National Archives or the SEC Historical Society if he didn't have a copy handy—and he probably had a lot of other info at his disposal. Artie concluded in his book that investors are pretty much helpless and ill-informed when it comes to this so-old-its-creaking practice. "When their broker recommends a fund, they don't know enough to ask: Are you suggesting this fund because your research shows it's the best investment for me, or because your firm is paid $1 million to push it?"

If you have Artie's book, don't bother to thumb through it to find the exciting story of how Artie acted on his hatred and thrashed all those broker-paying funds. It's not there. As top man at the SEC during the entire 1990s growth of the fund industry into a multitrillion-dollar behemoth, Artie sat back in his leather armchair and watched all those funds paying off brokers, and watched . . . and watched . . . and watched . . . zzzzzzz.

That's not exactly the story you get from reading *Take On the Street,* or the forceful condemnations of the fund industry that Artie provided the media as an oft-quoted pro-investor deity. In his book he bragged that "the SEC brought enforcement cases against some of the largest and most respected [mutual fund] companies during [his] tenure." He pointed out that he put the screws to Van Kampen Investment Advisory Corp. and Dreyfus Corp., two very large fund groups, for allegedly putting out advertisements exaggerating the performance of their funds. He didn't point out that Van Kampen got a soba-noodle slap— a meaningless censure and $125,000 in penalties. That's about one-hundredth of the penalties his successor and Spitzer would later impose in far less weighty situations. It was, adjusted for asset size, the equivalent of the "penalty" you'd pay for returning an overdue exercise video to the library.

Artie forgot to mention the Van Kampen soba-noodle slap, which was insanely puny even by pre-Spitzer standards. He went on to say that Dreyfus paid $3 million to settle its case, which would be about what that company spends on umpires for the corporate softball league. As he bragged about that "penalty," Artie had yet another memory lapse and forgot to mention that two-thirds of it was imposed by Spitzer.

Apparently Artie was distracted by something when he wrote the mutual fund chapters, because he forgot other stuff that might not have made him look very good. He forgot to talk about the other soba-noodle slaps he dealt out whenever fund miscreants came his way, which wasn't very often. The alleged wrongdoers got small fines, a good scolding, signed papers not admitting to anything, and went on their way. The funds involved included some—Invesco and Alliance Capital were among them—that staged a comeback a decade later in the late-trading extravaganza. They were also "large and most respected," at least as large and respected as Dreyfus and Van Kampen. How could he have forgotten?

By the time Bill Donaldson took the helm, Artie had already set the gold standard for doing nothing about mutual funds generally and fund payments to brokerages in particular. Donaldson provided the fund industry with needed continuity in the thumb-twirling, brow-knitting, and inaction department as he took over early in 2003. And just in time. In June of that year, just a few months after he came on board, the SEC received a kick in the slats in the form of an annoying, meddling GAO report.

The GAO said there was a thing called revenue sharing that needed attention. Its report observed that "such payments have been increasing and have raised concerns about how these payments may affect the overall expenses charged to fund investors." The House Capital Markets subcommittee, meanwhile, was sticking its nose into the subject of fees and payments to brokers and generally making a pest of itself. The subcommittee held oversight hearings on fund fees in March 2003, and two members of the subcommittee, Paul E. Kanjorski and Robert W. Ney, sent over to Donaldson a bunch of obnoxious questions. Donaldson, flush from a confirmation hearing that resembled a 1960s-style love-in, responded by sending on to the congressmen a memo he had received from his fundmeister Roye, successor to Barry Barbash of Enron-exemption fame.

Roye made it very clear that the SEC had no canine in this particular fight. He approached the subject of fees, expenses, and revenue-sharing arrangements with a kind of bored indifference, such as you might find in a bartender who has witnessed one too many fistfights. Roye was not even willing to pay lip service to the notion that such payments were problematic. The words "conflict of interest" were nowhere to be found in his analysis of the payments (except for a footnote saying that those conflicts were "addressed"). Roye devoted most of his assessment to a dry legal analysis that made the payments seem about as insignificant as the loose change that falls out of your pocket when you sit on the sofa.

The congressional inquirers asked about the impact of revenue-sharing arrangements on price competition. It was a question that Roye clearly preferred they had not asked. He wasn't going to touch that one with a ten-foot pole. It was, he said, "difficult to assess whether revenue-sharing payments generally have stimulated or inhibited price competition among funds." He then proceeded to duck and weave and dance around the subject for a few more sentences.

Several months after the congressional Q and A session, when the fund scandal erupted, the SEC finally "acted." Release Nos. 33-8358, 34-49148, IC-26341; File No. S7-06-04 was inserted into the Federal Register. Here was the culmination of almost four decades of study and hand wringing and shoulder shrugging and Levittal condemnation. I think this is so momentous that it requires a new paragraph:

The SEC required disclosure.

Isn't that just what you'd expect from an agency in the forefront of "change?" Now, you might not think that this was a change, seeing as how brokerages *already were* disclosing fund payments and NASD rules *already required* that they make some kind of disclosure. That's why brokerages like Morgan Stanley were nabbed. They weren't given stern scoldings and soba-noodle slaps because they were taking payoffs. It was because they hadn't disclosed the payoffs.

Observe the brilliant simplicity of this act of inaction. The SEC could have very simply said no—no to revenue-sharing, kickbacks, or whatever you want to call them. Instead, it said yes—but with a stern frown, a reassuring expression of continued concern, and lots of words.

The SEC's pirouette around the fund-kickback issue was not an isolated case of failure to regulate. For decades, as hemlines have crept up and down and as the sands of time have poured through the hourglass, the SEC's approach to regulation of anything it touches has been very much the same. It has withstood periods of tranquility and ferment. The pattern is as follows: a long-standing problem, a period of contemplation and repose, and, finally, a tepid "solution" or a request for more comment, all spaced months or years apart. In the process, time has healed all wounds and preserved the status quo.

It's not just mutual funds that get this treatment. It's the way the SEC approaches its job.

The only variation, post-scandals, is that the spin has been more effective as a result of flaccid media coverage. Even when proposals run into opposition despite their lameness and are meekly watered down, the media either doesn't notice or doesn't care. Remember what I said earlier: this isn't Iraq or the White House. The media is on board.

For example, the SEC shocked a lot of people in March 2004 when it suggested actually doing something about market timing. The SEC proposed a mandatory 2 percent redemption fee on fund redemptions within five days of a purchase, with the proceeds going to fund assets and not the fund manager. It was a pretty obvious way of putting an end to market timing—so obvious that it was endorsed by the mutual fund trade association, the ICI. It looked as if the impossible were about to happen, and that the SEC would actually do something about a problem. But when the rulemaking process ground to a halt a year later, the forces of inertia, as usual, carried the day. The SEC said, "Never mind," and backed off from the whole idea. The SEC decided that instead it would "require a fund's board of directors either to approve a redemption fee or to determine that a redemption fee is not necessary for the fund."

In effect, the SEC was slamming its fist on the table and saying, "Goddamn it! You guys absolutely have to stop market timing—unless you don't want to."

In a statement explaining the SEC's about-face, Roye pointed out that there had been four hundred comment letters and that "most investors did not like the proposed mandatory redemption fee and thought it would penalize many shareholders who were not engaged in market timing." Excuse me. "Most investors"? Had the SEC slipped the Gallup organization a few thousand bucks to conduct a survey of investors? Sure, a bunch of people had written letters opposing the idea, but they were short-term traders who had organized a letter-writing campaign, and it was so transparent that about a hundred of the "investor" letters were identically worded.*

Actually, the coup de grâce didn't come from a few self-interested fund traders. Major fund groups, including Fidelity and Vanguard, had met with Roye and other SEC officials, and were not at all crazy about the mandatory redemption fees. Now, not all of the criticisms and objections from fund groups and others were bogus by any means. A lot of them were pretty good, constructive suggestions. But the SEC, rather than make intelligent changes in the rule, decided that the best course of action was no course of action. The soon-to-be former head of fund regulation said the SEC would "leave the decision regarding whether a redemption fee is appropriate to those in the best position to make that decision—the fund directors." In other words, the buck was being passed back to the people who were responsible for the scuzzy trading in the first place.

---

* Letter-writing campaigns by special-interest groups and their dupes seem to have a hypnotic effect on the SEC, as we'll be seeing in Chapter 17.

The same thing happened to another post-scandal rule, also proposed with great fanfare and uncritical media hype, that would have required funds to receive all orders before four P.M. That would have closed a loophole exploited by some late traders. But the fund industry didn't like it and, hey, their wishes were Bill Donaldson's marching orders. In March 2005, long after the furor died down, Donaldson backed down.

One thing about the SEC—it is a polite agency. When it proceeds with a mutual fund rulemaking, it always behaves like a well-brought-up regulator, one that is polite and respectful. The SEC is mindful of its place, and doesn't get uppity. Take the rule issued in October 2004 banning directed brokerage, which is the same kickback arrangement as revenue sharing except that the payments come right out of the fund assets instead of being laundered through the investment advisor. All that funds have to do, if prevented from this kind of kickback arrangement, is to shift over to revenue sharing, which isn't being banned.

You'll be pleased to know that this hippotamus-size loophole, which a number of people outside the fund industry pointed out during the rulemaking process, has been duly noted. "Commenters also addressed concerns regarding revenue sharing," the SEC said in adopting the final rule. "We will take these and other comments we received into consideration as we evaluate whether and how to amend the rule further." Translation: "If you think we are going to actually do anything massa doesn't like, don't hold your breath."

That point was underlined in February 2005, when the SEC finally acted on its dumb revenue-sharing disclosure rule, which it had been staring at for more than a year. The SEC's action was typical—it acted by deciding not to act. The SEC decided that a year wasn't enough, and that more time and more public comment was needed, so that the SEC could figure out how to write a rule that would put the SEC's stamp of approval on kickbacks.

The SEC's sterling record of inaction-disguised-as-action reached new heights of splendor in its campaign to put a spit shine on mutual fund governance. Nothing else has covered the SEC in greater glory for regulation fans than its plan, adopted by a narrow vote in June 2004, to force funds to set aside 75 percent of board seats, and the post of chairman, for "independent" directors. It was passed by a split vote of the SEC commissioners, with Donaldson siding with Democratic members in favoring the rule, adding to his reputation for fearlessness and Levitt-like investor protection. Then there was that U.S. Chamber of Commerce lawsuit, which made the whole thing seem even more heroic.

When you survey the vast wasteland of trivia and red herrings that is the SEC's roster of regulations and proposed regulations, keep in mind that such things are roughly analogous to a traffic accident. If you've ever smashed up your car, you know that what matters is not the actual accident but what appears in the police report. What matters in the SEC regulatory agenda is not the purpose of the agenda—which is to maintain the status quo—but how it is portrayed in the media. The actual Bill Donaldson might have been a bumbling, somnolent nonregulator, but that was not what mattered where it counted, which was in the media. One of the reasons for Donaldson's embrace by the media was that he was a proponent of the virtues of pristine corporate governance, whether the governee was the New York Stock Exchange or mutual funds or companies generally. Donaldson's credentials in this regard are usually accepted without much reflection on his actual record, even though he headed the NYSE at a time when its supervision of floor trading was so lousy that Artie Levitt's SEC actually rapped it on the knuckles.

"Corporate governance" is the great corporate-speak buzzphrase of our times. It is a self-evident good thing, like "good government" and "standing up straight" and "chewing thoroughly before swallowing." Its primary incarnation, the "independent director," is "good for you," in much the same quasi-mythical sense as fish was supposed to be "brain food" when we were kids. When the subject of corporate governance has been subjected to rigorous analysis by researchers, independent directors fall into the same mushy category as antioxidants, echinacea, and vitamin C. Nobody has been able to prove that independent directors make much of a difference to how a company is run—the evidence is, to say the least, mixed—but that hasn't kept corporate governance from being grotesquely overemphasized.

There is certainly some anecdotal evidence that independent directors are more than just window dressing. After all, it was the independent directors of the New York Stock Exchange who eventually nudged and prodded Dick Grasso into calling it quits. (In a lawsuit, he claims that he was fired.) True, it was those same independent directors who had snored loudly, saliva dribbling onto their undershirts, while Grasso rammed through a compensation package that made Cortez's hunt for El Dorado seem like Gandhi's walk to the sea by comparison. It's a pretty sorry history, not that it matters. Corporations nowadays have to eat their spinach, and mutual funds are no exception.

This independent-board-member rule was a special love of Bill Donaldson's, who had headed a board at one time and had served on a few as an independent director. As a matter of fact, Donaldson was a prime example of the kind of independent guy you want on your board if you are a CEO and you don't want to be bothered very much. Don't forget that Donaldson was on the board of that corporate turd EasyLink Services, which as we've seen was dreadful enough to require touting by paid analysts. Just before Donaldson came to the SEC, the man appointed to head the new SEC accounting standards board, William Webster, turned out to have served as an independent director of a sickening little company called U.S. Technologies, whose CEO eventually was bundled off to prison.

Webster, like Donaldson, was the kind of good soldier you see filling the "independent" slots on corporate boards throughout the country. When U.S. Technologies auditors pointed out that the company's financial controls were crummy, Webster, as head of the auditing committee, fired them. Now, that's independent!

Having himself served as an independent director, Donaldson was anxious to bring the joys of independent corporate governance to mutual funds. What worked so well at U.S. Technologies and his old stomping grounds, EasyLink, clearly had a place amid the grim mutual fund landscape.

The only problem was that it was not necessary. Mutual fund governance was just fine, thank you very much.

Take the American Funds Distributors group, the Beaver Cleaver of a fund group that turned out to be a revenue sharer with "approximately fifty" unnamed brokerages. If its conduct was any measure of the quality of its governance, you've got to figure that American Funds' directors were insiders and management lackeys, bereft of the independence and jaw-jutting courage that a William Webster would bring to the fore. Let's take the American Funds flagship, the Growth Fund of America, founded in 1973, with 3.3 million customer accounts. This was one of the funds that Mr. Carter of San Dimas mentioned as having been pushed too severely by his broker at Smith Barney.

The Growth Fund of America board had nine members when the American Funds group was paying off those fifty or so unnamed brokerages. Seven of the nine directors—78 percent—were as independent and free as the wind. It was the same story at the group's other funds.

It was the same pristine picture at the Janus fund group. Its Mercury fund was involved in the very first late-trading scandal. At Janus, directors are called trustees. Seven trustees, and all except one were independent. That's 86 percent. And you have to figure that these were hardworking types, as each of these trustees—not unusual for funds in general—served on the boards of no less than *fifty-nine portfolios*.

Ditto at the Invesco Dynamics fund—that's the one where investors lost 34 percent at the same time hedge fund late traders saw a 110 percent return on their money, according to Spitzer. In 2003, all of the Invesco stock funds were under the loving care of eight independent directors, far outnumbering the three insider directors. True, that was under the 75 percent threshold Donaldson set, but not by much—73 percent of the board. But after the unpleasantness with Spitzer it was all fixed, and by 2005 Invesco had two insiders and fourteen outside directors on each fund board. A veritable model of propriety, with independent directors occupying 88 percent of board seats.

Oh, and don't think for a moment that Invesco Dynamics shareholders stood naked and unprotected while the fund was letting them be systematically screwed by late traders. On the contrary, in July 2002, Invesco laid down a code of ethics that was one of the toughest in the world. It's thorough. It covers every possible sin imaginable—except allowing some of its clients, such as a certain hedge fund cited by Spitzer, to engage in late trading that screws other clients. It's such a wonderful code of ethics that it is pretty much standard throughout the fund industry—so commonplace that the SEC decided in mid-2004 to pass a rule requiring codes of ethics for an industry that already had them and already had been ignoring them.

Superb governance is also to be found in pretty much all the other fund groups caught up in the scandals. You couldn't swing a cat in the boardroom of the sleaziest mutual fund without clawing a director who was "independent" in the sense of not being employed by, or doing business with, the fund company. Such pristine independence was the norm *while the scandals were taking place*.

Here's the percentage of independent directors on the boards of the major scandal-beset fund groups, *while* all the late trading and other nastiness was under way:

> *MFS Funds: 75 percent*
> *Nations Funds: 60 percent*
> *Strong Funds: 83 percent*
> *Alliance Capital Management: 86 percent*
> *Putnam: 77 percent*
> *Pilgrim Baxter: 75 percent*

Note the really good score for Pilgrim Baxter. Way to go, Pilgrim Baxter! Those guys really had some terrific corporate governance over there, at the very same time that their president and board chairman—Gary L. Pilgrim and Harold J. Baxter—were allegedly engaged in some really off-the-charts sliminess, allegedly screwing over the fund's investors by allegedly letting some of their hedge fund pals engage in late trading. Gary Pilgrim even had the chutzpah to allegedly invest in one of the hedge funds that was screwing his investors. Note my use of the word *allegedly,* and that brings me to the good part. Both dodged a bullet, agreeing to fines and bars from the industry, without having to admit or deny guilt. No criminal prosecution—not from the feds and not from Spitzer, who had the power to send folks to prison but rarely exercised it. Way to go, Mr. Pilgrim and Mr. Baxter!

Actually it wasn't just the scuzzball mutual funds that have terrific governance. Independent fund directors already comprise solid majorities of fund boards, and most have done so for many years. In 2002, Artie Levitt's SEC codified the status quo by requiring independent board majorities. The lion's share have long exceeded that 75 percent level set in Donaldson's new rule, the one that makes him look like a hero because it resulted in a suit from the U.S. Chamber of Commerce. True, most funds need to play a little musical chairs because they don't have an independent chairman, as the new SEC rule requires. But what's the difference? They're so top-heavy with independent directors that any selfish, grasping insider directors would be consistently and resoundingly outvoted by all those brave, forthright independents.

That is the fun part of these "fund governance" changes. They're the regulatory equivalent of the fake news shows that you see on Comedy Central. Nobody is supposed to believe that Samantha Bee is "Senior Baghdad Correspondent" on *The Daily Show with Jon Stewart,* and nobody was supposed to believe that Bill Donaldson was really a "market regulator." He was just playing it for laughs. Having been an independent director himself, he surely must have known that it doesn't matter in the real world if independent directors are 50 percent or 75 percent or even 100 percent of a fund's board. The ICI itself proposed back in 1999 that two-thirds of fund directors be independent. The ICI knows full well that having an "independent" fund board doesn't mean a thing—because if it did mean a thing, they wouldn't be proposing it, would they?

The inanity of "independent" fund boards has been established fact for ages, and was one of the central findings of the Freeman-Brown study in 2001. They observed in their analysis of the fund industry that even though "independent fund directors have the right to demand advisory or distribution fee cuts or to fire the fund's advisor or underwriter, those rights are virtually never exercised."

Fund boards have no reason to act as burrs under management saddles. Keep in mind that the Investment Company Act shortchanges investors by providing a lesser standard of fiduciary duty than do most state laws. The act is a veritable bulletproof shield protecting overreaching fund managers and lazy or inattentive fund directors. Among other things, it denies plaintiffs the right to a jury trial, and limits damages to the actual losses suffered by shareholders— thereby preventing the kind of punishing punitive damage awards that might kick crummy funds where it hurts. Sure, people can still sue in state court to take advantage of stricter state fiduciary duty standards—and chances are they will lose. The courts have found that the Investment Company Act supersedes state laws.

You'll lose in federal court too, more than likely, if you challenge fund taking. The landmark case on fund fees, which was decided by the Second Circuit Court of Appeals in 1982, found that a fee is no good only if it is "so disproportionately large that it bears no reasonable relationship to the services rendered and could not have been the product of arm's-length bargaining." This standard, which was established in the case of *Gartenberg v. Merrill Lynch Asset Management,* is sensible—until you realize that investors simply don't have access to the facts they need to pursue cases like this. Admissible evidence, the Freeman and Brown study observed, is not available, so, as a practical matter, fund practices are untouchable.

"Independent" directors aren't the answer to the fund industry's problems, any more than they were the answer to the problems of the NYSE or Enron or any of the other pillars of Corporate America where they sat quietly and did nothing. The Chamber of Commerce lawsuit against this ridiculous, meaningless, goofy, and unnecessary regulation has, however, performed a service—not to the public by any means, or even to a fund industry that could care less if this fund governance rule is passed. The service it performed for the SEC was to give the mistaken impression that the pinnacle of our self-regulatory pyramid, and its chairman Bill Donaldson, were doing something worthwhile for investors. That was the line, and it has been swallowed—along with the hook and the sinker—by the financial press.

Donaldson's emergence as another Investor's Champion became evident in early 2005, when he began to back off from some of his early proposals after the Street had begun to squawk. In February 2005, SEC flacks went on the offensive, arranging for Donaldson to have interviews—all on the same day, apparently—with every major media outlet in the country. This produced the usual glowing coverage and a particularly orgiastic outburst in *Business Week.*

The nation's leading financial weekly was so overjoyed by its access that it went a little overboard. *BW* portrayed Donaldson in the kind of terms that no flack would dare to use, as it would be too embarrassing: "crusader," "activist agenda," a "zealous enforcer" who "set a blistering pace," and, last but not least, the man who "cleaned up the mutual-fund mess."

If you've ever had a fender-bender, you might know what it's like to do something a little careless with the Chevy, and the cop on the beat isn't very bright and gives you a pass. That's how Donaldson must have felt when he read the *BW* story. What really happened is not important. What really matters is what's in the police report, or, in this case, the pages of *BW*.

A few months later, Donaldson retired. He left behind a legacy of achievement not just in the meaningless realm of mutual fund governance but in a rapidly growing corner of Wall Street that was of increasing consequence to investors—hedge funds. Those are a kind of supercharged mutual fund that used to be the exclusive preserve of the rich, but now are eager to share their blessings with you.

CHAPTER NINE

IT'S A BIRD, IT'S A PLANE . . .
IT'S SUPERINVESTOR!

I t happens when you least expect it. You may be at an alumni reunion where people are drinking too much, or perhaps you are at a party that you know you should have skipped. A "financial consultant" or "advisor" sidles up to you near the munchies, asks a few innocent-sounding questions, and purrs gently, "So . . . that means you are an *accredited investor!* Now, I have at my office a numbered offering memorandum I can send right over to you for the Millennium Partners Variable-Interest Market Neutral Alpha Partners Partnership III."

If anyone ever says that to you, take the nearest crudités and eject them firmly in the direction of the offending words. If bodily injury results—well, any jury would call it self-defense.

Maybe it sounds nice to be called an accredited investor, or another ominously flattering expression that someone might deploy in your presence, "sophisticated investor." Please, resist. Walk away. You don't want anyone calling you that. If either of those labels can be legitimately applied to you—and sometimes even if they cannot—you may wind up putting your money into a "private placement" for a company that can't get a loan from the bank, or you may find someone talking you into a barf-bag real estate partnership, or maybe a movie or venture-capital partnership that is the functional equivalent of shredding your cash and using it as mulch in the tomato garden.

Or you may wind up on the wrong end of the most overblown investment craze of turn-of-the-twenty-first-century America. You may become the latest casualty in a skirmish for the fortunes of America called the hedge fund. As a matter of fact, you may be a casualty even if you don't know you're a casualty.

Your pension fund, or the endowment of the college that is charging you through the nose for the education of your offspring, may be dragging you into Hedge Fund Mania. You should be kicking—and screaming.

Hedge funds are investment funds (sometimes called investment vehicles, as in the Porsches their managers buy with your money) that are designed for people and institutions that have a serious misfortune—the accumulation of substantial sums of money, both the theoretical "paper gains" variety and actual, no-kidding-around "wealth." If your net worth climbs to more than $1 million—even if it's mostly equity in a condo you can enjoy only by moving into a cardboard box—you are an accredited investor. Ditto if your salary is $200,000 a year ($300,000 if married), even if most of it goes to taxes or the kid's nursery school fund or alimony.

If mutual funds are the white bread of Wall Street, indistinguishable from one another except for the label, hedge funds are a custom-baked, pure-cream wedding cake, the one that celebrates your marriage to your fantasies. Very little on Wall Street is awesome, and hedge funds are truly awesome.

They are not awesome because of what they do, which is pretty much anything except parboil the firstborn of their partners. Hedge funds can sell short to bet on stock-price declines, make lofty macro bets by trading currencies and commodities and foreign stocks or real estate, borrow money to engage in all of this lofty wagering, perform all kinds of market-neutral strategies that make you sorry you slept through advanced calculus—and, of course, they can screw over mutual fund investors by late-trading their funds. They can do all that, or they can do nothing. They can stash all the money in CDs and go fishing if they want (and, for a lot of them, that wouldn't be a bad idea).

None of this makes them even particularly distinctive. Any investment bank's proprietary trading desk does most of that stuff, all the short-selling and macro wagering, and the big ones don't even have to say much about it in their SEC filings.

What draws the breath from the lungs is their proven ability at acquiring, and taking, your money. When it comes to achieving that objective, hedge funds are masters of not just this universe but any others that may lie beyond the Milky Way (even if, as some cosmologists believe, there are as many universes as there are galaxies, and as many galaxies as there are stars in the Milky Way, and as many stars in the Milky Way as there are Milky Ways or even Almond Joys in the Milky Way).

In 1990, a total of $50 billion was invested in hedge funds, while about $1.1 trillion was stashed away in mutual funds, including money market funds.

That was a reasonable enough ratio—twenty-two white-bread money-taking machines for the masses to one hedge fund for all those lucky accredited investors. By 2005, the mutual fund–hedge fund ratio had gone completely bonkers. Mutual funds had achieved a healthy gain in assets to $8.2 trillion, while hedge funds—as many as seven thousand of them, according to estimates—had climbed to $1 trillion under management, a twentyfold increase since 1990.

Several explanations are usually given for all this rampant growth, though probably "excuses" might be a better word. One that you might hear is that hedge funds are being pushed very heavily by brokerages, and that they are hot on a new class of hedge fund that invests in other hedge funds, and which are designed for as mass a market as the law allows. The only problem is the numbers involved. It's not that they're not good enough. They're too good.

In 1990, there were three funds of hedge funds, according to the scarce information available at the time. By 2002, there were 510 of them. Okay. That's plausible for a hot new financial product, and, of course, the 1990s were great years for Wall Street. However, look what happened during 2002, which was a totally sucky year, with terrorism and corporate scandal weighing down the market. Between January and September, the number of FOHFs zoomed to 675. While standard, off-the-line investment vehicles were clogging the showrooms, their salesmen sitting around reading newspapers, investors were lining up at Fund of Fund City, signing up for a brand-new Hedgemobile. Percentages are a little meaningless when applied to insanity, but that's a 32 percent increase in this subset of hedge funds alone, with an 84 percent increase in their assets.

It was the same craziness at the other end of the investor food chain—the professional investors who manage corporate pension funds and the endowments of charities and universities. The numbers are never any good—Bill Donaldson only had available two-year-old figures when he testified before Congress on hedge funds in mid-2004—but they definitely track a pattern of vast increases in hedge fund investment by large investors. About a fifth of corporate and public pension plans in the United States were using hedge funds in 2002, up from 15 percent in 2001, and other data showed pension fund investments in hedge funds growing from $13 billion in 1997 to more than $72 billion by 2004, an increase of more than 450 percent.

By the early part of the new millennium, hedge funds had become the third-largest investment class owned by university endowments, right after stocks and bonds. One study estimated that 12 percent of endowment and foundation money was deployed into hedge funds. The biggest endowments were drawn to those mothers like moths to a fireplace, with 20 percent of their assets in hedge funds in 2004, according to a survey by the National Association of College and University Business Officers. Sober and even spiritually overachieving institutions (Yeshiva University was one) were socking away more than half their spare cash into hedge funds. An institution founded by Thomas Jefferson, the University of Virginia, declared its independence from sanity by sticking 56 percent of its endowment into hedge funds. The champion of them all was a small, leafy, ivy-covered college of the "third choice" variety out in western New York state, Alfred University, which put almost three-quarters of its endowment into a fleet of these sleek, exclusive, wealth-loving investment vehicles.

There is no rational explanation for any of this. There is, however, a pretty good irrational explanation.

All this hedge fund mania is happening for the same reason intelligent, sane people subscribe to magazines that explore the secrets of Area 51, where the aliens are kept in deep freeze. The same reason impels thousands of hardworking, responsible, rational people every year into the streets of Tombstone, Arizona, to watch reenactments of the Gunfight at the O.K. Corral and wander through the streets at night to catch a glimpse of the ghost of Big Nose Kate. This is not to demean hedge funds (or Big Nose Kate), by the way. They are in good company—squarely in the annals of American folklore, along with Daniel Boone, Johnny Ringo, George Washington's coin toss across the Potomac, and the shooter at the grassy knoll.

Hedge funds are the only component of Wall Street that is built pretty much entirely upon myth. Few areas of financial endeavor have been a subject of so many hoary myths, moronic half-truths, goofy speculation, once-true falsehoods, and knucklehead fantasies—a self-perpetuating hagiographic narrative recounted in countless books, one more inane than the next, and even less countable newspaper and magazine articles, one more sycophantic than the next. Perhaps most egregious is the periodic spectacle of the press genuflecting in front of hedge fund "philanthropy," which rarely—Soros is a notable exception—involves a significant deployment of hedge fund wealth. It's not just the trade press. Even the *New York Times* is occasionally beguiled by the "generosity" of obscenely overpaid hedge fund managers.

Hedge funds are more than just loaded—they are "sexy." They are a sure way to make you rich, or at least to make money when all around you are losing theirs, and are run by people who have made themselves rich by being smarter than anyone else. Over the long term, if one had invested a small sum of money with them when they were "undiscovered," one could have become well and truly loaded. They are the geniuses who sit at the *Barron's* Round Table and are quoted by stock-market columnists and feted by the media as daring, swashbuckling traders who really know what is going on and do the smart thing in contravention to the conventional wisdom.

They are the "smart money." When markets crash, they are the ones who are buying, covering their short positions, having previously predicted the collapse. They may occasionally commit excesses, their dark side emerging when they prey on innocent small companies by the horrors of a practice called naked short-selling, which will be explored in all its violence and terror in Chapter 17. But generally they are benevolent, taking time out from the pursuit of riches and Bridgehampton polo by rooting out malfeasance and tipping off the SEC on countless frauds.

Among them is a special breed. Modest, eschewing all publicity, sometimes scholarly or volatile in the manner of genius, "secretive" and hence all the more worthy of media worship, are the heroic, the "legendary" *übermenschen* known as Superinvestors. Like Wotan, like Thor, like Sergeant Fury, laws do not stand in their way. Not laws of nature or man, and certainly not the Efficient Market Hypothesis. These are the names that are the objects of an infatuation beyond embarrassment, such as George Soros, Julian Robertson, Paul Tudor Jones, Michael Steinhardt, Bruce Kovner, and Louis Bacon. Those who dwell in the hedge fund world generally fall into two categories: Superinvestors and the "next" Superinvestors.

That's the myth. Usually the financial press, functioning in the role of the *griot* imparting the oral tradition, forgets to mention that the superstar investors tended to make their biggest bucks when they were managing small sums of money. Some of the biggest names in the business liquidated or wound down their funds when their assets swelled beyond reasonable size, the odds caught up with them, and their performance turned lousy. In the media, and sometimes in the marketing efforts of the naughtier fund promoters, individual hedge fund managers are often portrayed as continuing in the tradition of the Superinvestors.

This myth, though laughable, is no laughing matter. The 1998 failure of a massive house of cards called Long-Term Capital Management, a particularly opaque hedge fund, practically brought down the entire banking system. LTCM investors, among them a bunch of thoroughly snowed institutional types, suffered through a 92 percent decline in their holdings. LTCM could, and probably will, happen again. Hedge funds are looming ever larger in the global markets. It has been shown time and again—in lawsuits and indictments scattered throughout the country—that all too often, people who buy into hedge funds have only the haziest idea of what is being done with their money. All they know is that hedge funds are powerful and strong, wise and mysterious and wonderful.

The "powerful" part is certainly true. Since hedge funds often use humongous amounts of borrowed money, they can buy and sell a hell of a lot more stocks, bonds, futures contracts, and so on than is reflected in those asset numbers. Credit Suisse First Boston found that more than half of the trading on the New York Stock Exchange and the London stock exchange was believed to have originated from hedge funds.

As for the "wonderful" part—well, here are some of the things hedge funds do for the people and institutions who invest in them:

- They cause people to pay fees that would be considered highway robbery in even the most wack-a-doo mutual fund—and which have not shown any sign of declining despite all that humongous growth.
- They cause people to buy into "black box"—"gimme the money and I do what I want with it"—investment strategies.
- They cause people to give their money to creeps they haven't bothered to check out, the kind of people they wouldn't trust to run out and buy them a sandwich, much less manage their fortune.
- They cause people to sign contracts that are so one-sided they would make a credit-card lawyer blanch, including "lock up" clauses that keep their money confined to the funds for as many years as some fund managers should be confined to prison.
- They cause people to agree, sometimes eagerly, to be treated like slightly retarded schoolchildren and not be given any information about what is being done with their money.
- They cause people to buy investment products that are functionally equivalent to mutual funds. There's even a name for that, the "long only" hedge funds, which are basically hedge funds that do everything a mutual fund would, except that they overcharge you and give you the ability to tell your golfing buddies that you've invested in a hedge fund. These funds have been hyped in the media as conservative, when they're really quite the opposite. By not short-selling stocks, which would smooth out the bumps when the market gets rough, they are actually a

good deal *more* prone to market fluctuations than traditional hedge funds.

That brings me to the best part:

- They have people lining up for the dung sandwich described above, and in return they provide performance that is subpar, inconsistent, not worth all the risk, or all of the above.

Hedge funds have their own version of Mutualingo, a special vocabulary that is used to describe all the misconceptions and fantasies that have made them the Oreck ElectrikBroom of Wall Street, sucking up all the spare change and loose fortunes that have fallen under the couch. Like Mutualingo, the special language of hedge fund fallacies—Hedgefallatio—has replaced English to describe every aspect of the hedge fund industry.

So let's build up our word power again, and look at some common Hedgefallatio expressions.

Let's start with *hedge fund*. Sometimes you see headline writers make fun of that term, as in "clipped hedges" and other variations on that, and they have every right to do so because that is pure Hedgefallatio. I'm using it in this book to avoid confusion, but it is really not correct, and neither is the definition that you see in the press. Usually it is something like this: *"Hedge funds are unregulated private investment partnerships for the wealthy."*

Let's pull out the *Handbook of Hedgefallatio* and do a little deconstructing.

Hedge. Lots of hedge funds don't do any hedging at all, in the sense of taking securities positions—such as using options or selling short—to reduce the risk of their stock portfolios. Note, by the way, the use of the terms *lots of* and *hundreds of* whenever I or anyone else talks about hedge funds. That's because, as you'll be seeing, nobody keeps accurate statistics on hedge funds, and not even the self-regulatory pyramid has counted them.

Private Investment Partnerships. Not necessarily. Just about every major hedge fund, and many minor ones, has an offshore equivalent to attract overseas money, and these are generally not partnerships. They are usually structured as mutual funds.

Offshore is also Hedgefallatio, a tribute to the hedge fund manager's best friend, the U.S. tax code. Offshore funds are not situated on platforms in the Gulf of Mexico, as implied, but rather are a kind of wink-and-nod legal fiction employed by the hedge fund industry. In English, that means a fund that is based in the United States and staffed in the United States, but avoids the U.S. tax laws by keeping its "domicile" in a filing cabinet on some Caribbean island. George Soros's Quantum fund, which kept European central bankers up at night during the 1990s, and all his other funds were offshore entities, even though the only "shore" nearby was a muddy lake over at Central Park. Soros's funds were run from an office building at Seventh Avenue and Fifty-seventh Street in midtown Manhattan, but they were incorporated in the Netherlands Antilles, sharing a mailing address with a bunch of other U.S.-staffed "offshore funds."

A lot of the new fund-of-funds concoctions, offshore and domestic, are similarly structured as mutual funds. The word *private* is not necessarily correct. There are loopholes in the rules allowing funds to be marketed, under certain circumstances, to ordinary "nonaccredited" U.S. investors. But since thousands of ordinary folks are paper millionaires anyway because of the real estate boom, the distinction is growing less important. Over at the SEC, Bill Donaldson, following in the Artie Levitt tradition, decried the "retailization" of hedge funds while doing nothing about it.

Unregulated is also incorrect. Every single aspect of their lives is governed by, or exempted from, the Securities Act of 1933, the Investment Company Act of 1940, and other federal laws. Apart from that, many of the largest funds are run by people who file some forms with the SEC and are considered registered investment advisors, making them subject to on-site visits by the SEC. This is a fairly benign and tolerable kind of regulation that doesn't bother fund managers very much, so naturally enough a registered-investment-advisor requirement was the centerpiece of Bill Donaldson's silly "hedge fund oversight" program. We'll be coming back to Donaldson's approach to hedge funds in a few pages. It's a lot of fun, definitely worth the wait.

Hedge funds are also subject to a bunch of strictures because of the aforementioned exemptions. These are things that, theoretically, keep funds from doing stuff that they might want to do, such as advertising or selling to junior high school investment clubs. None of these rules is much of a bother—and if they were, you can bet the hedge fund industry would see to it that they were changed, and fast. The no-ad rule has been kept, but that's because it is a big joke. The law doesn't keep hedge funds from hiring public relations firms to flack the funds so aggressively that you'd think you were in the air over Berlin in 1940. The nice thing about these restrictions from the fund perspective is that they have a significant fringe benefit. In return for agreeing to rules against things that don't bother them too much, hedge funds are given the green light by regulators to tell you to drop dead when you want to find out what they are doing with your money, and they can take fees that are the envy of the free world.

So let's sum up for a moment here: Hedge funds don't hedge. A lot of them aren't private investment partnerships. A lot of them don't do anything special. They are definitely not unregulated. So what are they? That brings us to the English-language definition of *hedge fund,* which is as follows:

"Hedge funds are glorified mutual funds with fees that are high enough to choke a Clydesdale, Belgian, Percheron, or other draft-class horse."

As we saw in previous chapters, an equity mutual fund will take, on average, about 1.5 percent of your money, come rain or come shine (not counting commissions and other hidden goodies). Hedge funds take that, but they want more. Why? For the same reason your two-year-old wants another slice of cake. Your two-year-old would say, if you asked him, "Because I wanna!" Well, that's pretty much the answer from the hedge fund industry. They wanna. You are willing to give it to them, and the law allows it, so they take a performance fee that is usually expressed in the media as "20 percent of profits." That's 20 percent of all the income and capital gains, realized and unrealized, generated by the fund. Plus another 2 percent of assets on top of that—more than the typical mutual fund, you will note—the infamous "20 and 2."

The ostensible reason you pay them so much is because they are "smarter" and "more nimble" than mutual fund managers. Hedge fund managers are, by definition, the "smart money." That is another Hedgefallatio term that you see often in the financial press, usually intended to denote *"an uncommonly shrewd professional investor; e.g., a hedge fund manager."* The English definition is *"a person smart enough to talk you into paying high fees for uneven, often mediocre performance."*

According to research by Burton G. Malkiel and his colleague Atanu Saha, which was circulated in the academic world and a thoroughly annoyed hedge fund industry in 2005, all the terrific performance that you read about in the media has been puffed up like a goose at the slaughterhouse. Malkiel and Saha found that fund return numbers have been consistently misrepresented—really made to dance and climb into the trees—by a variety of methods. When the statistical steroids were removed, they found hedge funds underperformed the market, gaining 8.8 percent a year between 1995 and 2003, compared with 12.4 percent for the S&P 500. By comparison, hedge fund databases had shown funds beating the market during that entire period. The study could go back only to 1995, the authors said, *because no reliable data was available before 1995.*

What this means is that during the most glorious years of growth for the fund industry, when money was being poured into hedge funds at a crazy pace, and when the financial press was outdoing itself to glorify the fund industry, the numbers upon which all that money-pouring and fund-glorifying were based were a lot of ca-ca.

Malkiel and Saha found that the numbers afterward weren't much better. Their study described several serious problems with the way hedge fund indexes have been compiled over the years. They examined the oldest and most widely used index, from the TASS Research division of Tremont Advisers—there are a few others, all pretty much painting the same glorious picture of fund performance—and discovered that rouge and mascara had been applied to gussy up some otherwise drab numbers. Fund indexes, they found, systematically exclude funds that flame out and otherwise depress the numbers—what's known as survivorship bias—as well as a bunch of other things that weren't very nice at all.

Much of the skewing arose from the fact that hedge funds don't have an obligation to report their performance to anybody. (They're exempt from the law requiring that for mutual funds.) If they suck wind—well, that's something they can keep to themselves. They can report numbers to fund databases in a year when they're doing fine, and stop reporting the next year when they're not doing so well. Or just tell the databases, from day one, to get lost. It's a bit like college kids having the power to pick and choose which grades they can include in their GPA, or have no GPA at all. Naturally enough, funds tend to shout to the world how great they're doing only if they're doing great. If they are, they tell the fund databases the story of their terrific long-term performance, and their great past performance changes the indexes for previous years. It's almost as if the track record of fillies in the *Daily Racing Form* consisted only of the horses that won most of their races. This built-in, retroactive bias, called backfilling, is sort of like a tractor pushing dirt—which falls on the brains of wealthy but clueless investors. Backfilling made nonsense out of the "vast majority" of published fund statistics as recently as 1997, said the study, and only in 2001 did that statistical muck finally get swept out of hedge fund statistics.

Now, the authors didn't totally knock hedge funds. They found that the funds do serve a legit purpose in that they are not correlated to the S&P, and thus can be useful to diversify a portfolio. They added a caveat, however. Hedge funds, they said, are "extremely risky" because of the wide variation between outstanding funds and earth-pawing, dung-chewing doggies. "Investors in hedge funds," Malkiel and Saha concluded, "take on a substantial risk of selecting a very poorly performing fund or worse, a failing one." In 1997, fewer than two dozen hedge funds had assets of more than a billion dollars, according to an estimate by Morgan Stanley. By 2003, this number had grown to 193 bloated behemoths. With the number of megafunds on the rise, hedge fund performance is likely to get even worse. As we'll be seeing, the bigger and fatter a fund tends to be, the more risks it has to take—and the more likely it is to bite the big one.

There's a word for "likely to bite the big one" in finance. It is called kurtosis. This may sound like a form of acne, but it actually is used by statisticians to describe charts of fund performance. Such charts tend to look like a bell curve, with the highest part in the middle. *Kurtosis* describes the part of the curve to the left and right of the big fat lump in the center. Those are called tails. High kurtosis means "fat tails." What that means is that higher than normal numbers of funds perform well—and terribly.

High kurtosis, a kind of financial manic-depression, can be an even worse problem when combined with other risk factors—and hedge funds have those in spades, according to the Malkiel-Saha studies and others over the years. These have found that hedge funds show uneven persistence, so a winner one year has a good chance of turning subpar the next year. Studies of funds have found that a concept along the lines of kurtosis, called skewness, also works against many categories of hedge funds. You want high skewness, meaning a higher than average chance of picking a well-performing fund. On a chart of fund returns, that means a lot of fund returns are clustered in the higher numbers—a "fat right tail," as statisticians call it. "Negative skewness" means a higher than average chance of picking a dog.

Well, guess what? Hedge funds tend toward low skewness. Buy a hedge fund at random, particularly a category at the low end of the skewness trail, such as fixed-income arbitrage, and you are more likely than not to pick a stinker. One fund category heavily populated by Superinvestors and their wannabes, the global macro funds that can prowl the world for investment opportunities, had better than average skewness scores. But their kurtosis numbers were subpar, as was their performance generally. The global macro funds had an average performance (excluding dead and backfilled funds) of 7.3 percent a year between 1995 and 2003, lagging the market by five percentage points.

Oh, and those funds of funds that people were swarming to buy in 2002? Seems that these are the real runts of a generally crappy litter. It didn't matter whether backfilled returns were included or excluded. They were scrambling for the hind tit no matter how you counted their numbers. "Clearly, the typical Fund of Funds is not able to form a portfolio of individual hedge funds that can outperform the industry average after expenses," the authors said. Their average annual return was slightly worse than the global macro funds.

Needless to say, the fund industry screamed and hollered from the moment the Malkiel-Saha study started to make its rounds, in late 2004 and early 2005. The other hedge fund trackers protested that their indexes accurately reflected fund performance and said they didn't juice up their numbers—though the study anticipated such objections by saying that other fund indexes closely tracked the crummy TASS numbers. Despite all the hollering, there was no dispute that the pre-1995 hedge fund figures were unreliable. Critics of the study also didn't dispute other findings of the Malkiel-Saha study, including the factual basis for their view that funds are an extremely risky form of investment because they are so widely disparate in their performance. They disputed the "risky" characterization, noting that funds tended to beat the market during downturns, which was true enough. But they didn't quibble with the hard facts, the kurtosis and other mathematical indicators, which showed that investors scoping out hedge funds stand a better-than-decent chance of picking a mutt.

Now think about all this for a moment. A twentyfold increase since 1990 in an extremely risky investment? Hundreds of presumably cautious, presumably well-educated college endowments putting their money into funds that pose a substantial risk of turning belly to the wild blue?

Let's wander down memory lane and see if we can figure out what's gone wrong here.

CHAPTER TEN

HEDGE FUNDS: THE BIRTH OF A NOTION

Somewhere buried in the history of hedge funds is the answer to this underlying dilemma: How did a reasonably good way of managing money become so haphazard, perilous, and, often, just plain dumb?

It's really impossible to say with any certainty, evidence being so scarce, but there is a chance that, once upon a time, hedge funds were an intelligent place to put your money. There's very little data to support, or contradict, that proposition, the pre-1995 numbers being so lousy, but it's plausible enough. That's because hedge funds, as originally conceived, made a lot of sense in much the same way other antiquated 1940s institutions—such as the United Nations and urban renewal agencies—made sense as originally conceived.

Firm believers in efficient markets acknowledge that even though stock picking is generally an exercise in futility, there are inefficiencies in the markets—false perceptions contributing to stock-price anomalies—that sometimes can be exploited by sharp traders. As we saw earlier, Wall Street has embraced an antidote to the poison of the EMH, a theory of investing called behavioral finance, which holds that the market is subject to overemotional buying or selling that can be exploited by investors. EMH adherents agree that there are market inefficiencies, but that these occur randomly and that investors cannot consistently take advantage of them. Thus the EMH holds that "savvy stock pickers" and "proven stock-picking systems" are just random by-products of the laws of probability.

Hedge funds in their heyday, their Trygve Lie era, might have been able to give the EMH a run for its money. They were at one time small, nimble, and secretive enough to be able, theoretically, to exploit market inefficiencies systematically. Their business model was, and is, also sensible—in theory.

The creative genius underlying hedge funds lies in application of that word *hedge*. No question about it, early hedge funds lived up to their name. They hedged. Hedging is a sound thing to do if you know what you are doing, and is very much the antithesis of the kind of risk taking that hedge funds are known for nowadays. Hedge funds have changed so much from their origins that it makes you wonder why they are still called hedge funds. They should be called something else. Maybe "hedgeless funds," or maybe something that has two syllables and a similar sound, such as "retch funds."

The concept of hedging to reduce risk predates modern stock markets entirely. Rice farmers in Japan were hedging their crops in the seventeenth century, and by the 1630s you could buy and sell futures contracts on tulip bulbs in Europe. The problem, virtually from Day One, was that the same mechanisms that are used in hedging could also be used for speculation. An extreme example was the Dutch Tulip Bulb Mania of 1637, which is described in Charles Mackay's 1841 book, *Extraordinary Popular Delusions and the Madness of Crowds.* "Every one imagined that the passion for tulips would last for ever, and that the wealthy from every part of the world would send to Holland, and pay whatever prices were asked for them," said Mackay. All that one needed was a Dutch Artie Levitt, watching sternly from his leather armchair, to make the 1990s analogy complete.

The principle behind forward contracts was simple—the ability to sell something today for delivery tomorrow. Modern hedging arrived in the United States in 1848, with the founding of the Chicago Board of Trade. This provided farmers in the Midwest with a reliable way of selling their crops ahead of the harvest to lock in a price. If it turned out that the market price at the time of harvest was higher than the price of the contract, the farmers took a paper loss. Meanwhile, they'd already been paid for the contract, and all they had to do was deliver.

Hedging guarded against the possibility of a bumper crop causing prices to fall through the basement. That could mean ruin. It thus took some of the weather-dependent uncertainty out of farming.*

Nineteenth-century midwestern grain farmers probably didn't know it—no, make that *definitely* didn't know it—but they were bold pioneers on the frontiers of finance. The hedging in which they engaged was adopted, pretty much intact, by Wall Street financiers in the years preceding the crash of 1929. Like the

---

* Hedging via futures contracts is a good thing, and the futures industry would like you to think that it is a necessary thing, and that tampering with it would mean the demise of the entire financial system. Not so. For a while in 1936, government banned options on futures—a standard product nowadays—and in the 1950s, futures on onions were prohibited because of pressure from farmers in the Midwest. The world did not end.

honest, hardworking midwesterners from which they shamelessly stole this technique, trading desks of investment banks went long and short simultaneously.

The farmers went short when they sold the contract. *Short* is Street parlance for selling something you don't own, whether that is bushels of wheat or shares of stock. *Long* means owning something. The farmers became long when the wheat, sorghum, or corn sprouted out of the ground.

On the Street, traders would buy stocks that they felt were likely to increase in price, while short-selling roughly the same dollar amount of less desirable stocks. A more recent variation on this theme, called pairs trading, involves doing that with different stocks in the same industry. The aim is to take advantage of superior gains in the better stocks, while exploiting price declines in the lousier stocks.

There are plenty of disadvantages to doing this. First, and most obviously, is that you might pick the wrong stocks. The second possibility is that you might pick the right stocks and the market goes against you. In a market crash, your longs and your shorts decline, so you'll do a lot better than investors who are totally long. You'll be protected, or hedged, much the same as that nineteenth-century farmer who sold his corn ahead of a bumper crop.

In the kind of tulip-craze-type market rallies that we saw in the 1990s, a long-short strategy is hurt by all those short positions, because of the principle that "a rising tide lifts all boats." Still, short-selling was generally a sensible investment strategy—if, and only if, the fund manager had researched a stock thoroughly enough that he could get information not available to the general public. What's nice about the short-selling end of the transaction is that you gain in two ways—from any possible decline in the cost of the stocks, and also from interest you can scrape up from deploying the proceeds of the stock sale into Treasury bills or money-market instruments. So that gooses returns still further—again, assuming the trader is not a bum.

The first hedge funds used that basic formula—though how, and where, or by whom, is lost to history. We know that the term *hedge fund* was coined in the mid-sixties, and was first used to describe the investment fund that was founded in 1949 by a former financial journalist named Alfred Winslow Jones. Since hedge funds were considered rich men's playthings through the 1980s, they weren't counted or even thought about very much. Press coverage was scarce, and though these funds were definitely not totally unregulated, the SEC was definitely looking the other way. Nobody even knows for sure if Jones was the first hedge fund manager. The SEC, in a 2003 study of hedge funds, calls him "one of the first." What we do know is that Warren Buffett was another hedge fund manager in the sixties, thereby adding to the subsequent glory of the thing.

Aside from actually hedging, early hedge funds differed from ordinary investments in two primary respects—they could charge a performance fee, and one had to be rich to buy into them. One of the philosophical underpinnings behind securities regulation is that the very wealthy are not just different from you and me, but also smarter, perhaps more noble, and better able to take care of themselves. The "$1 million=accredited investor" equation was set in 1982, when $1 million really meant "rich enough to ignore." Today it just means "prosperous enough to be ripped off." By 2005, inflation, as measured by the Consumer Price Index, had eroded those 1982 dollars by a tiny fraction over one-half. So all the borderline millionaires who buy into hedge funds nowadays are comparative schleppers by 1982 standards.

Short-selling was what made hedge funds sexy. Mutual fund managers do not ordinarily engage in that kind of trading, so hedge fund managers had, again in theory, that much of an advantage over their white-bread brethren. Back in 1990, when there were only about $1 billion or so of them, hedge funds reeked of a kind of venturesome, snazzy, white-shoe snob appeal. They had a certain panache, a kind of genteel but iron-fisted British Secret Service reputation, because of their aversion to publicity—which was genuine at the time—and because of their willingness to go against the tide of Wall Street hype.

Until the early 1990s, hedge funds were under everybody's radar screen. They were hard to locate. There was no hedge fund association, no newsletter, none of the other outward manifestations of full-fledged industryhood— including no involvement in the scandals that wracked Wall Street in the eighties. Mike Milken, Drexel Burnham Lambert, and the rest had nothing to do with hedge funds. They were untouched by the insider-trading scandals of the time.

Those were the innocent years. They were so innocent, so clubby, so intimate, that hedge funds didn't shield their managers from liability. Now, *that's* innocent. They were the days when a good many managers, filling the role of liability-bearing general partners in the limited-partnership structure of most hedge funds, didn't incorporate to prevent themselves from being ripped to shreds in the event of a lawsuit. Another sign of how carefree things were was that hedge funds, by and large, didn't impose a mutual-fund-style management fee until the 1990s.

It took only a couple of years into the decade before such gentlemanly vestiges of a more genteel era went out the window. Hedge funds were fast becoming an industry, with all the manifestations thereof, including a bona fide scandal. It happened in 1991, and the subject of the scandal was a bond-trading scheme that was so routine that the people doing it didn't give it a second thought. Salomon Brothers, the investment bank and trading powerhouse, had a stranglehold over the U.S. Treasury bond market. Solly did what Wall Street firms do when they have a stranglehold over something, which is to tighten the noose until the eyes pop out and roll on the floor. Traders at Salomon apparently decided to control the market for Treasury notes—and they decided to let in some of their best customers.

As later set forth in a Justice Department lawsuit, two of the leading hedge funds of the time—Steinhardt Management Corp. and Caxton Corp.—"each bought large, leveraged long positions" in Treasury notes in April 1991. It was such a large position, $20 billion, that it was larger than the $12 billion in notes that the Treasury had actually issued. At the same time this was happening, other traders were going to short those notes. Shorting anything, a bond or a stock, involves borrowing something and then selling it. One of the risks of shorting is a short squeeze, which can happen when a major market participant controls the market in a stock, and forces the short-seller to buy back the stock at a higher price. That makes a profit for the short-squeezer and a loss for the short-seller. As alleged by the Justice Department, Steinhardt and Caxton were the short-squeezers—a bit ironic, by the way, because hedge funds are more often the victims than the perpetrators of short squeezes.

This wasn't some penny-stock promoter putting the arm on traders trying to dump their stock. The feds' accusations described a massive scheme. A short squeeze of Treasury bonds would actually move the market, pushing bond prices higher and interest rates lower. Something like that would require massive capital, verve, dedication—and brass balls. "Brass balls" was practically the middle name of the hedge fund managers involved. Steinhardt Management was run by Michael Steinhardt and Caxton was run by Bruce Kovner, both duly-certified, cape-wearing Superinvestors noted for their willingness to take massive bond and stock bets. Could Superinvestors have been making money by gangbanging the government bond market, cheek by jowl with some of the more cretinous traders at Salomon Brothers? They denied it—vigorously, I might add—even as Salomon Brothers itself was turned inside out for doing the same thing. They denied it right up to the minute that they settled, at which time they stopped denying it but didn't admit anything either.

In December 1994, the two firms reached a settlement with the Justice Department and the SEC, settling the allegations without admitting or denying that anything had happened. They agreed to pay penalties and forfeitures totaling $76 million.

Seven years later, Steinhardt started denying again. He had this to say in his memoirs: "While denying wrongdoing throughout, we had reached the point where we needed to move on. The continued distraction of protracted litigation had taken its toll." It does, doesn't it? Oh, well. At least it was all worth it, despite the "distraction" and legal fees and threat of criminal prosecution—waived by Artie Levitt's SEC and the Justice Department in return for no admissions to anything and some bucks. Not enough bucks, it seems. Steinhardt bragged: "Despite the enormous burden of the Treasury scandal, our bond bet had been a huge win for our investors. From mid-1990 through 1993, we had made more than $600 million on our interest rate view."

What all this proved (apart from the idiocy of settlement agreements not forcing people to admit guilt) was that hedge funds had arrived. They were now in the big leagues. They had cornered a portion of the bond market, or at least the Justice Department was still saying that even while Steinhardt was neither admitting nor denying in the agreement, and denying later in his memoirs. In announcing the settlement, Anne K. Bingaman, assistant attorney general in charge of the Justice Department's antitrust division, told a different story than Steinhardt did years later. She maintained in the Justice Department announcement of the settlement, nondenials notwithstanding, that "Steinhardt and Caxton joined to corner the market and to inflate the price of securities in the largest and most important securities market in the world."

The Salomon Brothers scandal had taught the hedge fund industry a whole bunch of lessons. One was that they had to cover their posteriors. That business about general partners having personal liability might have worked in the clubby, gentlemanly old days, when hedge funds were sold over cognac and cigars, but it simply would not do in this vibrant, modern, market-cornering era. As lawyers from the law firm of Arnold & Porter observed in October 1993 in a paper presented to a hedge fund conference, "Although there may be marketing reasons for the general partner to be an individual, this is generally undesirable, since, as a matter of law, the general partner has unlimited liability."

It certainly would be undesirable if the general partner's name happened to be David J. Askin.

CHAPTER ELEVEN

HOW TO STUFF A WILD HEDGE FUND

In the late 1980s, Wall Street redefined the all-American dream of home ownership. That was no longer to be just a cozy, green-clapboard Cape Cod–style home, with a tree house for Jimmy in the backyard and maybe a babbling brook somewhere on the premises. None of that crap. Wall Street was focusing on something a great deal more important—the income stream from the mortgage secured by that cozy, green-clapboard Cape Cod–style home. You too could own a piece of your neighbor's mortgage. You might not have the fun of sending a nasty note when your neighbor is a day late with his monthly payment, or enjoy the thrills of foreclosure if he loses his job, but you could enjoy a portion of the principal and interest stream from that mortgage. When the mortgage was finally burned in the fireplace, a little bit of you would go up the chimney.

Wall Street brought the blessings of home-mortgage ownership to all Americans by a process known as securitization. What that means is simple enough in principle, though the execution can be a bit messy. You take a contract that generates cash, and use it as the basis for a security that can be bought and sold on the open market. Securitized mortgages had been around since the 1970s, when government housing programs such as Fannie Mae started packaging them, but it wasn't until the late 1980s that Wall Street got really whipped up into a frenzy about them. Securitized mortgages had everything you could want from a financial vehicle: great gas mileage, plush interior, mag wheels—and, above all, high commissions. The leading manufacturers started cranking them off the assembly line. The Big Four were investment banks with large marketing arms that knew their way around a showroom and had a sterling reputation: Merrill Lynch, Bear Stearns, Drexel Burnham Lambert, and, right at the top of the list, the champion mortgage repackager of them all, Kidder, Peabody & Co.

Quite a bunch: a retail-wholesale powerhouse, an Eddie Haskell–like trading outfit, an even more mischievous junk bond merchant, and a firm that had gone through some rough spots (such as one of its brokers' involvement with *Wall Street Journal* insider-trader R. Foster Winans) but was now doing quite well.

Securitized mortgages—known as collateralized mortgage obligations, or CMOs—included both straightforward mortgage pools and all kinds of variations designed by the aforementioned brokerages. One of the things they did that made things more complicated—and profitable—was to peel off the interest from the principal, and sell the two separately. As any junkyard operator in East New York can tell you, a stripped car is worth more than the sum of its parts. It's the same thing, more or less, with mortgages.

Well, you know what happens when Wall Street wants to make a few bucks: The usual bad-mouthing resulted. The *Chicago Tribune* reported in September 1987 that "some" were on the loose again. Fortunately, the *Trib* had an expert on hand to refute them. "Some view these strange investment vehicles as 'Wall Street foisting speculative time bombs off on unsuspecting investors,'" said the *Trib,* quoting David J. Askin, "vice president and manager of the fixed-income research department" at Drexel Burnham. Not true, said Askin. The newspaper went on to say that, the views of "some" to the contrary notwithstanding, mortgage-backed securities were high-yielding and, above all, "safe."

The people who bought CMOs included some ordinary retail investors, but the primary market consisted of professional investors and traders for major investment houses—people brainy enough to understand the complexities of stripping and hedging and duration and risk and beta and theta and portfolio balancing. Among them were hedge funds, and by September 1991, one of the managers of a leading CMO hedge fund was that same David J. Askin.

Askin took over the management of a hedge fund called Granite Partners. In the coming months, there would be other CMO hedge funds, but Granite was always the biggest. Everything went just fine. In 1993, the Askin funds climbed 20 percent. After all, Askin was a twenty-four-carat mortgage-securities whiz, and he attracted twenty-four-karat investors—Nicholas J. Nicholas Jr., former CEO of Time Warner in its pre-AOL days; James L. Gray, former president of Warner Cable Communications; Playboy Enterprises chief financial officer, David I. Chemerow; the 3M Employee Retirement Income Plan; and even the Salami King of the Bronx, Isidore Pines, who ran the Hebrew National kosher food company.

These were wealthy people and institutions that were careful with their bucks, and, judging from Askin's résumé, he was about the best guy they could have running their securitized-mortgage portfolios. He had impeccable academic credentials, and he had risen through the ranks at first Merrill Lynch and then Drexel, where he developed what an official postmortem later described as "proprietary models for fixed income investing and was widely regarded as a quantitative oriented manager, with particular expertise in evaluating mortgage prepayments."

And then . . . Granite lived up to its name. The Askin funds were in Hedge Fund Memorial Park, all laid out neatly in adjoining plots. It was over. Sudden, quick, but not painless.

In April 1994, the Askin funds declared bankruptcy. Most of their $1.6 billion in CMO portfolios, as magnified by three-to-one leverage, had gone away. Poof!

How in heaven's name did that happen? After all, mortgage-backed securities were "safe," as no less an expert than David J. Askin was happy to admit. Besides, Askin was running Granite, Quartz et al. under optimal circumstances, such as existed only in hedge funds. As we saw in the last chapter, hedge funds are, in theory, an outstanding way of managing money, and Askin put that theory to practice. He was incentivized up the wazoo. He had as much freedom as a twenty-pound alley cat. He and his colleagues in hedge-fund-land had made the hedge-fund business model even more fantastic than it had been when A. W. Jones and Warren Buffett were slogging away at their buy-and-short strategies.

Askin worked out all the kinks, and by the time his funds conked out in April 1994, hedge funds were a lot better than the clubby, intimate, tweed-jacket kind of operation that they had been just a few years before. Only the good stuff (the so-high-you-get-dizzy fees and go-out-and-have-fun investment latitude) was retained. The bad stuff went out, and good riddance!

The really bad stuff had to do with that word *hedge*. No hedging for these guys. The Salomon Brothers bond-trading fiasco had demonstrated, for anyone who had cared to notice, how much fun hedge funds could have if they stopped hedging—how they could enjoy the benefits of even a rigged market and get away with it. They didn't have to tell the regulators, or even their investors, a damn thing they were doing. They were accountable to no one. Sure, there was regulatory heat from the Salomon disaster, but it was worth it. Hedge funds were able to exhibit the kind of screw-you attitude that is rarely found among money-making enterprises anywhere, except for maybe Colombian drug gangs or the Gambino crime family.

In 1990, according to some of the unreliable statistics then available, about 70 percent of hedge funds made money the old-fashioned way, by going long and short simultaneously. Then the erosion began, and hedging gradually faded away—to the point that by 2005, with the fund industry immensely bigger, "traditional" hedge-funds-that-hedge represented just one-third of all funds. Of course, since hedge funds are free to leave their investors in the dark and do pretty much whatever they want regardless of what their ostensible "style" may be—Long-Term Capital Management was an outstanding example of style-disregarding—no one can really say how many long-short hedge funds were still hedging.

Another stodgy convention that had become totally passé much faster, and was pretty much history by the early 1990s, was that old-fashioned, buck-stops-here "general partner is liable if anything bad happens" philosophy that helped keep fund managers on the path of righteousness in the old days. By the early 1990s, hedge funds everywhere were following the kind of good legal advice that was given by Arnold & Porter at that presentation in October 1993. No hedge fund manager was going to do anything so brain-dead as accepting personal responsibility if anything bad happened. The general partner of the flagship Granite Partners was another limited partnership, Askin Capital Management, and the general partner of that was something called Dashtar Corporation, with Askin finally materializing as the general partner of Dashtar. (The origins of the name are not known, but one might suspect it was a subliminal salute to the Dustin Hoffman–Warren Beatty disaster *Ishtar,* arguably the worst movie ever made.)

Just to make sure that nobody got confused on this liability point, the Granite fund made use of belt-and-suspenders language that was already popping up in hedge fund documents throughout the land. Investors in the fund agreed, when they plunked down their $1 million minimum investment, that they would "indemnify and hold harmless the partnership and General Partner and their Affiliates, officers, employees and agents to the extent permitted by law, for any and all costs, expenses, liabilities or losses (including legal expenses) which the indemnified party may incur under ERISA or otherwise if and to the extent . . ." and on and on. Combine that gem with other standard language allowing Askin to do anything he wanted, *including* parboiling the firstborn of his partners, and you get the general idea of the kind of glorious freedom Askin enjoyed.

Which is not to say that he made use of all of his freedom. Granite was supposed to be market neutral, which meant that it would achieve its stated objective of a stable 15 percent annual rate of return no matter what was happening in the bond market. The evidence suggests that he actually hewed pretty close to the fund's stated objective, or at least *tried* to do so.

Askin made every effort, apparently, to balance bullish securities with bearish securities, just as one would expect from a good hedge fund manager adhering to the A. W. Jones tradition. Askin later told the Bankruptcy Court trustee examining the funds' demise that, dyed-in-the-wool quant that he was, he used a "proprietary prepayment model" to help him buy stocks, as well as "sophisticated tools to select securities and balance his portfolio."

With all those sophisticated tools and models, it stands to reason that when the Fed raised short-term rates on February 4, 1994, Granite was as hedged against disaster as a bookie joint at Super Bowl time, and ready to withstand the punishment—not.

Something peculiar happened. We know that something peculiar happened only because of the exhausting and well-compensated labors of that Bankruptcy Court trustee, former New York City comptroller Harrison J. Goldin, who was paid a few million bucks to turn out a 375-page report in 1996. By then, the Granite mess was a kind of wretched memory and nobody much cared except for its creditors, their lawyers, and the accountants and experts who were paid to care.

The trustee, his lawyers, and his accountants pored over every scrap of paper involved in the life and death of the Askin funds, and actually hired Askin himself as a consultant to help the trustee figure out how he made a mess of things. The trustee's conclusion, after two years of dogged research with the assistance of the mess-maker himself, was that the biggest hedge fund disaster up to that time had occurred because there had been a misunderstanding somewhere along the line. That's right—a goof.

Apparently, just as you might pick up a quart of buttermilk at the store thinking it was eggnog, Askin bought securities that weren't what he thought they were. It seems that Askin thought his Granite fund was composed of securities that made it market neutral. But—uh-oh!—it wasn't. Darn it. His fund actually had a "bullish tilt" and was thus vulnerable to increases in interest rates, such as took place in February 1994. It seems that Askin, the toast of the quant world, actually "lacked adequate quantitative tools to measure that tilt."

As for that "proprietary prepayment model" that Askin said he had—well, Goldin respectfully disagreed with his consultant on that point. It's not that Goldin thought the model wasn't good enough. *He didn't think it existed.* Goldin reported that he couldn't find any evidence that there really was such a thing.

Some of the buttermilk that Askin thought was eggnog went by the name of inverse IOs. These were exotic CMO derivatives that tended to decline when interest rates rose. They were real stinkers to have in your portfolio when, say, the Fed decided to increase rates. Goldin found that Askin "may also have been misled by certain broker/dealer sales representatives" to believe that the inverse IOs were actually good things to own when rates went up. Goldin went on to say, in a kind of carefully worded kick in Kidder Peabody's posterior, that the funds could make a good case for misrepresentation against Kidder. The latter swiftly denied any naughtiness. Still, Askin might have wanted to take back what he said to the *Trib* in 1987, when he debunked that myth about "Wall Street foisting speculative time bombs off on unsuspecting investors."*

You have to admit, there's a certain charm in all this. If you rip away the MBA and the quant background and all the years analyzing and measuring and weighing mortgage-backed securities, it seems that Askin was just another guy in a green-clapboard Cape Cod, helpless before a fast-talking broker. As portrayed in the Goldin report, Askin was a kind of unsophisticated Rand Groves who was led down the garden path by his brokers. He bought stuff that he thought would zig when it was really supposed to zag. Could have happened to anyone.

In fact, shortly after the collapse, Askin's lawyer repeated a refrain familiar to *schlepper* investors everywhere—Wall Street was to blame. His client, he maintained, was forced out of business, with Askin in roughly the position of a homeowner who doesn't get much slack from the bank when he falls behind on his mortgage payments.

There was some basis for this complaint. After the Askin funds declined 20 percent in February 1994 (though he goofed there too and told investors it was just a 1 to 2 percent decline), his investors started to pull the plug—and so did those brokers who had sold him stuff on credit. Acting with the kind of compassion usually found among easy-terms furniture salesmen, Askin's brokers

---

* Not only was Askin one of those unsuspecting investors, but history was to record that Kidder was hoist by its own "unsuspecting" petard. The firm was pummeled by those same interest-rate fluctuations in 1994, and also by the alleged chicanery of CMO trader Joseph Jett. Kidder later maintained that Jett took advantage of complexities in the CMO biz to hoodwink the firm into thinking that he was a terrific trader, when he was really playing games with the computer system. Jett heatedly denied any wrongdoing.

called in the repo man. They socked Askin with a margin call, which is precisely what happens to you if you buy stock on credit and the price starts sinking and your account lacks sufficient collateral. If you read the fine print on the margin agreement, you'll find that the broker has the right to force you to put up more money, or to sell the stock. Askin tried to come up with the money, but he didn't have any luck because his clients were cashing out.

As Goldin gently put it, the "broker/dealers were unwilling to forbear exercising their contractual rights to liquidate the collateral upon the Funds' default." The brokers rented some U-Hauls, loaded up their IOs and the other cardboard-furniture merchandise, and the Askin funds were kaput. The brokers sold all those CMOs that they repossessed, thus depressing the market for CMOs generally and making the market for that stuff a lot less hot than it used to be. To make everything messier, as things went down the tubes Askin often guessed at the prices of the securities in his portfolio. That goes by the euphemism of "manager marks," which you have to admit sounds much nicer than "guesses." These were not accurate guesses, so his doing this did not make investors feel very affectionate toward him. But, then again, they didn't like the man very much anyway, not after he lost so much of their money.

One bright spot emerged from all this: The cause of higher education was advanced by the Askin disaster. Since Askin's brokers did not dot all the i's and cross all the t's as they cashed in all those CMOs, lawsuits were filed that dragged on through 2003. The resulting legal fees sent a whole generation of law firm partners' progeny through prep school and college.

There were no other silver linings because there were no consequences. Every parent, puppy owner, and victim of a financial disaster knows that without consequences a mess is going to happen again. Nobody involved in the Askin mess—not the hedge fund industry, not the investors therein, and certainly not the self-regulatory pyramid—learned a thing from it. That would have been enough, by the way. Not a ton of new regulations, just an understanding of what had happened, and a determination not to repeat it.

Didn't happen.

That was not for want of resource material. Thousands of acres of virgin woodland were swept off the face of the earth by the public record spewing forth from the Askin saga—a trustee report that's longer than this book, plus several thousand pages of filings in various courthouses by the aforementioned law firms, all about the Rise and Fall of David Askin. They are a veritable MBA course in the business practices of hedge funds and Wall Street firms.

Reduced to its essentials, the Askin failure could be deconstructed as follows:

1. *Askin's fund was supposed to be hedged, but wasn't.*
2. *He bought the wrong stuff.*
3. *He borrowed too much money.*
4. *When things turned bad, investor redemptions made things worse.*
5. *When his funds failed, he hurt the market generally.*

A number 6 might have been applicable at some point if Askin hadn't been run off the road by his brokers. The Askin funds, like most hedge funds, had high-water marks that don't allow a fund manager to take that 20 percent incentive fee until he makes up for losses in previous years. So if a fund manager runs a hedge fund that declines 10 percent one year, he has to push up the portfolio 11.1 percent before drawing a nickel in incentive fees. This sounds terrific, but in reality it sucks.

The high-water mark penalizes managers who engage in volatile investment strategies, in theory. In practice, it is the functional equivalent of handing out cyanide pills to people in depression clinics. Over the years, it has become nothing more than an encouragement for fund managers to close their funds. It's easy—just a few documents need to be filed with the state corporate-filings office, and of course the fund documents don't make the suicide process at all difficult.

You can't blame fund managers for putting an end to their funds when things go bad. After all, nobody wants to work for *bupkis*. They don't want to recoup old losses. That's just a marketing gimmick. They want a fresh start, so they can start charging fees again as if nothing happened. The old investors? Well, they're accredited and sophisticated, so they'll understand.

Hedge funds are prone to suicide because they are volatile. The old nursery rhyme sums up their fate: When they are good they are very, very good, and when they are bad they are horrid. Askin did a decent job when the market was doing well. When the market wasn't doing so well, as happens sometimes with hot markets like mortgage-backed securities, Askin was horrid because he was leveraged to the hilt with the wrong stuff. He wouldn't have been so horrid if he had been structured like . . . well, like a hedge fund. An old-fashioned *hedged*, long-short hedge fund.

The Askin meltdown caused a brief flurry of activity within the self-regulatory pyramid. A task force was organized by the President's Working Group on Financial Markets. The task force chewed things over for a few months and in September 1994 issued a report. It made a bunch of findings, of which two deserve highlighting: (1) hedge funds "could exacerbate market movements if the funds need to sell to meet margin calls or unwind leveraged positions"; (2) "It may be difficult for banks and broker-dealers to monitor the creditworthiness of hedge funds because they do not typically know the overall positions of hedge funds, which can change rapidly."

Four years after those words were written, Long-Term Capital Management put the financial system in jeopardy by following fairly closely in the footsteps of Askin and Granite. Rather than repeat the oft-told tale of LTCM, let's just examine the template at work here. Once you have the template, all you have to do is fill in the blanks:

- You have a Superinvestor, real or imagined. So all you have to do is erase the name of would-be Superinvestor David J. Askin and replace it with would-be Superinvestor John W. Meriwether.
- There is a catalyst. Instead of the catalyst being the Fed raising rates as the trigger to disaster, there was the Russian devaluation of the ruble in August 1998.
- Leverage. Instead of a $600 million hedge fund with buying power magnified by 3-to-1 leverage, there was a $4.8 billion hedge fund with buying power magnified by 25-to-1 leverage.

Other parts of the template were unchanged:

- Same limitations on general partner liability.
- Same up-the-wazoo incentives. LTCM investors agreed to a 25 percent incentive fee and a three-year lockup that chained them to the fund as it went down the drain.
- Same "market neutral" really being "market directional."
- Same nonexistent or inadequate "quantitative tools."
- Same market impact—except that instead of causing an upheaval in just one corner of the market, the LTCM disaster threatened scores of major financial institutions. That's because the counterparties to its insanely leveraged transactions included every major bank and brokerage firm. The Federal Reserve was forced to intervene, and to engineer a bailout of the fund by the private sector, to keep a few traders from hurting the economy.

The Askin Template is not the only template out there in hedge-fund-land. There are a bunch of others, some quite original but most of which had the very same elements that were established way back in 1994, when the Askin funds went belly-up. So study the list below carefully. All of these templates need to be kept in mind if you are one of those lucky accredited investors, or if your pension fund or college endowment is invested in a hedge fund:

- The Mispricing Template. This template makes full use of the "manager marks" aspect of the Askin disaster, to fail on that basis alone. The demise of the Kenneth Lipper hedge funds in early 2002 was based entirely upon that.
- The Goofy Leverage Template. Also known as the LTCM Subtemplate, this includes funds that managed to conk out because of overborrowing combined with bad bets. This template includes LTCM copycats such as Convergence Asset Management and High Risk Opportunities Fund, an $850 million LTCM wannabe that lost 30 percent of its value during six months of 1998, and struggled along until it was shut down in 2001.
- The Oops! Template. This one is growing increasingly popular among hedge fund managers, because it takes advantage of the glorious freedom that characterizes this sexy, adventurous, philanthropy-prone form of money-managerial endeavor. It is simple in its purity: The investor gives the hedge fund money, and the fund manager accidentally puts it in his pocket. Oops! It can take a while to discover such oversights because of all that glorious freedom I just mentioned (and because having lots of money is so nice!). A good example of the Oops! Template in action was the Bayou hedge fund group, whose co-founders pleaded guilty to fraud charges in September 2005, for their role in a nine-year, $450 million fraud. Oops!
- The Hubris Template. Also known as the Green Kryptonite Template, as it tends to infect the funds of Superinvestors and would-be Superinvestors after their superpowers attract billions of dollars in investor cash. To keep their performance on the go, they make huge bets that can smack them in the face when the Efficient Market Hypothesis catches up with them. It doesn't help that the high-water mark means they have to either withstand a lengthy period of no paychecks or say "Ta ta." See if you can guess which of those two alternatives they generally choose. Hint: It doesn't involve working for *bupkis*.

The first Superinvestor to blunder into the last template was Michael Steinhardt. He shut down his massively hyped $2.6 billion hedge fund group after making a massively arrogant wrong-way bet on overseas bonds, which caused his fund to sink 30 percent in just *three months* of 1994. His fund stayed in the toilet, and he shut it down in September 1995. He ended that year up 26 percent—which looks great until you realize that the S&P 500 had a 37.6 percent total return, after which it doesn't look so great. In fact, it looks lousy. Steinhardt bugged out despite not having a high-water mark—demonstrating that ego alone can turn an overhyped investment superstar into a former over-hyped investment superstar.

The next überinvestor to stick his foot in the "EMH trap" was my old pal Julian Robertson,* who shut down his even more humongously hyped Tiger funds in early 2000 as a result of lousy stock picking that caused him to pull off a considerable feat—double-digit losses at a time when the major stock indexes were racking up record gains. His funds peaked in August 1998, and investors found their Tiger holdings sliced nearly in half by the end of February 2000. Julian managed to take a fund group that had $23 billion in net assets in 1998 and turn it into a shriveling, on-the-run $6 billion fund group (after redemptions) in early 2000. Yep, it takes a really *active* portfolio manager to accomplish that during the biggest bull market in history. Later that year, George Soros and his loyal sidekick Stanley Druckenmiller (a kind of reflected-glory Superinvestor) had to reorganize the Quantum funds after being caught, hedgeless, in the tech-stock bust.

The hubris and the stupidity and the arrogance have continued to this day, filling template after template. You may even read about them in the back pages of the newspapers now and then, while the front pages chronicle how hedge funds have become the youthful, zestful Robin Hoods of Wall Street. Literally. Hedge fund managers organized the modestly named Robin Hood Foundation, which has an annual ball that has become a leading Wall Street social event. (Kind of makes you wonder how they'd feel about a real-life Robin Hood waylaying them on Dune Road.) Hedge fund managers have climbed to the highest rungs of the social ladder much as did investment bankers during the 1980s. It's all great stuff—until they fail. And fail they will, consistently.

* I should point out, in the interests of fairness and full disclosure, that Julian sued the author and his then-employer, *Business Week*, for libel in early 1997 after I reported on some earlier lousy performance by the Robertson funds. He later dropped the suit after his performance improved, and we ran an editor's note acknowledging that. Unfortunately for investors who took that as a buy signal, Julian proceeded to drive his funds off a cliff.

According to the Malkiel-Saha study, the average lifespan of the live hedge funds surveyed was sixty-two months. The average life of the dead ones was five years, with fund failures reaching a maximum at forty-eight months. As Saha observed at a seminar outlining his study, "failure is a real and palpable possibility for many hedge funds."

All of this makes hedge funds arguably one of the smartest, snazziest, sexiest things you can do with your money—as long as you don't mind losing it, either through high fees or dim-witted, arrogant investment strategies or even flat-out thievery. There's really not much doubt at all that an index fund you buy over the Internet is likely to do better than a hedge fund, and has the added virtue of being far more liquid and way, way less likely to fail. Buying an index fund, however, will not give you status. It does not provide scintillating cocktail party chatter, unless all involved have been drinking and have other things on their minds.

Unfortunately, status is not the only issue involved here. As first Askin and then LTCM proved, all that status has a price. Unrestrained trading by hedge funds is capable of dragging down the entire financial system. That hurts everybody, whether you are sophisticated, accredited, or keep your money in a tin box; whether you are driven by status or greed, are an efficient-markets maven, an advocate of behavioral finance, or perhaps just an ordinary person who wants to be left alone.

CHAPTER TWELVE

THE MONEY FLOATS IN—FROM YOUR WALLET

J onathan D. Iseson made his first, and only, appearance in the *New York Times* on June 1, 1999, when the Metropolitan section portrayed him as an example of the chichi financier who was giving the Hamptons their style and grace despite much recent lampooning and degradation by the big-hair set. "The money floats in on private helicopters and corporate jets and gleaming white yachts," the *Times* reported. " 'I just got it yesterday,' said Jonathan D. Iseson, a 42-year-old hedge fund manager from Manhasset, N.Y., docking his 48-foot cruiser at the Sag Harbor Yacht Club. He downsized from a 55-footer. 'I got rid of the wife, so I didn't need the space,' he explained."

A great wit too! And there was better to come. The hedge fund that the forty-two-year-old yacht-docker and wife-divorcer was piloting was the Blue Water Fund Ltd. In the months that followed the *Times* piece, the Blue Water Fund Ltd. sailed over the bounding waves. There is an old saw that goes something along the lines of "Where are the customers' yachts?" but it did not apply to Iseson or Blue Water. They had plenty of solid bucks coming their way, in the manner in which solid bucks are often last seen before they sink below the waves—on paper. In the first quarter of the new millennium, Blue Water was at the very top ranking of hedge funds tracked by MAR/Hedge, a leading hedge fund database, with a 140 percent gain. The problem was that this gain had resulted from one stock that was dominant in the Blue Water portfolio— dominant as in 55 percent of its net assets. That one stock was an Internet company called Netsol, and Blue Water's purchases of that stock had driven up its price and, thus, the value of Blue Water. A good strategy, but a little—maybe just a bit risky or overconcentrated, wouldn't you say?

Well, it all became public and the lawsuits came and lots of people got upset. The lawsuits, which charged fraud and stock manipulation—allegations very much denied by Iseson—were settled after the usual legal *sturm und drang*. Blue Water sailed over the horizon, and the publicity was mild enough that Iseson was able to move on to other fields of endeavor, doing convertible bond deals at a brokerage that doesn't like to publicize his Blue Water dalliance, and who can blame it? The regulators did nothing, so obviously nothing bad had happened.

Quite a story, Blue Water—and there are so many of them too: hedge funds that are bold and brave, and that may cut corners now and then, not always to the benefit of their clients and not always with a Katrina-sized gust of negative publicity.

All this is by way of saying that the portrayal of hedge funds in this book has been badly skewed, in the sense of being too gentle. We've only scratched the surface of how adventurous hedge funds have become. We haven't explored the Blue Waters of hedge-fund-land. We haven't explored the many mini-Askins and the hedge funds that are having even more fun with your money, the phony-baloneys and criminals and scamsters who screw investors using hedge funds.

We haven't delved into an even worse element that has been introduced into the equation—increasing numbers of hedge funds, including some gloriously underperforming funds-of-funds, that are sponsored by Wall Street megafirms and mutual funds. The perpetrators of this latest glory upon the investing public include every major brokerage house, from Merrill Lynch to Salomon Smith Barney, and big fund groups such as Wellington Management, Alliance Capital, and Invesco. Nowadays your "financial advisor" and mutual fund have plenty of nice, high-fee house hedge funds, including plenty of fee-upon-fee funds-of-funds, to add to the list of merchandise they can sell you.

We also haven't gotten to the cute little tricks that hedge funds perform, in addition to the not-so-cute, not-so-small tricks enumerated previously.

One of the more public-spirited hedge fund managers, an ex-newsman-turned-fund-manager named Harry Strunk, has compiled a list of the various ways hedge funds screw investors. Harry is widely known for an index that tracks short-sellers, and he also runs Treflie Capital Management LLC, in West Palm Beach. Here's a sampling from Harry's list:

- *Lockdowns.* We've already seen how hedge funds often have lockup provisions that don't let you take money out of the fund for a specified period of time. Usually the restriction lasts a year or so, after which you can withdraw on a quarterly basis (or sometimes annually). The more chutzpah-laden hedge fundies, like Long-Term Capital, like to keep your money for longer periods. My old buddy Julian Robertson had a lockup that kept investors in one of his funds, Ocelot, for five years—strapping them to their seats while the airship *Robertson* slammed into Efficient Markets Mountain. Way to go, Julian!

The lockdown is a variation on that. Harry explains it this way: "Usually involving a highly illiquid position, the manager protects the fund's performance by 'locking down' the illiquid position. He does this by withholding a percentage of a departing partner's funds, that portion which is invested in the illiquid security." What that means is that, whether the investor likes it or not, the investor's money is tied up with the fund he'd very much like to quit.

- *IPO grabbing*. That's what Harry calls a variation on a scheme that came to infect Wall Street in the late 1990s, when investment banks allocated shares in hot initial public offerings to key corporate officers—the ones in charge of hiring investment banks, that is. Some hedge fund managers have personal "side accounts" that sop up IPOs, the same ones being accumulated by their funds, for their own profit—sometimes as a reward for doing business with the brokerage.

- *Tax dumping*. Since there is a significant difference between short- and long-term capital gains, some hedge fund managers make an unfair allocation, dumping trades with short-term capital gains on partners who are cashing out. Harry observes that "managers sometimes use the rationale that they are doing what is best for the interests of the limited partners"—and, of course, the fund manager himself.

- *Quarterly fees*. Some of the more creative hedge fund managers are taking their 20 percent cut of the profits on a quarterly rather than an annual basis, thereby encouraging them to engage in risky short-term trading. Blue Water had a quarterly performance fee, Harry observes. But since the investors were tied in by a yearlong lockup, they couldn't yank out their funds after a quarter had flitted by. At the end of the year, the gain in Netsol had evaporated, and Blue Water hit Davy Jones's locker by mid-2001.

Let's see what the self-regulatory pyramid is doing about this stuff. The pyramid and its overseers in Congress, as well as the Federal Reserve Board of Governors, have all been toying with the idea of regulating (or, more precisely, toying with the idea of toying with the idea of regulating) hedge funds since the early 1990s. They really, really haven't wanted to do any toying or even thinking about toying with hedge fund regulation. But then the funds started misbehaving, again and again. It was a real pain in the butt.

Scandals can be so annoying, so disruptive to the orderly flow of paperwork. Just when the leather armchair is feeling comfy, and the lure of the post-government job is intruding upon even the deepest of afternoon naps, along comes a scandal with reporters calling and editorials screaming, and one must make believe that one gives a damn about hedge funds. Such are the demands of government service.

The first whiff of potential hedge fund lousiness took place during the Salomon Brothers bond-trading scandal in 1991. While the Solly bond market scandal was not a "hedge fund scandal" per se, it was plain at the time that hedge funds were making money along with Salomon as the latter was cornering the government bond market. Just about every leading Superinvestor of the era—Julian Robertson and George Soros as well as Steinhardt and Kovner of Caxton Corp.—was getting sued and investigated for a supposed role in the scandal. Robertson and Soros were eventually cleared, but, as we've seen, Steinhardt and Kovner were pursued for some years and accused of helping Salomon rig the market.

Something new was at work here—a form of investment that was feckless, maybe a tad irresponsible, and capable of causing problems.

Officials of the SEC, Federal Reserve, and Treasury Department roused themselves to action via a *Joint Report on the Government Securities Market* in January 1992. The report was an intelligent document. Among its findings:

> Events in the government securities market have shown that their capacity for leverage allows hedge funds to take large trading positions disproportionate to their capital base. Thus far, [hedge] fund managers have proved very adept at controlling their market risk, and their lending counterparties appear to consider them creditworthy. However, the sheer size of the positions taken by hedge funds raises concerns about systemic risk that these funds may introduce into the financial markets.

The report did everything but use the name *Askin* in predicting the hedge fund failure that lay in wait, two years down the road.

Prescient as that was, when it came to hedge funds the SEC was at the very foot of an Everest-size learning curve. That was evident only a few months after the *Joint Report* was issued, when the SEC was forced to cope with one of the perennial annoyances of bureaucratic life—congressional meddling. On March 18, 1992, the head of the House Telecommunications and Finance Committee, a nosy Massachusetts Democrat named Edward J. Markey, sent a letter to the Bush I administration SEC chairman, Richard C. Breeden. Markey wanted to get some authoritative answers to some basic questions on the subject of hedge funds. Breeden put his staff right on it and, three months later, sent over to Markey a staff memo that laid out all the "facts," such as they were. The study is interesting for what it reveals about the SEC's knowledge of the hedge fund industry, which was pretty close to nothing.

Breeden began by making one thing perfectly clear: Appearances to the contrary notwithstanding, hedge funds were nothing to get all worked up about. "Since 1987," he said in a letter to the Markey committee, "the Commission has apparently received no investor complaints and has instituted no enforcement actions against hedge funds."

"Apparently"? Well, come now, you can't expect the SEC to keep accurate records of investor complaints. In any event, this was about as clean a bill of health as the SEC could provide. The staff memo, attached to Breeden's letter, picked up on that "stop worrying and go away" theme. It began by presenting a vaguely worded history of the hedge fund industry culled from press clips, apparently the SEC's only source of info on hedge funds at the time, and moved headlong into a discussion of the here and now. The press clips were, alas, inadequate sources of data, particularly on such things as offshore funds, which the media wasn't covering very much at the time.

Unbeknownst to most of the civilized world and the regulators thereof, offshore variations on hedge funds, such as the Soros funds, were about to explode on the scene. Just one of the Soros funds, Quantum, had $3.1 billion under management at the start of 1992. During the year, the Soros funds—which, as you'll recall, were operated "off the shore" of the Lake at Central Park—would accumulate a massive short position in the British pound. Soros would cash out before the first golden leaves of autumn, causing teeth-gnashing throughout Europe and turning him into "the man who broke the Bank of England."

The SEC report devoted all of four nonchalant paragraphs to the offshore phenomenon (though Soros's Quantum Fund did appear in a list of hedge funds tacked on as an appendix, "taken from recent media articles from newspapers and periodicals"). The report observed that there were $250 billion in offshore funds—thereby making the whole discussion inane by lumping in ordinary non-U.S. mutual funds with U.S. hedge funds operated out of filing cabinets in the Caribbean. The SEC staff even had trouble finding elementary source materials. "According to media reports," the report said in a footnote, "there does exist a privately published list of offshore funds. The staff, however, was unable to obtain a copy of this list." That apparently is a reference to the *U.S. Offshore Funds Directory,* published by Antoine Bernheim, a pleasant gentleman whose phone number was, and is, listed in the Manhattan telephone directory.

The report went on to discuss the sources of cash for hedge funds, and did so in a way that would have completely misled any policymaker who made the mistake of believing it. The SEC staffers cast cold water on "media sources [that] recently have reported that some pension funds invest, or are considering investing, in hedge funds." No, said the report. Not happening. A footnote said that "it appears that registered investment companies do not invest significant assets in hedge funds" because of provisions of the Investment Company Act that "prevent excessive layering of fees." As those words were being written, pension funds were already becoming one of the hedge funds' biggest sources of cash. In fact, the SEC's 2003 study of the fund industry observed correctly that "pension funds were among the earliest hedge fund investors."

Having downplayed or scoffed at all the major trends that would drive hedge funds in the years to come, the SEC's 1992 study was no more useful as it turned to possible ways of riding herd over funds. For that, the study relied on an impending "large trader reporting system" that would supposedly put hedge funds under a microscope. The system had been in the works for a long time. It was not the SEC's idea, but was rammed past the agency's tonsils by Congress, in a law called the Market Reform Act of 1990. The system was designed to overcome information gaps that regulators encountered during the crash of October 1987 and a market downturn two years later. The aim was to help market overseers reconstruct and analyze trading activity, in the event that, God forbid, there should be another crash.

In the report, the "large trader reporting system" came in handy as something to which the staff could point, a thing that would deal with hedge fund secrecy and opacity. The Markey committee was assured that "the Commission will be able to gain considerable information regarding hedge funds that are large traders in the equity markets as a result of its proposed large trader reporting system." Such a system "should provide the Commission with access to information that is more tailored to systemic risk concerns, without unduly burdening private investors."

Now, at this point some of you may be thinking, "Gee, why haven't I ever heard of such a thing?" The reason is that it doesn't exist. Hedge funds didn't like the idea, so it didn't happen. Such is our self-regulatory pyramid in inaction, with the accent on *self*. Regulation with the consent of the regulated—has a Jeffersonian sound to it, don't you think? In order for a regulatee (or, in this case, a putative nonregulatee) to exert the necessary muscle, it is necessary to have a full-fledged lobbying arm in Washington, and by the early 1990s that goal had been realized. Hedge funds now had their own lobbyists, some hired by individual hedge funds, and their own trade association, the Managed Funds Association. The MFA was founded in 1991, just in the nick of time, you might say, and proceeded, along with other hedge fund lobbyists, to help the SEC and other regulators come up with excuses to not regulate the hedge fund industry.

The large trader reporting system was quietly shelved in the time-tested Washington way—by doing nothing. Artie Levitt's SEC simply never adopted implementing regulations. No reasons were given at the time. No reasons were necessary. Congress could pass the law, but it could not enforce it. As Stalin supposedly said in a similar situation, "The pope? How many divisions has he got?" The advantage of not doing something, as opposed to affirmatively saying no, is that one is rarely asked why one doesn't do something. The hedge fund industry did not like this idea one bit—said it would be difficult to implement and maintain and also that there were other mechanisms out there able to monitor stock market activity—so it was not done. Besides, it might have actually done what it set out to do, and shed some light on hedge funds, at least as far as their stock dealings were concerned. That would never do.

Congress finally roused itself in the mid-1990s, slammed its fist on the table, and shouted, "Damn it! Time to do something about hedge funds!" Our legislators decided that it was high time to make it *easier* for hedge funds to bulk up on assets, and to *reduce* oversight of the funds.

It happened in 1996. Hedge funds were now a $200 billion industry, getting bigger, and desirous of getting bigger still. At the urging of the MFA and other hedge fund lobbyists, Congress decided that the time had come to improve the lifestyles of hedge fund managers. Thus was born the National Securities Markets Improvements Act of 1996. (Note the word *improvements* in the title of the bill, as in "improved hedge fund revenues.") Previously hedge funds had a restriction of one hundred investors per fund. That went out the window, and the asset base (and resulting fees) of hedge funds were now "improved" fivefold, with the number of investors allowed per fund increasing from one hundred to five hundred, as long as each investor had up to $5 million worth of investments sitting in his portfolio.

The law also provided an additional "improvement" that made hedge fund managers everywhere stand tall: It greatly reduced state regulation of offers and sales of hedge fund securities. Just what hedge funds needed in the mid-1990s—less oversight!

In fairness to Congress, I should point out that all these wonderful improvements had no effect on the LTCM disaster one way or the other. However, hedge fund lobbyists really showed their stuff when it came to damage control after LTCM, ensuring that every single regulatory response to Meriwether & Co. was quietly but effectively shelved. Again, the swift sword of inaction was the fund industry's most effective weapon.

In 2000, the Commodity Futures Trading Commission issued a proposal that would have gone a long way toward shedding light on the activities of the biggest hedge funds. What happened next was dazzling, probably the most impressive act of inaction to take place anywhere on the globe until a few years later, when the forces of evaporation caused the waters of Lake Powell to recede, exposing the glories of Glen Canyon. This time, the force of nature at work was the sheer power of bureaucratic entropy.

Acting as recommended by one of the numerous committees formed after LTCM, the CFTC proposed a rule requiring operators of large commodities-trading "pools" to report periodically to regulators on their finances and risk. These are not fecund bodies of water where cattle, swine, and other "commodities" come to drink, but actually regulator-speak for some of the biggest hedge funds. Many are considered commodity pools because they dabble globally in currencies and futures contracts. With such oxen unwilling to be gored, the rule came under attack from the MFA. The result was immediate, sustained, and, I might add, effective inaction.

In the absence of any strong interest group (such as the U.S. government) pushing in favor, the rule was allowed to evaporate. It sat on the CFTC's Semiannual Regulatory Agenda until late 2002, marked "Next action undetermined," and was finally withdrawn in March 2003, a few weeks after its twilight-zone status was publicized in *Business Week*.

By 2003, the theory and practice of hedge fund inaction, which had begun under SEC chairman Richard Breeden and was refined by the stasis-loving Investor's Champion Artie Levitt, was being further improved by Bill Donaldson. With the hedge fund industry now pressing up toward the trillion-dollar mark, there was work not to be done. Total inaction, the favored methodology during the Levitt era, now gave way to a Donaldson specialty—inaction disguised as action.

By now, Street firms were falling over themselves to get prime brokerage bucks from hedge funds—a particularly lucrative business in which Wall Street firms handle trades, paperwork, and other administrative tasks for hedge funds. Brokerages were pushing low-minimum funds of hedge funds with horse-choking fees. Donaldson, in one of several stern speeches on the subject, referred to this as the "retailization of hedge funds."

A good example of this was being bestowed upon the lucky customers of Merrill Lynch in 2005. To invest, all you needed was a million bucks—"including the value of your home," Merrill was careful to point out. Since real estate was engaged in a boom of an insanity not seen since the IPO mania in the late 1990s, that meant that pretty much anyone living in a Manhattan co-op bigger than a peanut shell was now a millionaire. Whoopee! They could now prance around, rejoicing like James Dean covered with oil in *Giant*, and buy what Merrill had to offer. Its Multi-Strategy Hedge Opportunities fund of funds (minimum initial investment $25,000, minimum subsequent investment $10,000) was a doozy. Here's how the charges stacked up:

1. *A sales charge of up to 3 percent for an investment of $100,000, scaled down to below 1 percent for $1 million and up*
2. *A management fee of 1.5 percent*
3. *A "member service fee" of 0.25 percent*
4. *"Administrative fees" of 0.32 percent*
5. *"Other fees" of 1.03 percent*

That was it. Not too bad, huh? Total fees were being capped at 3 percent during 2005, as an extra added incentive. Of course, you have to tack on the fees skimmed off by the hedge funds, commodity pools, and so on in which this fund invests, which included management fees of 1 to 3 percent *plus* incentive fees of 15 to 25 percent of profits.

Bill Donaldson gave many speeches attacking "retailization" of hedge funds. When it came time for inaction, what he did was require, in a rule he pushed through the SEC in October 2004, that hedge funds register as investment advisors with the SEC. That'll fix 'em! Not.

Instead of doing anything about the fee circus described above, or forcing funds to provide meaningful disclosure to regulators and protection for their investors, Donaldson's rule did absolutely nothing to deal with any of the problems that have plagued hedge funds. Nothing was done to keep crooks from running hedge funds, or to stave off systemic risks from runaway leverage. In fact, 40 percent of hedge funds were *already* run by registered investment advisors, voluntarily. As for the 60 percent that were holdouts, the rule wouldn't do much of anything that mattered to customers.

Not only did the rule fail to do anything about crooked funds—which tend to be too small to be affected by the rule anyway—it actually expanded the potential market for hedge funds. Since pension funds tend to invest only in hedge funds that are run by registered investment advisors, SEC commissioner Cynthia A. Glassman noted, "Mandatory registration of all advisers will expand the potential universe and thereby afford even more opportunities for investment in hedge funds." Other critics said that the meaningless registration requirement would give a kind of "*Good Housekeeping* Seal of Approval" on hedge funds. This kind of sensible opposition to bureaucratic wheel-spinning, by the way, later caused Glassman to be snidely referred to in the media as one of the "two Republican commissioners" who voted against Donaldson and stood in the way of progress. I challenge anyone to find anything particularly Democratic or Republican about a regulation that won't work.

Proponents of the rule noted that it would raise the wealth requirement for investors in those 60 percent of hedge funds that are not registered. That's because there already was a rule requiring that investors in registered funds have a net worth of $1.5 million, or at least $750,000 under management with the investment advisor. That looks good, until you realize how easy it is for hedge funds to get around this limitation.

That brings us to the pièce de résistance, the Roach Motel Encouragement Rule that Donaldson enacted as part of his inane registration requirement. Remember those ridiculous lockups that we discussed earlier—such as the one that proved so horrendous for the people who bought into LTCM and Julian Robertson's Ocelot fund? Lockups are so egregious, so downright disgusting, that you'd think that Bill Donaldson (whose old firm Donaldson, Lufkin & Jenrette marketed Ocelot to hapless investors in 1997) would come down hard on such things. Instead he actually *encouraged* lockups. He wrote into the rule a loophole that exempts funds with lockups of two years or more.

In other words, if a hedge fund manager is particularly greedy and grasping, he gets off the hook! He doesn't have to bother registering his fund, and he's not subject to that $1.5 million net worth limit. He gets a pass, thanks to the new Investor's Champion, Bill Donaldson.

You'd have thought that Donaldson and the SEC would have noticed how dumb this rule truly was. However, to call it dumb assumes that Donaldson and the SEC really wanted to do something to curb hedge fund abuses. It wasn't dumb if their intent, from Day One, was to do nothing. You've got to admit—as an act of nonregulation, it is a work of genius.

CHAPTER THIRTEEN

BEAR IN THE WOODS

Wall Street can be admirable when it sets its mind to the task. Just take a look at the full-page, full-color advertisement that appeared in two consecutive issues of the *New York Times* Sunday Business section, on April 10 and 17, 2005:

> **Bear Stearns: Voted**
> **America's Most Admired**
> **Securities Company.**
> **Again.**

For the second time in three years, Bear Stearns had the honor of being at the very top of a list, published in *Fortune* magazine, which said that—well, look at that word. *Admired!* Bear is viewed with genuine affection by its peers in the securities industry, much as you might look back tearfully on a beloved schoolteacher or mentor or parish priest. The rest of the world has Mother Teresa; Wall Street has Bear Stearns. Its financials for the first fiscal quarter of 2005—well, if they gave out a Nobel Prize for Consistent Profitability, Bear would have walked away with it. Every page of its Form 10-Q quarterly report for the three months ending February 28, 2005, as well as its Form 10-K annual report for the year ending November 30, 2004, reeked with the stuff of Profit Greatness.

One of the main reasons Bear did so well in early 2005 was its prominent but by no means dominant role in the business of underwriting bond issues for state and local governments. The overall size of the municipal bond business is well into the Trillion Dollar Club—$2 trillion and counting. Bear didn't break out all the numbers, but it is willing to tell us that during the first quarter of 2005, a total of $172 million of its $379 million in profits came from its various underwriting activities, with municipal bond underwriting being an unspecified, but substantial, corner of the business. That wasn't bad for an uneven year, when trading volume was on the wane because of a shaky market. Bear's muni mastery continued for the rest of 2005.

Munis are the Norman Bates of Wall Street: They seem mild-mannered on the surface, but when you get to know them—well, they can sure be surprising! Munis lack the glamour of hedge funds, but they bring out the mischievous streak in even the most staid Wall Street firms—and Bear is anything but staid. As a matter of fact, that is why it is so profitable, and admired. Munis have added considerably to Bear Stearns's reputation for being rambunctious and for what is sometimes politely described as "pushing the envelope."

This is not a knock but a compliment—one that Bear has earned many times over. This firm had no qualms about being the leading banker and trade executor for the worst of Wall Street's boiler rooms back in the 1990s. Somebody had to clear their trades and issue statements to customers—emblazoned with the clearing firm's name. Somebody had to make money providing legitimacy to the worst creeps in Wall Street history.

This was more than just a reasonably profitable business. It was an *admirable* business. Anyone can make money doing things that are nice and decent and safe. But it takes a gutsy firm, an envelope-pushing firm, to make money doing things that aren't so nice and aren't so decent or safe. As we saw earlier, Bear worked cheek by jowl with one of the slimiest Wall Street investor-ripoff firms of the 1990s, A.R. Baron. Later the SEC alleged—and was still muttering these words to itself when it was all over—that Bear's actions "were a cause of Baron's fraud" and that Bear "aided and abetted" Baron in various instances of slip-sliding past the securities laws. Bear was able to allegedly do stuff like that, and *get away with it.*

In August 1999, Bear reached a settlement with the SEC that cemented the firm's reputation for squeezing against the envelope and won the admiration of the entire securities industry. Without admitting or denying a thing, Bear paid $35 million, one-tenth of its profits in a good fiscal quarter, and made it all go away. It was a soba-noodle slap to end all soba-noodle slaps, doled out by the Investor's Champion, Artie Levitt. For some reason, Artie forgot to say anything about it in his book (you know, the one he should have called *Take On the Street—Or How I Ignored the Worst Stock Market Abuses in History*).

Clearly, Bear does not break out in hives worrying about the morality of things. If you don't believe me, try spending a couple of hours meeting with Bear Stearns's clearing officials, as I did at the height of the late-1990s boiler-room scandals. Or, if you don't have the opportunity to do that, turn to page 17 of the Form 10-K annual report for 2004, and look for the subject heading "Legal Proceedings" at the bottom of the page. There you will find some leftover boiler-room lawsuits, still racking up the legal fees after all these years, some New York Stock Exchange floor-trader lawsuits, some Enron lawsuits, some IPO allocation lawsuits, some mutual fund inquiries and investigations and lawsuits. Everything in order—allegations denied; inquiries and investigations fully cooperated with. The list just goes on and on until you get toward the bottom:

Municipal Bond Offering Matters

Bear Stearns has been notified by the Chicago office of the SEC of a formal investigation into its municipal bond offering practices, which has been focused on the municipal underwriting business conducted through the Chicago office of Bear Stearns. Bear Stearns has also received subpoenas and requests for information relating to its municipal underwriting business conducted through the Chicago office of Bear Stearns from the United States Attorney's Office for the Northern District of Illinois; the State of Illinois, Office of Executive Inspector General; the Illinois Securities Department; and the Office of the Attorney General of Illinois.

Bear Stearns is cooperating with each of these investigations or inquiries.

Of course they are. This is a law-abiding company, most of the time. What the feds and the state of Illinois were investigating were allegations that Bear was being naughty out in the sticks—"shitting in the woods," to use a classic bear-related expression—just as it was allegedly naughty when it climbed on a Sealy with A.R. Baron, Sterling Foster, and other wallet-harvesting factories.

It seems that an investment banker in Bear's Chicago office named P. Nicholas Hurtgen, a man with a strong background in local government, helped raise money for the Milwaukee county executive in early 2003, right after Bear won a $100 million county bond deal. Bear, while not the low bidder for the job, was the *best* bidder. "County officials later located various records documenting that Bear Stearns was the unanimous choice of a bid-evaluation group composed of county employees," reported the Milwaukee *Journal Sentinel*, which has been all over this story while the national media and financial press have been busy with other things.

It also emerged that Bear Stearns paid a consulting firm headed by a Republican National Committeeman $809,000 to help it get a $10 billion bond issue that helped the firm garner an $8 million fee, and correspondence later surfaced that raised questions concerning what the RNC guy did for those bucks. Meanwhile, a whistle-blower suit filed by two Illinois hospital executives accused Bear of getting that bond deal by paying kickbacks. Bear responded to all of this by saying it was cooperating with investigators and was "confident of the integrity of [its] business." Bear continued saying that even after Hurtgen was arrested by the feds in May 2005 and charged with multiple counts of mail fraud and wire fraud, with an extortion count thrown in for good measure. Hurtgen and another defendant, a building contractor, were charged with scheming to get "multimillion dollar contracts for their businesses through construction kickbacks or other fraudulent deals."

The term of art that is utilized with respect to the foregoing is "pay-to-play." That refers to a whole bunch of things, some legal and some not, which, taken together, amount to a kind of K-Y jelly, lubricating the entire municipal securities market, all $2 trillion and counting of it. It describes how things are done whenever your local elected officials come in close proximity to Wall Street, whether the latter comes a-courting for municipal-bond business or pension-fund-management business or anything. The aforementioned business is purchased, cash on the barrelhead, by paying the people you elect into office, and/or the people they appoint, and/or their friends, lawyers, consultants, girlfriends, boyfriends, and others who have made the right career and life choices.

As in the case of payments to brokers by mutual fund companies, the principle here is "disclosure as absolution." As long as the correct forms are filled out, it is legal for large Wall Street firms, as well as local banks and bond firms, to spread money around state capitals and local governments through lawyers and consultants, in return for muni-bond underwriting business—very much the way it was legal for Bear Stearns to clear trades for the scuzziest boiler rooms, and to let these felon-invested firms use its name on their customer statements as a cover for thievery.

Pay-to-play is happening everywhere, whether you know it or not— whether your hometown newspaper has been all over the subject, like that feisty Milwaukee paper, or, as is more likely, is ignoring it entirely. The national news media and the financial press haven't been paying attention to the subject, even on a busy day such as May 9, 2005—the day Hurtgen was indicted and a Philadelphia official was convicted in its muni-bond scandal. A doubleheader, but it hardly aroused much interest outside Philadelphia and Chicago.

Like some of the other Wall Street terminology that we have previously examined, the phrase *pay-to-play* does not quite capture what is involved here. The expression actually originated in Washington, where nondescriptive terminology is a way of life, as a rhetorical device that allows courteous, dinnertime discourse concerning a subject that might make a lot of people want to go out and throw up. Note the semantic gentility of the word *play*, which brings forth images of Wall Street executives skipping rope or tossing a ball around the playground. The implication is that they are *playing*, and that they have to *pay* in order to *play*.

In reality, the objective is to *take*—to acquire fees from the underwriting of municipal bonds. To do so requires that they *pay off*. Thus what we have here, for the public officials and their pals, is a kind of legal graft that has an old and honored place in the history of our cities. As a Tammany Hall politician named George Washington Plunkitt expressed the concept a century ago, "I seen my opportunities, and I took 'em." In pay-to-play, the opportunities are on both sides, very much in the American tradition.

You'll be happy to know our self-regulatory pyramid has acted decisively against pay-to-play. In April 1994, the Municipal Securities Rulemaking Board, created by Congress as the self-regulatory organization for the muni-bond business, passed a rule that bars firms from municipal-bond deals within two years of a muni dealer contributing money to a public official who could influence the underwriter-selection process.

This rule, known as G-37, was actually a pretty good rule. It read well. It made a lot of sense. It was also universally beloved, as evidenced by the fact that it went unscathed through the SEC bureaucratic machinery, a rulemaking process that can reduce the most delicious T-bone steak of a regulation into a mass of disgusting, useless bile (or worse). Now, that could mean only one of two things:

1. **This was such an outstanding rule that its righteousness was undeniable.**

   or

2. **Wall Street could figure out a way around the rule.**

Let us turn to an expert on the intricacies of municipal finance to resolve this issue. His name was Ronald A. White, and he was a lawyer in the city of Philadelphia. On February 21, 2003, years after enactment of G-37, in a telephone conversation that was rudely intercepted by the FBI, White said as follows:

> Like, like on big [municipal bond] deals where like say . . . let's say Paine Webber or J.P. Morgan where they take the leads, we make them share it. Even though it's only one person really runnin' the books . . . It's an opportunity for, you know, the other people to get, you know, kind of more involved monetarily, you know what I mean? . . . Uh, and, and, and everybody, I mean, is happy because I mean, if these guys are makin' say two million or, you know, somethin' like that on these deals? . . . And they, and they gotta give up say, you know, six or seven hundred, that, I don't, I don't see a lot of resistance from 'em, and they're kind of happy to do it.

As you might surmise from the tenor of the foregoing, pay-to-play seems to have survived G-37 intact. White was more than just a fellow you would hire for a couple of hundred bucks to draft a will. This gentleman, now deceased, was what is known as a go-to guy, and in Philadelphia he was the guy you went to if you wanted to underwrite municipal bonds.

As for G-37 . . . well, what about it? G-37 effectively prohibits muni-bond firms from giving campaign contributions to public officials. G-37 was not being violated. White was not a public official. He was a go-to guy. Since G-37 prohibited direct payments to politicians through their campaign funds, middlemen like White—consultants and attorneys—took over the job of funneling campaign contributions from Wall Street firms, local muni-bond dealers, and banks. Sometimes, as happened in Philadelphia, things got a bit out of hand, and those middlemen became conduits for good old-fashioned bribes.

No one at Paine Webber was implicated in any wrongdoing—White might have just thrown in that name at random—but that can't be said for JPMorgan. In June 2004, a U.S. grand jury in Philadelphia handed up an indictment charging White, two Morgan bankers, and a bunch of people with an assortment of felonies, all having to do with what White was discussing. That is, muni-bond firms being "happy" to pay for business. The indictment alleged an elaborate scheme in which a city official directed bond business to firms in return for kickbacks. Guilty pleas came from the two Morgan bankers—whose employer usually plays the wise, mature Ward Cleaver of Wall Street to Bear's envelope-pushing Eddie Haskell. (Bear, it must be noted, was not involved in the Philadelphia case.) Two muni execs at Commerce Bancorp and a former city treasurer were convicted of fraud and conspiracy after a jury trial that got a lot of local attention, even if it wasn't very newsworthy just a few miles up the Northeast Corridor.

Morgan itself was not implicated, and it does seem pretty clear that the firm really didn't cotton to what its two bankers were doing. Still, the bankers asserted during an internal investigation that go-to guys like White were commonplace.

Commonplace—and legal. It was legal for UBS Financial Services to get muni-bond deals in California, Georgia, Kansas, Oklahoma, and West Viriginia by paying $460,000 a year to a politically connected Washington consulting firm. (UBS says its use of consultants is 100 percent kosher.) JPMorgan, which has since sworn off consultant-hiring after its Philly experience, hired a former speaker of the California state assembly to get state bond deals.

In New Jersey, Bear Stearns was able to get some lucrative bond deals by using a well-connected New Jersey lawyer named Jack Arseneault—a close ally of New Jersey's former governor James E. McGreevey. Arseneault really knew how to bring home the bacon for his consultees at Bear, according to Bear's filings with the federal muni-watchers. In 2003, he was credited with snaring for Bear a $1.7 billion bond deal that netted Bear $6.4 million in fees, for which Arseneault got a nice piece of change, $250,000. When all that came out in the local papers, Arseneault's services were dispensed with, and he was dropped from the payroll as of November 30, 2004.

Still, he must have been missed, and sorely, if you take a look at the kind of great work that he performed for Bear in just his last year on the job (officially defined in government filings as providing "general consulting services assisting [Bear Stearns] in developing new business and new business contacts in the State of New Jersey").

According to Bear's filings with the MSRB, Arseneault helped Bear get eight great muni gigs for Bear Stearns in New Jersey in 2004 alone. They were:

- Senior Manager, bond issue by the New Jersey Housing and Mortgage Finance Agency

- Senior Manager, bond issue by the Garden State Preservation Trust (one each in the second and third quarters of 2004)
- Senior Manager, bond issue by the New Jersey Transportation Trust Authority (twice in the third quarter of 2004)
- Co-Manager, bond issue by the New Jersey Transportation Trust Authority
- Co–Senior Manager, bond issue by the New Jersey Economic Development Authority (in the third and fourth quarters of 2004)

Arseneault earned just under $1 million during 2004. In his last two months on the job he was paid $120,000, of which $20,000 was a monthly retainer and $100,000 was "a discretionary payment, no portion of which was specifically attributable to any single municipal securities transaction listed above."

If you're ever looking for one of those self-help books about starting up your own consulting business, don't get one unless it suggests that you "become a pal of the governor of New Jersey."

Arseneault must have done a lot of good stuff for that money. The only problem is that New Jersey says he didn't have anything to do with getting Bear muni business in the Garden State. A spokesman for the New Jersey state treasurer's office told me that state officials dealt only with Bear Stearns officials—and not Arseneault. Since Bear would not be a subject of earnings-related admiration if it just threw money at people for no reason, that raises the question of why it would pay $1 million to some guy who's a friend of the governor. Think about that. Why would they do such a thing? Beats me. You know, I spent a long time thinking about it, and I just haven't the slightest idea. Do you? I called both Arseneault and Bear to ask if they could help me figure this out and, darn it, they wouldn't call me back. I guess maybe they couldn't figure it out either.

So, the mystery persists, perhaps till the end of time. While you are mulling over that question, I urge you *not* to give any thought to what happened in Philadelphia. If you're doing that—stop! You might be influenced to give a very impolite, uncharitable answer to that question. Besides, nobody appears to be investigating how Bear got all that work in Jersey, so nothing bad happened. Best to forget the whole thing—until it comes knocking at the door of your state capitol.

When the Philadelphia and Illinois muni-bond scandals and similar controversies reared their embarrassing heads in 2004 and 2005, the self-regulatory pyramid had even less impetus than usual to do anything.

Neither the media nor Eliot Spitzer was interested, and since Eliot was running for governor, it was pretty clear that this was a hot potato he was likely to avoid (Mrs. Spitzer not having raised a fool). Still, it had been a while. Total inactivity, no matter how tempting (and relaxing), is rarely a viable alternative for the pyramid. It had been almost six years since pay-to-play had been the subject of sustained, vigorous inaction. Clearly its time had come.

The last time the pyramid had not attacked pay-to-play was back in 1999. Artie Levitt, who always liked to cite that G-37 regulation in his speeches at the time, was making noise about bringing the blessings of clean ethics to munibond lawyers. It was standard practice then (as it is now and probably will be until the ice caps melt) for politically connected law firms to win appointments as counsel for state bond underwritings, or to get legal work for state pension funds, in return for campaign contributions. Well, you know Artie. He loves to give speeches. He gave a bunch of speeches on the subject and scowled and knitted his brow—and, as usual, he backed down. Instead, as one law journal commentator later put it, the American Bar Association "was allowed to substitute its own rule that is highly subjective and unenforceable."

Nice work, Artie! Something else he forgot to mention in his book, along with another rule he introduced with great fanfare at the time that went nowhere—a proposal that would have banned pay-to-play in the awarding of city and state pension-fund business. The affected parties didn't want it, and that was that. It died unmourned and unnoticed, sort of like a coleus you forgot to water.

So in March 2005, in reaction to all the unpleasantness in Philadelphia and elsewhere making the whole consultant-hiring business look pretty bad, the MSRB acted. Now, you may have noticed that a template is at work in situations such as this—that is, situations in which bad stuff is happening, and the pyramid's bureaucrats are moved to rise from their leather armchairs. In this case, we have a municipal-bond market being milked by Wall Street. As you have seen in this book, the response of our self-regulatory pyramid is invariably weak, tentative, wrongheaded, or just plain stupid. In this case, however, we have to toss the template out the window.

The MSRB actually issued a rule that is, by regulatory standards, not bad at all. Let's not go overboard and call it effective, but it really is not as much of a waste of virgin forest as are most market regulations. The MSRB saw that consultants posed a problem, and did something about it. This organization didn't propose more disclosure or licensing or registration or forcing consultants to wear uniforms or file papers or any of the other kind of dim-witted stuff that regulators usually do when presented with a problem. The MSRB *banned consultants entirely.*

The regulator of the muni-bond business didn't shuck and jive. It acted. Muni consultants are a thing of the past. A good thing. An improvement.

The only problem is that it won't work.

Oh, well. It was good while it lasted, wasn't it?

Banning consultants was a good idea. The problem resided in two gaping loopholes embedded in the rule. Lawyers aren't covered, and firms can simply get around this rule by putting their "consultants" on payroll. Another loophole is that it does not cover dealers in municipal-bond derivatives, called swaps. In a swap, local governments agree to pay muni dealers a floating rate of interest on their debt. The muni dealers pay local governments a fixed rate of interest—"swapping" one form of interest for another. That enables the government agency to repay its bondholders and keeps interest costs nice and predictable. Everything is all ducky when short-term rates are low, as they were for most recent years. When they increase, they can prove to be stinkers—for the muni-bond issuer, that is. For the swap dealer it is not so bad.

What makes swaps nice from the muni dealer's perspective is that they are not regulated by the MSRB. The words *muni swap* may sound like "municipal security" to you, but they don't sound like "municipal security" to the rule-making board. The MSRB views them as derivatives, which means they are regulated only by Providence, as in "Let's pray they don't screw around with them."

Still, you have to give the MSRB credit for passing a good rule, a rule that makes sense. It won't work, but ask yourself a question—doesn't "A for effort" mean anything in this hurly-burly world?

You can't really get sore at the MSRB because pay-to-play can't really be fixed by the federal government or our self-regulatory pyramid. Local governments have to act. There is a simple solution.

Right now, the vast majority of muni-bond awards are doled out on a negotiated basis, which means that the firm is selected first, and it then negotiates the financing terms with the governmental agency. Advocates of this method of doing business say that it keeps costs down, because the municipality and the underwriter can time the offering for the best market conditions, and the firm can presell the issue before it hits the market. That supposedly makes it better for the municipality. It certainly is a better way of doing business from the perspective of the underwriter, because the spread—the profit the firm garners from the bond deal—is not subject to competition.

There's no evidence that either the negotiated method or its alternative—going out for competitive bids—is better than the other. Studies of the subject have come up with mixed results. What we do know is that negotiated deals haven't always been the predominant way of awarding municipal-bond contracts. In 1970, 83 percent of municipal-bond deals were awarded competitively. By 1993 that number had declined to 25 percent. Since then, that number has shrunk still further, to the point that some muni-bond dealers report no competitive deals in their filings with the MSRB.

Commenting on the Philly scandal guilty verdicts in his column on the Bloomberg wire, journalist Joe Mysak observed that "you almost wonder why so many bankers actually prefer to do business this way, fighting for negotiated awards, rather than competing at auction sale, where the best bid wins the bonds."

Well, I suppose that if one were really mean and cynical about it, one would conclude that the dilemma that stumped Joe is resolvable as follows: If negotiated deals came to an end, so would pay-to-play. Sure, there are ways around even competitive bidding (bid rigging, for one), but that is the only way of really attacking the problem. If you care, that is.

That's the ultimate issue here. There are a lot more important issues facing the world today than your elected officials or their pals getting rich from muni-bond deals. There always have been and always will be, which is why pay-to-play persists, and isn't going away unless you want it to go away. The solution is at your town hall or state capital. If you don't give a damn, you can bet that the people there won't give a damn. After all, they're the ones sopping up the gravy, not you. All you do is pay the tab.

CHAPTER FOURTEEN

THE ANSWER: FREED-UP MARKETS

T he municipal-bond morass is one of the best examples you can find of the principle that I set forth at the beginning of this book: Heaping on more regulations is not the cure for Wall Street's obsession with your wallet. The MSRB and SEC can pass muni-bond rule after muni-bond rule, but it won't mean a thing as long as the regulators are captured by the industry and the system itself is inherently screwed up.

The muni mess exemplifies something else that is evident from all that we've seen. Despite securities industry rhetoric to the contrary, the Street doesn't really want free markets. Muni-bond dealers don't want competitive bidding. Sure, they come up with all kinds of excuses about why negotiated deals are better for the issuer. Bottom line: Taxpayers don't get the best interest rate on the bonds their governments sell, and corruption and pay-to-play persist.

Sure, free markets are just fine by the Street—unless they get in the way of profits, and then free markets aren't so fine. Until the Justice Department put an end to the practice in 1996, brokerage firms that bought and sold Nasdaq stocks—market makers, as they are called—routinely fixed prices. The market makers didn't want a free market. They wanted freedom—in this case, freedom to fix prices. The NASD, which ran Nasdaq, didn't care. The Justice Department had to step in because Artie Levitt's SEC was, as usual, asleep at the switch. Artie says in his book that when he headed the Amex, which was from 1978 to 1989, customer cheating by Nasdaq dealers—charging too much when selling and paying too little when buying—was "common knowledge" on the Street. The Amex estimated customer losses at $2 billion a year from those practices, later found to be a result of price fixing. Yet even though he knew customers were being systematically screwed, Artie's SEC took no action until the Justice Department launched its antitrust probe.

That's the way it works. The Street wants freedom at your expense, freedom to abuse, freedom to restrict *your* freedom of choice. It goes something like this:

- Brokerage firms want the freedom to disguise their brokers as financial advisors. They want the freedom to deny you your constitutional rights, so that you don't have the freedom to access the courts if you have a dispute with your broker. If you don't like any of that, you have freedom—to not open an account at any Wall Street firm, because *all* of them do the same thing. That's the kind of free market the Street likes—the "my way or the highway" free market.
- Hedge funds want the freedom to charge you ridiculous sums of money in return for mediocre performance with no accountability, and the freedom to turn the markets upside down whenever they goof up.
- Mutual funds want the freedom to pay off brokerages to sell their wares. They want the freedom to skim off billions of dollars in fees for doing a consistently lousy job of managing your money, and without coming clean about what they are doing with all those bucks.

So it is all the way down the line, in every single problem or mess that we've examined in this book.

The other common thread that has run through this book is the extent to which the Street has taken over the regulatory process. The logical outcome of the capture theory I mentioned earlier is that scandals keep repeating, in what academics call a cycle of scandal. We saw the latter in action at the New York Stock Exchange, where laughably poor oversight has meant that floor traders keep breaking the law, over and over again. We saw the cycles peddling away again in the mutual fund scandals, in which late-trading schemes from the 1930s and earlier were rerun periodically in the decades that followed. We'll be seeing the reruns rolled out again, big time, in our examination of microcap fraud in the next chapter.

Capture theory maintains that the political process of regulation is essentially dictated by the industry, and that any efforts to promote the common good, no matter how sincere, rarely succeed. We've seen that theory in action today, but I would hesitate to say that securities regulation has *always* been a captive of Wall Street. Beware of the free-market advocates who reflexively oppose any new stock market regulation. In all likelihood they're just carrying water for Wall Street. Like it or not, there are times when the self-regulatory pyramid just has to step in. A drowning man needs a lifeguard, even if his boat is leaky.

There's a school of thought that this nation actually once had an effective securities-regulation apparatus, back when the markets were a lot smaller and when business was more effectively cowed than it is today. When the SEC was first created in 1934, it was by all accounts a kick-ass operation, staffed by feisty Jewish lawyers who were Semitically disqualified from working on the Street. It was headed in its early years by a reformed market-manipulator named Joseph P. Kennedy, and later by a tough young New Dealer from out west, future Supreme Court Justice William O. Douglas. (Doctors say that reading Douglas's straight-shooting autobiography, *Go East, Young Man,* within twenty-four hours of Artie Levitt's self-aggrandizing *Take On the Street* can cause toxic shock syndrome.) True, the seeds for later scandals were germinating and sprouting buds during the early SEC era, as we saw in our romp down memory lane in mutual-fund-land. But the fund industry was a tiny thing in those days, not the omnipotent, multigazillion-dollar behemoth that we have today.

Something happened to the SEC over the years, just as something happens to a lot of us as we get older. All too often we abandon the principles we had when we were young. That may not matter a lot if you're a crotchety old guy with a bad conscience, but it's bad news if you're a middle-aged regulatory agency. It doesn't matter how it happened, but if the federal bureaucracy was ever the answer, it isn't anymore. The answer is a fair market—a freed-up market where consumer choice and the markets themselves are the main agents of liberation.

Still, the feds can't just fold up their tents and go home. Freeing up the markets, liberating them from the rules and practices that benefit Wall Street, will take action from the government. Effective mutual fund oversight, curbing microcap fraudsters, ending the Street's stranglehold over arbitration, and reining in the hedge funds' leverage is a job for the feds and for state and local regulators and law enforcement. Spitzer proved that even a small force of underpaid lawyers in one state can have a visible influence on Wall Street.

So even though you ultimately are the answer, you can't do it alone. That's the bad news. The good news is that you have more power than you think. You can nudge the self-regulatory pyramid to get off its rump and act. You can effectively protect yourself from scams of all kinds, and you can even change the system. As you'll be seeing in Chapter 17, people acting in your name, using the techniques you could be using to help investors, have already changed the system—for the worse.

They couldn't do it alone. They've had a lot of help from the people who are supposed to be watching your back.

CHAPTER FIFTEEN

CLUELESS IN MICROCAPLAND

Microcap fraud is the alternate-universe *Law and Order* of Wall Street.

It just goes on and on, season after season, episode after episode, rerun constantly, and in every episode Jerry Orbach never catches the crook, and Sam Waterston is invariably humiliated in court. Sometimes it seems as if a new variety of small-cap fraud-scandal surfaces, but it's really just a new season of that great old show.

Small-stock scams have been around for about as long as there have been stocks, albeit in various guises. In the 1950s they surfaced as trade in the shares of worthless mining stocks, thereby giving Utah and Denver brokerages a sturdy and not always fair reputation for skinning investors. In the 1980s microcap fraud was still largely centered out west and became known as penny-stock fraud, leading the SEC to set up a Penny Stock Task Force in 1988 to grapple with this issue. In the 1990s, microcap fraud retreated back to lower Manhattan, where the boiler rooms were staffed by cadres of New York street toughs, sometimes with Mob links. That was the era when microcap fraud really came into its own, with stock scamsters to be found not just in New York but virtually everywhere, and it exploded from an estimated $2-billion-a-year fraud in 1989 to a much larger phenomenon, perhaps a $10 billion annual ripoff, a decade later.

Today, all you have to do is turn on your computer and log on to the Internet, and there they are, those pesky little devils, the successors to the pesky little devils that bedeviled your great-grandparents. In 2005, financial fraud accounted for 9 to 11 percent of global spam, double the amount of the year before, according to one spam-watching survey. At times, the number shoots up to 15 percent of the billions of pieces of junk clogging Internet mailboxes.

Investment spams are a high-tech version of one of the oldest come-ons known to Wall Street. "There is a type of promoter or manipulator that believes in tips first, last and all the time," said Edwin Lefèvre in his 1923 memoir, *Reminiscences of a Stock Operator*. Lefèvre noted that "tip-seekers and tip-takers are invariably tip-passers, [so] tip-broadcasting becomes an endless-chain advertising." The Internet brought all that "endless-chain advertising" into just about every American home, and quite a few overseas.

One of the most celebrated microcap-stock pushers, a teenager from New Jersey named Jonathan Lebed, is a good example of this phenomenon. Lebed was the subject of a widely publicized SEC enforcement action in the final days of the Artie Levitt administration. Following unwittingly but very precisely in the footsteps of the "tip-passers" cited by Lefèvre, Lebed found that he could make a lot of money by posting anonymous comments about dog-puke stocks on Internet message boards. All he had to do was take a position in the stock, post a load of ca-ca under various pseudonyms, and cash out.

One postmortem, a sympathetic article in the *New York Times Magazine*, excused Lebed's conduct by saying that he was engaging in the same conduct as Wall Street analysts who pumped stocks on CNBC. The SEC complaint told another story. It maintained that Lebed, who settled the charges without admitting or denying the allegations, had "purchased large blocks of thinly traded microcap stocks and, within hours of making such purchases, sent numerous false and/or misleading messages, or 'spam,' over the Internet touting the stocks he had just purchased." In other words, it was straight-up pump-and-dump stock fraud. Nor was there anything particularly noteworthy about teenagers engaging in stock fraud. Kids only a few years older than Lebed were staffing chop-house phone banks throughout the 1990s.

Not only did Lebed express no remorse whatsoever, but he used all the publicity—most of it sought by Artie Levitt*—to his advantage. In the best traditions of caught-but-not-subdued microcap-stock pushers throughout history, Lebed picked up where he left off and moved his operations into the legal end of the microcap-shilling business. By 2002 he was shamelessly trading on his past lies and fraud by running an email list, promoting dreadful little stocks in

---

* Actually this was a rare example of Artie's publicity hunger backfiring just a bit. His grasp of the Lebed case was so tenuous, and his comments so rehearsed and robotic, that he was chopped into bits in that *Times Magazine* article.

return for cash and free-stock payments. He clearly adored the publicity he received over the years, and proudly posted the *Times* piece and other media coverage on his Web site. For years afterward he was still running his lucrative little stock-hype business, pumping stocks on his Web site and email list more aggressively and more profitably than ever. The SEC took no action, because there was no action to be taken.

Lebed had learned his lesson. As we saw in the case of mutual fund payoffs to brokerages, the self-regulatory pyramid abides by the principle that disclosure is a self-absolving confession. In his new career, Lebed disclosed when he took positions in stocks and when he was paid to make recommendations. So he could hype stocks legally, and there wasn't a thing anyone could or should do about it—except avoid his stock picks like the plague.

Lebed went legit easily because disclosure is easy and, above all, ineffective. Disclosures, after all, have about as much impact on investors as the earliest cigarette warning labels had on nicotine addicts, back when they said only that smoking "may be hazardous to your health." Even so, a remarkable number of small-cap pitches don't bother to slap on the SEC-mandated disclosures. Failure to mention compensation at the bottom of spams, newsletters and such practically screams, "I'm breaking the law!"

When you think about it, though, it becomes obvious why even the easy-to-follow laws are broken in microcapland. The laws are broken because they are not enforced, and they are not enforced because the media doesn't care. The financial press (with a few exceptions, such as Christopher Byron* of the *New York Post,* John R. Emshwiller of the *Wall Street Journal,* Herb Greenberg of MarketWatch, and Carol Remond of Dow Jones Newswires) has ignored or written off microcap fraud as a thing of the past, or as a kind of excusable market "excess."

The low point in the media's coverage of 1990s microcap fraud (the 1980s low point is a couple of chapters away) was probably reached in December 1995. The *Wall Street Journal* wrote about Wall Street boiler rooms—then at their peak—as if they were a kind of cute, Runyonesque, slightly overenthusiastic bull-market phenomenon. "Despite a regulatory crackdown on so-called rogue brokers who hop from firm to firm amid customer complaints, there remains a Wild West flavor in some off-the-beaten-path corners of the investing

---

* Commenting on an SEC microcap "initiative," and responding to a *BW* puff piece on the subject, Byron said this: "What we have here isn't a bold new anything from the SEC, it's simply the latest effort at public-relations damage control from a bunch of Beltway bureaucrats who've missed the boat on virtually every major Wall Street swindle for the last 30 years." (*New York Post,* March 15, 2005.) Such on-target commentary is becoming rare in the financial press.

business," said a story entitled "Wall Street Is Sometimes the Wild West." The story went on to describe one boiler room outfit as "tiny" and another, the odious, Mob-linked First Hanover Securities, as "equally obscure" (*obscurity,* in this case, being a code word for "I've never heard of it").

After recounting a series of blood-curdling events, including the defrauding of a customer and a violent episode that left a broker charged with assault, this is how the nation's leading financial publication described the phenomenon of hoodlums peddling microcap stocks on Wall Street: "The whole incident points up a recurring issue in the securities industry, analysts say. Brokers can move from firm to firm with impunity." That was it. The "issue" was that brokers moved around too much—not that the microcap market was infested with criminals. So it should come as no great surprise that a few months after this horrid story appeared, a few traders tried to arouse the interest of the *Journal* in the inside details of Mob infiltration of Wall Street firms—and the *Journal,* after some initial interest, did nothing.

First Hanover was not the first or even the worst scambucket firm to pull the wool over the eyes of the financial press. The biggest scammer firms, Hanover Sterling and Stratton Oakmont, occasionally surfaced in the press— but were almost invariably described as ordinary Wall Street firms, without even a hint of the practices that would later get them exposed as criminal enterprises. During a period in which the microcap scamsters were at their most brazen, hardly a word appeared about microcap fraud. And for a good reason— the SEC and NASD were telling the world that microcap fraud was on the wane. After all, the penny-stock firms of the eighties—Hibbard Brown, First Jersey, Blinder Robinson, and so forth—were all out of business. A "sweep" of penny-stock firms conducted in 1993 by the SEC, NASD, and state regulators found "only traces of past widespread abusive practices."

Isn't that fantastic? Penny-stock fraud wiped out! All thanks to our self-regulatory pyramid and their overseers in Congress. In 1990, Congress passed legislation called the Penny Stock Reform Act, which gave the SEC, NASD, and other regulators power to force brokerage firms to give customers notice of the potential dangers of penny-stock investing, and an opportunity to change their minds after they bought a penny stock. One of the authors of this landmark legislation, Senator Richard Bryan, a Democrat from Nevada, was justifiably proud when the results of the sweep were announced in June 1994. "This report is proof that we took the right action in passing legislation to curb this abusive practice and protect small investors," Bryan said at the time. "America's small investors are the backbone of America's businesses. If small investors are afraid to invest because of fears of widespread fraud and abuse, a major source of capital for business dries up."

Bryan was certainly not alone in pronouncing that microcap fraud was dead. I was told by NASD and SEC officials in 1996 that small-stock fraud was no longer considered much of a problem. It wasn't at all unusual, well into the 1990s, for sleazy, manipulated microcap stocks to receive favorable mention in stock market columns.

On the surface, a law that subjects penny stocks to disclosure—a law specifically aimed at protecting investors in such stocks—seems like a pretty good idea. The only problem was that the Penny Stock Reform Act didn't work. In fact, it is actually an excellent example of how the government has done a lousy job of protecting you from microcap scamsters. It's not that they can't, or won't. It's that they don't have the slightest idea of how to deal with the problem—not in 1990, and not today.

The law was passed—as such laws usually are passed—as a belated reaction to a problem of previous years. If was a lot like the doc prescribing antibiotics for the flu a couple of years after you recovered. In the 1980s, when the penny stock firms mentioned earlier were ripping off investors with impunity, there was such a hue and cry that Congress decided that the available legal remedies were not sufficient. Our lawmakers consulted with the self-regulatory pyramid, and enacted the Penny Stock Reform Act in 1990, after the penny stock craze was pretty much over and new varieties of microcap fraud were already under way.

Read with full knowledge of subsequent events, the PSRA has a charming, quaint quality to it. It was a bit like a diary that you wrote when you were a child, full of hopes and dreams. It's entirely possible that the framers of this legislation sincerely believed, like children—dim-witted children—that boiler-room crooks would act like good little children too, and give their customers a "penny-stock disclosure document," all nice and properly filled out, and that everybody would live happily ever after.

Likewise, even a child might have been able to see the problem. As put into effect by SEC regulations, the law applied only to stocks that were priced below five dollars. That was the main problem in the 1980s—stocks under five dollars. The catch was that these were manipulated stocks, so the *share price of the stocks was determined by the scamsters*. All the scam artists had to do was increase the price of the shares, and the law would not be a problem.

That seems almost childishly obvious today. It was also childishly obvious at the time.

Years later, Randolph Beatty, dean of the accounting school at the University of Southern California, told me of the time he attended a seminar in Washington organized by the North American Securities Administrators Association. This was the late 1980s, and the good people at NASAA wanted to figure out ways of combating penny-stock fraud. The idea of drafting a law that targeted the under-five-dollar stocks was a major topic of discussion.

Beatty patiently explained the folly of the idea to the participants, which included a sizable contingent from the SEC. He really tried. "These lawyers didn't understand the economics of it, even when it was explained to them," he recounted.

Really? Did it take a degree in economics to understand how rock-dumb this idea truly was? Maybe. Or maybe it wasn't stupidity but simply indifference. Maybe lawmakers and regulators knew that the idea of focusing on *manipulated* stocks that trade under five dollars was a dumb idea—and didn't care. After all, "they had to do something," notes Beatty. Besides, like many works of fantasy, the Penny Stock Reform Act read well.

"This bill ranks with the most important legislation we will consider this year," said Congressman Matthew J. Rinaldo, a New Jersey Republican who cosponsored the legislation, not long after the law was passed. "It will bring the longstanding national disgrace of an inadequately regulated penny stock market to a close," said the congressman, bless his heart.

Having eliminated microcap fraud the most effective way imaginable—by defining it incorrectly—the self-regulatory pyramid was able to proclaim an impressive victory. A GAO report said as follows in 1993:

> Between the end of the third quarter of 1988 and the end of the second quarter of 1992, SEC data showed that the number of broker-dealers trading in penny stocks decreased by 49 percent, from 324 to 165; the total capital of penny stock broker-dealers decreased by 59 percent, from $583 million to $240 million; and quarterly trading gains and commissions of penny stock broker-dealers on transactions in over-the-counter securities decreased by 37 percent, from $258 million to $162 million. SEC data also showed a decline in the number of complaints received by SEC about penny stock broker-dealers from a high of 3,863 in 1989 to 822 in 1991.

All this was true. *Penny-stock fraud* was no longer much of a problem. But *microcap fraud*—involving stocks priced a tiny bit higher—was a bigger problem than ever. As those words were being written in 1993, the massive boiler rooms of the 1990s were running full steam and ripping people off throughout the country. Prosecutions and enforcement actions years later would show that 1993 was the beginning of the Golden Age of Microcap Fraud, and that the NASD and SEC were soundly snoozing when they weren't patting themselves on the back.

As Beatty had anticipated, microcap scam artists were taking the simple precaution of moving their shares into the five-dollars-and-above price range. They could do that because of amazingly stupid enabling regulations enacted by the SEC. After all, the PSRA itself didn't define penny stocks as being under five dollars. That was the bright idea of the SEC, then under the brilliant leadership of Richard C. Breeden, and the definition stayed unchanged under the Investor's Champion, Artie Levitt.*

To its credit, the GAO warned in its 1993 report that "the decline in penny stock activity does not mean that the penny stock fraud and abuse problems have been resolved or are no longer a matter of regulatory concern." The GAO said it had been told by "law enforcement sources" that "penny stock issuers are trying to avoid the new penny stock rules by using phony financial information to price stocks just above $5, so that the stocks no longer meet the penny stock definition." Those few words, buried in an otherwise upbeat eighty-page report, received little attention at the time.

The law had another loophole, exempting securities trading on national securities exchanges. The exemption for Amex and Nasdaq stocks meant the law did not apply to dozens of microcaps traded on those two markets. That didn't matter, however, for the simple reason that the law itself didn't mean much. That was obvious from the get-go, clueless GAO report notwithstanding. Academics began to churn out a succession of critical studies. The first warning bells were sounded in 1993, when the weaknesses of the penny-stock law were described in a widely ignored article in the *Columbia Business Law Review*. A

---

* The ordinarily voluble Levitt is curiously silent on the subject of microcap fraud in his memoirs. Perhaps he didn't think any self-aggrandizement on that subject was necessary, because the media had already done the job for him. One example was a September 1997 story in *Business Week*, in which Levitt—"one of the most powerful and effective SEC chairmen in memory"—was credited with "cleaning up unsavory behavior in the over-the-counter market and cracking down on rogue brokers." In what must have confused any readers who noticed, I took the opposite position in a cover story three months later—a piece on the rise of chop houses called "Ripoff!"—saying that regulators had "barely dented" a very real and growing problem.

2000 study, published in the *Indiana Law Journal,* concluded that the Penny Stock Act "has proven to be mostly a paper tiger due to substantial loopholes." The last nails on the coffin of the law were hammered in by Beatty and his colleague Padma Kadiyala in 2003. The two pored over data concerning the effect of the penny-stock law on the IPO market, and found that it had only a "cosmetic effect" by reducing the number of IPOs that sold for under five dollars. In fact, there was a "migration of speculative issuers into the non-penny range." The study found a surge in IPOs priced between ten and twenty dollars. They also found that the probability of a lawsuit concerning a lousy IPO *increased* after the penny-stock law was passed. Beatty and Kadiyala looked at another measure of issuer quality, the bid-ask spread—that is, the difference between the prices at which you can buy and sell the same stocks at the same time. Generally, the narrower the spread, the better it is for investors. Bid-ask spreads for IPOs got wider—worse for investors—after the law was enacted.

As microcap-scam artists continued to ply their wares during the first Gulf War and the Clinton prosperity and the bull market and the Internet boom and the Internet bust and then the second Gulf War, the foolish, ineffective PSRA receded into history as a kind of dumb footnote, to be politely ridiculed by academicians like Beatty and ignored by the scamsters it was supposed to curb. It was ignored by the media, which said not one word about the failures of the law. It was ignored everywhere in the world except at the SEC.

On January 16, 2004, long after the PSRA had faded from even the most anal-retentive memories, SEC regulation writers caused entire forests of trees— tender young saplings and great, towering monuments to nature's greatness—to be felled for the purpose of adding twenty-two pages to the Federal Register. The SEC had decided to exhume the coffin of the PSRA and slap a new coat of mascara on the corpse.

By now it was obvious that stocks did not suddenly lapse into delinquency because their prices were under five dollars, and that stocks above that price were often among the worst frauds. None of these facts, apparently, had been absorbed by the SEC despite its participation in a few dozen microcap prosecutions during the preceding decade—and even though the 2004 rule-revamp proposal itself conceded that "a persistent pattern of abuse continues to exist with regard to the trading of these low-price, thinly traded securities."

Why had the SEC decided to dredge up the penny-stock rules from their eternal rest? Well, it seems that the SEC had finally realized that stocks listed on junior tiers of markets—subsidiaries of stock markets with looser listing standards—could slide by its useless penny-stock rules. Nasdaq had applied to be certified as a national securities exchange, and since the OTC Bulletin Board—where a lot of microcap stocks were traded—was taken over by Nasdaq in 2000, that meant its subsidiary OTC market could be exempt from the penny-stock rules.

That's it, folks. That and some rewording of meaningless disclosure forms that are supposed to be given to penny-stock investors, and a little other tinkering, and you have our SEC in the full flower of wheel-spinning. The SEC was proposing rule amendments for the sake of proposing rule amendments—not because it seriously believed that proposing meaningless amendments to a meaningless regulation was going to have any effect on microcap fraud or penny-stock fraud.

Why waste time amending rules that made no sense in 1990 and even less sense in 2004? Beatty has a theory: "Because," he says, "it was somebody's job."

Now, you might wonder what the SEC meant, in proposing its ridiculous rule amendments, when it talked about a "persistent pattern of abuse." What did that mean in terms of investor losses? The SEC didn't say.

Putting a dollar figure on the scope of microcap ripoffs is always a little dicey. After all, the crooks involved don't exactly take out tombstone advertising in the *Wall Street Journal* to trumpet their latest scores. In 1989, state regulators estimated that losses from microcap fraud were running at $2 billion a year, and their estimate for losses from chop houses in the 1990s was $6 billion. In 1997, the number that regulators were using was $10 billion a year. All these numbers are pretty much no better than educated guesses. One fairly reliable gauge of scam activity does exist—the volume of stocks traded on the OTC Bulletin Board. That is the repository for stocks in companies that aren't solid enough to make it to the Nasdaq SmallCap Market or even the American Stock Exchange.

According to the GAO study of penny stocks in 1993, OTC trading profits and commissions from penny stocks, good and bad, were about $3 billion a year. If that $2 billion state number from 1989 was still in the ballpark, it would suggest that about two-thirds of penny-stock trading profits and commissions were a product of fraud.

Back in the 1980s, small-cap stock fraud was concentrated on the OTC market. Today it's spread around to the Amex, the Nasdaq SmallCap Market, and the Pink Sheet stocks too lousy to make it to the OTC. Even so, OTC dollar-volume numbers are a good gauge of microcap fraud. They are really quite startling.

If you go back to 1996, when the boiler rooms were running full steam under the noses of an indifferent self-regulatory pyramid, $38.5 billion in stocks traded on the OTC Bulletin Board. The number climbed, egged on by a crazy bull market plus the disease of Internet message boards and email spams, until OTC volume peaked at $101 billion during 2000. Well, the market miasma hurt the dregs as well as the blue chips, so OTC dollar volume plummeted to just $15.6 billion in 2001 and leveled out at about that number in 2002.

Since then the market has shown a bit of spunk, but not the OTC. Nope, those stocks haven't just done well. They have completely gone nuts.

Volume on the OTC Bulletin Board has not just recovered to the levels back in the fraud golden era of the 1990s, but has zoomed off the charts. In 2004, OTC dollar volume was *triple* the amount in 2002 and substantially higher than 1990s levels—$51 billion. (Nasdaq, by contrast, experienced a far more modest gain since the 1990s.) Trading slacked off a bit during the first four months of 2005, but surged during the summer—climbing 22 percent in May through October of 2005 over the year before.

So, if past is prologue—and on Wall Street, past is *always* prologue—the pump-and-dump crowd is enjoying yet another golden era.

Now, to be fair, people who like OTC stocks point out that the vast majority of OTC stocks and stock dealers are as honest as the day is long, totally non-manipulated, and safe for even babies and nursing mothers to purchase. Many OTC stocks are struggling but honest and legit entrepreneurial companies with a good idea but only the sketchiest of financial backing. Others are the publicly traded stubs of nice old companies that have largely become private. So let's buy that argument and arbitrarily exempt 90 percent of the over-the-counter market from any kind of fraud contagion. That still would mean that microcap fraud can be conservatively estimated to be a $5-billion-a-year ripoff.

The media has, lamentably, neglected this area—but there are some brilliant exceptions. In addition to the work of Chris Byron and the other reporters I mentioned earlier, there was a terrific series of articles on overseas boiler rooms by Christopher Carey in the *St. Louis Post-Dispatch* in June 2004. But if you just follow the national news media and your local paper's wire service coverage, chances are you don't know there is even a possibility of a problem.

One reason is the tendency of the press to let the SEC and the self-regulatory pyramid set the news agenda. The problem with relying on the SEC's well-lubed PR machinery, or press releases from U.S. Attorneys' offices, to dictate coverage of the underside of the markets is that the SEC and law enforcement usually pursue lawbreakers after the ripoffs have been completed. The SEC's enforcement staff is getting better—they've been halting trading in doggy stocks with greater frequency—but the regulatory machinery remains creaky except on the hot-button headline issues of the day.

Most of the major 1980s penny-stock schemes did not result in criminal prosecutions until the 1990s—long after the ripoffs occurred—and prosecutors didn't target the 1990s abuses until the tail end of the decade. The court system being as it is, some of the penny-stock prosecutions left over from the eighties, such as one involving some mutts we'll be examining in the next chapter, were still clogging the appellate courts in the late 1990s. The biggest busts of the 1990s crop of scam brokers—including the massive "Wall Street Mafia" roundup—took place in 1999 and 2000. One microcap scam that surfaced in 2001, involving abuses in a form of financing called the PIPE, wasn't a subject of SEC action until four years later.

Another reason for lagging coverage is simple economics. Newsroom budgets being as they are, very few publications have the resources—or, when they have the resources, the interest—of the *New York Times*, which let Diana Henriques spend the greater part of a year examining ripoffs of military servicemen by sellers of investment products. Still, there are encouraging signs. Dow Jones Newswires commendably allowed Carol Remond to roam at will through the microcap netherworld, as a result of which she won the Gerald Loeb Award in financial journalism in 2005. Carol's winning the award will, I hope, change some of the "large-bore, small-bore" prejudices that I mentioned at the beginning of this book. But don't bet on it. Carol's work was terrific, but received scant attention and virtually no follow-up from the rest of the financial press. Old newsroom prejudices are hard to overcome.

Faced with a continued onslaught of microcap fraud, the self-regulatory pyramid is facing down the hordes of crooks with more than just the nonsensical Penny Stock Reform Act. They also rely upon a regulatory weapon that is the functional equivalent of the flintlock pistol—the civil suit, usually settled by the payment of a fine and a promise to not do anything bad again, without admitting or denying liability.

The problem with this approach is that microcap scamsters don't mind being sued. Hell, they are not always deterred by even the threat of criminal prosecution.* When civil penalties are imposed, they do not pay them. In the

---

* In my 2003 book, *Born to Steal,* I described how one scam artist, Louis Pasciuto, continued to engage in scams long after the FBI began closing in. Boiler rooms kept operating even after a full-press law enforcement effort snared Pasciuto and dozens of others.

past—security procedures have since been tightened up—when they needed a NASD broker license, they would pay people to take the test. When they are banned from the securities industry, they continue to sell stocks. When they are punished, they stay in business, operating within the confines of the law or not, usually without drawing much regulatory follow-up. That was a common theme in all of the rogue-broker and stock-promoter crackdowns of recent years.

The philosophy behind investor protection laws was summed up this way by William O. Douglas, the ass-kicking SEC boss in the 1930s, in his memoir *Go East, Young Man:*

> The large percentage of stockholders on the small side accentuated the need for investor protection. The problem reminded me of the golden-mantled ground squirrel in the Cascades who is the anchor man in the food chain. He is to predators what hamburger is to man. His enemies are many, including the coyote. In the capitalistic system the unsophisticated small investor is the ground squirrel, and the coyote has always been numerous.

The remedy, as dictated by the Securities Act of 1933 and 1934, is disclosure. But as Douglas acknowledged in his autobiography, the "two SEC acts . . . provided only fair warning of the approach of the predator through full disclosure." If the investor did not analyze what was disclosed, and if his broker didn't analyze it for him, then—well, good luck getting out of the Cascades.

There is, by the way, nothing wrong with that. Investors aren't ground squirrels, so you can't really blame the Wile E. Coyotes, and you can't even blame the Elmer Fudds at the SEC. Nobody forces you to buy microcap stocks. The SEC may not be particularly competent, it may waste time and the money you throw at the government on April 15—but even if it were headed by the latter-day equivalent of William O. Douglas, avoiding crooks would still be your responsibility.

After all, the microcap markets are a dangerous neighborhood. You can't blame the cops if you walk with a wad of bills protruding from your shirt pocket and some hood comes along and takes it.

Let's say someone sends you an email urging you to buy a stock, and says the following at the bottom of the email, as Jonathan Lebed did in one of his mid-2005 hypes, a wretched little OTC company called mPhase Technologies (stock symbol XDSL). mPhase, a nanotechnology company—the "big big, new

new idea" of 2005—had tried to boost its share price in late 2004 with the help of rent-an-analysts at Taglich Brothers, and by May 2005 . . . well, this is what it was reduced to doing:

> My firm Lebed & Lara, LLC, has been compensated by XDSL 100,000 restricted shares which have since been registered and 175,000 warrants to purchase shares at $0.35 for our previous one-year investor relations contract. We just signed a new one-year investor relations contract with XDSL and were compensated an additional 300,000 restricted shares. Never invest into a stock we discuss unless you can afford to lose your entire investment. For our full disclaimer go to: http://www.lebed.biz/disclaimer.htm

If you went to that disclaimer, you would find the usual standard language, such as "Lebed.biz is an independent membership service that specializes in providing information on stocks that in the opinion of Jonathan Lebed have investment potential," and "all opinions expressed by Lebed.biz/Jonathan Lebed are not a solicitation to buy, sell, or hold securities" (which means, I guess, that all the hype in his emails falls under the category of "investor education").

Lebed went well beyond the requirements of the law in making these disclosures. He posted on his site articles that told the much-told tale of his youthful scrapes with the SEC. He provided a link to the text of the famous consent decree that he signed with the SEC in 2000. He provided photographs showing that he was just a kid who lived in New Jersey and had a bad haircut. He was twenty in 2005, older than some of the kids who worked at Hanover Sterling, Greenway, A.R. Baron, and other infamous boiler rooms, but he didn't conceal his age the way they did. On the contrary, his youth and his SEC consent decree were crucial parts of his business plan and marketing strategy.

If you bought a Jonathan Lebed stock, you got precisely what was coming to you. You got a stock recommended by a guy with a high school education who was paid to make recommendations, and whose only claim to fame was neither admitting nor denying that he committed securities fraud when he was fifteen years old.

That's the free market for you. There's only one problem with this picture: The microcap market isn't a free market.

Again, our paradigm applies. Microcap-stock pushers don't really want a free market. What they want is the freedom to push their wares, so that OTC dollar volume—and their bank accounts—swell to ever-higher levels. They want the freedom to push stocks on you without being snared by the market forces that would operate in a truly free market—the market antibodies that are capable of fighting scamsters.

CHAPTER SIXTEEN

THE HOLISTIC APPROACH
TO CORPORATE CRIME

Doing battle with stock scamsters and corporate creeps requires a warrior with a unique combination of qualities:

1. The *tenacity* of an Amazon River leech
2. The *information hunger* of a gossip columnist on deadline
3. The *market savvy* of a rag merchant
   and, last but not least,
4. The *greed* of a Wal-Mart buyer in China

A smattering of people possess the first three criteria: some regulators and prosecutors, a few journalists, and a handful of market-savvy, pistol-toting FBI men and Postal Inspection Service agents. However, few of these people have—or, if they have, are allowed to exercise—that essential fourth ingredient that is required if you want a full-time, 24/7, record-scouring, private-eye-hiring, journalist-nagging, whistle-blowing, ferocious, irritating, scam-fighting machine. What you need are people who have a profit motive—short-sellers. Only short-sellers make money by rooting out corporate crime of all kinds.

They are the free-market solution to stock fraud. They are the boas you throw into the attic to hunt rats, the ladybugs you carefully return to the garden if you find one on your hoe. They are a holistic, natural, sandals and vitamin C approach that works when more orthodox approaches fall flat.

Short-sellers arouse profoundly mixed feelings on Wall Street. Although almost every major brokerage engages in some kind of short-selling, traders who do nothing but short-sell occupy one of the less-prestigious fringes of the securities industry. You don't see short-sellers in the Styles section of the Sunday *New York Times,* photographed alongside slinky beauties in the VIP section at the grand-opening reception of the Edwin Lefèvre Pavilion of NYU Medical Center. The Street profits from them and pays lip service to the desirability of short-selling, while at the same time keeping its distance, much as you would from a poor relation who can't hold a job. The self-regulatory pyramid alternates between ignoring short-sellers, prosecuting them, and sitting back passively while the shorts spoon-feed them information that they usually ignore.

Right now the pyramid, and particularly the SEC, has shifted over to hostility, under pressure from a coalition of microcap-stock pushers and their dupes. Regulators have actually made life *harder* for shorts at just the wrong time—when the rig-happy microcap market is exploding, and when the market in general often shows the kind of rampant hype that it exhibited in the Internet and IPO frenzy of the 1990s.

That's not very smart—in fact, it's downright idiotic—because the market needs short-sellers. Just about every major corporate and accounting scandal in recent memory that involved a publicly traded company was initially uncovered by short-sellers. Not by the media, not by the self-regulatory pyramid, and not by Eliot Spitzer. At least as important are the day-to-day hypes and lower-level frauds that shorts uncover, passing on tips to the press and to regulators.

Shorts, and newsletters catering to short-sellers, were investigating accounting abuses long before it was fashionable. If allowed to do their work without government meddling, they are capable of being the only market participants—alongside an aroused, educated, phone-slamming and spam-deleting public—that can counteract the perennial plague of stock hype and fraud. In some cases they are swifter than the FBI and federal prosecutors—and certainly more effective than the SEC and NASD—because all those guys usually show up after the smoke has cleared and the robbers have run off with the loot. Shorts can actually stop the crooks dead in their tracks.

All that being said, shorts don't deserve halos. Some of them live up to their reputations by being, well, scum. One short once offered to give me the lowdown on a major public figure—if I wrote a story lambasting a reporter he didn't like. (I don't know the merits of his beef with the reporter, but what he offered me on that public figure was a lot of crap.) Other shorts have been occasionally accused of extorting money from companies. Others lie, cheat, and steal—in other words, they act like the Wall Streeters that they are.

One rogue short who received a lot of attention was a Texas trader named Amr Elgindy, who in January 2005 was convicted of getting info by bribing an

FBI agent (he's appealing the conviction). Elgindy was actually a pretty good scam fighter, but he couldn't resist the lure of easy bucks. An occupational hazard, I guess.

Another short with a knack for getting himself into trouble—he has had more run-ins with authority figures over the years than Leo Gorcey in the old Bowery Boys movies—is a fellow by the name of Manuel Asensio. Manuel appeared more or less out of nowhere in the mid-1990s. I had the rather dubious distinction of giving him some of his earliest publicity, and over the years have watched him go from stock to stock, controversy to controversy, mess to mess, and lawsuit to lawsuit. It's been sad, or perhaps a better word might be *expected*. He's a bright guy, but he is a bit like a car with a chronically malfunctioning radiator. Manuel can't seem to go very far without letting off steam, and it usually blows right back in his face.

The Manuel I knew when I was at *BW* liked to affect a street-smart Antonio Banderas persona, but at heart he was a wannabe white-shoe type who belonged to the Harvard Club, hired a PR firm at one point, and liked to hold conference calls with the media—just like the grown-ups. Manuel, however, had that malfunctioning radiator, or slipping fanbelt, or leaking water pump— I just don't know. Out it always came, the steam. Thus it would be Company X "launches another outlandish promotion" and Company Y's "reported earnings raise serious legitimacy concerns." All in public statements for the whole world to read and enjoy, or not enjoy, as the case may be.

Hey, nothing wrong with any of this. The First Amendment entitled Manuel to his moments of steam. He was the first short in memory to put out press releases promoting his recommendations—a perfectly valid and, in my view, even laudable practice. It got him plenty of attention, plenty of clippings he'd put on his Web site. It also got him an anti-Asensio Web site of his very own, asensioexposed.com, which published his disciplinary record in full. It got him plenty of attention from the NASD, which in January 2005 issued a ruling kicking Manuel out of the securities industry. By then he had closed his shorting operation.

The charge was that Manuel's steam was a bit too hot. He allegedly made "unwarranted or misleading" statements in research reports, and was accused of not providing the NASD with requested information. Manuel is appealing the decision. Fortunately for the markets, if not for the image of short-selling generally, an NASD ban, if upheld, will not keep the guy from shorting. I hope Asensio returns to vigorous, outspoken short-selling no matter what, because I think that he and guys like him play a valuable if irritating role in the market. But for his own good, he might want to do something about that radiator thing I mentioned.

Other shorts have also been penalized by the regulators every now and then. But one thing that you will not find, despite all the racket being put out by anti-shorting forces, is even the most unscrupulous short-selling, even the obnoxious Asensio at his alleged worst, doing any tangible harm to investors. In fact, naughty as they sometimes are, there's no getting around the fact that shorts fulfill an essential economic function, one that ought to gladden the hearts of believers in free markets everywhere. Economists have always maintained that short-sellers provide a vital role in the market. You need a bearish viewpoint if you want a stock's price to include all available information. That's one of the underpinnings of the market's pricing mechanisms.

To understand why short-sellers are so important, why they need to be nurtured and pampered and allowed to thrive, you have to understand what they do, and—at least as important—what they *don't* do. Short-sellers don't cause market crashes, and they don't hurt investors in stocks that are freely traded in the open market—as opposed to fool's-gold microcaps that are rigged by rogue brokers or hyped to absurd levels on the Internet. Sure, there is such a thing as a "bear raid." They happen. You should pray that a stock in your portfolio is so afflicted, if it is a legitimate and not a rigged stock. If it is rigged, then it doesn't matter if there is a bear raid or not—you'll be taken to the cleaners sooner or later.

It's easy to blame short-sellers (or "program trading," or "hedge funds," or "Jews," or "Commies," or "capitalists," or whomever we may find distasteful) when we lose money. It's human nature. A good example of that took place after the crash of 1929. A handful of shorts profited, and years later people were still upset. "Much has been said recently about the evils of short selling, and proposals have been made to prohibit it by state or federal law," said the authors of a book called *High and Low Financiers,* an examination of "Some Notorious Swindlers and Their Abuses of Our Modern Stock Selling System," back in 1932.

The muckraking authors of that book—lawyers who worked for Spitzer's antecedents at the New York attorney general's Securities Bureau in 1929 and 1930—refused to bad-mouth the shorts. They called short-selling a "useful break on excessive speculation or manipulation." This was a brave sentiment during the Great Depression, when stocks were in the doldrums and there was a widespread belief that short-sellers put them there.

What caused the 1929 crash, and all market setbacks, was that the market became overheated in the first place. The fault for that was speculators and manipulators—not the shorts. The market was widely rigged before the 1929 crash, but the culprits were syndicates, or pools, that combined their resources to drive up the prices of certain stock sectors. Also contributing to the frenzied speculation was unrestricted leverage. Traders would buy stocks on margin using borrowed money—frequently putting up only one dollar for every ten bucks' worth of stock they bought. Yet, the authors of *High and Low Financiers* observed that it was the shorts, not the margin lenders, who were getting all the knocks: "There would be more justification," they wrote, "for a ban on all purchases on margin, which has never been seriously proposed."

Academic researchers have been dissecting short-sellers for quite some time, to see what makes them tick and to find the black heart that is supposed to reside therein, and have never found it. What they have found, repeatedly, monotonously, is perfectly innocent and, usually, beneficial—for bulls as well as bears. For example, researchers at Vanderbilt University studied all 101 global stock markets, and found that when short-selling restrictions are removed, share prices don't decline. They *rise*. That's because short-selling improves the overall quality of a market, increasing liquidity and reducing volatility. Nor did they find that stock market crashes take place more frequently in markets that allow short-selling.

An "efficient, fairly priced stock market" is one of the "good things" that responsible people are supposed to want, along with "fair employment practices" and "a solvent Social Security system." People are supposed to want all that good stuff, but in fact they don't. I can string academic papers on the benefits of "equal employment opportunities" from here to Jupiter, and it won't matter. People want a "job," not a system that offers "equal employment opportunity for all." They want a "monthly check," not "a solvent Social Security system."

Shorts make markets more efficient but they root for stocks to go down, and nobody wants stocks they own to decline. That's like wanting your children to die. We want our children and our stocks to grow up big and strong, so they can support us in our old age. It's an emotional thing. No less a Wall Street expert than the author and consultant Charles D. Ellis—an official Street sage, appointed by Bill Donaldson to chair the SEC's investor education effort—put it this way in his book *Winning the Loser's Game:* "We smile when our stocks go up and frown or kick the cat when our stocks go down. And our feelings get stronger and stronger the more—and faster—the prices of our stocks rise and fall."

Falling in love with stocks is a common flaw in large and small investors alike. In fact, even market superstars have fallen in love with their stocks, only to be left in the lurch when the stocks did not love them back. Two of the big hedge fund stars of the 1990s, Michael Steinhardt and my pal Julian Robertson, were left at the altar by the same stock—US Airways—some years apart, with Robertson really going *meshuga* and buying up a 25 percent stake in that dog of an airline, and not unloading even as the stock plummeted 55 percent because of all the usual airline-related problems.* Now, is that love, or what? Steinhardt and Robertson were truly the Tarleton twins of lovesick investors back then, with US Airways playing the fickle Scarlett O'Hara. Then came Stanley Druckenmiller, the George Soros deputy who had once been viewed everywhere as the cold, stalwart type, the Ashley Wilkes of Wall Street. His passion was technology stocks at just precisely the wrong time—who said only amateurs are lousy market timers?—and he wound up dragging down Soros's Quantum Fund in 2000 because of his general codependence and neediness whenever a cute, well-endowed microchip stock beckoned. In investing, as in life and *Gone with the Wind,* it is always better to stomp off like Rhett Butler than to be left panting in the doorway or chewing radishes in the fields.

Short-sellers arrived briefly—very briefly—as heroes in the wake of Enron, back in the days when people were falling out of love with stocks generally. But even then, their contribution was only grudgingly acknowledged. In their account of the *Journal*'s coverage of the Enron saga, reporters Rebecca Smith and John R. Emshwiller described shorts as "shadowy denizens of Wall Street," and lamented that there are "lots of ruthless shorts who will spread rumors, hoping to instigate a sell-off that will make them money." Though Emshwiller found them "smarter and harder working than the average analyst," his coauthor, Smith, didn't like them. "The whole business seemed somewhat unsavory to her."

Prejudice against shorts among the financial press is understandable, because writing anything negative about a big company can result in considerable heat—as Bethany McLean found when she was pursuing her early negative Enron story in *Fortune*. All things being equal, it gets a reporter considerably less grief to write a positive rather than a negative piece on an Enron or a Tyco—*before,* that is, such companies become piñatas. It's easy to forget that these were once reputable companies that posed a serious lawsuit threat against any financial journalist who dared to probe their inner workings.

The problem is that nobody knows for sure which companies might become piñatas down the road. The word *Enron* is synonymous with "crook"

---

* "Mr. Robertson still hasn't sold a share of US Airways, faithful to the airline," the *Wall Street Journal* reported on the day Robertson went out of business in March 2000. The *Journal* quoted "one person familiar with the matter" as saying Robertson was "too long to be wrong." On Wall Street, love means never having to say you're sorry—or wrong.

today, but in the financial press it used to be synonymous with "powerful, nasty company that hires powerful, nasty lawyers." I'm told by colleagues at *Business Week* (I was on leave at the time) that in early 2001 a *BW* reporter took a hard look at Enron's trading operations, but was unable to persuade *BW* editors to publish her reporting about what was then a perfectly respectable company. *BW* instead ran a favorable cover story focusing on the "derring-do" of Enron's future felon Jeff Skilling. The Enron cover haunted *BW* for years afterward not only because it was spectacularly off base, as became obvious in the months ahead, but because of a reason known only within the magazine—that *BW* had missed a chance to rain on Enron's parade. *Fortune* more or less broke the Enron story in March 2001—with the company, naturally, blaming shorts for badmouthing it. But only the month before, *Fortune* named Enron the "Most Innovative Company in America" for the sixth year in a row.

Short-sellers make their living by trying to uncover scams before they become public knowledge. Whether they are right or wrong, they benefit investors. I know, it's counterintuitive. But you have to keep saying to yourself, over and over again: <u>Short-selling always benefits investors.</u> Another principle needs to be underlined: <u>The smaller the stock, the bigger the investor benefit from short-selling.</u> There is no way anyone other than a scam artist can be hurt by a short-seller. All the propaganda to the contrary, and there is plenty of it out there, this is one of the biggest con jobs being perpetrated by the microcap-stock pushers, their allies and dupes.

To understand how shorts gum up the works for stock promoters and cruddy brokers, and *only* for stock promoters and cruddy brokers, let's look at the mechanics of short-selling.

In order to short a stock, you borrow and then sell it. The stock is borrowed from other people's accounts without their knowledge—it's allowed by the standard language of brokerage agreements for margin accounts. Now, a lot of people have trouble with this "borrow and then sell" concept, and I don't blame them. After all, most people wouldn't borrow a book from the library and then sell it. That wouldn't be nice. It probably also wouldn't be legal.

Just for the heck of it, let's imagine for a moment that it were legal. Let's say you borrow from the library a newly published bestseller that retails for thirty dollars. You believe that this book doesn't have much value as a collectible, that it's really just a flash in the pan, so you sell it to a used-book dealer for ten dollars.

Let's say the library doesn't impose fines, so you have time to test out your hypothesis concerning this book's lack of lasting value. You wait a few months and find you were right. The same book that was retailing at thirty dollars, and which you sold at ten dollars, is now selling for one dollar at a yard sale, so you buy it and return it to the library. You've made a nine-dollar profit.

That may seem like easy money, and it is. I hate to tell you this if you bought this book on the day it was published, but books almost always depreciate immediately. Stocks, of course, are an entirely different animal—sometimes rising quite dramatically in price, either because the market itself is rising or because the stock is terrific, or rigged. That makes short-selling hazardous. In fact, the smaller the stock—and thus the more crucial the role of shorts in deflating hype—the riskier it is, because small stocks are notoriously prone to manipulation. One common scam is the short squeeze. That happens when a stock is deliberately made scarce through various mechanisms.

Let's go back to the book-shorting analogy for a second. Let's say a publisher out there is tired of guys like you undercutting his prices by borrowing his books from the library and then selling them. So he gets an idea. He sends out to the libraries a book in which he has planted a huge mistake—a libelous comment. Then he sends out a panicky notice calling back the books so that they can be pulped. The publisher knows that if he recalls the book and pulps it, any remaining unpulped copies of that book will be scarce, and thus valuable—really hurting you lousy book-shorters!*

You sold the book for ten dollars, and now, because it is scarce, it is worth a lot more. You want to wait until the price of the book declines, because you feel it is a crummy book and it eventually will be worthless. But the library says, "Uh-uh." It wants the *original* book back right away. So you shop around and buy it on the open market for, say, fifty dollars. Or maybe the library just buys it from the nearest used-book seller for eighty dollars, and bills you for that. You take a pretty heavy loss either way. If there are a lot of people like you who shorted this book, you'll all be in the used-book stores at the same time, driving up the price of the book.

What I've just described is a short squeeze. The library buying the book and billing you is called a buy-in when it happens with stocks. This manipulative conduct is a common occurrence—and the SEC, rather than curbing short squeezes to prevent artificial price inflation, is actually *encouraging* squeezes to wipe out microcap shorting. We'll be coming to that in the next chapter.

The problem with short squeezes is that small investors get hurt. Short squeezes push shorts out of the market, thereby allowing rigs to flourish.

---

* Something roughly similar to that actually happened. A book called *Trading with the Enemy*, an account by a former employee of hedge fund manager and cable TV guru Jim Cramer, had to be recalled because of a serious error—and the few unpulped copies did become collector's items. Needless to say, that error was not deliberately planted by the publisher, which practically had kittens when it was uncovered.

Speaking of restrictions on short-selling generally, Yale University's Owen A. Lamont said, "The evidence is consistent with the idea that short sale constraints allow very substantial overpricing, and that this overpricing gets corrected only slowly over many months."

Fortunately, the constant threat of short squeezes is somewhat offset by the other edge of the two-edged sword of short-selling. That edge, the one that is death to the stock swindler, is that short-selling sometimes has the effect of temporarily—I repeat, *temporarily*—reducing share prices, which often can be sufficient to put the kibosh on stock-fraud schemes.

That word *temporary* needs to be emphasized because the downward pressure on stock prices from short-selling is what gets people mad at shorts. If a stock is not an artificially inflated ripoff, the shares will rebound if shorting hurts the price. Short-induced price declines don't happen at all in large-cap issues, and are restrained for stocks generally because of the uptick rule, a New Deal-era restriction that allows shorting of exchange-traded and Nasdaq stocks only at a higher price than the preceding trade. Despite the uptick rule—which is viewed as so expendable by the SEC that its enforcement was suspended during 2005, as you'll be seeing—shorting still exerts some downward pressure on stock prices, and that gets people upset for no good reason.

If you like a stock enough to buy it, what difference does it make that somebody is pushing down the price—any more than it would if you were dealing with rare books or Depression glass or vintage *Sergeant Fury* comic books? While you may not be happy that people are bad-mouthing your fave stock or author or collectible, you know that they're all really valuable, and you'll snap up even more at their current depressed prices.

Glassware and comic books are obviously different from stocks, but the principle is the same. A short-seller's machinations, or the hype of a stock promoter for that matter, should not change your opinion of the company. If the underlying fundamentals of the company are good, if it really is making a better mousetrap or has found a cure for herpes, the stock price will eventually recognize that. That same principle applies, by the way, whether you are a believer in the Efficient Market Hypothesis or value investing or behavorial finance. There is no real disagreement among all schools of market analysis that if a stock's price is out of whack because it is *manipulated* downward or upward, it will eventually revert to the price that reflects its genuine, nonmanipulated value.

That principle was expressed eloquently way back in 1923, long before academics systematically put the markets under a microscope, by the author of *Reminiscences of a Stock Operator*. Edwin Lefèvre put it this way: "As I have said a thousand times, no manipulation can put stocks down and keep them down." If a bear raider were to push a stock below its intrinsic value, Lefèvre noted, "the raider would at once be up against the best kind of inside buying. The people who know what a stock is worth will always buy it when it is selling at bargain prices."

Lefèvre was right. But he could say it a million times and it wouldn't matter, such is the prejudice against short-sellers.

In scams, the determinant of a stock's price is not information but manipulation. The market price is rigged, either by controlling the mechanisms by which the stock is bought or sold and/or by inducing people to buy the stock at ever-higher prices. The latter is carried out by some combination of the following: hyping the stock on the Internet, pushing the stock in a media campaign, or having salesmen at a boiler room cold-calling you or your uncle in Florida or cousin in Donegal.

Short-sellers disrupt scams by horning in on the scamsters, selling the shares that are involved in the manipulations, and generally making a mess of the thieves' carefully scripted schemes. One of the few documented examples of shorts in action, busting up a major stock scam, came in early 1995. Traders systematically shorted the stocks being sold by Hanover Sterling & Co., one of the leading boiler rooms of the 1990s—a major stock-fraud operation that geared up in the early part of the decade, at the same time the SEC and NASD were assuring the public that penny-stock fraud was a thing of the past.

By incessantly selling the shares of Hanover stocks, shorts drove down the prices of the shares, making it impossible for Hanover brokers to rip off the public. That's because their scheme was predicated on an inflated share price. The Hanover stocks had a built-in commission—a humongous, illegal commission that was split between Hanover and the broker. In *Born to Steal,* my account of the chop-house world, I described how the massive profit, or chop, for one Hanover stock consisted of three dollars of the eight-dollar share price. If the eight-dollar share price could not be maintained, the whole scam would have crumbled into dust.

If you're engaged in a stock rig, the last thing that you need is for the free market to intrude. Remember our template: "Freedom, not free markets." In this case, the freedom to steal. Such were the economic underpinnings of vast swaths of the microcap market in the 1990s, and the same holds true today. Microcap-stock promoters and Internet stock pushers—who are usually paid with cheap stock or stock-purchase warrants—want the freedom to shill their stocks without anyone getting in the way of their rigs.

When Hanover collapsed, the people at the NASD were mad. They weren't mad at Hanover. They weren't mad at sky-high commissions. They didn't even know about the sky-high commissions. What made them mad was that a member firm, Hanover Sterling, was put out of business, and short-sellers appeared to be the culprit. The firm was their priority, not the firm's victims. That's how screwed up the self-regulatory pyramid's priorities were at the time, and they have not changed measurably since then when it comes to microcap fraud.

The NASD investigated Hanover's demise by taking testimony from key personnel, including a fellow who was one of the hidden owners of the firm. His name was Bobby Catoggio. Mind you, this wasn't some suit counting beans in a quiet office. This was the head of trading for Hanover, the guy who told the brokers every day how much swag they were going to rip off from their customers. It was quite a spectacle: an "aggrieved party," later identified by law enforcement as a Mob associate, who was a crook of such magnitude that in 2001 he was sentenced to 141 months in prison and ordered to pay $80 million in restitution to his victims.

In an interview with the NASD in May 1995, Catoggio was righteously indignant. He was furious that short-sellers, functioning *in loco NASD,* had accomplished what the snoozing regulators would have done, had they been competent. It was world-class gall. It was also illuminating. A transcript of this mutt's NASD testimony provides a rare inside account of how short-selling helps the markets by interrupting stock schemes.

Catoggio told the NASD that "for about six weeks before we were closed we were getting hit with large amounts of sell orders from the Street." Note those words—*the Street.* That means "other than Hanover Sterling and its accomplices." Since Hanover stocks were rigs, since the shares were kept high so that the built-in profit (chop) was substantial, Hanover was forced to buy all those stocks being sold short, and buy and buy and buy—until it ran out of money. Its clearing firm, Adler Coleman, collapsed at the same time as a result.

The only reason the shorts seriously hurt these stocks was because they were manipulated. If the prices of Hanover stocks had been determined by market forces, if even a crazy market—such as the Internet bubble—had driven the prices upward, a raid by short-sellers would not have been sufficient to drive down the prices of the shares. The market would have come to Hanover's rescue. Just as Edwin Lefèvre said decades ago, the bear raider would have been "up against the best kind of inside buying." That didn't happen because there was no market for these stocks outside Hanover. Its prices were artificially boosted to provide under-the-table payoffs, or rips, to the brokers.

The shorts gave Hanover a taste of the free market—and it was bitter as hell.

The people who put Hanover out of business weren't angels. Some of them were traders at Sovereign Equity Management Group, a brokerage that prosecutors later contended was controlled by Phil Abramo, a capo in the De-Cavalcante crime family. The DeCavalcante crime family and the other shorts were not in the investor-protection business. Yet, purely out of greed, they were able to do something that the NASD and SEC weren't contemplating, which was to shut down a firm that was ripping off investors.

By putting Hanover out of business, the shorts protected investors from being ripped off by the firm in the future. They didn't hurt Hanover's current investors because they were doomed anyway. Customers were not allowed to sell their shares at elevated prices—Hanover had strict rules against that, like most chop houses. The purpose of a rig is to make money for the broker, not for the customer.

Except for standing around with their hands in their pockets and investi-gating the wrong people, the denizens of our self-regulatory pyramid reacted to the Hanover fraud in classic, somnolent fashion. Hanover's principals and bro-kers melted away, moving on to other firms, where they ripped off investors un-til the law-enforcement crackdown years later.

The Hanover stocks were special stocks, and special stocks require a special kind of short-selling. There is only one way to short-sell the schlock stocks that most richly deserve to be shorted. The technique that put Hanover out of busi-ness was known as naked short-selling.

As rigged stocks, the Hanover shares were controlled entirely by the scam-sters. We've already seen how shares must be borrowed if they are to be shorted. So how did the shorts borrow Hanover shares for the purpose of selling them short? Simple. They didn't borrow them. They just sold stocks that didn't exist. That is the only way to disrupt stock rigs.

We'll be dealing with naked shorting in the next chapter. Suffice to say, for the time being, that there's no question that naked shorting bends, or even breaks, the rules that govern short-selling. That is not because naked shorting is wrong. It is because the rules are wrong. Rule-breaking as it is, naked shorting performs the greater good of allowing the free markets into a region of the mar-ket that is the least free, the most prone to manipulation, and the most in need of bearish input into the price-discovery mechanism. Naked shorting breaks a window that lets in some fresh air and lets out the stench.

Opponents of naked shorting, however, have duped a lot of people into believing that the problem isn't overinflated stocks. They want you to believe that the problem is overinflated stocks collapsing. What their arguments ignore is that *overinflated stocks always collapse when the rig ends*. It's inevitable. It happens 100 percent of the time. Naked short-selling, when it exists, just accelerates the process—which is good for investors, because the sooner an overinflated stock collapses, the sooner the rig is stopped. What difference does it make whether a rig is stopped by a regulator or a naked short-seller?

In fact, a fine line separates naked shorting from ordinary, perfectly legal trading. Brokers sometimes have to do that—sell stocks to their customers that are not in the inventory. None other than Bobby Catoggio lamented that he didn't go short when he sold his customers Hanover's scuzzball stocks. It was pretty routine among the chop houses for brokers to sell more stocks to their customers than they had in inventory.

A lot of the guff surrounding naked short-selling involves that word. *Naked* is a Street term that means "unhedged." Every day, thousands of people engage in the perfectly legal practice of selling call options, in which they agree to sell a stock at a certain price. A good many of them don't own the stock they've agreed to sell. This is called writing a naked call option. That's risky, but you can do it if you fill out the right forms, and it's perfectly legal. Selling a call option on a stock that you do own is called writing a covered call.

See? You can get "naked" yourself, right there in the privacy of your brokerage account, and nobody will hold it against you.

Being a naked short-seller of a stock is similar to selling a naked call option. In both situations one creates a position in one's portfolio that didn't previously exist, for the purpose of betting on the future price movement of the stock. The difference is that naked shorting of stocks is something only professional investors—mainly brokerages—have been able to do, by exploiting loopholes in the existing rules.

If anything, regulators should be working to make it easier for people to short microcaps, so that you or I or anyone can do so. Sure, buying individual stocks is a bad idea. Buying microcap stocks is an even worse idea. But since people have the ability to buy those doggies, they should be able to short them too. If a certain stock is a pile of dung, that is all the more reason to short it, whether or not the shares are available to be borrowed. It wasn't fair that only a few market players, some allegedly Mob-affiliated, were able to make a bearish bet against Hanover Sterling stocks. If it had been possible for any investor to short those stocks as easily as buy them, the Hanover rig would have been nipped in the bud and thousands of investors would not have been ripped off. The same holds true for just about every stock rig.

In his 2001 book *Sold Short,* the usually unrestrained Manuel Asensio doesn't say anything about naked short-selling per se. But he does make a valid point: It should be allowed. Or, as he put it in his book, daintily not using the term, the borrowing requirement for short-selling should be abolished. Asensio argued, "If traders can prove they have sufficient funds to cover fully the risk of any upward price movement, why should it matter whether their particular broker or any broker happens to have shares of that stock available to borrow on a particular day?" Asensio's Web site includes a well-reasoned analysis of short-selling's impact on stock fraud. He's right. Unfortunately, Asensio is such a loose cannon that his perfectly valid views on the subject have received scant attention.

No matter how much you may dislike individual short-sellers, they are good for you, like spinach. They are the Greek chorus, the naysayers, the whistle-blowers. They are inconvenient but necessary. Short-selling isn't rocket science, and neither is its effect on the markets. It's just as Lefèvre said long ago, in *Reminiscences,* as he contemplated how a bear raid can help investors: "There is nothing mysterious about this. The reason is plain to everybody who will take the trouble to think about it half a minute."

That's all you need to do: Think about it half a minute. Unfortunately that's a lot more thinking than has been devoted to the subject of short-selling by regulators or, too often, the financial press.

CHAPTER SEVENTEEN

THE BALONEY BLITZKRIEG

I n its edition of May 11, 1987, *Business Week* described an intriguing new development in the struggle between microcap-stock promoters and short-sellers. An article by veteran financial writer Chris Welles reported that brokerages under attack by short-sellers, particularly naked short-sellers, had been fighting back. "The infighting is 'very bitter, very personal, and very ugly,'" the magazine reported. The owner of a firm called Creative Securities, which went belly-up in 1985, supposedly because of concerted stark-naked shorting, had filed lawsuits against a brokerage and a journalist accused of being in cahoots with the shorts. Another victim of rapacious shorts, the "small New York firm" Haas Securities, was cited by Welles as an example of how "firms have successfully resisted apparent bear raids." Despite a negative (and, *BW* implied, short-inspired) article in *Barron's,* the prices of Haas stocks hadn't budged.

Why had the shorts behaved so horribly? Why were they persecuting innocent small companies and blameless brokerages? *BW*'s explanation: Microcap fraud was a thing of the past. "The bull market has not produced a lush supply of the shorts' perennial favorites—tiny, overhyped OTC stocks," said Welles. As a result, shorts were "having to bend their criteria and get involved in companies that are more legitimate." Not to worry. The justifiably outraged brokerages were fighting back—and taking their battle to Washington.

It was a remarkable article that would probably have gotten you good and mad—if you happened to be a customer (a better word might be *victim*) of the brokerage mentioned so favorably in the article. As later emerged in civil and criminal cases, the "small New York firm" that had "successfully resisted" shorts, Haas Securities, was in the midst of a $644 million stock-rigging scheme involving all of the Haas stocks cited by *BW* as bear-raid victims. Haas president Stanley Aslanian Jr. later pleaded guilty to securities fraud, and he and his cohorts served prison terms.* It seems that Haas had indeed successfully resisted the shorts—by engaging in the classic investor-gouging, market-manipulating techniques of the microcap-stock fraud that Welles said wasn't happening anymore. As for the lawsuits filed by that feisty guy from Creative Securities—all were later thrown out of court. Another co-founder of Creative was convicted of stock fraud and sentenced to prison.

The short-bashers did manage to get Washington's attention, albeit briefly. After a couple of years of robust pressure, the House Banking Committee held hearings in December 1989 on short-selling abuses. It was a gala event. Typical of the irresponsible rhetoric that was thrown around at the hearings, a Republican congressman named J. Dennis Hastert, the future Speaker of the House of Representatives, described short-selling as "the most blatant thuggery we've had come before this committee in a long time." That caused economist Owen A. Lamont to wonder aloud, in his Yale study of long-short battling years later, "Who was the victim and who was the thug?"

During the hearings, the SEC's associate director of enforcement, John Sturc, testified that "many of the complaints we receive about alleged illegal short-selling come from companies and corporate officers who are themselves under investigation by the Commission or others for possible violations of the securities or other laws." Officials from three public companies testified against short-selling. In subsequent years, Lamont noted in his study, the presidents of two of these three companies were prosecuted for fraud. Sturc's rebuttal of the short-bashing testimony was so effective that one committee member, California congressman and future SEC chairman Christopher Cox, remarked, "Is this subcommittee being snowed?"

The answer was yes. Though naked shorting was against the rules, it was widely viewed by the self-regulatory pyramid back then as a kind of necessary evil—to be tacitly tolerated, and prosecuted only on rare occasions. In the face of this benign regulatory indifference, fueled by the sleaziness of some anti-shorting loudmouths, the anti-short forces faded away. Regulators publicly took the position that naked shorting was a rare occurrence in the markets. This was, in a

---

* *Barron's* swiftly ran a story shredding the *BW* piece, and Welles shot back with a letter attacking the *Barron's* piece, and *Barron's* shot back with an editor's note attacking Welles's response to the *Barron's* story attacking *Business Week*.

sense, a position the regulators had to take. Naked shorting was, after all, not permitted by the rules governing the markets. So they just turned a blind eye to it.

In mid-1987, for instance, an NASD official told *Barron's* that the NASD had received only "ten or so" complaints about naked shorting since the fall of 1986, and couldn't substantiate a single one of them. Imagine that. No naked shorting at all—despite all the shorting that was taking place, as the SEC later acknowledged, against the unborrowable stocks involved in the massive Haas scam?

It was ludicrous—a clear case of regulatory nonfeasance. However, anyone who wanted to keep the stock scamsters at bay could only hope that this nonfeasance would continue forever. There was every reason for optimism. After all, apathy and denial are the two mighty left arms of the self-regulatory pyramid. Put the brakes on short-selling? You couldn't expect the pyramid to do that, even if it were a *good* idea.

Restricting naked short-selling of microcap stocks, the only free-market mechanism capable of taking on stock scamsters, was a bad idea in 1989. It was a bad idea in 1990, and 1991, and every year without exception up to and including 2004. By then it was an even worse idea—because, as we've seen, the microcap market was exploding in the years after the market declines of 2001 and 2002. The dangers of microcap fraud, and the beneficial impact of shorting on stock schemes, were even more widely known than they were in the late 1980s.

Yet something happened in the intervening fifteen years that had gotten the self-regulatory pyramid to start up its engines, click into high gear, and rush into a brick wall. In July 2004, the SEC passed something called Regulation SHO, which effectively put an end to naked short-selling. By early 2005, the most thinly traded, abuse-prone microcap stocks were effectively immunized against the only market force capable of countering the rampant hype and stock-rigging schemes that infest the microcap market.

Why had the SEC done something so dumb? What could possibly have motivated this agency to take such an abysmally ill-advised action, fully fifteen years after its own deputy head of enforcement had testified that complaints about naked shorting tended to come from crummy companies seeking to shift the blame for their own inadequacies?

The reason is a little frightening. The SEC was knuckling under to an aroused quasi-public. Not a genuine public, but rather a phony public, and what makes it scary is that the SEC couldn't tell the difference. A motley coalition of microcap-company officials, deluded investors in doggy microcap stocks, stock promoters, and OTC stock publicists exerted pressure on the self-regulatory pyramid and, ultimately, won. They won, but you lost, if you are foolish enough to venture into the microcap market.

In the process, they provided an excellent example of how a pressure group with nothing on its side—not the facts, not a great many people, nor even a particularly massive amount of money—can carry the day with our self-regulatory pyramid. You just have to be smart—and know what buttons to push. No, I take that back. You just have to know what buttons to push.

After the 1989 House hearings, the campaign against naked shorting went into a kind of remission. There was an occasional flurry of anti-shorting publicity during the 1990s, but nothing much came of such things. Occasionally, cruddy microcap companies would seek to torpedo the shorts by asking their shareholders to request the stock certificates for their shares from their brokers. Doing that screws the shorts by forcing them to close out their positions.* However, through most of the 1990s there was no concerted anti-shorting campaign of the kind that had flared up in the 1980s. The only anti-short activist of note in the mid- to late 1990s was a stock promoter named Ray Dirks, who occasionally publicized the "Shortbuster's Club"—the name he gave to stocks he was pushing on the basis of their high short interest. However, Dirks's aim was to distribute propaganda about marginal stocks pushed by a brokerage firm with which he was associated, not to change the system. Dirks's blathering received little attention, and the self-regulatory pyramid continued to do nothing.

It probably didn't help the short-bashers that Haas's successors in the stock-scam business continued to bear out Sturc's point, by being the ones to scream the loudest about short-selling. The short raid on Hanover Sterling got some media attention, but it didn't rise to the cloud-cuckoo level of the Haas coverage in 1987. Similarly, the media paid little attention when a firm with a name as dishonest as its sales practices—State Street Capital Markets Corp.†—complained in 1996 that naked short-sellers were attacking its stocks. It later was revealed in extensive civil and criminal proceedings, including a March 2000 indictment of several Mob figures, that State was controlled by Mob-linked scam artists, and that its stocks were manipulated up the wazoo.

---

* Stock can be loaned out to short-sellers only from margin accounts in which the shares are held in book-entry form, otherwise known as "Street name." If a shareholder asks for his stock certificates, the stock cannot be loaned to the shorts, and any stock that is already loaned is called back—thereby forcing shorts to buy back the stock they had sold short. That is a quintessential short squeeze.
† No relation to the reputable Boston money management firm State Street Corp. The dirty State Street was also known as White Rock Partners.

It didn't hurt the shorts (though it didn't help much either) that academic studies continued to demonstrate throughout the 1990s that short-selling was a positive force in the markets. One significant academic probe of short-selling, published in 1997, examined shorting on Nasdaq at a time when there were no restrictions on selling during market declines. Researchers at three universities concluded that criticism of short-selling simply had no basis in fact: Shorts, they found, did not destabilize markets by selling into falling markets and exacerbating price drops. As usual, this study and others like it received little attention outside academia.

Then came the market downturn of 2001 and 2002. Nasdaq stocks were pummeled, OTC volume collapsed, and so did the prices of OTC stocks. A few distant rumblings could be heard, as the short-bashers began a new campaign aimed at blaming everybody but the scuzzy companies themselves for their falling share prices. Beginning in 2002, it was almost as if the loony "long-versus-short" days of 1987 were being played out again. Company after company began to call for investors to obtain the stock certificates for their shares as a way of manufacturing short squeezes.

Among the most voluble of the OTC short-bashers were two obscure companies, Universal Express and GeneMax. In 2002 and 2003, these two companies were putting out scads of press releases railing against naked short-sellers. They also commenced lawsuits against brokerages and others the two companies blamed for conspiring with the shorts to push down their share prices, and the suits generated still more press releases. These companies were unrelated, and their campaigns against short-sellers were separate and uncoordinated. They had only one thing in common: a hatred of short-sellers. No, make that two things in common: a hatred of short-sellers and the fact that their stocks weren't very good investments. Both were dogs as stocks and money losers as companies. Even one of Gayle Essary's rent-an-analysts could cough up only a "speculative" rating on Universal Express in its last analyst report in July 2003.

A lot of the anti-shorting noise was blaring from a stock-promotion firm that handled GeneMax's investor relations, and was so cozy with GeneMax that it had the same address. The name of that firm was called Investor Communications International. ICI, which represented a bunch of other OTC firms in addition to GeneMax, formed a National Association Against Naked Short-Selling. Its membership included GeneMax and other ICI clients. By January 2003 the NAANS had a Web site up and running and spewing forth the following line of drivel:

**This is a call to action for all OTC Bulletin Board
listed public companies . . .**

Corporate America is under siege! Not by terrorism, but rather by
an unethical market practice that is destroying emerging public
companies and undermining the trust of small investors. It's called
naked short selling and it is illegal, according to the rules of the
NASD and US Securities and Exchange Commission (SEC). The
problem is that this fact hasn't stopped the broad group of Market
Makers, Clearing Houses and Securities firms that are still using
this practice to ruin hundreds and hundreds of companies across
the country all in the name of profits.

It was a repetition of the hooey that was pushed, without success, by the anti-
short people in the late 1980s. But there was something new. The appeal had a
clever twist.

What followed—under the heading "What can you do to defend your
company?"—was mainly a description of what the *NAANS* could do, and indeed was about to do. What it had in mind had only rarely been attempted by
the short-haters: a concerted campaign of old-fashioned, all-American flesh-
pressing, buttonholing, and lobbying. In addition to meeting with members of
Congress and "leading government representatives to rally support from within
the highest levels of government," NAANS planned to start a PR campaign to
"win the support of the government and the investing public."

It was a stroke of public-relations genius. After all, short-selling was inherently unpopular, and its impact on the microcap market was not widely known
or understood, making it ripe for attack. By March 2003, the NAANS had
come up with an even better way to spin naked shorting. It was a *"devastating
counterfeit stock scheme."*

It was so brilliant, so imaginative, and so downright wrong that the staid
Wall Street paper-pushers at the Depository Trust & Clearing Corporation, a
not-for-profit company that handles the mechanics of trading for Wall Street
firms, had to post a rebuttal on its Web site vigorously denying this off-the-wall
accusation—which had been raised in a lawsuit against DTCC that had been
tossed out of court.

The DTCC noted, just as the SEC's Sturc had pointed out to Congress
years before, that many of the firms that were hollering about naked shorting
had "little or no revenue, according to their financial reports, and substantial
losses, for periods of seven or eight years." The DTCC pointed out that one of

these companies had been cited for failing to file financial statements since 2001. Another had been chided by the SEC for press releases that spun fairy tales about nonexistent business plans. "They will do anything they can do that takes people's attention off that kind of record," said DTCC first deputy general counsel Larry Thompson, "especially if they can convince a law firm to take the case on a contingency basis, which is what has happened."

The DTCC was right—not that it mattered. The hysterical stock-counterfeiting charge was so enticing that it appeared to pique the interest of the news program *Dateline NBC,* according to emails and posts that flooded the Web in 2004 and 2005. The story went out over the Web throughout the early part of 2005 that NBC had put together a massive exposé of stock counterfeiting. There was even an "airdate"—April 10, 2005—that was repeatedly trumpeted on Gayle Essary's FinancialWire and even a Universal Express press release. When that day came and went without the show being aired, the short-bashing community howled in protest, and some saw the hidden, invidious hand of the dastardly Depository Trust & Clearing Corporation.

Only a small number of people were spreading these silly tales. Gayle Essary pushed the anti-naked-shorting line hard in his FinancialWire news service, hacking away at naked shorting as a "national financial scandal." Gayle's contribution to the cause was a drumbeat of "coverage" and a label, "Stock-Gate," which was catchy enough but didn't get much attention except from the true believers. Still, Gayle made good use of it. "In yet another stunning development in the StockGate saga that has roiled the financial industry," was how Gayle, a master of understatement, began an April 2005 FinancialWire item on naked shorting. Gayle also made considerable hay from the nonairing of the *Dateline NBC* report, a routine delay he slammed as a "First Amendment issue." Gayle named the "powerful and reclusive" DTCC as a "prime suspect" in what he described as the "sudden and inexplicable 'indefinite postponement'" of "what was expected to have been a shocking expose of the DTCC's purported role now and over the years in the counterfeiting of electronic certificates supporting illegal naked short sales."

Another major anti-shorting campaigner was Richard A. Altomare, CEO of the short-fighting Universal Express. Altomare's company was at least as adept at putting out press releases as it was at its core business of shipping stuff. Universal Express churned out a bunch of increasingly outraged statements throughout 2003 lashing out at the curse of naked short-selling. One missive that Universal sent out to the media in October 2003 exhibited the kind of cool, dispassionate reasoning one had come to expect from the short-bashers. This one called naked shorting "economic terrorism" and announced that Altomare was heading to Washington, in suitably Capraesque fashion, to press his case with lawmakers and the SEC.

In late 2003 and early 2004, this invigorating picture of folksy populism was darkened. Word crept out on the Internet, and was picked up by the media, that the president of ICI was named in SEC documents as a stock promoter named Brent Pierce, who was barred for fifteen years by securities regulators in Vancouver.* ICI's links to GeneMax also were publicized, as was the relationship between GeneMax's sometime CFO James D. Davidson and a stock-touting newsletter publisher called Agora Inc.—which Davidson founded and which was charged with stock fraud by the SEC in April 2003. (Davidson wasn't charged, and Agora was still fighting the charges two years later.)

Similar difficulties befell the shipping-and-press-release magnate. The SEC sued Altomare, his company, and others for stock fraud in March 2004. The suit sought to bar Altomare from serving as an officer of any public company in the future, asserting that Universal issued a series of false press releases from May 2002 to April 2003, and "thereafter made other false statements in public interviews, press releases, and Universal's filings with the Commission." The SEC also said that the company's claims of naked short-selling were unsubstantiated.

Well, you can rest assured that none of this had any effect on the flow of anti-shorting propaganda from Universal Express or its crusading CEO. The SEC suit made Universal Express even more teed off. The company erupted with outrage at what it described as SEC retaliation for its outspoken anti-naked-shorting stance, and the rest of the short-bashing community rallied around. If anything, the rhetoric climbed up a notch, as Universal publicized its own suit against the SEC, filed a few weeks before the SEC legal salvo in March 2004. No, the company asserted in legal papers, that was not a preemptive move. Clearly it would take more than a mere SEC lawsuit to deter people quite so dedicated and persistent.

For a long time it seemed that the short-bashers' vigorous pursuit of publicity was a failure. There was little of the half-witted press coverage of the

---

* ICI, understandably, has not clutched Brent Pierce to its corporate bosom. SEC documents in 1999 and 2002 listed him as president. ICI said in January 2003 that Pierce was currently a consultant to ICI, and that he was "the owner of ICI during a brief period of 2000 for purposes related to litigation" (whatever that means). In March 2003, ICI said Pierce was "neither a director nor officer of ICI."

kind that had been bestowed on the short-bashing stock swindlers at Haas years before. In retrospect—given the short-bashers' effectiveness and the harm they ultimately caused to the microcap markets—there probably *should* have been media attention, but not the kind of media attention desired by the anti-shorters. The exceptions to the near-universal media indifference were sparse, and included *Forbes,* Carol Remond of Dow Jones Newswires—but not her corporate brethren at the *Wall Street Journal*—and Herb Greenberg of MarketWatch.com.* Another rare voice of reason came from the Internet blog of Mark Cuban, owner of the Dallas Mavericks and a critic of the campaign against naked shorting. *Barron's,* which practically owned the story in the late eighties, didn't have much to say on the subject this time around. The *New York Times* weighed in with a gently critical piece on the anti-naked-shorters, but only after Regulation SHO was a reality.

The ICI and its "coalition" faded away during 2004, but the anti-shorting campaign was taken up by others, grabbing the flag before it touched the ground. Cynically dishonest Web sites appeared with misleading watchdog-type names, such as investigatethesec.com, aimed at advancing the harebrained "stock counterfeiting" cock-and-bull story. Anti-shorting emails flowed like a Niagara of raw virtual sewage to the media, regulators, and anyone who seemed even slightly interested, or not interested at all.

Their contents were the usual combination of lies, exaggerations, and sheer fantasy. A typical 2004 missive, churned out by one of the leading Patrick Henrys of the anti-short campaign, read as follows:

> At the present time everybody from President Bush, into the halls of Congress, through to the Department of Justice and settling in the Chair of Bill Donaldson are aware of the abusive practice of Naked Shorting and the impact this is having on small business. Wall Street has completely rewrote the economics of supply and demand as it relates to Securities trading and has created massive imbalance on the books of our Broker Dealers by overselling small business stocks without ever settling the trades. The SEC went so far as to admit that stocks were oversold to a point where trade settlement failures exceeded the entire float of publicly traded companies.

---

* I'll modestly consign to a footnote my pro-naked-shorting piece, "Don't Force the Shorts to Get Dressed," which ran in *BW* on December 8, 2003.

The endless stream of repetitive, shrill, and increasingly bizarre arguments might have made it seem, to those on the receiving end, as if they were working as USDA inspectors at an Oscar Mayer meat-processing plant. It was like the old TV commercial jingle, "My baloney has a first name, it's N-A-K-E-D. My baloney has a second name, it's . . ." It was just baloney, more baloney, and still more baloney—and as it continued through 2003, the sheer weight of it all was beginning to take effect. The opponents of naked shorting were doing more than just sending tired arguments and idiotic rhetoric by email. They were personally delivering their baloney to the SEC and members of Congress.

On October 28, 2003, the SEC caved in. The pinnacle of our self-regulatory pyramid decided that the time had come to shut down K Street and hold a Baloney Festival. The SEC published for comment a rule proposal that would put the brakes on naked short-selling. Regulation SHO was born.

Now, it must be underlined at this point that the only thing that had changed from previous years was the Baloney Blitzkrieg I just described. This is crucial, because it speaks volumes about the impact of a sustained campaign on the self-regulatory pyramid. Nothing else had happened to warrant Regulation SHO. There had been no sudden spate of naked shorting, no new evidence, no gigantic scandal in the headlines, no market crash that demanded a scapegoat, no dramatic academic or GAO or regulatory study that demonstrated graphically how the microcap-stock market was in the grips of naked short-sellers. In fact, the SEC rule writers were unusually succinct when it came to describing the evidence that there was an actual problem they were trying to fix.

That's because there wasn't any evidence.

Although the rule proposal made reference to "increased instances of 'naked' short selling," the SEC was able to site a grand total of only *one* naked-shorting case in the rule proposal. That involved a hedge fund called Rhino Advisors, which allegedly manipulated downward the shares in a company called Sedona to cash in on a debenture. Hardly a bear-raid situation or an example of "stock counterfeiting"—a bit of sheer crapola nowhere mentioned in the SEC rule proposal, or, for that matter, anywhere outside the fantasies of the short-bashers.

If the SEC bureaucrats were going to get those persistent baloney-pushing short-bashers off their backs, they would have to get the Street on their side, or at least not in opposition. After all, our self-regulatory pyramid knows who's boss—they don't call our system of securities regulation "captured by the industry" for nothing. The SEC softened any impact on the Street by including in its proposal a two-year suspension of enforcement of the uptick rule—which bans shorting when prices are falling—for the largest and most widely traded stocks. (To be exact, the SEC proposed a technical change in the uptick rule, and a pilot program suspending all restrictions for the biggest stocks.) By so doing, the SEC was able to keep the Street happy, because large firms do a lot of short-selling of large companies but only rarely short-sell microcaps.

Bill Donaldson's SEC could breathe a sigh of relief. Wall Street's reaction was mixed. While the Street clearly preferred the status quo, it could live with naked-shorting restrictions, with some minor changes that were incorporated in the proposal. Not a word was said in favor of naked shorting as a curb on market abuses—not by the Street establishment, not by the Securities Industry Association, and not by the large Street firms that sent in comment letters.

In contrast to the Street's mild reaction, and the polite, deferential responses the SEC usually gets to its rule proposals, the bulk of comments were mass-produced from supposed members of the public and had all the subtlety, and intellectual finesse, of email spams—which is precisely what some of them were. By 2003, the SEC was accepting comments by email. They didn't have to be signed. They didn't even have to make sense. One person was free to use five, six, a dozen, or a hundred email addresses to push the same repetitive argument, and the SEC had no way of knowing.

So this is what the SEC got, by the dozens:

Dear Sirs,

*THE SEC (THE BIG QUESTION MARK—PROACTIVE-
REACTIVE—IDLE??)*

For those living the battle cry of positive pro-active reforms out of the Securities and Exchange Commission, may expect to wait a long time. The fact is, the SEC, as recently observed, cannot bring them selves to enforce existing rules or enact appropriate legislation to curtail the rampant fraudulent practices of Wall Street.

The SEC received 21 comment letters/emails with that precise wording—the agency's comment compilers called it "Letter Type B"—as well as dozens of others conveying the same elegant-as-peanut-butter message in boilerplate letters from people who were all fired up about naked short-selling but didn't quite know why. In all, the SEC received 462 comment letters/emails, the vast majority of which were produced by the Baloney Brigade. The SEC found itself having to prepare a sixty-two-page summary of the baloney barrage, most of which had a common denominator. "Despite contrasting opinions," the SEC summary said, "the comments appeared to share an underlying concern with the use of manipulative devices as a means to control stock prices."

The status quo, tempting as it might be, could not remain unchanged in the face of all this supposed public outrage—when, that is, it could be addressed without discomfiting the regulators' friends and future employers on Wall Street. Meanwhile, the villains of this regulatory drama, the supposed utilizers of "manipulative devices" to "control stock prices"—the naked shorts—were caught in a vise. They were violating the rules. They couldn't exactly admit to doing that, could they? One can go on and on about how naked shorting helps the free market, but going public with a defense of naked shorting won't do you any good if it means that you have to fend off the SEC or NASD as a result. A couple of shorts contributed cogent but—hardly helping their case—anonymous comment letters via email, and there were letters from law firms representing understandably unidentified clientele.

The few comment letters opposing Regulation SHO had a sad, pathetic, almost pleading tone. Is this really happening? Is it really necessary to tell the SEC that cutting back on naked shorting will hurt, not help, the markets, and that the main problem with microcap stocks—one that the SEC itself had proven time and again—was not short-selling but rather upward price manipulation?

The Washington law firm of Pickard and Djinis, representing an unidentified Canadian investment dealer, made a rare rational argument by noting that Regulation SHO "will remove an important market constraint on pricing inefficiencies and upward manipulations attempted or occurring with respect to such securities." In fact, said the firm, the proposed rule "plays directly into the hands of such manipulators. Indeed, the regulation actually would have the effect of encouraging manipulative tactics that involve restricting the supply of securities."

The few intelligent comments pointed out the utter absence of evidence that naked shorting hurt the markets. There were only "sketchily alleged and apparently unproven 'abuses' by short sellers," said the law firm of Feldman Weinstein LLP on behalf of a client or clients unknown. The firm went on to plead with the SEC not to put "a series of new tools at the hands of the promoters of penny-stock 'pump and dump' schemes to work their frauds."

At the very moment those soon-to-be-ignored words were being fruitlessly committed into writing, the SEC had plenty of evidence to rebut the wild accusations of the short-scapegoating baloney purveyors. One study was in the process of being conducted for the SEC by a visiting economist, Leslie Boni of the University of New Mexico. She found that Regulation SHO would hurt the liquidity of the market as a whole—with OTC and Pink Sheet stocks among the hardest hit. Boni found that naked shorting took place more frequently than had been previously believed, and that cutting back on it would mean "illiquid, expensive-to-borrow stocks may be more likely to experience temporary short squeezes and increased price volatility."

Microcap-stock pushers and the Baloney Brigade may not care, but you should care—and the SEC is legally obliged to care—about that kind of stuff. Lack of liquidity is *always* bad for investors. This evidence of Regulation SHO's potential harm to the market* was published after the dirty deed was done, but the intellectual vacuity of Regulation SHO was obvious long before it was proposed. Besides, you don't need a study by the Physics Department of the Massachusetts Institute of Technology, replete with Venn diagrams and foot-pound calculations, to know that gazing down the hose of a running vacuum cleaner is not a good idea.

The fundamental flaw with the Boni study and the few anti-SHO letters was that they were true and contained facts—and such irrelevancies were ground into dust like the French army in 1940 by the persistent, well-organized Baloney Blitzkrieg. In July 2004, exactly nine months after Regulation SHO was proposed—a veritable rapier-thrust by SEC standards—the rule was adopted, with some changes but with its most damaging anti-shorting provisions intact.

The new rules didn't completely outlaw naked short-selling, but made it costly and troublesome, effectively crippling it as a microcap trading strategy. Beginning on January 3, 2005, a broker could not allow a short sale of a stock unless he had "reasonable grounds to believe that the security can be borrowed so that it can be delivered" when due. Just to make sure that the shorts didn't sleaze their way around that requirement, the SEC cleverly required regulators farther down the pyramid to publish lists of "threshold" securities—stocks in

---

* Opponents of naked shorting seized on Boni's conclusion that naked shorting was more widespread than previously believed, but ignored the stuff about short curbs increasing volatility and hurting liquidity.

which there are an abundance of "fails to deliver." That is, stocks sold but not actually delivered. That includes naked short sales—because you can't deliver a stock you didn't borrow in the first place. (Fails can be caused by a lot of things other than naked shorting, however—something foes of short-selling usually ignore.)

Clearing firms—the big outfits that handle trades for the smaller brokerages—were now required to close out fails involving threshold stocks if the fail persisted for ten days. The SEC had proposed two days, but the Securities Industry Association, speaking for the Street, had said that was too short and ten days would be better—so ten days it was. However, the SIA had no objection to the threshold lists, so that was that. The threshold lists remained.

Short-sellers who engage in microcap shorting tell me that the rules were a snazzy contrast to much of what emerges from the SEC. Regulation SHO was well-drafted and effective. Shorts who bet against unborrowable microcaps now risked being squeezed like a lemon, and that was not a risk worth taking. Even the stocks that could be borrowed became costly to borrow. Thanks to this gratuitous SEC meddling with the free markets, brokers started charging for the privilege of loaning out scarce small-cap stocks to short-sellers, making the whole process uneconomical for vast numbers of stocks.

The wretched impact of Regulation SHO became evident well before the worst parts of the new rule took effect in January 2005. By then, the shorts had already quietly folded up their tents and stalked off without a word, leaving the microcap market to the promoters, paid-research hype-masters, and fraudsters. After Regulation SHO, shorts quietly confined themselves to shorting stocks that they could borrow. The worst stocks, the manipulated stocks, couldn't be shorted anymore because they couldn't be borrowed, so the shorting in them dried up. Today a Hanover Sterling would be unmolested by shorts, free to rip off the public.

You can't blame the shorts for cutting out. The free market is not a charity bake sale. Market participants are in it to make money for themselves—whether their impact is bad, indifferent, or, as in this case, good for the markets and good for small investors.

It was a clear victory, but the short-bashers weren't satisfied. The Baloney Brigade rolled on, crushing the white flags of the enemy beneath the treads of their Sherman tanks.

The reason victory had not brought peace was that the victors had not, and would never, achieve their objective—which was to elevate the prices of the worst stocks in the world. With the short-sellers all but extinct, anticipated short squeezes did not take place, so prices of slimeball stocks usually did not go up. Still, that was no reason to stop the Baloney Blitzkrieg. On the contrary, there was every reason to continue it. Naked shorting was more necessary as a scapegoat than ever before. It was a permanent war for the sake of having a permanent enemy and a permanent scapegoat, very much as in George Orwell's *1984*.

So the war continued. It is still being waged as I write these words, and it will no doubt be waged after these pages have turned yellow with age, and will be waged when your children and grandchildren bounce their great-grandchildren on their knees. Great battles are like that, particularly when they are waged in the realm of fantasy.

Among the leaders of the anti-shorting forces in the post-victory offensive, standing upright in a staff car, was the press-release-happy OTC shipping magnate Rich Altomare of Universal Express, wearing his multipronged SEC litigation as a badge of honor. In April 2005, his company issued a press release announcing positive developments in its lawsuit against the SEC. Compensatory damages in the suit were "now estimated to exceed $1.4 Billion." The suit "will now be considered by the United States Court of Appeals for the Eleventh Circuit, the second highest Court in America. We anticipate that this venue will be less expensive with a shorter deliberation outcome than a full Jury trial of such importance, which would have been appealed inevitably by either side." The reason the suit was moving to an appellate court was not mentioned—it had been thrown out of a lower court. A mere detail when massive fraud was under way!

"Imagine that trillions of shares," the press release continued, "questionable compensation to the SEC, billions of dollars of un-owned securities stolen from thousands of companies and hundreds of thousands of stockholders should all be 'grandfathered' simply because the SEC decreed it should, without financial settlement of these massive illegal short stock positions!"

It had to be imagined, because it wasn't happening.

In the early months of 2005, after it became apparent that ending naked shorting wasn't having an immediate and visible price-boosting effect, the Web page of something called the National Coalition Against Naked Shorting materialized out of the clear blue sky. NCANS billed itself as a "grassroots advocacy group composed of small investors who are tired of the predatory hedge funds on Wall Street violating the rules against naked shorting." Note another old scapegoat, hedge funds, being hauled into the picture. There were plenty of reasons to be concerned about hedge funds, but naked shorting wasn't one of them. As for that "grassroots" thing, the roots were in the soil of the great state of Utah, where NCANS was funded by a businessman named Patrick Byrne. He ran a firm called Overstock.com that was an innocent victim of perfidious naked shorting.

Byrne swiftly emerged as the Douglas MacArthur of the Baloney Blitzkrieg. His Tojo, the villain behind what he claimed was naked shorting of Overstock, was what he described as a "Sith Lord"—a character from the *Star Wars* movies. Some scoffed, but it made perfect sense. Naked shorting was an imaginary problem. So why not blame it all on an imaginary villain?

The short-bashers focused their still considerable energies on the lists of stocks that were supposed to have shouted "Squeeze me!"—the threshold lists. Since these were not being squeezed like a roll of Charmin in those old TV commercials, resentment was building.

One of the short-bashers' 2005 poster children was the donut-franchise company Krispy Kreme. The company's stock was on the threshold lists in early 2005, and yet its price remained stubbornly depressed. How could that be?

There were two possible reasons:

1. *Regulation SHO wasn't working.*
2. *Krispy Kreme's accounting was under investigation by the SEC and federal prosecutors, and the company announced in January 2005 that investors should not rely on its last five years of financial statements.*

Well, I don't have to tell you which of these two possible explanations was the one pushed by the Baloney Brigade, do I?

The NCANS Web site, after pointing out that Krispy Kreme was "down 85% since last fall and 40% since it became a threshold security," went on to observe:

> This indicates to me at least that the covering of the fails is being done at the expense of the investor, wherein the market makers and specialists systematically abuse their privilege, and drive the prices of the SHO companies into the ground to shake out the small investors, thereby providing the necessary shares to solve their big customers' problems.

True, and it could also mean that the shorts were not being squeezed because there were no shorts to squeeze.

With the NCANS, Altomare, and Byrne leading the way, the increasingly surreal, comical-if-it-wasn't-so-dangerous struggle against naked short-selling marched on. Byrne's bankroll meant that the short-busters could occasionally run full-page ads in newspapers such as the *Washington Post,* and that they had an ally in Utah Republican Senator Robert Bennett, who grilled a hapless Bill Donaldson on Regulation SHO at a Senate Banking Committee hearing in April 2005. Still more senators and members of Congress—a few, but that was all you needed—enlisted in the Baloney Brigade.

In mid-2005, the foes of naked shorting made the mistake of consuming their own baloney, and deluded themselves into thinking that there really was a "grassroots coalition" of "investors" who were upset about naked shorting. Demonstrations were organized in Washington and New York in June 2005, at which only a handful of people showed up. A mere dozen could be rustled up to make fools of themselves in front of the NASD building in New York, according to an account in Reuters. Not that it mattered. As advocates of bad causes around the world can tell you, if Reuters shows up, it's a success. So another demonstration was planned, this one in front of the headquarters of the evil DTCC.

The Baloney Blitzkrieg marshaled its forces in front of the DTCC headquarters, at 55 Water Street in lower Manhattan, on July 29, 2005. Providence smiled upon these silly people, bestowing upon them an entirely undeserved break in a heat wave that was plaguing the city. The forces of baloney came prepared with their own camera crew—a fellow named Oscar, who had obtained the police permit for the demonstration, was on hand to film a documentary about this blight upon the nation's markets. The demonstrators were dressed as they would for a backyard barbecue, and proceeded to skewer the truth for a few hours as they paraded in front of bored office workers, carrying yellow-on-black signs with slogans such as COUNTERFEITING STOCKS IS A CRIME and COUNTERFEIT SECURITIES ARE DESTROYING AMERICA. A brochure was handed out—"WALL STREET'S NEXT NIGHTMARE! *FINANCIAL TERRORISM*"—as New York police, diverted from watching for the real thing, looked on impassively.

The spectators, mostly office workers on rational errands such as obtaining coffee from the takeout across the street, were puzzled by all the bizarre anger being directed in their general direction. "Naked shorting? We don't do that here," said one puzzled gent, an older man, to his friends. He might have been from DTCC or he might have been from Standard & Poor's, which occupies space in the same building. Whichever his employer, his sentiments were, of course, correct.

The paid-research guy Gayle Essary was there—not joining the demonstration, he told me, as befits a newsman—handing out leaflets on his own crusade against DTCC, which he blamed for his FinancialWire "news" service being yanked by a newspaper that distributed it over the Yahoo! wire. Gayle was dressed with dignity in a gray suit, and another man showed respect for the occasion by coming to the demonstration in an undertaker-dark suit, smoking a cigar, accompanied by his similarly attired son, both as somber as professional mourners. He described himself as a self-employed provider of financial services, and railed against naked short-selling as I took notes and the two of us were filmed by Oscar's cameraman.

It was a good-natured crowd—people who had a cause, and were exercising their right to demonstrate. These people cared about their cause. One of them had composed a country song, "The Ballad of Naked Shortee," or words to that effect, and it blared on occasion from a speaker, giving the whole demonstration a kind of tailgate-party, down-home, festive air. These were people who, thankfully, did not take themselves too seriously. I doubted—until I talked to them—that they truly believed the nonsense on their signs. One female participant in the demonstration wore a realistic-looking bare-behind prosthesis and a sign saying DTCC—COVER YOUR SHAME! Another participant, who described himself as a "self-employed security consultant," drove up in a black Ford Focus, upon which were scrawled the words STOCKGATE and THE SEC SUCKS and DO YOU OWN REAL STOCKS? and GOT CMKX?

CMKX was the stock symbol of a Las Vegas company called CMKM Diamonds, and appeared to be a subject of angst for these demonstrators. I learned that most of them were participants in an online chat room devoted to CMKM and its woes—its persecution by the SEC, the "counterfeiting" of its stock. The plight of CMKM was on caps and on signs as well as on the Ford Focus, and one fellow—who would give me his Internet handle but not his name—had it emblazoned on a red T-shirt.

The Ford Focus guy, Barry Shipes, explained that he had bought the company with that particular stock symbol about a year before, and that the stock had declined. He blamed the shorts. "I absolutely feel in my heart of hearts that this company has been naked-shorted on a daily basis by millions and millions of shares." My suggestion that this alleged short-selling presented a buying opportunity was rejected by Mr. Snipes. Later I found out that he had some basis for this position. The stock's days in the market were, apparently, numbered.

The SEC had ordered a temporary trading halt in the company's stock in March 2005, claiming that CMKM had not filed the annual and quarterly reports required by law. The last time it had done so, in September 2002, the company's financial statements had a charming, piggy-bank quality to them that would arouse the paternal feelings in most any investor, because most any investor not residing on skid row would have more money in the bank. At the time, CMKM had total assets of $344, all in cash, and total liabilities of $1,672. The absence of financial statements since then did not bother the people on the picket line, but this did: In May 2005, SEC administrative law judge Brenda P. Murray had held a hearing to determine whether the registration of the company's shares should be suspended or revoked.

Several demonstrators made angry references to the hearing, but it wasn't until after I looked up the decision that I could understand what they were talking about. Then it was my turn to be puzzled. By my reading of Murray's decision, it was a little surprising that the demonstrators were picketing DTCC and not the CMKM headquarters in Vegas.

They might have had trouble finding it. According to Murray's decision, CMKM's supposed executive offices were "occupied only by a hot rod shop." Murray did not even seem to buy that the company had an actual business, saying it was "purportedly engaged in the business of mineral exploration." CMKM's chairman, CEO, and cochairman of the two-person board of directors, Urban Casavant, refused to testify, invoking his Fifth Amendment right against self-incrimination.

None of this troubled the demonstrators. Neither did the SEC judge's finding that CMKM had not been totally honest and forthcoming with either the people on the picket line or the agency. Murray ruled that the company had told the SEC it didn't have to file with the agency when it really did. She said it had "deprived shareholders and investors of material information," and "promoted the company to investors through informal news releases and public statements that contained false information," and "operated in secret, revealing scant information to the investing public regarding its purported multi-million dollar transactions and stock issuances." Murray said a lot more in her fourteen-page decision, all unflattering stuff like that, which had nothing to do with naked shorting and hence did not bother the demonstrators.

What made the demonstrators' indifference even stranger was that this decision had not been handed down somewhere in the dim mists of time. It had been issued on July 12, 2005, a little more than two weeks before.

Assuming these were actual investors in the company and not paid shills—

I had no reason to assume the latter—then people who had innocently purchased shares in a crummy company had channeled their rage against a nonexistent enemy. It was weird. No, it was more than weird. It was sick.

There is a silver lining to all this. There has to be, if one has any faith in the existence of a merciful, forgiving Supreme Being presiding over an orderly universe. The short-bashers' Baloney Blitzkrieg demonstrates how the immobile, status quo-loving self-regulatory pyramid can be pushed into action if pressured to do so—even by a small band of self-interested loudmouths. Imagine what can happen if broad numbers of investors, representing the thousands of ripped-off and teed-off investors, were to use the same techniques of the phony, cynical—but dismayingly effective—short-bashers, this time to protest *real* abuses, not victimless, craftily manipulated baloney. The mind boggles.

CHAPTER EIGHTEEN

FIGHTING BACK

T he naked short-sellers had an Achilles' heel: Publicity was simply not in their best interests. Publicity attracts lawsuits, harassment from short-haters, and regulatory attention of the kind that sent Amr Elgindy and Manuel Asensio on trips down the Via Dolorosa (with flagellation thrown in at no extra charge). When Regulation SHO materialized in the distance like the mother ship in *Mars Attacks!*, naked shorts knew they had to keep their mouths shut or prepare to be zapped with death rays. Not a single naked short-seller was prepared to come out of the closet and scream, "We're naked, we're short, and we're proud!"

The Baloney Blitzkrieg also exposed the myopia of supposed investor advocates. Eliot Spitzer wasn't coming anywhere near this one. The institutional investors who had proven effective in areas of far less concern to investors, such as the Dick Grasso saga, were AWOL. Ditto for the American Association of Individual Investors and Consumer Federation of America. Ditto for the American Association of Retired Persons—even though senior citizens are perennial victims of stock scams—and the other scattered, disorganized investor advocates.

One longtime advocate for the small investor was particularly disappointing. The North American Securities Administrators Association, which ordinarily can be expected to stand up for investors, signed up for a hitch with the Baloney Brigade. NASAA was early and forthright in publicizing the menace of microcap fraud in the mid-1990s, and though state regulators didn't show much clout before Spitzer, their hearts were usually in the right place. Not this time. Here's an excerpt from NASAA's comment letter on Regulation SHO: "From the time the so-called 'naked short selling' controversy was initially identified in early 2003 by national commentators, a NASAA Project Group has monitored this issue from the perspective of its impact on small-business issuers, the securities of which are traded in the over-the-counter market, as well as their public stockholders, who have contended that the trading market for their shares has been adversely affected by manipulative short selling activity."

"National commentators"? Though the media had hardly been shrieking on the subject, most of the media coverage had been skeptical at best, and the coverage in 2003 highlighted the questionable character of the naked-short advocates. "Impact on small-business issuers"? "Public stockholders"? It was as if the Baloney Blitzkrieg were spreading a disease and NASAA had caught it—an acute case of "naked-shorting astigmatism." NASAA had a choice—it could have sided with investors, or it could have backed the issuers and promoters of OTC stocks. NASAA chose the OTC-stock crowd, and by late 2005 the group was firmly in the anti-naked-shorting camp. It was a disgraceful performance.

If the forces that have traditionally restrained Wall Street cannot be counted on to protect your rights, you have to step into the breach. You may be wondering, "Isn't that why I pay taxes? Isn't that what the SEC is for?" It is. That's the problem.

The conventional wisdom is along the lines of, "Well, we're stuck with it." In a *New Yorker* column on the boiler-room kingpin Allen Wolfson, James Surowiecki observed in June 2005 that the "current system depends in large part on an assortment of short sellers . . . Web sites, and investigative journalists to sniff out scams. But this vigilante system doesn't work very well." Surowiecki observed that "investors don't have the tools for uncovering fraud that the SEC has. We don't depend on private citizens to stop street crime. Why should we depend on them to stop crime on the Street?"

The answer is that we have no other choice—and that it's not just crime on the Street that requires citizen intervention but the whole gamut of issues facing investors. Comparisons with the Old West are a little too facile—nobody is getting shot off his horse like John H. Tunstall in the Lincoln County War—but the situation is broadly analogous. When the law is weak or unavailable or openly siding with the bad guys, what's the public to do? The natural reaction is to step into the breach. When the citizen—investor or short-seller—works lawfully to supplement law enforcement or regulators, that can and should be encouraged.

Besides, what if Surowiecki's premise is incorrect? What if ordinary citizens have as many of the tools for uncovering fraud as the SEC, and sometimes do a better job of using them?

The Internet is the powerful, and underutilized, tool that Wall Street would dearly love for you not to use. You need to take back the Internet from the Baloney Blitzkrieg, the stock hucksters, spam pushers, and Wall Street touts. If they can create a phony "coalition" against naked short-selling, why can't there be a real coalition to bring back naked short-selling, or abolish Regulation SHO, or get rid of pay-to-play, or force mutual funds to stop taking money from brokerages? Or a coalition to put an end to mandatory securities arbitration? Or a coalition to fight unfair mutual fund fees or microcap fraud or hedge fund leverage or any number of real—as opposed to imaginary, phony-baloney—problems?

Think of it: a *real* coalition, coalescing around a *real* problem. Such coalitions might begin in the virtual realm but move swiftly over to the real world, as the Howard Dean campaign demonstrated in 2004. The Internet has its limitations, but one undeniable attribute is that it is superb at rallying the troops and bringing together people from disparate backgrounds.

Properly used, the Internet can apply serious pressure on the people with their hands in your pocket. Exposure is their Achilles' heel too. We saw glimpses of that in the last chapter—the skeletons that were in the closets (or sometimes sitting in the living rooms) of some of the companies and stock promoters who were fighting the naked shorters. They're afraid of exposure, and will fight harshly against it, not because they are violating a few house rules while serving the common good, as are the naked shorters, but because they serve a narrow interest group—themselves.

You can get under the skin of the most arrogant, secretive—and sometimes even criminal—people on Wall Street. You have power, and are feared. All you have to do is tell the truth.

CHAPTER NINETEEN

AN OUTBREAK OF
INFORMATIONAL BACTERIA

On October 23 and 25, 1994, an unidentified subscriber to the Prodigy online service got a little nasty. Actually, more than a little nasty. Actually, *a lot* nasty. Irresponsibly nasty, one would conclude at first glance.

He or she—the identity of the person is lost to history—posted incendiary remarks in the Money Talk bulletin board, the same online forum in which future paid-research mogul Gayle Essary was exploring the wonders of day trading. The Internet was still in its hobbyist-geek phase, and the action, such as it was, could mainly be found on Prodigy, America Online, and the other large commercial dial-up services, of which Prodigy was the largest back then. A potential audience of two million people could read all the unflattering stuff that somebody unloaded on an obscure brokerage exec named Daniel M. Porush, his employer, a Long Island firm called Stratton Oakmont, and a Stratton IPO in the stock of a company called Solomon-Page Group Ltd. According to this unknown person, the Solomon-Page IPO was a "major criminal fraud," Porush was a "soon to be proven criminal," and Stratton was a "cult of brokers who either lie for a living or get fired."

Now, that was a bit much, even by the insult-happy standards of computer bulletin boards and the Internet, in which one of first terms to be coined, back in the 1980s, was *flame,* which means "a virulently attacking post." However, this was a battle that Stratton had to wage. Just a few months before the Prodigy attack, Stratton had successfully beaten back an SEC lawsuit, filed in March 1992, that claimed Stratton used "boiler room tactics" and defrauded the public. Thanks to the SEC, the firm was getting back on its feet. Stratton was desperately battling to keep afloat, and potential customers simply could not be allowed to believe that either the firm or its underwritings were criminal or fraudulent.

While, technically speaking, Stratton had reached a settlement with the agency, in reality it was a Stratton victory—perhaps the biggest to be won against the SEC by an alleged securities transgressor during Artie Levitt's tenure (and you can be sure he didn't boast about it in his memoirs). Stratton's lawyer, a media-savvy ex-SEC regional administrator named Ira Lee Sorkin, had run rings around his former employers, portraying the firm as misunderstood, maybe slightly aggressive, but not at all criminal or fraudulent. It worked. Even though its entire management team received suspensions or expulsions, the firm itself could stay in business, with an "independent consultant" reviewing its "policies, practices and procedures."

The consultant "will help make Stratton even more compliant than it already is," Sorkin told the *New York Times*. Porush received a one-year suspension and paid a $100,000 penalty, without admitting or denying anything, as the firm continued fighting hard, issuing press releases and protesting its innocence. "Stratton Oakmont remains a fully operational, well-capitalized broker-dealer and looks forward to continuing to serve fully its clients. The firm's underwriting and brokerage activities will continue without interruption," Stratton said in a press release announcing the settlement.

So when those nasty words appeared on Prodigy in October 1994, Porush had to do what motivational speakers call "acting as if." He had to act as if he wasn't a criminal, and as if the SEC hadn't given a mammoth boiler-room operation a lease on life to continue to rip off the public.

It was a stunningly successful strategy. In the months to come, dispatches from Stratton's righteously indignant defense of its reputation interspersed with news about the SEC's continued tussling with Stratton. News of the lawsuit continued, muddying the waters, even after Stratton openly defied the consultant report ("impractical and irresponsible," fumed Sorkin), drawing yet another lawsuit from the SEC. In July 1995, Porush, still "acting as if," invited in *Newsday* to complain about "the lies and smears that newspapers keep printing every time the Securities and Exchange Commission sues his firm . . . [and] every time a fed-up investor vents his spleen in an online bulletin board."

It was more than just good PR.

The difficulty with writings such as those that appeared on Prodigy was fundamental to the character of Wall Street, in which fortunes rise and fall on the basis of imagery, and in which imagery is fragile and transitory. What you or I would call free speech is not viewed as a fundamental constitutional right, but rather as a form of bacteria. The bacillus of free speech can be friendly, in the manner of organisms that turn sour milk into cheese, or malevolent. A good example of friendly informational bacteria was the Baloney Blitzkrieg, or the puff pieces on various subjects that you see every day in the financial press.

Friendly informational bacteria serve only one purpose—to promote the intake of United States currency into the object of praise and prevent its outflow. Malevolent informational bacteria have quite the opposite effect. They cause United States currency to remain in the wallet, to *not* flow out, nourish, and enrich.

Informational bacteria could not be more malevolent than the organisms that were being spread via Prodigy. There was something new here—something troubling and dangerous. Instead of the usual bacillus spreaders of the media, who could often be subdued by a stiffly worded letter, what was happening on Prodigy was potentially far more difficult to handle. Ordinary people, especially anonymous ordinary people, were not vulnerable to the kinds of leverage that work against the press. They were far more prone to multiply. They needed to be crushed.

The quarantine-and-disinfection procedure was effectuated in the New York State Supreme Court in Nassau County. In October 1995, after some legal skirmishing, Prodigy settled. A joint press release soothed Porush's hurt feelings thusly: "Prodigy is sorry if the offensive statements concerning Stratton and Mr. Porush, which were posted on Prodigy's Money Talk bulletin board by an unauthorized and unidentified individual, in any way caused injury to their reputation." Carefully worded, nothing admitted, but it didn't matter because the word *sorry* was used, which was enough. Victory.

No money changed hands. No money had to change hands.

The purpose of the lawsuit was not to get money but to prevent the spread of bacteria. Disinfection was the only thing that mattered. Disinfection had taken place. Stratton Oakmont had rebuffed an attack of resistant informational bacteria, and by so doing had established itself as a litigator, a process-generator. Its critics were on notice, and an apology was on record that could be shown to investors in the wares that Stratton was selling.

Stratton continued in business for another two years until it collapsed under the weight of its own criminality, and Porush and his partners were all carted off to federal prison. In 1999, Porush and other Stratton execs pleaded guilty to securities fraud and money laundering for manipulating a bunch of Stratton IPOs, including Solomon-Page Group Ltd. Stratton really *was* a den of thieves. Porush really *was* a criminal. The Solomon-Page IPO really *was* rigged. If prospective Stratton customers had listened to the anonymous person on Prodigy, they would have avoided millions of dollars in ripoffs.

Looking back, you really have to admire *Porush v. Prodigy* as a marvelous bit of hypocritical asymmetry. Remember that, as Taglich Brothers, young David Wolfson, and countless brokerage firms and hedge funds and mutual funds and other Wall Streeters have learned, breaking a few house rules on Wall Street—or even some fairly significant laws—does not mean having to say you're sorry. Still, here it was, an apology *to* Stratton Oakmont and *to* Daniel Porush, the kind of man who never had to say he was sorry—except when prodded to do so by his attorneys, just before a federal judge sentenced him to four years in prison and seven years of supervised release, on ten counts of securities fraud and money laundering.*

The truth was out about Prodigy a full two years before Stratton was belatedly shuttered by the NASD, five years before the massive Stratton indictments, and seven years before Porush pleaded guilty. Only one reporter followed up on the Prodigy whistle-blower's allegations—Susan Antilla of the *New York Times,* who wrote two pieces about the Solomon-Page IPO. There was no other follow-up. Defamation suits will do that—they have a chilling effect.

In fact, the only legal ruling that emerged from the case was bad for online-service providers, because it found them potentially capable of being held liable as publishers of the nasty stuff that people sometimes said in online comments. In 1996, with the enactment of the Communications Decency Act, Congress closed this legal chink in the armor of the ISPs, but the point was proven. You had to watch your step online—or be sued.

Porush v. Prodigy was a losing battle, as battles such as this usually are. Still, it was more than a demonstration of raw hypocrisy on the part of a criminal and typically abysmal negligence on the part of Artie Levitt's SEC, which let Stratton off the hook to rampage through the markets for another two years. It was also the earliest demonstration of the power that investors can wield by simply telling the truth.

For the first time in history, investors were capable of functioning as a kind of third force—spreading malevolent informational bacteria on their own, without first gaining the confidence of a member of the media.

They could even do their bacillus-spreading anonymously.

---

* This deliciously ironic moment went largely unnoticed by the media. "At yesterday's hearing, Porush, calling himself 'humbled and humiliated,' apologized to Stratton's customers, who he said 'didn't get a level playing field' at the brokerage," said *Newsday,* the only news media outlet to cover his May 2002 sentencing. Judge John Gleeson responded that he didn't believe Porush was sorry.

Anonymity makes a lot of people recoil, and for good reason. Anonymous information is inherently unreliable. Anonymous opinions are inherently suspect. But anonymous tips, fleshed out and verified, are the meat and potatoes of cops, investigators, and reporters. Anonymity—to borrow an expression from an insincerely contrite Dan Porush—levels the playing field when you are writing about people who are rich with stolen money and not above using their swag to hire lawyers to shut you up.

In 1994, with the Internet in its infancy, weblogs didn't exist and Internet message boards were only just cranking up. By the end of the 1990s, the Internet was providing investors with ways of counteracting Wall Street hype, often behind a protective shield of anonymity, ferreting out criminals and connecting with other investors.

That brings us to the next recorded outbreak of malevolent informational bacteria. Despite myriad disinfection attempts, this particular scourge was never totally eradicated. It is still going on—arguably the longest epidemic of its kind in history—and it provides an ongoing lesson in investor power. It shows that the tools are there. All you have to do is use them. And all that the people with the power—the regulators and the media—have to do is to pay attention.

The story of this outbreak of malevolent informational bacteria begins in 1998. At that time, in Australia, Norway, Ireland, and elsewhere in Europe, people were getting calls from a new arrival on the transnational cold-calling scene. Its name was Amber Securities. One of the people at the receiving end of the calls was an Australian named Scott Bowen. The stock that Amber tried to sell Bowen was a scrappy little motorcycle company called Titan Motorcycles of America. That's one of the companies that was mentioned in our earlier exploration of the overseas boiler rooms, one of the stocks whose virtuosity was by now familiar to a great many people with working telephones in the lush green west of Ireland.

Bowen did not buy any stock in Titan when it was first pitched to him. But in June 1999 he took the plunge with another stock from the U.S. OTC market, a California company called ZiaSun Technologies. As Bowen later told the tale, he purchased a thousand shares of ZiaSun from Amber, which by now had changed its name to the more businesslike Capital Assets Ltd. ZiaSun had its finger in several pies, most very promising and Internet-related. In the ensuing months, Bowen claimed, he was persuaded to buy more promising-looking stocks—Chequemate International Inc., Loraca International, CastPro Inc., and a company partly owned by ZiaSun called Asia4Sale. Like ZiaSun, all had been doing quite well in the market. ZiaSun shares, for example, had quadrupled in less than a year to more than twenty dollars by mid-1999.

Then came the microcap crash, the one that got the naked-short Baloney Blitzkrieg all revved up. Among the casualties was ZiaSun, which was down to six dollars a year later.

Bowen was upset. As upset people often do in such situations, he sued pretty much everyone he thought was culpable, including ZiaSun. According to his allegations in his suit against ZiaSun and other defendants (all of whom hotly denied wrongdoing), the impetus for the stock-price rise was, he contended, a "pyramid scheme" in which stocks were pushed on Bowen and other shareholders throughout the world.

Bowen maintained that the impetus for his stock purchases came from a "financial and investment consultant" for Amber/Capital named Lynn Briggs. The Australian contended that Briggs told him that no investor had ever lost money with those companies because of Amber/Capital's "close association and intimate knowledge" of the companies. Bowen also alleged in the suit that another individual with a starring role in this little drama, who "directed" Briggs and other brokers who peddled the stocks, was a person named Bryant Cragun. He was a former ZiaSun CEO who lived in California and had become an investment advisor and fund-raiser for all the companies sold to Bowen, ZiaSun included. All told, Bowen bought exactly $365,625.50 in stocks, according to his suit.

It was a pretty routine Wall Street tale. Man buys stock, man loses money, man doesn't get his money back. Ordinarily it would end at about this point, usually with the suit tossed out of court—as indeed happened to Bowen's suit against ZiaSun et al. Bowen simply didn't have enough evidence to support his pyramid-scheme allegation and to connect all the dots, so a judge eighty-sixed the suit. But the story did not end there. The war that Bowen lost continued on the Internet, and was still being slugged out years later.

Like most companies peddled by overseas boiler rooms, ZiaSun was perfectly legitimate. It had real operations, real earnings, and actual people working for it. However, the company's founders had ties to the boiler rooms, and the company had business dealings with several of them. They were the kinds of ties that, if they had been highlighted and brought to the attention of people like Bowen, would probably have resulted in people like Bowen not buying the stock. The problem from the investor standpoint was that nobody was writing about ZiaSun, not bringing those interesting connections to the attention of the investing public.

Nobody was writing about them except people like you.

Unbeknownst to Bowen, a lot of people were speaking out about ZiaSun. They weren't the big-mouth pension fund managers whose self-righteous and often hypocritical squawking helped bring down Dick Grasso. No, they were what the self-regulatory pyramid and media condescend to call "small investors." In late 1998, months before Bowen and other overseas investors were being pushed the stock of ZiaSun, a discussion about the company commenced on the Internet. The chatter on the popular, cacophonous Silicon Investor Web site began on November 5, 1998, when a fellow who bought ZiaSun shares (from a broker who also sold him stock in a scrappy little motorcycle company; see if you can guess its name: it begins with a "T") created a message-board topic on the company.

At first all was harmonious and innocuous. That changed in the spring of 1999.

The first bouts of nastiness were little more than the online equivalent of mosquito bites. Some were flames, very much of the kind that got Dan Porush all riled up in righteous anger.

"Personally I think this company is a SCAM!" said one anonymous critic on the SI board.

Soon the attacks became more specific, more barbed, more effective. The SCAM! ranter later explained in another post that he "called investor relations one morning last week and had six different people return [his] call telling [him] how great the company was." Another anonymous message observed similarities between ZiaSun and another Internet play that had been widely criticized on SI. It also detailed apparent links and similarities between the companies. Several other messages linked ZiaSun to Amber Securities, and implied that neither was a paragon of virtue. Another alleged that ZiaSun had been promoting its products in Internet newsgroups, via mass-volume spam postings.

While all this was happening in early 1999, the people whose job it was to protect investors from boiler rooms were nowhere in sight. Back in 1999, the total amount of energy expended in the United States—or the rest of the world, for that matter—on overseas boiler rooms was a big, fat zero. Nobody who was supposed to ferret out such things, not the self-regulatory pyramid or law enforcement or the media, had said even one negative word about any of the people who sold Bowen those $365,000 in stocks. The self-regulatory pyramid, after years of consent decrees and knuckle-raps of the kind Stratton had received, was only just getting serious about allegations of fraud from U.S. investors. The global victims would have to wait, maybe forever.

This was a vacuum, the kind of vacuum that had arisen so often in the past when the stock pushers peddle their wares, but for the first time in history it was being filled. It was being attacked with informational bacteria—the malevolent kind. The kind that keeps investors from plunking down their cash. Fully two months before Bowen bought ZiaSun and other stocks from the renamed Amber Securities, the alarm was already being sounded, if you knew where to hear it. The bell ringers weren't Artie Levitt's SEC and not myself or anyone else in the media at the time. People were doing more than yelling. They were using powerful Internet search tools to investigate—sometimes going down blind alleys but sometimes hitting nails on the head.

Something changed. It wasn't just flaming anymore. When ZiaSun boosters—including ZiaSun employees and a stock promoter from the Cayman Islands—talked up the company in Silicon Investor and other investor message-board Web sites, they were answered by more than just jibes. The responses were often articulate and well reasoned.

The SI people combed through the growing Internet availability of public records and address information—once the exclusive province of regulators and federal agents, investigative reporters and private detectives. They disclosed their findings to denigrate ZiaSun's prospects and repeatedly hammer away at Amber Securities, other reputed boiler rooms, and the people connected to them. The list of targets eventually grew to encompass Bryant Cragun and Lynn Briggs, who Scott Bowen in Australia had unsuccessfully sought to blame for his stock purchases.

Following SI's ZiaSun message board was a bit like watching a constantly evolving argument among a group of petulant, sometimes threatening busybodies and lunatics. Through it all, actual information was being exchanged, and some of it was pretty good.

On April 8, 1999, one message on the SI board zeroed in on ZiaSun's investor-relations firm, which did work for a bunch of boiler-room favorites (including a spunky little motorcycle company), and had the same address as ZiaSun. That's hardly the kind of thing you want to see in an OTC stock, if you are a small investor. Others noted that Amber was selling stocks in Australia without being registered with Australian authorities. In the coming months, other messages would say that Lynn Briggs, former president of ZiaSun, had once been a broker for P.T. Dolok Permai, and that P.T. Dolok was also known as International Asset Management. When action was finally taken overseas, they would spread the word that IAM had been raided by Thai authorities and that both firms had been blacklisted by Australian and New Zealand regulators for selling securities without a license.

The SI crowd would call attention to documents indicating that IAM had raised funds for an "IPO" for ZiaSun when it had the name of Best Way USA, and was distributing an "IPO prospectus"—the problem being that Best Way USA never actually had an IPO.* The SI messages also traced the colorful history of Bryant Cragun, who was chairman of an offshore stock pusher called Oxford International Management from 1991 to 1997, and who was later linked in court documents to IAM and P.T. Dolok Permai as well. Along the way, they uncovered in an Internet archive a May 1998 Web page for IAM, which included a roster of IAM brokers. It's there where one can find Edward J. Loessi, future CEO Council founding member, whose surprised reaction to appearing on said roster I noted on page 41.

The people who should take a bow for digging out all this stuff, giving these goodies and a lot more to the media and also to the regulators when they finally woke up to the problem, were condemned by ZiaSun and its defenders as short-sellers eager to attack the stock. That has an element of truth to it, as at least one professional trader was involved in the SI online debate. And it may well be that some of the anti-ZiaSun zealousness was brought on by a thirst for short-side profits. But even if it were 100 percent true, that would probably be one of the best arguments in favor of short-selling of microcap and OTC Bulletin Board stocks. Anything that serves as a counterweight to all the rampant hype and manipulation, anything that will induce investors to publicize the shortcomings of questionable stocks, should be welcomed and encouraged. But as we have seen, the SEC made it harder to short small-company stocks—thereby discouraging shorts from participating in the online dialogue about microcap stocks.

Now that the shorts have absconded from microcaps, thanks to the geniuses at the SEC, the gumshoes who have been tracking down the offshore boiler rooms and their ilk—and are continuing to work hard to uncover rotten companies—are strictly amateurs. They are ordinary citizens of this country—and sometimes not even of this country—who are filling in where law enforcement has been slow to tread.

These people come from all walks of life and various points on the globe, but they have two things in common. One is that they are fed up. Another is

---

* The company later contended that it had no knowledge of the "IPO."

that they have a panache that is very deeply ingrained in the American spirit. Calling what they do "vigilantism" is not quite precise, and neither is it 100 percent correct to say that the SEC and other regulators are playing the Dean Jagger role in *Bad Day at Black Rock,* the sheriff with a guilty conscience and a bottle of gin. But it's close. The difference is that old-style vigilantism was violent, illegal. Not the Internet vigilantes. However, the reaction has been violent—not physically, but by use of the modern-day equivalent of the gunfight at high noon.

CHAPTER TWENTY

THE GUNFIGHT AT ZIASUN CORRAL

The people doggedly pursuing boiler rooms and scam artists on the Internet are the kind of individuals who are familiar to anyone who has ever lived in a close-knit city neighborhood or a small town with a lively civic life. They are the pests. They are the busybodies who, sometimes out of sheer mulishness or personal vindictiveness, simply refuse to leave well enough alone. In small towns they are politely called gadflies and civic activists, and not so politely called cranks and hotheads. They pester town zoning boards and library committees, sometimes for sound reasons and sometimes for no reason at all. They want the sidewalk repaired, the sewer bills lowered, the hiring practices investigated.

They are, in other words, absolutely essential to a vibrant democracy.

Today's investor activists are also pests. Necessary pests.

The prime mover behind much of ZiaSun's online scrutiny was a lean, gaunt, tall fellow in his early forties named Floyd D. Schneider. Floyd lived in a nice part of northern New Jersey and he was a mortgage broker by profession. Meeting the man, you'd never know that he was a veritable hound dog of the boiler-room world, a man of extraordinary memory, blessed with a prodigious attention to detail.

Floyd is in this for fun. He is not an investor. Well, that's what he says, and it makes sense. Most of the stocks in which he is interested are awful stocks, and thanks to the SEC they cannot be shorted by even professional investors. He gave up investing a long time ago, in the late 1990s, when he formed a Web site devoted to exposing scams. It was called TheTruthseeker.com, and he shut it down in 2000 because of the *tsuris* I'll be coming to in a moment. Though he has shared information with short-sellers, Floyd denies that he has ever shorted stocks. No, Floyd appears to be just a civic-minded guy, a hobbyist, a man who does things out of principle. You have to give him that. He is a man who shoots straight and will join the posse, even if it is only him.

One difference between him and Gary Cooper, whom he resembles from a distance, is that Floyd is not a man of few words. He is a man of many words, which he disseminates by email and postings on Silicon Investor nowadays. His SI handle, famous throughout his significant but unknown readership of fellow investors, regulators, enemies and admirers, is "Truthseeker."

Why, apart from an occasional fifteen minutes of recognition, does he do it—seek truth (or spread untruths, as his detractors allege)? There really is no good answer, just as there was no answer from that other fifties movie icon, James Stewart, in his wheelchair in *Rear Window*, when Raymond Burr confronted him and asked, "What do you want?" What does Floyd Schneider want? Probably nothing except that he likes to do it. It gives him satisfaction and it also is in his citizenship genes. There also might be—oh, maybe just a wee bit of vengeance involved in his work, as he has been bothered by people he has bothered, and he is not afraid to bother them right back.

It probably helps just a little that his gumshoe work has made him a kind of minor-league celebrity. He is not publicity-shy, and has been written about on occasion. When Amr Elgindy, a Texas short-seller, was put on trial in late 2004 for allegedly bribing an FBI agent, an SEC investigator named Brett Baker testified under cross-examination that Floyd was one of his sources of information. It made the Dow Jones wire. Floyd was not displeased.

ZiaSun is his nemesis. He doesn't like ZiaSun (and its various corporate successors, ZiaSun being no more) and ZiaSun et al. don't like him. I use the present tense deliberately—and the pluperfect, perfect, and future grammatical tenses apply as well, where appropriate. Nowhere, outside of maybe the Arab-Israeli conflict or the historic enmity between aficionados of vinyl records and compact discs, is permanent conflict almost assured. The ZiaSun-Floyd enmity began not too long after ZiaSun realized that it needed to intervene in the fight that was under way at Silicon Investor, and decided to participate. Just a few days after the online attacks began in earnest, on April 7, 1999, ZiaSun chief executive Anthony L. Tobin posted a message of his own.

"I have been alerted by several people that there is much discussion of ZSUN, and myself, taking place on these message boards, so I have taken the time to browse through," said Tobin, projecting an attitude of detached annoyance. He went on to observe that "some of the postings are amusing, some are rather shocking. Some are outright lies." He then yanked out the bogeyman—short-sellers. They were behind the negative posts, he said. People have a right to make money, he went on, but "I don't believe that traders should be allowed to profit from defamation of a company or a person. This is something that Zia-Sun and some of its larger shareholders are looking into through legal counsel."

Uh-oh. Legal counsel—the modern-day equivalent of the Jack Palance character in *Shane,* dressed in black and grinning and dangerous. These small investors, the ones saying nasty things about ZiaSun, were flirting with danger—and Alan Ladd was nowhere in sight.

These people, these nobodies, these Internet dirt farmers and sheepherders, were dangerous to the ranchers and gunslingers in this particular feud. The little people were on notice that they could be shot down without further warning, their bodies dropping into the mud. Fighting words were being spoken, and ZiaSun was not about to sit still for such talk. *Porush v. Prodigy* had proven the reaction that a few rash words could provoke, even when accurate.

In June 1999, ZiaSun, and later Cragun, rode into town, drew their six-shooters, and sued those nasty Silicon Investor users. Floyd, acting in the Van Heflin role of the homesteader who rallies the good people of the valley, was the No. 1 defendant.

This was considerably more complex litigation than the *Porush-Prodigy* suit. For one thing, the defendants and other Silicon Investor denizens made it complicated by keeping up the attack. An injunction was sought and awarded. A countersuit was filed by one of the message posters, an investor from Greece. And then, in October 2000, it all came to a halt. The suit was settled.

The ranchers had won. The homesteaders were loading up their Conestogas and leaving the valley.

The Greek investor got sixty thousand dollars. But apart from that, it was a smashing victory for ZiaSun. True, the defendants—the Ziasun Eight, as they grandiosely called themselves—didn't have to pay any damages, and duly trumpeted that in a press release. But monetary damages weren't the objective of the lawsuit, just as it wasn't for Dan Porush. The plaintiffs were suitably triumphant in their press release: "Through this settlement, ZiaSun, Tobin and Cragun succeeded in stopping a pattern of derogatory statements that harmed the company and drove down stock prices."

The operative word was "stopping." The defendants agreed to a total and perpetual gag order, a disinfection mechanism that no court would have ordered, and which would never have been agreed to by any but the most wimpy or cash-starved media company. The ZiaSun Eight weren't a media company. Almost all were those "small investors" that the Street is supposed to adore. They had taken on Wall Street, and Wall Street had fought back, and attorneys' fees are crushing when the germicide that is used against you is a defamation suit.

The defendants had no choice. They could continue to be soaked by legal fees, or they could agree to a series of "refrains." So they agreed. You would too. From the date of the agreement until the end of time, they would refrain:

> from publishing to any third party, directly, indirectly, or through any third party intermediary, any statement, opinion or other communication . . . about . . . Bryant Cragun; ZiaSun Technologies, Inc.; Anthony Tobin; Loraca International, Inc.; Chequemate International, Inc.; Titan Motorcycles of America, Inc.; Asia4Sale; Online Investors Advantage; Dynatech International, Inc.; any plaintiff or cross-defendant in [either of the lawsuits]; any member of Bryant Cragun's or Anthony Tobin's family who defendants know or reasonably should know is related to Cragun or Tobin; any individual or entity who defendants know, reasonably should know, or ever have suggested is related to Bryant Cragun or Anthony Tobin; any person defendants know or reasonably should know is an officer, director, employee, agent, subsidiary, or shareholder of any of the companies identified above; or any person defendants know or reasonably should know is an employee, agent, attorney, accountant, heir, successor, assign, or representative of Bryant Cragun, ZiaSun, or Anthony Tobin.

What happened to the First Amendment in all this?

"The defendants have agreed to waive any First Amendment claims they may have regarding the types of statements covered in the agreement," ZiaSun lawyer Christopher Howard proudly proclaimed in the ZiaSun press release. "That's something you can obtain only through an agreement. No court in the country can order a party to waive First Amendment protection."

Now, isn't that something? Just shows you how terrific a lawsuit can be when you're a company and the defendant is some poor slob who says something you don't like on the Internet. You can force a guy to do pretty much anything—give up his rights, shut his mouth forever, or maybe even eat ground glass under certain circumstances.

Note the wording of the settlement. Pretty broad. Silence forever not just about ZiaSun but about all the companies and people that the defendants had linked to ZiaSun. That happened to include some of the same stocks that Scott Bowen, the Australian investor, had made the mistake of buying. It also happened to include the boiler room Amber Securities, because that was an "entity who defendants . . . have suggested is related to Bryant Cragun," and any others that may take the place ("successor") of all the people and entities the SI people didn't like, forever and ever, until the sun sucks the earth into its fiery bosom and the last boiler room and lawyer are turned to ashes.

Note too the reference to "cross-defendants." ZiaSun also wanted people to shut up about those folks as well. They were the people who were countersued by that Greek investor. He had brought into this litigation a rather colorful cast of characters. One was Lynn Briggs, the boiler-room salesman and ex–ZiaSun exec. No more talk about him was allowed.

The media was AWOL while most of this was going on. There was some routine coverage in the wire services, but if you're expecting there was a hue and cry from the guardians of the First Amendment, guess again.

Now, this is not to say that the media were completely indifferent to ZiaSun. After extracting a vow of silence from its online critics, ZiaSun went on to greater glory. CNBC and *Business Week* both had deals with a company called Telescan, under which the latter firm offered investment seminars to the general public in conjunction with those two organizations. When Telescan merged with ZiaSun in 2001, both media outfits had deals with the successor company—therefore covered by the gag order—called INVESTools.

The workshops are a pleasant way of whiling away the afternoon if you are retired or unemployed—the two dominant characteristics of the audience at a CNBC University (that is, INVESTools) "investor education seminar" that I attended in New York a while back. Probably the most notable aspect of the seminar was that it wasn't a seminar at all, but rather a four-hour sales pitch for the *real* seminar, which cost thirty-five hundred dollars. There was some talk about using a combination of technical (stock charting) and fundamental (corporate performance) factors in stock picking—and CNBC University had that available in a Web site, if you attended the real seminar. There was talk about the investment technique known as covered-call writing, in which investors sell call options on stocks they own. What that means is that if you own shares of, say, IBM, you can get paid a few hundred bucks if you agree to sell the shares at a particular price. The fellow presiding at the seminar, a very well-dressed gent who looked to be in his late thirties, said that doing this was equivalent to collecting rent on stocks in your portfolio—and that if I attended that thirty-five-hundred-dollar seminar, I'd find out the right way to do it. The only problem was that probably a hundred or so books could teach one to do the same thing at a fraction of the cost, and with enough money left over to buy plenty of shares in a sensible index fund.

It would be a shame if any of my fellow seminar attendees actually went out and did any of that covered-call selling. That's because you get paid the most "rent" when you sell calls on volatile stocks. They might learn the hard way that *volatile* means "most likely to drop into the basement." And if the stocks rose just as dramatically, their gains would be limited. A little knowledge, they say, is a dangerous thing.

Oh, well. The cookies and coffee were free, at least. They were very good cookies. The coffee was a little weak. A *CNBC Guide to Money & Markets* was given to all participants, and it is a good little book. CNBC has since dropped out of its deal with INVESTools, so you'll have to attend an INVESTools or BusinessWeek Investor Workshop if you like cookies and have a few hours to kill.

You won't learn anything about investing—unless you take the dangerously little knowledge provided and make the mistake of selling covered calls. But you'll get to see a whole lot of investors, chewing cookies, who were the kind of people sued by the corporate predecessors of the people who put out those nice cookies. If you're lucky, you'll come out of the seminar with your blood sugar below 150 and your hand on your wallet.

There's an epilogue to Floyd's story. There always is an epilogue when it comes to Floyd. After the battle with ZiaSun was settled, Floyd moved on to other targets. Today, he remains an avid amateur sleuth—and defendant. It has gotten him sued on at least one other occasion. One, still pending, concerns some uncomplimentary things he said about a company called Matrixx Initiatives. The other—well, I say "at least one" because the other is a little murky.

On December 21, 1999, a press release was generated by a stock promotion outfit called the Investor Relations Group, saying that Floyd and his then–Web site, TheTruthseeker.com, had said a bunch of nasty things. "As the world wide web grows, investors are consulting financially related Internet sites for information," said the press release issued by Dian Griesel, president and CEO. "These sites have a responsibility as great as any other genre of press to disseminate truthful, accurate, fact-checked information. Yet, there is no truth, accuracy nor facts in any of the statements made about my company by Floyd Schneider, Author of TheTruthseeker.com."

Fine—except that Floyd was never served with any lawsuit. When he heard about the suit, he called the attorney who was pursuing the case. "I tell him that if it's frivolous, the attorney has got to pay damages," said Floyd. "I go, 'This is ridiculous.' So he gets back to me. He's willing to settle it—now he just put out a press release, suing me for four million dollars—he's willing to settle it for his attorney's fees, which are about five thousand dollars. I told him to go to hell, stuff it, I'll see you in court, and that was the last I heard of him."

Ms. Griesel would not return a call seeking an explanation for this mysterious nonlawsuit lawsuit. But, then again, there isn't very much to say. When a lawsuit is a bacillus-eradication mechanism, and when the bacteria are being spread by some ordinary guy, some mortgage broker who likes to post on the Internet, there's not much point in serving lawsuit papers when a press release will suffice.

Sometimes press releases won't do the trick. In one of the most recent outbreaks of malignant informational bacteria, the financial press itself was enlisted, and with stunning success.

TURNING ON THE LIGHTS AT YALE

E ver hear of something called Farallon? It's a safe bet that the answer is no, which is good, from the Farallon perspective, because you are not supposed to know that it exists. "Farallon" may sound like a brand of stain-resistant carpeting, but it is actually an operator of hedge funds and is located in San Francisco. It doesn't have to disclose a darn thing to *you*, of course, but, as of early 2005, it was reported to have about $12.5 billion under management. That made Farallon among the very biggest hedge fund operators in the entire world, possibly the largest. Thirteen billion dollars is a lot of money when you can do whatever you want with it and not tell anybody about it, and use as much leverage as your conscience permits. As we've seen in previous chapters, hedge fund operators are the last absolute dictators in the world, answerable to no one. They're sort of like ship captains, except they can't perform marriages and are only too happy to push aside the women and kids and jump into the lifeboats when the weather gets a little rough.

Like most hedge funds, Farallon adheres to what might be described as the "reverse Willy Loman" school of nondisclosure: *Attention must not be paid!* This is not to say that the reputable people who run Farallon—I mean it; these guys have shoes so white you can use them as shaving mirrors—won't insert that name into a carefully chosen media outlet when exceptional circumstances arise. On such occasions they submit themselves, like a child dragged to the bathroom for an enema, to a vaccination against negative-information bacteria. That distasteful chore was most recently performed in a Wall Street trade publication called *Institutional Investor,* in its issue of February 14, 2005. The date held no special significance, for you might say that every day is Valentine's Day at *Institutional Investor*. *II*'s content—smooth as a baby's bottom, deferential as a midshipman—was reflected in its acronym: *Aye aye!*

"Day after day, month after month, for five long years, Thomas Steyer showed up at work wearing the same tie, a vibrant red plaid with navy, green and white stripes." So began the humorous anecdote at the beginning of the 7,260-word article.* After pointing to the white shoes worn by Farallon CEO Steyer, ex–risk arbitrageur at Goldman Sachs, the rest of the article reads, as hedge fund manager profiles usually do, as if it had been written by Rodgers and Hammerstein. Farallon was a superbly managed hedge fund ("determination, willfulness and self-confidence are on full display"), a beautifully performing (according to "sources" with uncannily precise information) hedge fund. And, above all—walking in the storm, but keeping its head up high—it was an unfairly attacked hedge fund.

Here we have the exigent circumstances that necessitated the inoculation. It seems that the bane of boiler rooms and stock promoters had come to hedge funds. An outbreak of negative-information bacilli needed to be suppressed and prevented from spreading, so as not to infect the perceptions of the world at large.

In the past, Steyer sought privacy "as doggedly as he does undervalued assets," but those days were no more. He could maintain his privacy in Argentina, Indonesia, and Russia, but not on the campus and in the computers of Yale University, which invests an undisclosed but large percentage of its $12.7 billion endowment with Farallon. There were people at Yale who just wouldn't leave Farallon in peace. *II* observed that Steyer was being "demonized by a gaggle of former graduate students with time to burn and a proclivity for building Web sites." They were portrayed as a kind of Baloney Blitzkrieg, with *II* heaping on the Yalies the kind of ridicule the anti-naked-shorting cranks deserved, but did not receive, from *II* or pretty much anyone else in the media.

The "gaggle" was doing nasty things and making statements that were sometimes "over the top" and "misleading." It was so . . . *hurtful.* "The protests hurt on a personal level," said *II*. Steyer was more than just a decent man. *II* pointed out that he was a "voluble Democrat" and a "key fundraiser for John Kerry's presidential campaign" who maintained a sympathy for the oppressed that you would expect from such an individual. What you had here, in the view of *II,* was a bunch of damn fools bothering a good man.

Probably to avoid adding to the emotional wound already suffered by

---

* The punch line, which I must omit for space reasons, involved the purchase of neckties.

Steyer, *II* left out the worst part, something that would really get the blood boiling of anyone who cares deeply about the privacy of hedge fund managers and Democratic fund-raisers. The Farallon protesters had gotten their grimy hands on Farallon's top-secret partnership documents and had the unmitigated gall to *post them on the Internet!*

Not to worry. The Steyer piece was as effective as a vaccination, even if it was pretty execrable as journalism. No further publicity of any kind about Farallon—not on the Yale campaign or anything else concerning this signifi- cant hedge fund operation—subsequently appeared in the media. This was, after all, a 7,260-word profile. While *II* was not a direct competitor of the *New York Times,* the *Wall Street Journal,* or the major business magazines, it was closely read by their staffs and the sources of their staffs, and no self- respecting reporter is going to suggest a feature story on a subject that had re- ceived such exhaustive "ink." Not even Jonas Salk could have come up with a more effective magic bullet. When the *Times* profiled the manager of the Yale endowment in August 2005, the article didn't even mention Farallon, much less the anti-Farallon campaign. Success!

Clinically efficacious as it was, anyone reading the *II* piece with an open mind might have been bothered by a few things.

For instance, why was this "gaggle" of people at Yale being so nosy? Was there no public purpose whatsoever for anyone at that prestigious presidential training ground, or outside it for that matter, wanting to know what was being done with Yale's substantial endowment, particularly its hedge fund invest- ments? Were these "former graduate students with time on their hands" just a bunch of trust-fund slackers adding "embarrassing hedge funds" to their idle- rich gambols? Or was there a serious, substantial, even public-spirited motiva- tion at work here?

In fact, these supposedly wild-eyed kids, without necessarily knowing it, were working in the best interests of the people with the most at stake in the endowment. I refer, of course, to future generations of Yalies. The Yale endow- ment is more important than ever in funding the institution, providing more than twice the share of revenue provided by tuition and fees. So Yale students, and their parents, directly suffer if the Yale endowment stumbles, because they'll have to make up the difference if Yale's investments hit the skids. Faral- lon, neckties and all, white shoes and all, is prone to all the hedge fund vicissi- tudes that we've seen in this book. It may be the most terrific thing to hit New Haven since *Oklahoma!* went into rehearsals, but even more terrific hedge funds have stumbled in the past, dragging down their investors with it.

Here's why the Yale-Farallon disclosure people were on the right track—showing the kind of aggressive curiosity that you might do well to emulate with your college, whether you are a student, a faculty member, an employee, an alumnus, or, above all, a parent who has to pay the tuition bill:

- College and university endowments like Yale's love hedge funds, and are buying them at an increasing pace. Of the $267 billion or so in college endowments, it has been estimated that fully 12 percent are deployed into hedge funds, and the number is growing.
- Hedge funds don't necessarily love colleges. We explored in earlier chapters how hedge funds have a way of imploding, leaving their investors holding the bag—and college and university endowments have suffered from all of the major hedge fund blowups of recent years, including Long-Term Capital Management.
- Colleges and universities, even public ones, are notoriously uninformative when it comes to disclosing what they are doing with endowment money. Investing in secretive, collapse-prone hedge funds piles opacity upon opacity.

Last but not least:

- As should come as no surprise to anyone who takes the Efficient Market Hypothesis seriously, endowments perform no better than managers of mutual funds. Or hedge funds, for that matter.

The average endowment manager lagged the S&P 500 by two percentage points over ten years, according to a survey by the National Association of College and University Business Officers in early 2005. They beat the S&P over a five-year period, but still were not able to outpace inflation and provide for their institutions' needs. "When inflation and yearly endowment spending rates are considered, the five-year average 3.8 percent investment return rate for institutions [participating in the survey] translates into a decline in endowment investment earning potential over time," even when strong 2004 gains are taken into account, said NACUBO.

That last point, by the way, explains the first point—why endowment managers are desperately scratching for higher returns, usually without success, by putting ever-greater sums of money into hedge funds. Yet it's been proven time and again by the efficient-market types that scrambling for higher-than-market returns is a losing battle, and that the market will beat you most of the time. Those are the house odds. They stink for active money managers.

So all these are good reasons for members of the Yale community to be curious about Yale's dealings with Farallon and other hedge funds. However, it should be noted that none of these reasons was the initial motivating factor behind the "gaggle" of Yalies who dared to put Tom Steyer's fund under a microscope. Contrary to *II*'s portrayal of them as hysterical dilettantes and cynical union activists, these were actually serious, committed graduate students—mainly current students, by the way, not the former ones, with its sixties outside-agitator imagery, alleged in the *II* piece.

One of the principal student activists running the Farallon campaign at Yale was Andrea Johnson. She was a fairly typical student at the two-year graduate course of study at the Yale School of Forestry—serious, socially aware, a Colorado native, and a bit beyond the college-kid range at twenty-eight years old. Andrea never read the *II* story because Wall Street trade organs devoted to favorable-bacilli inoculation are not among her ordinary reading matter. She is interested in stuff like community-based environmental initiatives, not money-manager back rubs. In fact, until this whole Farallon business arose, she had never even heard of hedge funds. Like most nonfinancial types, she is not interested in such stuff until it comes breathing down her neck—as it did in this case.

What got people like Andrea interested in Farallon was a quintessential New West tale, kind of the thing you'd read about in John Nichols's New Mexico novels, only messier. The mindset in the rural West today is very much like the Old West in one respect: You mind your own business, but if someone messes with you or your neighbors, you don't back down. As a Coloradoan, Andrea didn't much like the idea that her school was involved in a scheme that didn't exactly reek of good-neighborliness. In 2002, word crept out in the Colorado media and Yale student press that the university had been involved in a bit of a mess in her home state. It was the kind of mess that used to get people reaching for their Winchesters, back in the more straightforward days of western history.

In the 1990s, Yale, in partnership with Farallon, wanted to take water from a patch of land called the Baca Ranch in the San Luis Valley of southern Colorado, and sell all that precious moisture to the Denver suburbs. Yale's involvement in the thing was not revealed at the time.

Now, anyone who has ever seen a George Stevens movie can tell you that water is a bit of a troublesome issue out west. Apparently the people at Yale, and

Farallon, didn't watch many George Stevens movies. Not surprisingly, the idea of outsiders coming in and pumping out water tended to cause resentment among environmentalists and, of course, residents of the San Luis Valley. They fought it and the plan died, unmourned, in 2001.

Nice little mess, wouldn't you say? Dumb too. Even if the Baca Ranch plan was as innocent as a newborn lamb, as its defenders said it was, it certainly *sounded* stupid, which was almost as bad.

I'll mercifully fast-forward to early 2004. By now, the Baca Ranch water-pumping idiocy had died down. There was a transaction with the Nature Conservatory that defused the whole thing, more or less. But there was another element that became evident fairly quickly to the Yalies pursuing this issue, which included forestry students like Andrea, other activists, and union organizers seeking to needle Yale. They realized that not just the whole Baca Ranch episode was conducted behind closed doors, but that pretty much every aspect of the Yale endowment, particularly its dealings with hedge funds such as Farallon, was shrouded in secrecy. After all, Yale's dealings with Farallon over the Baca Ranch had emerged only after the deal was deep-sixed.

So in early 2004, these noninvesting, financially agnostic Yale environmental and community-activist types became investor advocates—and good ones, very much worthy of being subjected to attack by informational antibodies. As they researched the Yale-Farallon links from an environmental standpoint, they got peeved at stuff that is familiar to anyone who has read this far in this book, but came as quite a surprise to people unfamiliar with hedge-fund-land. (Students at Yale's School of Management, who might have provided some technical expertise, steered clear of all this, as best as I can tell.)

What bugged them the most was the lack of transparency of the whole thing. The students felt that they were groping around in the dark. Andrea later recalled, "If we kept attacking Yale investment by investment by investment, it's not really—it's putting out fires. And the larger issue is that we don't know where Yale's money is. We know even less than in the past. Twenty years ago we could kind of find out where a fair portion of Yale's money was because it was in public equities that you could track on the stock market, because they have to report if they have more than so much of a public holding." But by 2005, she said, students could identify only a small percentage of the endowment—2 percent—invested directly under Yale's name in domestic public equities. Instead, they have "a ton in absolute returns." That is, hedge funds. But precisely how that ton is distributed is something they have never been able to pin down.

As you'll recall, hedge funds are a land of Superinvestors and would-be Superinvestors, who take particular joy in their ability not to disclose anything to anybody. College endowments aren't much better. The students found that Yale administrators didn't like to discuss the endowment in any detail, particularly when it came to hedge funds, and also that Yale's disclosures were opaque. Andrea and the student researchers were unable to get the university to disclose the identity of the hedge funds in which Yale invested, or how much was in Farallon. It didn't help the cause of transparency that David Swensen, the manager of the endowment, was viewed as something of a Superinvestor himself, with his 16 percent annual return, realized since coming on board in 1983, definitely putting him in the first ranks of endowment managers.

Swensen's superstar status is reflected in occasional media puff pieces, and in his pay. If the student researchers had wanted to be really intrusive, they could have pulled Yale's IRS Form 990 off a public database and plastered his salary on the Internet. In 2003—the most recent year available—Swensen was paid a little more than $1 million in salary and benefits. While not very much by the insane standards of Wall Street, that made Swensen the highest paid employee of Yale, earning considerably more than the $695,000 in pay and benefits earned by Yale's president, Richard C. Levin.

As you can see, Yale does disclose stuff—if the feds require it, as they do with salary data for tax-exempt nonprofits. But, like most university endowments, it doesn't disclose what it doesn't have to disclose. Yale does not disclose its actual investments to the people who pay its bills, but rather puts out an annual report that is a study in obfuscation. In the 2004 report, for instance, the university's hedge fund investments are not separately broken out, but instead appear under the quixotic name of "Absolute Return" investments—the term that understandably befuddled Andrea. Those are indeed hedge funds, but without the name actually being used. To make the whole thing even foggier, the endowment uses two benchmarks for that asset class—a passive one, consisting of one-year Treasuries, and an active one, consisting of, sure enough, hedge funds. In 2004, 26 percent of the endowment was in these absolute-return investments, which would put Yale's investment in hedge funds just north of $3 billion. The words *hedge fund* do not show up in the endowment's annual report.

So the students et al. had ample, rational reason to feel a bit frustrated, and to go on the offensive, as college students tend to do when thwarted by authority. What Andrea describes as researchers at the Yale student union, presumably with the help of moles in the Yale administration, got out those Farallon part-nership documents, and put out their own Web site, www.unfarallon.com. En-couraged by the Yalies, students at other colleges with Farallon investments, such as Stanford University, began to push for more transparency in their own endow-ments as well. In March 2004, the Yale student activists committed a public rela-tions boner of their own, by organizing a silly sixties-style demonstration. "Chanting 'What do we want? Disclosure!' and 'Farallon has got to go,' over 60 concerned students, community members and alumni marched on the Yale In-vestment Office Wednesday afternoon." So reported the *Yale Daily News* on March 4, 2004.

Yale viewed the student activism with a kind of paternal contempt, ignor-ing the protests. They didn't have to change a thing or disclose a thing, and they didn't. When I called them about this, spokespeople for the university and Farallon sought to spin the Yale student activists as the cat's paws of steely-eyed union activists unsuccessfully seeking to represent university employees. Their activities were winding down, I was told, and were no longer worth mentioning.

I had no better luck than the students in trying to extract information out of the university and Farallon. A Yale spokesperson, the one assigned to dealing with pesky press inquiries on the endowment, would not even ac-knowledge that "absolute returns" meant hedge funds, in very much the way the British government would not acknowledge the existence of MI6. Faral-lon's spokesperson had nothing to say on the subject either, which is a bit more understandable.

The student activists believe that Yale might have as much as $2 billion invested just in Farallon—if so, the lion's share of its absolute returns in just one fund. A bit of an overconcentration—if so. But the Yale Form 990 for 2003 lists only $500 million in Farallon partnerships. However, that does not seem to be a complete list, and, as I said, I can roast their tootsies over an open flame and Yale's not coughing up that secret. Neither Steyer nor Swensen would be interviewed for this book on the campaign for more trans-parency at Yale.

That is not an unreasonable position, by the way. Hedge funds have a right to privacy, and college endowments have only the sparsest disclosure obliga-tions. They can pretty well disclose what they wish—and students, faculty members, parents, alumni, and steely-eyed union activists have as much right to push and prod and embarrass them to turn on the lights.

A little bit of good, old-fashioned southwestern sunshine would have prevented Yale from getting involved in a mess called Baca Ranch. And a few rays of light might not do Yale, and other college and university endowments, any harm at all—not as long as only their consciences, if any, prevent white-shoe money managers from turning their portfolios into replicas of Long-Term Capital Management, or worse.

THE SECOND BATTLE OF TRENTON

On July 22, 2005, Rand Groves was back in Trenton, in the Superior Court of the State of New Jersey, Mercer County, Civil Division, courtroom 3E. The kids were off from school, so he brought the whole family—his wife, his wife's mother, his two teenage sons, and his daughter. This was judgment day, the final reckoning on his case, as set forth in his motion for summary judgment and Merrill Lynch's cross-motion seeking the same thing. The hearing was scheduled for ten o'clock in the morning. The courtroom door was locked at the appointed hour, so Groves and his family waited quietly in the sunny corridor, calm and orderly amid a few dozen squawking, disorderly litigants from a domestic-relations tribunal down the hall. Groves was in his best suit, the children dressed as if for church. Things were looking up. He was reasonably optimistic.

After a protracted search, he had found a lawyer willing to take on his fight against Merrill Lynch on a contingency, pay-only-if-you win, fee arrangement—a feisty small-town lawyer named G. Martin Meyers. It was an egregious case, Meyers believed. Fabricated evidence, crucial blank tapes. It was, when it came to the facts, the kind of case lawyers dream about. On the law—well, that was something else entirely. Anyone looking at this case objectively would suspect—no, would know—that this case simply flew in the face of decades of carefully constructed jurisprudence that made it all but impossible for an investor to overturn an arbitration on appeal. That was a point that Merrill Lynch emphasized, quite persuasively, in its twenty-three-page brief arguing for dismissal of the case. The law had changed, for the better most legal scholars would argue, since those distant days of ancient history when George Washington met with his generals across the street.

After the First Battle of Trenton had ended in victory for the colonists, the British regrouped and attacked from the north. Washington was outnumbered, his troops were melting away, and he simply could not afford to lose Trenton to Lord Cornwallis, who had marched in from Princeton. The British attacked at a creek called Assunpink. They were repulsed. They attacked again and were repulsed again. Each time the line was held with heavy losses to the British. Had Cornwallis stormed the bridge, Trenton would have been lost—and with it, possibly, the revolution. The entire course of world history may well have been decided right there, at a little creek in New Jersey. With his troops holding the British at the creek, Washington decided on the evening of January 2, 1777, across the street from the courthouse, to move his troops along country roads and outflank the British. He attacked from the rear, near Princeton, and won a glorious victory.

With the triumphs in Trenton and then Princeton, a string of American defeats and retreats had come to an end. Several generations of American students (including the Trenton High School class of 1903, which erected that plaque across from the courthouse on Washington's Birthday, 1902) would learn that their independence, their freedom, was guaranteed by the Second Battle of Trenton, a crucial turning point of the Revolutionary War.

Groves needed at least as unlikely a victory in order to succeed for a second time in Trenton. He was cautiously optimistic. He had no other choice. His losses in 2000 and 2001, for which he blamed Merrill, had sent him into a financial tailspin. He had found a job in Florida, but he owed money to the New Jersey tax people as a result of his long-vanished options nest egg. Much depended upon reversal of the arbitration case and, hopefully, restoration of the money that he felt was lost because of Merrill's negligence. He had to win, and now that he was in an American courtroom, instead of a Wall Street arbitration forum, he firmly believed that fair play would prevail.

Judge Mary C. Jacobson was a last-minute replacement for another judge who had recused himself. Groves and his lawyer had not asked for the recusal, and they did not know why it had happened. It was, in a strange way, reassuring. Fundamental principles of American justice require that judges not preside over cases in which they have a conflict of interest, or even an appearance of a conflict of interest. Potential jurors are questioned closely to exclude those with any connection to the parties. This rigorous pursuit of fairness is one of the things that make lawyers, and even some laypeople, misty-eyed about the American court system. "Fundamental fairness" and "due process" are not mere clichés. They mean something. They are a reality.

By the middle of 2005, George W. Bush's plan for an Ownership Society had receded into memory, as his Social Security privatization plan met sustained opposition in Congress and was, for the time at least, moribund. Trade associations for the securities and mutual fund industry, for whom this would be a massive boon, planted stories in the media advancing the preposterous theory that they could not profit from the "low fees" promised by Social Security privatization. (Ignoring the principle that one penny multiplied by a trillion is at least as advantageous as ten billion multiplied by one dollar.) Still, the ethos that the president had encapsulated remained alive. The stock market was coming back to life, slowly. The Street was cranking up its advertising. Microcap stocks were booming. People were forgetting the kinds of complaints they had, the ones that Groves had unsuccessfully advanced just a few years before.

Neither Groves nor Meyers knew a thing about Judge Jacobson. They knew that she had been an assistant attorney general, which they viewed as a plus. When the courtroom doors opened, they and Groves's family sat in the courtroom waiting for her to rule on motions in three other cases, and the two men had an opportunity to assess her demeanor. She was an obscure jurist of middling reputation—ranking 175th out of 366 judges in a *New Jersey Law Journal* survey of lawyers several months before. But she seemed anxious to bring up her score (8.01 versus a statewide average of 7.85). She was cheerful, pleasant, courteous. A good judge.

Judge Jacobson appeared to be a compromiser, a conciliator, a "split the baby" judge. You might even think, when their time came and she proceeded to rip Groves's case to shreds, that she did so reluctantly. You could almost sense that she wanted to say, "Yes, Rand Groves. I will grant you some kind of relief. I will consider the evidence again, overturn what was unfair, and make things right for you." Maybe she didn't feel that way. But she seemed to feel that way, and appearances count, at least for a little, when you are facing financial ruin and your only immediate legal recourse is being flushed down the toilet.

The law was against him. Merrill Lynch had made that point. Reading the brief that Merrill filed, one could see that Merrill was . . . well, "right" doesn't seem to fit. Merrill was *correct.* Groves and his lawyer had hoped that the sheer weight of the adverse facts would carry the day, that and a more expansive reading of New Jersey arbitration law than this judge (or, quite possibly, any judge) was willing to provide.

Groves was impassive as he walked out of the courtroom after the judge ruled from the bench, being careful to thank the attorneys for both parties for their cogent, well-written briefs. His family showed no emotion as their breadwinner lost his absolutely, positively (appeal being a distant long shot, though it would be tried) final chance at overturning an arbitration decision that they considered, with some justification, to be manifestly unfair. These were well-controlled, perfectly behaved, nice people who did not believe in public displays of emotion.

New Jersey law—black-letter law, the lawyers say—made winning this case all but impossible. The New Jersey Arbitration Act, N.J.S.A. 2A:24-1, *et seq.* is so strong as to crush almost any challenge to an arbitration decision, no matter how unfair. Its four major provisions allow courts to overturn arbitration decisions only in cases of corruption or misconduct or refusing to hear evidence. The fact that brokerage customers such as Groves have no choice in the matter—either agree to arbitration or be gone—is not recognized by the law.

Groves's case had hung by its fingernails on ten words from subsection (c) of the act—an arbitration may be overturned as a result of "any other misbehaviors prejudicial to the rights of any party." A little wiggle room there, in that "any other" language. Erasure of the tape—the one with the "gotcha" moment, which was, to Groves, proof that evidence was fabricated by the broker—simply didn't make the grade. Merrill had argued, and the judge agreed, that the arbitrators had heard that "gotcha" moment and didn't need the tape. Besides, even if the tape had been available, it didn't matter. Merrill Lynch made that point in its brief: "Under the Arbitration Act," Merrill argued, "a court cannot vacate an arbitration award because it disagrees with the arbitration panel's findings of fact or conclusions of law." Again, the judge agreed. Again, it was a hard point to contradict. The law was as clear as a bell. Many cases said the same thing. Some cases even said that an erased tape was not sufficient to get a case overturned. The law is the law.

Judge Jacobson could not substitute her assessment of the broker's credibility for the arbitration panel's—and Meyers could talk about "blatant admission of fabrication of evidence" until he was blue in the face. It didn't matter. The law was against him. The arbitrators were not required to disbelieve witnesses just because, as the judge evenhandedly put it, "his credibility is called into question." "Nobody has shown me any case law saying that," said Judge Jacobson. Again, correct.

Rand Groves had lost his second battle of Trenton long before he stepped into the courtroom—not by days or months but by decades. His loss went unnoticed in the financial press, which as usual was focusing on the nuts and bolts of American capitalism—the swaying, terrorism-wary markets; the ongoing saga of Morgan Stanley's executive reshuffling; and, buried inside, the latest spasms from the perennial Dick Grasso saga. Maybe Grasso would settle. Maybe Grasso would not settle. The media was pulling petals off daisies on this one. Dick Grasso, two years after his departure, was still large bore. Arbitration was small bore, old news, no story. Groves did not exist, not for the regulators and certainly not for Wall Street, now that he had been sucked dry and tossed aside. Not even *NJBIZ* published a follow-up.

Three weeks after Groves's defeat, my repeated requests for comment from the firm and Ross came to naught. Then I received the following email from Merrill Lynch spokesman Mark Herr:

Mr. Weiss,

I understand you wish to talk about the litigation brought by Mr. Groves against Merrill Lynch and our employee, Lew Ross. Is it fair for me to assume that you know that an arbitration panel found for Merrill Lynch and Mr. Ross and denied Mr. Groves' claims? In a similar vein, is it fair for me to assume that you are aware, further, that when Mr. Groves sought to have the panel's ruling in favor of Merrill Lynch and Mr. Ross set aside by a Superior Court judge in New Jersey state court, the judge in that proceeding also found for Merrill Lynch and Mr. Ross?

Yes, it would be fair. Or, to use a better word, *correct.*

Some weeks later, Herr sent me another email setting forth Merrill's position on the Rand Groves case. Clearly, Merrill was fed up with Groves and sick and tired of his bellyaching. "There is no reason to believe Mr. Groves was treated unfairly or that his case had any merit," said the statement. As far as Merrill was concerned, the hearing before Judge Jacobson in Trenton, the one that was conducted on razor-thin legal grounds and was doomed before it started, was akin to a full-blown trial on the merits. Groves had had "two bites at the litigation apple and both times impartial tribunals rejected his theories." In Merrill's view, the one-sentence decision, the one Judge Jacobson had called "frustrating" in its brevity, was a complete vindication, a finding that its broker Lew Ross "did nothing wrong." Groves's appeal was framed in grotesque terms, setting forth, Merrill alleged, "a conspiracy theory worthy of Oliver Stone and just as inaccurate, untrue and false." Note the rhetorical use of repetition, with the word "inaccurate" used with two synonyms of identical meaning, underlining the righteousness of Merrill's position and its justifiable anger at the courtroom depredations of its ungrateful ex-client.

Groves read the statement, which I sent to him for his comment, with his usual combination of stoicism and anger. (Or, as Merrill might have put it, with "anger, upset and dismay.") It was a gross distortion of the record, he told me. It was unfair. Still, the damage had been done, and he wasn't about to get upset about yet another insult, another injustice. Groves was pressing on with an appeal of Judge Jacobson's ruling, still hoping for a miracle, and prepared to file for bankruptcy.

The media had not forgotten Wall Street—that it could chew up and spit out the small fry. A little more than a week after Groves lost his second battle of Trenton, on July 31, 2005, the newsmagazine show *Dateline NBC* led off a two-hour broadcast with a fourteen-minute segment on what it described as a particularly invidious peril to all investors.

"He was just a man with a dream—a dream that came true—his hot new invention—backed by Wall Street," said the announcer, his voice over images of an ordinary-looking man, middle-aged, wearing steel-rimmed glasses—the spitting image of Rand Groves. "I was worth forty-two million dollars on paper," said the man.

"And then," the announcer continued, "suddenly, mysteriously, it all fell apart. Some say the big guys got big bucks and the little guys got taken." A man with a Texas accent appeared, saying, "There was lying, cheating, and stealing."

If you were watching this story unfold that summer night, you had to believe that what was happening on the Street was a crookedness that was massive in its cruelty and danger to the public interest. After all, this was prime network real estate, the coveted first segment of a major newsmagazine show, and, at almost a quarter of an hour, it held the air for an eternity by network standards. Like all competent broadcasting, it focused on the plight of a single person, heroic but "mysteriously" victimized. He was not Rand Groves but rather a gent named Rodney Young, and the company he founded to develop his "hot new invention" was Eagletech Communications. CNBC correspondent Ron Insana, one of the Street's leading broadcasters, came on camera to explain:

> There's an old saying in business, "If you build a better mousetrap, people will beat a path to your door." Rodney Young used to believe that, but that was before his four-year odyssey through the world of starting a company—a wild ride that took him through some very murky corners of the stock market. His is a cautionary tale every investor should hear before buying another share in a small-company stock.

The story that Insana proceeded to tell was gripping. After going public in a 1996 IPO, Eagletech's share price had climbed from thirty-two cents to fifteen dollars within the space of four months, which Insana explained was "a remarkable performance for a start-up company." The company received $1.2 million in financing from what Insana described as "early investors." Things were looking good, Insana said. "The stock's rapid rise got the attention of small investors throughout the country on the lookout for the next hot tech stock."

And then, suddenly, it was all over. The stock came crashing down. "Something, or someone, had destroyed Eagletech," said Insana. "The question was how—and why."

The answer to this question, we learn, is a financial plague that an Eagletech lawyer named John O'Quinn, the fellow from Texas, says has "put as many as a thousand companies into bankruptcy," resulting in "market losses of more than four hundred billion dollars." Yep, massive stuff—this was, after all, a lawyer who had taken on the tobacco industry, *Dateline NBC* pointed out. Large bore by any definition. Surely, with numbers like this, you know what was completely and solely to blame for Eagletech's misfortunes.

Why, naked short-selling, of course!

The Baloney Brigade was on the march, and with this *Dateline NBC* broadcast had achieved an objective that it had been carefully plotting for more than a year—the conquest of a network television newsmagazine.

There was only one problem with the broadcast, which anyone could have determined by spending approximately fifteen minutes on the Internet. Let's just say it left out some stuff:

- The registration of Eagletech shares had just been revoked for failure to file required reports with the SEC.
- Eagletech stock had climbed not because this was such a great company, but because it was manipulated by stock swindlers who allegedly gained control of 92 percent of the company's unrestricted shares. According to an SEC enforcement action and a federal indictment, both filed in February 2005 and neither of which were mentioned in the broadcast, Eagletech stock was rigged by a crew of New York–based stock swindlers, including a reputed Columbo crime-family associate named Frank Persico, who had previously pleaded guilty to racketeering.
- Persico and another of the sixteen accused Eagletech manipulators had pleaded guilty to fraud charges by the time of the broadcast, and another guilty plea would follow in October 2005.

- Eagletech, though not accused of any wrongdoing—and probably unaware of the scams—was not a passive bystander. According to the SEC action, the scam artists were invited to raise money for the company.
- The alleged scamsters were accused by the feds of paying brokers in cash, under the table, up to 50 percent of the price of the stock to push Eagletech on unwary investors throughout the country. The purpose of the kickbacks was to "artificially increase the price of Eagletech stock and [another] stock and to profit from the manipulation of the prices of those stocks."
- The $1.2 million in early financing was from these alleged stock swindlers, and the swindlers used that early financing to cheat unwary investors.
- The scam artists allegedly used a variety of manipulative schemes to drive up Eagletech shares, including refusing to let investors sell the shares.
- Neither the SEC complaint nor the indictment, which did everything but throw the kitchen sink at the alleged perpetrators of the Eagletech scheme, *said even one word about naked short-selling.*

Eagletech's collapse was not even the slightest bit "mysterious." Its shares were rigged in a classic pump-and-dump stock scam. Such stocks always tumble when the rig is over.

As you can see, *Dateline NBC* might have had a pretty good story here of real alleged criminality, one with real victims. Or it could have turned over all that primetime network real estate to a real investor concern, such as the systematic deprival of investors' constitutional rights when they have a complaint against brokers. Instead, *Dateline NBC* hopped on the lead APC of the Baloney Brigade.

It was a stupendous victory. But the Baloney Brigade, as usual, drew no solace from its triumph.

The broadcast, you see, had not used the phony buzzword being pushed by the Baloney Brigade—"stock counterfeiting." "The now infamous and previously 'postponed' . . . 'Dateline NBC' expose aired Sunday night to a cacophony of yawns and disbelief, according to CEOs of companies decimated by naked short selling who contacted FinancialWire after its airing," Gayle Essary's FinancialWire reported the following day. " 'NBC just needed to get the program off the shelf, even though it was a journalistic "sell-out," ' said one CEO in an email to FinancialWire."

The Baloney Brigade was marching on.

All this didn't happen overnight.

Rand Groves's right to have his complaint against Merrill heard in an

American courtroom, a right guaranteed by the six thousand farmers and tradesmen who fought with Washington at Trenton, was chipped away for decades. It took more than one or two or a dozen unjust arbitrations or Wall Street scandals or mutual fund or hedge fund scams to erode investor protections, more than just one or two dumb SEC regulations, and more than just a couple of instances of flaccid, wrongheaded, or execrable financial journalism.

It all happened slowly, in court cases and regulatory proceedings and, above all, a series of little things that *didn't* happen—SEC rules and acts of Congress that weren't passed, speeches that Artie Levitt didn't give, cases that Eliot Spitzer didn't file, articles the financial press didn't write. Last and by no means least, there was the ruckus that investors didn't make—unless they themselves wound up ensnared in the system, by which time it was too late.

Your rights weren't given away, or even taken away. They just withered away, and you didn't know it was happening, even as you let it happen. It's not entirely your fault, by the way. Yes, if you worked at it, you could have found out that the loudmouths of the Baloney Brigade were claiming to speak for you. But you didn't even know where to look—or that whenever you hear the words *naked short-selling,* the word that should form in your head is *baloney.*

The Street and its dupes have set the agenda. But you can take the agenda right back from them. You need to fight back. You can't do it all, but you are the essential ingredient. Without sustained public pressure, nothing is going to happen.

In this book I've outlined a lot of what needs to be done. A lot of it is really pretty obvious once you know the facts, and is a question of individual choice.

You can sit idly by, or you can do something about the arbitration system. The NASD likes to tamper with the system and make "improvements" that don't change the essential unfairness of the system. In 2004, the definition of *public arbitrator* was altered to make that less of a charade, and remove people with more than twenty years of faithful service to the Street from serving as "members of the public." But the fundamental character of the system remained untouched. Tell the NASD, your congressman, and the SEC that the time for window dressing is past. You want the arbitration system to be voluntary—and you want that done now.

Now that you are aware of how mutual funds soak you, the choice is yours: to continue to play a loser's game and try to beat the market, or to invest your money in a low-cost index fund or an exchange-traded fund.

You can invest in a hedge fund, now that the inflated value of your co-op shares has pushed your net worth into the ranks of the accredited investors. Or you can say "No, thanks," and try to find another way of expressing your social status.

You can allow the people who run your state and local governments to enrich their pals through negotiated bond deals, or you can tell them to switch to competitive bidding.

You can wield the power that you have, and maybe have some fun in the process. You can make a difference by going online and playing a role in exposing stock fraud, or one of the many other forms of investor ripoffs and injustice that are taking place all around you.

You can give the Baloney Brigade a run for the money. You don't have to be a rich guy like Mark Cuban, owner of the Dallas Mavericks, to start up your own blog or to gain access to the Internet—either to research or to sound off. Blogs are there for the asking, totally free of charge. Don't just write about your summer vacation. Write about your experiences with Wall Street. Tell people about your blog. Word will get out.

You can tell the media to stop focusing on trivia, and to cover things that matter to you. If your favorite newspaper or financial publication has abandoned hard-hitting reporting that protects you, and instead is publishing puff pieces on moguls or boring inside-baseball articles on subjects that don't affect you, write to the editor. Tell him to publish articles for *you*, not for his advertisers or his reporters' sources. The people who run newspapers and magazines read letters from readers and take them very seriously, if the letters are coherent and aren't rants or part of an organized letter-writing campaign.

Above all, you can use the system to make yourself heard. You can offer a comment on an SEC rulemaking. You can nag your representatives in Congress. Don't leave all that letter-writing and rule-commenting to the Street and the Baloney Brigade. Start your own brigade. You can name it yourself. Maybe the Sanity Brigade. If you meet the bad guys and their dupes in the field of battle, you will definitely win. In the end, the truth always wins.

It will take a while. Their livelihood is at stake. They're not giving up.

Gayle Essary was upset by the *Dateline NBC* broadcast, and also troubled by the failure of NBC to broadcast a few days later, as had been expected, an interview with a former Commerce Department official who had come up with "proof" of naked short-selling of Eagletech. It was an interesting chain of events, he told me. First the *Dateline NBC* broadcast was mysteriously chopped in size and delayed, months of reporting disregarded, and then the non-broadcast of the interview with the ex-Commerce official. Strange.

Still, Gayle was upbeat. He was always upbeat, always looking for new angles, new ventures, or new variations on old ones. Gayle had been working hard and had come up with a brilliant idea, one in keeping with the times—the resurgent market, the explosion in the OTC, the nation's unquenchable hunger for above-market returns.

Three days after the *Dateline NBC* broadcast, Gayle put the following item on his FinancialWire:

"Ever Wonder What Happened To That Ornery Critter, 'The Waaco Kid'? He's Baaaack.

"Every once in awhile, someone muses, 'Whatever happened to the Waaco Kid?,' that ornery critter who was once the toast of 'Low Society' and a stockpicker extraordinare for individual traders—never investors—who were looking for a place to quite literally gamble on from 5% to 25% of their portfolios.

"It has taken four years to track down and locate the persnickety codger," Gayle reported, but all's well. "Okay, 'pick us a couple of stocks,' he was told, in exchange for an article contribution from time to time, and the rest, at least until the market opens again today, is history."

NOTES

Introduction: The Battle of Trenton

ix   **It would be against all:** The landmark 1987 Supreme Court case *Shearson/American Express Inc. v. McMahon* (482 U.S. 220) closed the door tightly on investor lawsuits against brokers, by requiring arbitration even in cases involving securities fraud. (Groves's case didn't involve fraud.) "The strong federal policy in favor of arbitration is by now well-established," observed the Fourth Circuit Court of Appeals in its May 2000 ruling on *Smith Barney v. Critical Health Systems,* citing the *Shearson* case. *Smith Barney* illustrates Wall Street's insistence upon not just arbitration but the Wall Street brand of arbitration. Critical Care had wanted to bring its case before the American Arbitration Association, which was allowed by fine print in brokerage agreements that made reference to the rules of the American Stock Exchange. This was known as the "Amex window" because Amex rules allowed customers to bring cases before the AAA. The Street fought hard and successfully, in this and other court cases, to close the Amex window and force investors into Wall Street's brand of arbitration.

x   **Whenever anyone has sought:** Even an innocuous attempt to impose common-sense conflict-of-interest rules was fought passionately by Wall Street regulators. In compliance with a law passed in 2001, the California Judicial Council required arbitrators in July 2002 to divulge a checklist of all business, personal, and professional ties that could represent conflicts of interest. The NASD and NYSE both reacted by stopping arbitrations in California, and then fought successfully in court, with the support of the SEC, to have the rules overturned. See E. Scott Reckard, "NASD Rules Preempt State Law," *Los Angeles Times,* May 25, 2005.

x   **Rand Groves was unlikely fodder for such a confrontation:** Details of his complaint against Merrill derived from case documents in *Rand Groves v. Merrill Lynch Pierce Fenner & Smith Inc., Llewellyn G. Ross and National Association of Securities Dealers, Inc.,* Superior Court of New Jersey, Law Division—Mercer County, Docket No. L-147104, June 4, 2004. Also author interviews with Rand Groves, and his attorneys, G. Martin Meyers and Jonathan Colman.

xiv   **The Securities Industry Association maintains:** "Why Arbitration Is Better Than the Courts," statement, Securities Industry Association, January 2004; interviews with securities lawyers.

xiv   **According to the NASD:** "Fact Sheet on NASD Dispute Resolution Inc.," NASD Regulation, July 2004.

xix   **Or, as one federal appellate court pointed out:** Ruling of the Third Circuit Court of Appeals in *Newark Stereotypers' Union No. 18 v. Newark Morning Ledger Co.,* 397 F.2d 594 at 598–99 (1968).

xix   **I had just written a story:** "Are Investors Walled Off from Justice?" by Gary Weiss, *Business Week,* March 22, 2004.

xx   **Tyco, which *Business Week* glorified:** "The Most Aggressive CEO," by William C. Symonds, *Business Week,* May 28, 2001. The profile of this "little-known but remarkably successful $38 billion conglomerate" described Tyco as "what today may qualify as the leanest operation in Corporate America." A different tone was taken in "The Rise and Fall of Dennis Kozlowski," by Anthony Bianco in the issue of December 23, 2002, which described a man "unhinged by greed" and "a rogue CEO for the ages."

xx   **A weekly business publication called *NJBIZ:*** "When Value Vanishes," by William T. Quinn, *NJBIZ,* August 2, 2004. The letter from a Merrill spokesman appeared in the August 16 issue.

xxiii   **He failed miserably:** For example, Levitt was an outspoken critic of Wall Street research, delivering many speeches on the subject and denouncing analysts in his book. See Chapter 3 ("Analyze This") of *Take On the Street,* by Arthur Levitt with Paula Dwyer (New York: Pantheon Books, 2002). However, a number of critics have observed that when Levitt actually had the power to do so, he did not bring so much as a single case against a major Wall Street firm involving fraudulent research. See *Blood on the Street,* by Charles Gasparino (New York: Free Press, 2005), p. 195.

xxiv   **One lasting legacy:** "Exemption Won in 1997 Set Stage for Enron Woes," by Stephen Labaton, *New York Times,* January 22, 2002.

xxiv   **At the conclusion of his term:** "The Investor's Champion," by Mike McNamee, Paula Dwyer, and Christopher Schmitt, *Business Week,* September 25, 2000. The article, illustrated with a sketch of Artie brandishing an Arthurian sword, praised Levitt as "the most aggressive securities cop in history." See also "SEC's Levitt Gets Big Applause from Small Investors," by Judith Burns, Dow Jones Newswires, October 13, 2000. For a more skeptical view of his battle with accountants, the focus of the *BW* piece, see *Unaccountable: How the Accounting Profession Forfeited a Public Trust,* by Mike Brewster (New York: Wiley, 2003).

xxvii   **By 2003, the press:** "The Hole Story: How Krispy Kreme Became the Hottest Brand in America," by Andy Serwer, *Fortune,* July 7, 2003. See "Merchants of Hype: Is the Media's Focus on Good News Masking a Bad Economy?" by Ellsworth Quarrels, *Across the Board,* November 1, 2003. Mind you, this was not an exercise in 20-20 hindsight. *Across the Board* was pillorying this syrupy 4,000-word story several months *before* Krispy Kreme hit the fryolator for alleged accounting irregularities. See also "A Hole in Krispy Kreme's Story," by Andy Serwer, *Fortune,* June 14, 2004; "Report Shows How Krispy Kreme Sweetened Results," by Mark Maremont and Rick Brooks, *Wall Street Journal,* August 11, 2005.

xxvii   ***New York Times* media columnist David Carr:** "Bad Business for Magazines About Business," by David Carr, *New York Times,* May 30, 2005.

xxviii   **When he was SEC chairman:** "Bush S.E.C. Pick Is Seen As Friend to Corporations," by Stephen Labaton, *New York Times,* June 3, 2005.

xxviii   **The financial media:** "The Man Who Moves Markets: Inside the World of Super-investor George Soros," by Gary Weiss, *Business Week,* August 23, 1993.

xxix   **Chances are, Wall Street is a part of your life whether you like it or not:** Frederick E. Rowe, a money manager in Dallas and the chairman of the Texas Pension Review Board, put it this way in an interview with the *New York Times:* "President Bush talks about transitioning to an ownership society. Well, we already have an ownership society, and the people who are owners don't know they're the owners. The owners are the people in America who hope to retire, and who are retired, and who depend upon a stream of income that their deferred investments generate. And they don't have many advocates." "Calpers Ouster Puts Focus on How Funds Wield Power," by Mary Williams Walsh, *New York Times,* December 2, 2004.

xxix **In 1962, the Federal Reserve:** "Survey of Financial Characteristics of Consumers," *Federal Reserve Bulletin,* March 1964.

xxix **According to the most recent figures:** "Equity Ownership in America, 2002," Investment Company Institute and Securities Industry Association, survey conducted in January 2002.

Chapter One: Mr. Grasso's Neighborhood

2 **The markets are so rude and chaotic:** Applications of chaos theory to the markets have been the subject of dozens of books and articles. See *Trading Chaos: Maximize Profits with Proven Technical Techniques,* by Justine Gregory-Williams and Bill M. Williams, 2nd ed. (New York: Wiley, 2004). See also "The Man from C.H.A.O.S.," by William Green, *Fast Company,* November 1995.

3 **Wall Street firms don't want you to know this:** Brad M. Barber and Terrance Odean, "Trading Is Hazardous to Your Wealth: The Common Stock Investment Performance of Individual Investors," *Journal of Finance,* April 2000.

3 **Probably the most dramatic:** "Defined Benefit vs. 401(k): The Returns for 2000–2002," Watson Wyatt Worldwide, October 2004; "A Lesson for Social Security: Many Mismanage Their 401(k)s," by Tom Lauricella, *Wall Street Journal,* December 1, 2004.

3 **All that:** "You Can Do It," by Gary Weiss and Jeffrey M. Laderman, *Business Week,* May 31, 1993. The Motley Fool investment Web site, which is in business to cater to investor greed and pipedreams, continued the "you can do it" mantra in a self-serving article, "Painfully Obvious Stock Tips," by Rich Smith, April 20, 2005. The article goes on to belittle index funds, and concludes that investors can do better than average— by subscribing to Motley Fool, of course! Money back if not delighted.

4 **In May 2005:** "Amex Says President Has Stepped Down; No Successor Named," by Dow Jones Newswires, *Wall Street Journal,* May 3, 2005. The *Journal* was so indifferent to the story, briefly noted on page 4 of its Money & Investing section, that it didn't even assign a reporter.

4 **Real estate agents put the value:** "The Amex: Worth More Dead Than Alive?" by Mara Der Hovanesian, *Business Week,* November 29, 2004.

5 **What made Grasso:** Dick Grasso's legacy flourished under the SEC reign of his predecessor at the NYSE, Bill Donaldson, who rammed through market structure rules that would retain the NYSE's hegemony. The *Wall*

Street Journal observed on April 4, 2005, in an editorial entitled "Donaldson's Dinosaur," "SEC Chairman William Donaldson is the powerful man he is because the U.S. has the most competitive financial markets in the world. So we have to wonder why he is about to use that power to preserve a monopoly for the very symbol of that capitalism, the New York Stock Exchange." Not that it matters to most investors (which is why we're dealing with this in a footnote), but the answer to the *Journal*'s dilemma was this: The NYSE is a monopoly because it *is* the very symbol of capitalism. That means it has heap big clout. See "Big Board Still Carries a Big Stick," by Aaron Lucchetti, *Wall Street Journal,* April 5, 2005.

7   **The NYSE and its defenders:** A typical assertion of the party line came from John Reed, who briefly served as NYSE chairman, in testimony before the House Capital Markets subcommittee at the height of the Grasso scandal, October 16, 2003. Reed said: "The role of the auction market [NYSE-speak for the specialist system], every time it has been studied, has always been seen to have positive benefits for both investors and issuers." (Of course, Reed testified earlier in the day that "we, in the New York Stock Exchange, are good regulators," so maybe he was still kidding around.)

7   **They have a duty:** The specialists and the exchange usually put it this way: "We supply liquidity when necessary to the proper operation of the market, acting as buyer or seller in the absence of public demand to buy or sell in those stocks"—Robert B. Fagenson, vice-chairman of Van der Moolen Specialists USA, Inc., and vice-chairman of the board of directors of the Specialist Association of the New York Stock Exchange, in testimony before the Senate Banking Committee on February 14, 2001.

7   **Well, here's what the NYSE's:** If you look carefully—*very* carefully—on the NYSE Web site, you'll find the stabilization numbers, updated annually, at this URL: http://www.nysedata.com/factbook/viewer_edition.asp?mode=table&key=19&category=4.

8   **Marios found that in 1990:** Interview with Marios Panayides in June 2005. Marios is gathering the data for a paper, which will be titled "Specialist Stabilizing Actions in the Transaction Process."

11   **Grasso was perfectly straightforward:** See "The $140 Million Man," by Gary Weiss, *Business Week,* September 15, 2003.

Chapter Two: How to Be a Wall Street Prophet

16 **Dick Grasso, now three years into his term:** Grasso quote from "NYSE Summarily Suspends Eight Members and Four Member Firms; U.S. Attorney's Office and SEC Also Take Action Against Members and Others," New York Stock Exchange press release, February 25, 1998.

18 **D'Alessio and his lawyer:** The legal documents quoted in this chapter are mainly from the voluminous filings in two cases, *U.S.A. v. Oakford et al.*, Docket No. 98 Cr. 144, and *SEC v. Oakford*, Docket No. 98 Civ. 1366, both in the U.S. District Court for the Southern District of New York. The civil suit brought by D'Alessio against the SEC, appealing his NYSE sanctions, was *D'Alessio v. SEC*, 380 F.3d 112, decided by the Second Circuit Court of Appeals on August 16, 2004.

18 **There was some media coverage of:** "A Street Scandal That May Not Die," by Gary Weiss, *Business Week*, August 9, 1999; see also "SEC, U.S. Attorney Query the NYSE Anew on 1990s Illegal Trades," by Robert Kowalski, TheStreet.com, February 16, 2001, and many other stories on the subject by Kowalski and Dan Colarusso.

18 **When *Fortune* lambasted Grasso:** "The Fall of the House of Grasso," by Peter Elkind, *Fortune,* October 4, 2004.

19 **The August 2004 appellate court ruling:** In addition to ruling on *D'Alessio v. SEC,* the Second Circuit in 2004 issued a similarly worded decision in *MFS Securities Corp. v. SEC,* brought by the floor brokers Mark and John Savarese.

19 **Beginning in "at least" 1991:** *In the Matter of New York Stock Exchange, Inc., Respondent,* Securities and Exchange Commission, Administrative Proceeding File No. 3-9925, June 29, 1999.

20 **When he sued the NYSE:** Complaint in *D'Alessio v. New York Stock Exchange et al.,* U.S. District Court for the Southern District of New York, Docket No. 99 cv 605616.

20 **Kwalwasser's SEC testimony later:** Opinion and Order in *U.S.A. v. Oakford,* December 13, 1999.

20 **As an appellate court ruling:** *MFS Securities Corp. v. SEC.*

23 **Yep, all that was going on:** See "NASD-Y Habits Will Have to Change," by Michael Schroeder, *Business Week,* August 26, 1996. *BW* said that "SEC negotiators were stunned that a week before the pact, Ketchum was disputing the issue at the heart of the probe: the existence of a 'pricing convention' in which brokers colluded to keep bid and ask prices artificially

wide to line their pockets at investors' expense." Sounds like a great choice to head enforcement at the NYSE, wouldn't you say?

Chapter Three: The Best Analysts Money Can Buy

25 **Spending on research:** "The Time for the Quant Is Now," by Mark W. Riepe, *Journal of Financial Planning,* April 2005.

25 **So when the Nasdaq:** "Stock Research 'For Hire' Offered," by Deborah Lohse, San Jose *Mercury News,* June 8, 2005; "New Nasdaq Research Project Raises Objectivity Questions," by David Enrich, Dow Jones Newswires, June 7, 2005.

25 **Gayle, who hails from Texas:** Interview with Gayle Essary, October 2004.

27 **For that we have to thank:** Brad M. Barber, Reuven Lehavy, and Brett Trueman, "Comparing the Stock Recommendation Performance of Investment Banks and Independent Research Firms," working paper, August 2004.

27 **Paid research firms:** "Buying Wall Street's Attention," by Gary Weiss, *Business Week,* January 27, 2003; "Amid Shrinking Research Pool, Companies Buy Their Coverage," by Susanne Craig, *Wall Street Journal,* March 26, 2003; "What's Research and What's Promotion," by David Baines, *Vancouver Sun,* May 12, 2004.

29 **Before coming to the SEC:** "SEC Nominee Donaldson Also Has Penny Stock Experience," by Brent Mudry, *Canada Stockwatch,* December 20, 2002; "A Thorny Question for Donaldson," by Gary Weiss, *Business Week,* January 13, 2003.

29 **The SEC said:** *In the Matter of EasyLink Services Corp. et al.,* Securities Exchange Act of 1934, Release No. 51506, April 7, 2005. By then Donaldson was an investor icon in the Levitt tradition, so the very serious allegations contained in the release, and the mild penalties imposed, were almost entirely ignored in the press.

29 **The analyst community's:** "Best Practice Guidelines Governing Analyst/Corporate Issuer Relations," CFA Centre for Financial Market Integrity/National Investor Relations Institute, December 2004.

32 **Gayle apparently forgot:** "Waaco Kid on the 4th: Give Boston Harbor Back to British; Ten Undervalued Small Cap Stocks for the Second Half of 97; Planned Website Because 'Waaco's Momma Didn't Raise No Fool,'" press release, Business Wire, July 7, 1997.

32 **Even at this early moment:** "A Closer Look at the Waaco Kid and His

Internet Gang," by Erle Norton, *TheStreet.com,* June 5, 1997. Erle had a considerably more skeptical take on Gayle than my probably too gentle earlier piece, "The New Grapevine Is Online," *Business Week,* May 27, 1996.

33 **Or you might have wound up:** "Tiny Genesis Fall Shows Dangers of Internet Investing," by Rebecca Buckman, Dow Jones Newswires, May 9, 1997.

34 **The IRI did good things:** "Investors Research Institute, Inc., Announces 113 Public Companies Pledge 'Best Practices in Investor Relations,' Higher Standards of 'Accessibility,' 'Scrutiny,' 'Disclosure,'" press release, Business Wire, January 25, 1999.

34 **By 2004:** "Lifting the Lid: Paid-for Research Scores with Investors," by Ritu Kara, Reuters, July 15, 2004.

34 **According to a 2002:** "The Cost of Coverage/Credibility," *IRUpdate,* National Investor Relations Institute, April 2002.

36 **As time went on:** Various analyst reports issued by Investrend Communications Inc.

36 **It is certainly:** "Starnet Took Bets, Warrants Disclose," by David Baines, *Vancouver Sun,* August 24, 1999.

36 **Instead, John slapped:** "Starnet Communication, Inc., Update," John M. Dutton, analyst, PAR research report, August 23, 1999.

37 **Nowhere on the site was it mentioned:** *In the Matter of John A. Carley et al.,* Administrative Proceeding File No. 3-11626, Securities and Exchange Commission, Initial Decision, July 18, 2005.

37 **They took a hard look:** *In the Matter of John A. Carley et al.,* Order Instituting Adminstrative and Cease-and-Desist Proceeding, September 1, 2004.

39 **In September 2004:** *In the Matter of Taglich Brothers Inc. and Richard C. Oh,* Securities and Exchange Commission, Securities Act of 1933 Release No. 8489, September 15, 2004.

40 **The SEC, fresh from its triumph:** *In the Matter of John M. Dutton,* Securities and Exchange Commission, Securities Act of 1933 Release No. 8524, January 19, 2005.

40 **Ditto for a soba-noodle slap:** *In the Matter of Corcom Companies Inc., dba Bluefire Partners Inc., Bluefire Research, Inc., and William P. Bartkowski,* Securities and Exchange Commission, Securities Act of 1933 Release No. 8584, July 6, 2005.

Chapter Four: Dialing the Globe for Dollars

43 **In 1997, word began to creep:** "Farmer Regrets His Faith in Offshore Share Tipsters," by Gail Seekamp, *Sunday Business Post*, Dublin, April 13, 1997.

44 **The shares that were being pushed:** Details of the Irish stock scam from correspondence and documentation provided to the author from Ireland.

45 **Here's a statistic:** *International Cold Calling Investment Scams,* Australian Securities & Investments Commission, June 2002. See the ASIC Web site, http://www.asic.gov.au/asic/asic.nsf, and the Web site of the New Zealand Securities Commission, http://www.sec-com.govt.nz/.

46 **After paying a $4 million fine:** Kott's most recent accomplishment was outmaneuvering the U.S. criminal justice system. He was originally indicted on forty-eight counts of securities-law violations, but was let off in May 2004 with a guilty plea to two counts and no jail time. See "How a Big Securities-Fraud Case Unravels," by John R. Emshwiller, *Wall Street Journal,* August 15, 2005. He was getting his name in the papers despite the guilty plea. See "SEC Probes Mamma.com over Kott," by Bertrand Marotte, *Globe and Mail* (Toronto), January 11, 2005. Kott could have been sentenced to eighteen months in prison, but prosecutors recommended, despite his having not cooperated, a "downward departure" under sentencing guidelines, and he was sentenced to probation. It's interesting to contrast this with the harsh treatment of Louis Pasciuto, subject of my book *Born to Steal,* whose bail was revoked when the book was published despite his extensive cooperation against dozens of mobsters and crooked brokers. Prosecutors claimed this was for his "own safety," but critics of the decision believed he was being punished for angering prosecutors. See the Afterword of the book's paperback edition (New York: Warner Books, 2004).

46 **Another early Vasco da Gama:** "The Penny Stock Scandal," by Pete Engardio and Gail DeGeorge, *Business Week,* January 23, 1989; "The Mob on Wall Street," by Gary Weiss, *Business Week,* December 16, 1996.

47 **The SEC obtained:** *SEC v. Kimmes,* 753 F. Supp. 695 (N.D. Ill. 1990). See also order dated June 23, 1993, *SEC v. Thomas F. Quinn,* United States Court of Appeals for the Seventh Circuit, Docket No. 92-2657.

47 **Tommy moved on:** *The Pretender: How Martin Frankel Fooled the Financial World and Led the Feds on One of the Most Publicized Manhunts in History,* by Ellen Pollock (New York: Free Press, 2002).

48 **Some years later:** *International Cold Calling Investment Scams.*

50   **One of the firms:** "Trapped Without Trial," by Rod Usher, *Time* (European edition), April 13, 1998.

50   **Even though the Thais:** "Public Prosecutor Filed Charges against 7 Executives of the Brinton Group for Conducting Unlicensed Securities Businesses," No. 29/2001, press release, the Securities and Exchange Commission, Thailand, September 24, 2001; "Conviction on Boiler Room Case—The Brinton Group," No. 42/2004, press release, the Securities and Exchange Commission, Thailand, June 10, 2004; see also "Beyond the SEC's Reach, Firms Sell Obscure Issues to Foreign Investors," by John R. Emshwiller and Christopher Cooper, *Wall Street Journal,* August 16, 2000.

51   **The 2003 case:** *S.E.C. v. David M. Wolfson et al.,* Docket No. 03-CV-914, U.S. District Court, Utah, October 16, 2003.

51   **In 2002, David Wolfson:** *SEC v. Allen Z. Wolfson, et al.,* Docket No. 02-CV-1086, U.S. District Court, Utah, September 30, 2002; see also "Cops and Robbers," by James Surowiecki, *The New Yorker,* June 27, 2005.

Chapter Five: The Ghost of Mutual Funds Past

53   **Charles Joseph Kerns Sr.:** "Former Palm Beach Resident Sentenced to 27 Years," by John T. Fakler, *South Florida Business Journal,* December 27, 2004; "Defendant Charles Kerns Sentenced to 27 Years in Prison for Role in Securities Fraud Scheme," press release, U.S. Attorney for the Southern District of Florida, December 22, 2004; www.charleskerns.com and linked Web sites.

54   **Let's go back:** "Spitzer Alleges Mutual Funds Allowed Fraudulent Trading," by Randall Smith and Tom Lauricella, *Wall Street Journal,* September 4, 2003.

55   **In October 2002:** Statement by Paul G. Haaga Jr. "Maintaining the Industry's Reputation and Our Investors' Confidence in Difficult Times," Investment Company Institute, October 2002.

56   *Business Week* **expressed:** "Breach of Trust," by Paula Dwyer, *Business Week,* December 15, 2003.

58   **In that year:** *Regulation by Prosecution: The Securities and Exchange Commission v. Corporate America,* by Roberta S. Karmel (New York: Simon & Schuster, 1982), p. 279.

58   **It's a mighty big till:** *Trends in Mutual Fund Investing,* Investment Company Institute, June 2005.

61   **"Insiders and favored":** *Protecting Investors: A Half Century of Investment*

Company Regulation, Division of Investment Management, Securities and Exchange Commission, May 1992, p. 300.

61 **An SEC study:** Conclusions of SEC Investment Trust Study, quoted in *Public Policy Implications of Investment Company Growth,* report to the House Committee on Interstate and Foreign Commerce by the Securities and Exchange Commission, December 2, 1966, pp. 64–65.

62 **The SEC's 1992 history:** *Protecting Investors,* p. 301, note 43.

62 **A former SEC fund:** "Memories from Early Days of the Securities and Exchange Commission," by Karl C. Smeltzer, oral history, SEC Historical Society, June 2004.

63 **Fred Alger Management:** The firm's vice-chairman, James Connelly Jr., paid $400,000 in SEC penalties and pleaded guilty to state charges of tampering with evidence. See *In the Matter of James Patrick Connelly, Jr.,* Administrative Proceeding File No. 3-11303, October 16, 2003; *People v. Connelly,* felony complaint, Criminal Court of the City of New York, New York County, October 15, 2003.

63 **Such as October 28, 1997:** "Your International Fund May Have the 'Arbs Welcome' Sign Out," by Mercer Bullard, TheStreet.com, June 10, 2000.

64 **Let's turn to:** "Remembering the Past: Mutual Funds and the Lessons of the Wonder Years," text of speech by Barry P. Barbash before the 1997 ICI Securities Law Procedures Conference, Washington, D.C., December 4, 1997.

64 **An SEC lawyer:** Scheidt's 1999 letter to Tyle is posted on the SEC Web site, at http://www.sec.gov/divisions/investment/guidance/tyle120899.htm, as is the 2001 letter, which is at http://www.sec.gov/divisions/investment/guidance/tyle043001.htm.

65 **According to studies at Stanford:** The $400 million estimate—Eric Zitzewitz, "How Widespread Is Late Trading in Mutual Funds?" Stanford Graduate School of Business, September 2003 (revised draft, November 2004); the $4 billion market-timing estimate was also by Zitzewitz— "Who Cares About Shareholders? Arbitrage-Proofing Mutual Funds," *Journal of Law, Economics & Organization,* October 2003.

Chapter Six: Happiness Is a Warm Fund Manager

67 **His advice:** *Feeling Good: The New Mood Therapy,* by David D. Burns, M.D. (New York: Avon Books, 1999), p. 352.

67 **If you had shares in:** "Reflections on the Efficient Market Hypothesis: 30 Years Later," by Burton G. Malkiel, *The Financial Review,* 40, 2005.

68   **One study:** "Survivorship Bias and Mutual Fund Performance," by Edwin J. Elton, Martin J. Gruber, and Christopher R. Blake, *The Review of Financial Studies,* winter 1996.

69   **Then a consultant:** "Putnam May Owe $100 Million," by John Hechinger, *Wall Street Journal,* February 2, 2005.

70   **In early 2005:** "Strong Finish," by Ian McDonald, *Wall Street Journal,* January 6, 2005; "Mutual Funds Exit 2004 on a Positive Note," by Karen Wallace, Morningstar.com, December 31, 2004; "For Value Funds, a Tough Act to Follow," by Roben Farzad, *New York Times,* January 9, 2005.

71   **Another set of statistics:** *Standard & Poor's Indices Versus Active Funds Scorecard, Fourth Quarter, 2004,* Standard & Poor's, January 18, 2005.

74   **His book:** *A Random Walk Down Wall Street,* by Burton G. Malkiel, rev. ed. (New York: W.W. Norton, 2003).

74   **The EMH originated:** "Efficient Capital Markets: A Review of Theory and Empirical Work," by Eugene Fama, *Journal of Finance,* 25:2, 1970.

76   **At the time:** Memo to Limited Partners, Tiger Management LLC, from Julian Robertson, March 30, 2000; see also "What Really Killed Robertson's Tiger," by Gary Weiss, *Business Week,* April 17, 2000.

76   **Yet well into the new:** Typical is this passage from a profile of Michael Steinhardt: "On Wall Street, Steinhardt was almost as much a legend as George Soros. He battled Warren Buffett in a threatened bid to control airline USAir, and paid a $40 million fine to settle charges that he disrupted U.S. Treasury-bill trading, according to the Justice Department." ("Millionaire Steinhardt Says Art Is Riskier Than Hedge Funds," by Linda Sandler, Bloomberg news service, June 7, 2005.) This misidentifies Steinhardt, and not his company, as the fine-payer. And, more to the point, it omits that Steinhardt closed his funds after immense losses and two years of being creamed by the indexes, that his investments in USAir were a disaster, and that he was fined for allegedly cornering, not "disrupting," the market in two-year notes (not "bills"). See also "The Tiger in Winter," by Stephen Taub, *Institutional Investor,* December 2002. *II* glossed over the collapse of the Robertson funds, saying that he "issued warning after dire warning" about an upcoming decline of tech stocks— but left out that he failed to position his portfolios to profit from a tech stock decline.

76   **In December 2002:** "The Tiger in Winter." Now, in fairness to *II,* I must point out that I wrote a story about Robertson some years before that was even worse: "The World's Best Money Manager," *Business Week Assets,*

November/December 1990. His subsequent implosion certainly belied that title.

77　**According to fund data:** Malkiel, "Reflections," pp. 5–6.

Chapter Seven: Mutual Funds Aren't Bullies

79　**Mutual funds have long embraced:** See (and I mean that literally—it's a great film noir) *Deadline at Dawn* (director, Harold Clurman; RKO, 1945).

82　**Or, as one of:** "Mutual Fund Advisory Fees: The Cost of Conflicts of Interest," by John P. Freeman and Stewart L. Brown, *The Journal of Corporation Law,* December 2001.

82　**As is usual:** Data from Morningstar, Inc.; "Top Funds at Fire-Sale Prices," by Timothy Middleton, MSN Money, September 7, 2004.

83　**Even the ICI:** In reaction to the hubbub over fees, the ICI published a paper intended to show that fees had declined. It did so by factoring in "distribution costs"—including sales charges, or "loads," which used to be as high as 8 percent and have pretty much gone out the window. By skewing the numbers that way, the ICI showed that what it described as "total shareholder cost" declined from 2.25 to 1.25 percentage points between 1980 and 2003. But if you take out sales loads, you find that fund operating expenses—"expenses used to support investment management, fund administration, and shareholder servicing"—rose from 0.77 percentage points, when the fund industry was tiny in 1980, to 0.88 in 2003, when funds were a multitrillion-dollar behemoth. See *Total Shareholder Cost of Mutual Funds, 2003,* Investment Company Institute, December 2004.

84　**The numbers work out:** *Mutual Funds: Additional Disclosures Could Increase Transparency of Fees and Other Practices,* GAO-04-317T, statement of Richard J. Hillman before the Senate Governmental Affairs Committee, January 2004.

84　**The ICI actually:** *2004 Mutual Fund Factbook,* Investment Company Institute, May 2004, p. 8. In the 2005 edition of the *Factbook,* the ICI wisely dropped the first sentence with the "very high standard" malarkey.

85　**Staffers of the:** Remarks of Senator Peter G. Fitzgerald (R-Ill.), Oversight Hearing on Mutual Funds: Hidden Fees, Misgovernance and Other Practices That Harm Investors, Senate Governmental Affairs Committee, January 27, 2004 (transcript, p. 20).

85 **Bear became known:** See *In the Matter of Bear Stearns Securities Corp.,* Administrative Proceeding File No. 3-9962, August 5, 1999. As for Eddie Haskell, I respectfully refer the reader to the official Leave It to Beaver Web site, at http://www.leaveittobeaver.org/gang/gang_eddie.htm, which states as follows: "He is a model white-collar delinquent, a creep who goads people into trouble rather than perpetrating the crime himself." Since Mr. Haskell was never found guilty of any wrongdoing, the word "alleged" should be inserted at relevant points in the foregoing.

86 **But when the American Funds:** *NASD Department of Enforcement v. American Funds Distributors, Inc.,* Disciplinary Proceeding No. CE3050003, NASD, February 16, 2005.

86 **One inkling:** Comments of John C. Carter, SEC File No. S7-06-04, June 10, 2004.

87 **That has been an:** *In the Matter of Morgan Stanley DW Inc.,* Administrative Proceeding File No. 3-11335, November 17, 2003; "Morgan Stanley Settles with SEC, NASD," by Brooke A. Masters and Kathleen Day, *Washington Post,* November 18, 2003.

88 **As a conservative:** Oversight Hearing on Mutual Funds, Senate Governmental Affairs Committee, p. 27.

88 **In March 2005:** *In the Matter of Citigroup Global Markets, Inc.,* Administrative Proceeding File No. 3-11869, Securities and Exchange Commission, March 23, 2005.

89 **Smith Barney listed:** The list can be found at http://www.smithbarney .com/products_services/mutual_funds/investor_information/revenue share.html.

91 **There is actually some:** "Fund Returns and Trading Expenses: Evidence on the Value of Active Fund Management," by John M.R. Chalmers, Roger M. Edelen, Gregory B. Kadlec, working paper, August 30, 2001.

92 **The MarketWatch:** "Work in Progress: SEC's Next Fund-industry Regulator to Inherit Challenges," by John Spence and Robert Schroeder, MarketWatch, February 24, 2005.

Chapter Eight: Mutual Fund Payback Time—Not

96 **In his book:** *Take On the Street,* by Arthur Levitt with Paula Dwyer (New York: Pantheon Books, 2002), p. 45.

96 **Artie forgot to mention:** *In the Matter of Van Kampen Investment Advisory Corp. and Alan Sachtleben,* Administrative Proceeding File

No. 3-10002, Securities and Exchange Commission, September 8, 1999.

96 **As he bragged:** *In the Matter of The Dreyfus Corporation and Michael L. Schonberg,* Administrative Proceeding File No. 3-10201, Securities and Exchange Commission, May 10, 2000. "Major Financial Services Firm Settles Mutual Fund Case," press release, office of Attorney General, state of New York, May 10, 2000. Dreyfus shamelessly treated the whole thing as a public relations victory. See "Dreyfus Deserves More Than a Slap on the Wrist," by Gary Weiss, *Business Week,* May 29, 2000.

97 **In June of that year:** *Mutual Funds: Greater Transparency Needed in Disclosures to Investors,* General Accounting Office, GAO-03-763, June 2003, p. 4.

97 **Donaldson, flush from:** "Memorandum to Chairman William H. Donaldson from Paul F. Roye, Division of Investment Management, Date: June 11, 2003, Re: Correspondence from Congressmen Paul E. Kanjorski and Robert W. Ney," from House Capital Markets Subcommittee.

99 **The SEC proposed:** *Mandatory Redemption Fees for Redeemable Fund Securities,* Securities and Exchange Commission, Release No. IC-26375A, File No. S7-11-04, March 5, 2004.

99 **In a statement:** "Redemption Fees for Redeemable Securities," opening statement of Paul F. Roye, director, Division of Investment Management, Securities and Exchange Commission, March 3, 2005. Even some people in the fund industry were shocked by the SEC's capitulation. "Here we are a year and a half after the scandals, and all we've got so far is a voluntary measure," said Russ Kinnel, director of fund research for Morningstar, quoted in "SEC Votes to Back Off on Market Timing Fees," by Jonathan Peterson, *Los Angeles Times,* March 4, 2005.

100 **The same thing happened:** *Amendments to Rules Governing Pricing of Mutual Fund Shares,* Securities and Exchange Commission, Release No. IC-26288, File No. S7-27-03, December 11, 2003.

100 **That point was underlined:** *Reopening of comment period and supplemental request for comment,* Release Nos. 33-8544, 34-51274, IC-26778; File No. S7-06-04, Securities and Exchange Commission, February 28, 2005.

100 **Nothing else has covered the SEC:** *Investment Company Governance,* Release No. IC-26323, File No. S7-03-04, Securities and Exchange Commission, January 15, 2004; see also "SEC is Sued Over Fund-Board Rule," by Deborah Solomon, *Wall Street Journal,* September 3, 2004.

101 **When the subject of corporate governance:** See *The Non-Correlation Between Board Independence and Long-Term Firm Performance,* by Sanjai

Bhagat and Bernard Black, *Journal of Corporate Law,* vol. 27 (2002). Bhagat and Black found no relationship between board independence and long-term corporate profitability.

102 **Just before Donaldson:** "Former U.S. Technologies CEO Sentenced to 125 Months in Federal Prison for Securities Fraud Schemes," press release, U.S. Attorney for the Southern District of New York, February 25, 2005.

102 **Mutual fund governance:** Fund board composition information derived from Securities and Exchange Commission filings.

103 **Note the really good score:** *In the Matter of Pilgrim Baxter & Assoc., Ltd.,* Administrative Proceeding File No. 3-11524, Securities and Exchange Commission, June 21, 2004.

104 **The ICI itself:** "ICI Board Adopts Resolution Urging Fund Industry to Strengthen Governance," press release, Investment Company Institute, July 7, 1999.

105 **This standard:** The Gartenberg case can be found at 694 F.2d 923 (2d Cir. 1982). See discussion in "Mutual Fund Advisory Fees: The Cost of Conflicts of Interest," by John P. Freeman and Stewart L. Brown, *The Journal of Corporation Law,* December 2001, pp. 643–53.

105 **Donaldson's emergence:** "Donaldson's Balancing Act," by Amy Borrus, with Mike McNamee, *Business Week,* February 28, 2005. The piece reported that Donaldson "plans to keep practicing what he preaches at the SEC's Washington headquarters for at least another year." He left three months later. Contrast with other, less sycophantic news accounts that were generated by Donaldson's PR offensive: "SEC Chief Is Open to Revising Rules, Yet Stiff Fines Stay," by Deborah Solomon, *Wall Street Journal,* February 10, 2005; "SEC Chief, Under Cross-Pressure, Sees Some Modest Changes," by Stephen Labaton and Jenny Anderson, *New York Times,* February 10, 2005; "SEC Chief Says Proxy Rule Needs Rewriting," by Ben White, *Washington Post,* February 10, 2005. (Apparently February 9 was a busy day for Bill Donaldson!)

Chapter Nine: It's a Bird, It's a Plane . . . It's Superinvestor!

108 **In 1990, a total of $50 billion:** "Hedge Funds: Risk and Return," by Burton G. Malkiel and Atanu Saha, working paper, December 1, 2004; 1990 mutual fund figure from *2004 Mutual Fund Factbook,* Investment Company Institute, p. 55.

109 **In 1990, there were:** "The Millionaires Club," by Gary Weiss, *Business Week Assets* (undated but published in late 1990). *Assets* was a short-lived personal-finance magazine published as a supplement to *Business Week*. Data on growth of hedge funds in 2002 from *Implications of the Growth of Hedge Funds*, staff report to the Securities and Exchange Commission, September 2003, p. 68.

109 **About a fifth:** Testimony of William H. Donaldson before the Senate Committee on Banking, Housing, and Urban Affairs, July 15, 2004.

109 **One study estimated:** Data from research by LGT Capital Partners, June 2004.

110 **The biggest endowments:** NACUBO statistics reported in "Endowment Assets in Fiscal 2004," by Elise Coroneos, *MAR/Hedge*, March 2005.

110 **Even the *New York Times*:** "Fund Managers Raising the Ante in Philanthropy," by Jenny Anderson, *New York Times*, August 3, 2005. The front-page article reported that at one recent charity event, "the crowd of 4,000 at the Jacob K. Javits Convention Center in May raised an eye-popping $32 million." That worked out to $8,000 a head, which hardly represented much of a sacrifice for the hedge fund crowd.

111 **The 1998 failure:** See *Hedge Funds, Leverage, and the Lessons of Long-Term Capital Management*, Report of the President's Working Group on Financial Markets, April 1999.

111 **LTCM could:** The high concentration of funds in some global markets—80 to 90 percent of the participants in some markets, according to the International Monetary Fund—has troubled some observers. See "Could a Few Hedge Funds Spoil the Party?" by Anna Bernasek, *New York Times*, July 3, 2005.

113 ***Offshore* is also Hedgefallatio:** A detailed discussion of the whys, wherefores, hows, and whatnots of hedge fund structure can be found in "Selecting the Appropriate Type of Hedge Fund," by Jeffrey C. Blockinger and Prufesh R. Modhera, *Review of Securities & Commodities Regulation*, September 25, 2002. For more on Soros, see "The Man Who Moves Markets: Inside the World of Super-investor George Soros," by Gary Weiss, *Business Week*, August 23, 1993.

115 **According to research:** See "Hedge Funds: Risk and Return."

118 **Needless to say:** "Historical Hedge Fund Returns Fairly Represent Performance," by George Van with Zhiyi Song, Van Hedge Fund Advisors International LLC, January 2005.

Chapter Ten: Hedge Funds: The Birth of a Notion

120 **The concept of hedging:** "A Brief History of Derivatives," *Derivatives Quarterly*, winter 1995.

121 **We know that:** "The Legacy," by Lawrence C. Strauss, *Barron's*, May 31, 1994.

123 **Salomon Brothers:** *Joint Report on the Government Securities Market*, board of governors of the Federal Reserve System, Department of the Treasury, and Securities and Exchange Commission, January 1992.

123 **As later set forth:** *United States of America v. Steinhardt Management Co. and Caxton Corp.*, U.S. District Court, Southern District of New York, Docket No. 94 Civ. 9044. See also joint Justice Department–SEC announcement, December 16, 1994.

124 **Seven years later:** *No Bull: My Life In and Out of the Markets*, by Michael Steinhardt (New York: Wiley, 2001), p. 231.

124 **As lawyers:** "The Legal Structure and Regulation of Investment Partnerships," by Victoria E. Schonfeld and Daniel W. Sasaki, Arnold & Porter, paper, October 1, 1993 (presented to a seminar in New York City called "Starting, Managing and Investing in Hedge Funds," October 21 to 22, 1993).

Chapter Eleven: How to Stuff a Wild Hedge Fund

125 **The Big Four were:** "Will Another Shoe Drop at Kidder," by Leah Nathans Spiro, *Business Week*, May 23, 1994; "The $700 Million Mystery," by Gary Weiss, *Business Week*, December 18, 1995; see also Final Report of Harrison J. Goldin, Trustee, *In re Granite Partners, L.P.*, Chapter 11 Case No. 94 B 41683/85, April 18, 1996.

126 **The *Chicago Tribune*:** "Interest Grows in Mortgage Securities," by Pat Widder, *Chicago Tribune*, September 28, 1987.

126 **Askin took over:** The details of the Askin saga in this chapter are from the voluminous court record, including the Final Report of Harrison J. Goldin, filings in the Granite Chapter 11 bankruptcy, and in *Kidder Peabody & Co. v. Unigestion International and Askin Capital Management, et al.*, Docket No. 94 Civ 3241. A good early press account is "The $600 Million Man," by Jack Willoughby, *Investment Dealers' Digest*, September 12, 1994.

128 **In 1990:** See "The Millionaires Club," by Gary Weiss, *Business Week Assets*, undated, 1990.

131 **One bright spot:** "Merrill to Pay $6M to Settle Granite Funds Suit," by Colleen DeBaise, Dow Jones Newswires, March 20, 2003.

132 **A task force:** *An Assessment of Developments with Potential Implications for Market Price Dynamics and Systemic Risk,* President's Working Group on Financial Markets, September 27, 1994; see also testimony of Richard R. Lindsey, director, Division of Market Regulation, Securities and Exchange Commission, before the House Committee on Banking and Financial Services, concerning Hedge Fund Activities in the U.S. Financial Markets, October 1, 1998.

134 **The Oops! Template:** "Bayou Funds Chiefs Plead Guilty in Federal Court to Defrauding Investors in $450 Million Hedge Fund Collapse," press release, U.S. Attorney for the Southern District of New York, September 29, 2005; complaint in *Jewish Federation of Metropolitan Chicago v. Bayou Mgmt LLC et al.,* U.S. District Court, District of Connecticut, Docket. No. 05-cv-01401, September 2, 2005.

135 **The first Superinvestor:** *No Bull: My Life In and Out of the Markets,* by Michael Steinhardt (New York: Wiley, 2001), pp. 227, 233, 241.

135 **The next überinvestor:** "Tiger Is Licking Its Wounds," by Gary Weiss, *Business Week,* March 13, 2000; "Humbled Tiger," by Jaye Scholl, *Barron's,* April 3, 2000; "What Really Killed Robertson's Tiger," by Gary Weiss, *Business Week,* April 17, 2000.

Chapter Twelve: The Money Floats In—From Your Wallet

137 **Jonathan D. Iseson:** "Still Chic? The Hamptons Feud and Fret, but Keep On Beckoning," by David Barstow, *New York Times,* June 1, 1999.

137 **The problem was:** The Blue Water saga received scant attention in the media, and the full majesty of its journey through hedge-fund-land emerges in legal papers. See the filings in *Tremont International et al. v. Blue Water Fund, Ltd. et al.,* U.S. District Court, Eastern District of New York, Docket No. 00-cv-03768. See also "Blue Water, Hedge Fund's Top-Performing Manager, Sued for Fraud," Bloomberg, July 2, 2000; "The Peddlers," by Josephine Lee, *Forbes,* August 6, 2001; "Why Hedge-Fund.net Is Getting Tarred by a Legal Tangle," by David Shook, Business Week Online, July 26, 2000.

138 **One of the more:** Interviews with Harry Strunk and materials generously provided to me by Harry, 2004 and 2005.

141 **Breeden put his staff:** Letter to Edward J. Markey from Richard C. Breeden, dated June 12, 1992.

143 **Besides, it might have actually done:** An SEC official testified years later that the trader reporting system would have had "little relevancy" to the Long-Term Capital Management disaster, which did not involve stocks. See testimony of Richard R. Lindsey, director, Division of Market Regulation, Securities and Exchange Commission, before the House Committee on Banking and Financial Services, concerning Hedge Fund Activities in the U.S. Financial Markets, October 1, 1998. That's a good all-purpose excuse, by the way, that could apply to a great many things the SEC doesn't do: "What's the point? It wouldn't have done any good."

144 **In 2000, the Commodity:** "Hedge Funds vs. the SEC," by Gary Weiss, *Business Week,* March 3, 2003.

145 **Its Multi-Strategy Hedge:** Merrill Lynch Web site, August 2005: http://www.mlim.ml.com/usa/Template.asp?id=AN4&rurl=/content/retail/html/multi-strategy-solutions.htm.

145 **When it came time:** *Registration Under the Advisers Act of Certain Hedge Fund Advisers,* Release No. IA-2266, File No. S7-30-04, Securities and Exchange Commission, July 28, 2004.

146 **Since pension funds:** Glassman address to the thirteenth annual Public Fund Boards Forum, San Francisco, December 6, 2004.

Chapter Thirteen: Bear in the Woods

149 **In August 1999:** *In the Matter of Bear Stearns Securities Corp.,* Administrative Proceeding File No. 3-9962, August 5, 1999.

151 **It seems that:** "Bear's Muni Deals Post Test for Rule Makers," by Aaron Lucchetti and Diya Gulapalli, *Wall Street Journal,* January 5, 2005.

151 **"County officials:** "Panel Urges Stricter County Bid Rules," by David Umhoefer, *Milwaukee Journal Sentinel,* November 29, 2004; see also "Bond Deal Records Missing," by David Umhoefer, *Milwaukee Journal Sentinel,* July 14, 2004.

151 **It also emerged:** "Bear, Stearns Letter Reveals 'Bob' Did Nothing for $800k 'Success Fee,'" *Illinois Leader,* June 30, 2004; "Bear Stearns Officer Resigns Amid Probes," *Wall Street Journal,* July 16, 2004; "Bear Stearns Unit Probed over Alleged Hospital Graft," Associated Press, October 19, 2004.

151 **Bear continued saying:** "Fraud Charges Faced by Ex-Aide of Bear Stearns," by Joseph T. Hallinan, *Wall Street Journal,* May 10, 2005.

153 **Let us turn:** FBI transcript of intercepted conversations, introduced in Philadelphia municipal corruption trial (see below).

153 **In June 2004:** *USA v. Ronald A. White,* U.S. District Court for the Eastern District of Pennsylvania, Docket No. 04-cr-370; "As Banks Bid for City Bond Work, 'Pay to Play' Tradition Endures," by Mark Whitehouse, *Wall Street Journal,* March 25, 2005.

154 **Commonplace—and legal:** G-37 forms filed by UBS Financial Services with the Municipal Securities Rulemaking Board. "Insiders Are Cashing In on State's Bond Market," by Evan Halper, *Los Angeles Times,* September 27, 2004; see also "SEC Asks What Political Consultants Do for the Money," by Joe Mysak, Bloomberg, August 20, 2004.

154 **In New Jersey:** Attachment to Form G-37/G-38, filed by Bear Stearns for consultant Jack Arseneault for 2004, Municipal Securities Rulemaking Board. "Underwriter terminates McGreevey middleman," by Dunstan McNichol, *Star-Ledger,* February 16, 2005; See also "Budget-balancing bond deals cost 19.2M in fees," by Dunstan McNichol, *Star-Ledger,* December 31, 2004.

156 **Instead, as one law journal:** Review of *Take On the Street,* by Richard W. Painter, *Michigan Law Review,* May 1, 2003. Painter was referring to Model Rules of Professional Conduct, R. 7.6 (2003), which provides that "[a] lawyer or law firm shall not accept a government legal engagement or an appointment by a judge if the lawyer or law firm makes a political contribution or solicits political contributions for the purpose of obtaining or being considered for that type of legal engagement or appointment." Try proving that.

156 **So in March 2005:** Release No. 34-51561, File No. SR-MSRB-2005-04, Securities and Exchange Commission, April 15, 2005; "Municipal Bond Regulator to Bar Hiring Consultants," by Darrell Preston and Eddie Baeb, Bloomberg, March 15, 2005.

157 **Another loophole:** "Muni Cleanup Just Might Be Sweeping Corruption Along," by Karen Richardson, *Wall Street Journal,* April 25, 2005.

158 **Studies of the subject:** See, for example, "Another Look at the Effect of Method of Sale on the Interest Cost in the Municipal Bond Market—A Certification Model," by Jun Peng and Peter F. Brucato Jr., *Public Budgeting & Finance,* March 2003. The authors of this study went to a lot of trouble and found that negotiated bond deals were neither better nor worse than competitive ones.

Chapter Fourteen: The Answer: Freed-up Markets

160 **The other common:** It's also, no doubt unintentionally, a pervasive theme in Artie Levitt's book. Richard Painter's review in *Michigan Law Review* observes that it is a blow-by-blow look at a regulatory agency knuckling under to the people it regulates: "Although academic work on regulatory capture theory is abundant, a behind-the-scenes account of how capture actually takes place is rare." *Michigan Law Review,* May 1, 2003. See also "After a Boom, There Will Be Scandal. Count on It," by Kurt Eichenwald, *New York Times,* December 16, 2002. However, as you are seeing, scandals are determined by media spin more than they are by market cycles.

161 **It was headed:** *Go East, Young Man,* by William O. Douglas, paperback ed. (New York: Dell, 1974).

Chapter Fifteen: Clueless in Microcapland

162 **In 2005, financial fraud:** Survey by Commtouch, developer of antispam software, released April 13, 2005.

163 **Lebed was the subject:** *In the Matter of Jonathan G. Lebed,* Administrative Proceeding File No. 3-10291, Securities and Exchange Commission, September 20, 2000.

163 **One postmortem:** "Jonathan Lebed: Stock Manipulator, S.E.C. Nemesis—and 15," by Michael Lewis, *New York Times Magazine,* February 25, 2001.

164 **Lebed had learned:** Emails sent by Lebed to the author and others on his email list, 2002 to 2005.

164 **The low point:** "Wall Street Is Sometimes the Wild West," by William Power, *Wall Street Journal,* February 1, 1995.

165 **So it should come:** Interviews with confidential sources, 1996.

165 **A "sweep" of penny-stock:** "SEC Reports Drop in Penny Stock Fraud," statement by Sen. Richard Bryan, June 30, 1994; "Regulators Say Penny Stock Abuses Greatly Reduced," Reuters, June 29, 1994.

167 **Years later:** Author interview with Randolph Beatty, 2005.

167 **"This bill ranks":** Congressional Record, October 1, 1990.

167 **A GAO report:** *Penny Stocks: Regulatory Actions to Reduce Potential for Fraud and Abuse,* General Accounting Office, GAO/GGD 93–59, p. 20.

168 **They could do that:** The penny-stock definition can be found in the Code of Federal Regulations at 17 CFR 240.3a51-1.

168 **That didn't matter:** See "Broker-Dealer Regulation Under the New Penny Stock Disclosure Rules: An Appraisal," by O. Douglas Hernandez Jr., *Columbia Business Law Review,* 1993; " 'Click Here to Buy the Next Microsoft': The Penny Stock Rules, Online Microcap Fraud, and the Unwary Investor," by Kevin C. Bartels, *Indiana Law Journal,* 2000; "Impact of the Penny Stock Reform Act of 1990 on the Initial Public Offering Market," by Randolph Beatty and Padma Kadiyala, *Journal of Law and Economics,* October 2003.

168 **(footnote) One example was:** "Hardball at the SEC: Arthur Levitt is stepping on toes. Is that really such a bad thing?" by Paula Dwyer, *Business Week,* September 29, 1997; "Ripoff! The secret world of chop stocks—and how small investors are getting fleeced," by Gary Weiss, *Business Week,* December 15, 1997.

169 **On January 16, 2004:** *Amendments to the Penny Stock Rules,* Release No. 34-49037, File No. S7-02-04, Securities and Exchange Commission, January 16, 2004.

170 **After all:** *Putting Investors First: The Role of State Regulators,* North American Securities Administrators Association, 2003; "Ripoff!"

171 **If you go back to 1996:** Trading statistics from the OTC Bulletin Board Web site, www.otcbb.com.

173 **The philosophy:** *Go East, Young Man,* by William O. Douglas (New York: Dell, 1974), p. 272.

173 **Let's say someone:** Lebed email, distributed via his Internet list, May 25, 2005.

Chapter Sixteen: The Holistic Approach to Corporate Crime

177 **Just about every major:** See statement of James Chanos, president of Kynikos Associates, before the SEC Roundtable on Hedge Funds, May 15, 2003.

177 **One rogue short:** Indictment in *USA v. Amr I. Elgindy et al.,* U.S. District Court, Eastern District of New York; "Stock Trader Elgindy Is Convicted of Securities Fraud, Extortion," by John R. Emshwiller, *Wall Street Journal,* January 25, 2005.

178 **Out it always:** Asensio & Co. press releases, 2001 and 2002. See also *Sold Short: Uncovering Deception in the Markets,* by Manuel P. Asensio with Jack Bart (New York: Wiley, 2001).

178 **It got him:** See *NASD Department of Enforcement v. Asensio Brokerage Services, Inc., n/k/a Integral Securities, Inc., and Manuel Peter Asensio,* Disciplinary Proceeding No. CAF030067, Hearing Panel Decision, January 4, 2005.

179 **A good example:** *High and Low Financiers,* by Watson Washburn and Edmund S. De Long (Indianapolis: Bobbs-Merrill, 1932), p.265.

179 **The fault for that:** For a graphic, entertaining description of the precrash manipulations, see *The Day the Bubble Burst: The Social History of the Wall Street Crash of 1929,* by Gordon Thomas and Max Morgan-Witts, paperback ed. (New York: Penguin, 1981).

180 **For example:** "The World Price of Short Selling," by Anchada Charoenrook and Hazem Daouk, working paper, rev. version, October 2004.

180 **Two of the big hedge fund:** "US Air Headache: Robertson Is in Good Company," by Susan Pulliam and Mitchell Pacelle, *Wall Street Journal,* August 4, 1999; footnote: see "Tiger Makes It Official: Hedge Funds Will Shut Down," by Gregory Zuckerman and Paul Beckett, *Wall Street Journal,* March 31, 2000.

181 **In their account:** *24 Days,* by Rebecca Smith and John R. Emshwiller (New York: Harper Business, 2003), p. 40.

182 *BW* **instead ran:** "Power Broker," by Wendy Zellner, *Business Week,* February 12, 2001. A typical line from a sidebar on Skilling: "From an early age, Skilling, the son of a sales manager for an Illinois valve company, showed the same kind of supreme confidence and derring-do that are his trademarks now." See also "The Fall of Enron," by Wendy Zellner and Stephanie Anderson Forest, *Business Week,* December 17, 2001.

184 **Speaking of restrictions:** "Go down fighting: Short sellers vs. firms," by Owen A. Lamont, working paper, rev. draft, July 2004.

184 **Edwin Lefèvre:** *Reminiscences of a Stock Operator,* by Edwin Lefèvre (New York: George H. Doran, 1923; republished, Burlington: Books of Wall Street, 1980), p. 194.

186 **In an interview:** NASD transcript of interview with Robert Catoggio, May 23, 1995.

188 **What their arguments:** Enron, WorldCom, and the other crop of large-scale frauds are a prime example of that principle, and not even the looniest anti-short-sellers were claiming that naked short-selling caused those dogs to turn south.

189 **In his 2001 book:** *Sold Short: Uncovering Deception in the Markets,* by Manuel P. Asensio with Jack Bart (New York: Wiley, 2001), p. 241.

Chapter Seventeen: The Baloney Blitzkrieg

190 **In its edition:** "Stock Wars: The Longs vs. The Shorts," by Chris Welles, *Business Week,* May 11, 1987.

190 **As later emerged:** The SEC found that Haas stocks collapsed, thereby ending the manipulation, "as a result of net capital violations and cessation of its clearing relationship"—not because of shorts, naked or otherwise. See *In the Matter of Eugene Laff, Stanley Aslanian, Jr., and Lawrence Caito,* Administrative Proceeding File No. 3-9654, Securities and Exchange Commission, order dated March 18, 1999.

191 **As for the lawsuits:** "Editor of Barron's Is Cleared in a Suit by Investment Firm," *Wall Street Journal,* December 5, 1988.

191 **Typical of the irresponsible:** "Naked Shorts and Bare Facts—A House Committee Tries to Sort out Truth from Fantasy," by Edward A. Wyatt, *Barron's,* January 1, 1990.

191 **During the hearings:** Prepared statement of Richard G. Ketchum, director, Division of Market Regulation, and John H. Sturc, associate director, Division of Enforcement, Securities and Exchange Commission, before the House Committee on Government Affairs, Subcommittee on Commerce, Consumer, and Monetary Affairs, December 6, 1989.

191 **(footnote) *Barron's* swiftly ran:** "De-pressing Story—Read All About the Big Expose That Wasn't," by Jonathan R. Laing, *Barron's,* May 18, 1987; see also letter to the editor from Chris Welles, *Barron's,* May 25, 1987, and editor's note in response.

192 **In mid-1987:** See "De-pressing Story."

192 **In July 2004:** You can find this bureaucratic idiocy nestled in the Code of Federal Regulations at 17 CFR, parts 240, 241, and 242. The SEC identifier is Release No. 34-50103, File No. S7-23-03.

193 **It later was revealed:** See *USA v. Coppa et al.,* U.S. District Court for the Eastern District of New York, Docket No. 01-cr-3031.

194 **It didn't hurt the shorts:** "Short Selling and Trading Abuses on Nasdaq," by Timothy R. Smaby, Robert L. Albert, and H. David Robison, *Financial Services Review,* vol. 6, no. 1, 1997.

194 **Among the most voluble:** "GeneMax Corp. Announces Naked Short Selling Lawsuit Against Broker-Dealers, Market Makers and Clearing Agents," press release, PR Newswire, October 3, 2002; "GeneMax battles short sellers: Says it's target of bold campaign," *Globe and Mail,* November 18, 2002; "Universal Express-USXP-Declares War on 'Naked Short

Selling,'" press release, Business Wire, September 23, 2003; "Universal Blames Shorts, But What of Dilution?" by Carol S. Remond, Dow Jones Newswires, October 6, 2003. See also Investrend Research Note, Universal Express, July 14, 2003.

194 **A lot of the anti-shorting noise:** Web site of the National Association Against Naked Short Selling, January 2003, March 2003; "Don't Force the Shorts to Get Dressed," by Gary Weiss, *Business Week,* December 8, 2003.

195 **It was so brilliant:** "Naked Short Selling and the Stock Borrow Program," a "Q and A" with DTCC First Deputy General Counsel Larry Thompson, DTCC Web site, March 2005, posted at http://www.dtcc .com/Publications/dtcc/mar05/index.htm.

196 **There was even:** "Universal Express to Support 'Dateline,'" press release, Business Wire, March 29, 2005; "StockGate: 12 Days to Dateline NBC While Influential Washington Group Weighs In," FinancialWire, March 30, 2005; "StockGate: 10 Days to Dateline NBC As New Naked Short Selling Video Surfaces," FinancialWire, March 31, 2005; "StockGate: 6 Days to Dateline NBC and NCANS Accuses SEC Official of Lying to Senate," FinancialWire," April 4, 2005.

196 **"In yet another":** "StockGate Shocker: DTCC Stuns with Admission It Interfered with News Media," FinancialWire, April 13, 2005.

196 **One missive:** Email to media, October 21, 2003.

197 **Word crept out:** *In the matter of the Securities Act, S.B.C. 1985, chapter 83, and in the matter of Gordon Brent Pierce,* order under Section 144, Superintendent of Brokers, British Columbia, June 8, 1993; "Lawsuit Calls into Question GeneMax Float," by Carol S. Remond and Steve D. Jones, Dow Jones Newswires, March 14, 2003; see also Definitive Information Statement (Form 14C), filed at the SEC by Hadro Resources Inc., dated December 16, 2002, which lists Pierce as president of ICI. Footnote: "Investor Communications International, Inc., Announces Corrections to Investrend Communications, Inc., Financial Wire of January 23, 2003," press release, PR Newswire, January 24, 2003; "Investor Communications International, Inc., Announces Further Corrections to Inaccurate Reporting Conducted by Steve Jones and Carol Remond," press release, PR Newswire, March 17, 2003.

197 **ICI's links:** *SEC. v. Agora, Inc., Pirate Investor, LLC and Frank Porter Stansberry,* Docket No. MJG 03 1042, U.S. District Court, District of Maryland, April 14, 2003.

197 **Similar difficulties:** *SEC v. Universal Express, Inc., et al.,* Docket No. 04 CV 02322, U.S. District Court, Southern District of New York, March 24, 2004.

197 **If anything, the rhetoric:** *Universal Express v. SEC et al.,* U.S. District Court, Southern District of Florida, Docket No. 04-20481, March 2, 2004.

198 **Another rare voice of reason:** See "The Naked Shorts Get Some Clothes," Blog Maverick, http://www.blogmaverick.com/entry/1234000 833040434/, April 2005; "A New S.E.C. Rule Fails to Raise Share Prices, and Some Are Angry," by Floyd Norris, *New York Times,* February 18, 2005.

199 **On October 28, 2003:** *Short Sales,* Release No. 34-48709, File No. S7-23-03, Securities and Exchange Commission, October 28, 2003.

200 **Wall Street's reaction:** See, e.g., comment letters of Securities Industry Association and Security Traders Association, File No. S7-23-03.

202 **One study was:** "Strategic Delivery Failures in U.S. Equity Markets," by Leslie Boni, working paper, November 13, 2004.

202 **The new rules:** Final Rule, *Short Sales,* SEC Release No. 34-50103, July 28, 2004; "New Rules to Put Squeeze on Shorts," by Henry Sender, *Wall Street Journal,* January 27, 2005.

204 **In April 2005:** "Universal Express' Lawsuit of $1.4 Billion USD to Move SEC to United States Appellate Court," press release, Business Wire, April 4, 2005; "Federal judge Dismisses Universal Express Suit," by John T. Fakler, *South Florida Business Journal,* April 8, 2005.

205 **As for that "grassroots":** "The Emperor's New Shorts," by Justin Lahart, *Wall Street Journal,* March 2, 2005.

205 **2. Krispy Kreme's accounting:** Later in 2005, an internal report blasted Krispy Kreme to smithereens: "Report Shows How Krispy Kreme Sweetened Results," by Mark Maremont and Rick Brooks, *Wall Street Journal,* August 11, 2005. Damn those naked shorts!

206 **Demonstrations were organized:** "Small Protest in N.Y. Against 'Naked' Short Selling," Reuters, June 7, 2005.

208 **The SEC had ordered:** *In the Matter of CMKM Diamonds, Inc.,* Administrative Proceeding File No. 3-11858, Securities and Exchange Commission, March 16, 2005; see also Initial Decision, dated July 12, 2005.

Chapter Eighteen: Fighting Back

211 **In a *New Yorker*:** See "Cops and Robbers," by James Surowiecki, *The New Yorker,* June 27, 2005.

Chapter Nineteen: An Outbreak of Informational Bacteria

213 **On October 23 and 25:** *Stratton Oakmont Inc. and Daniel Porush v. Prodigy Services Co.,* New York State Supreme Court, Nassau County, Index No. 31063/94, see order dated May 24, 1995.

214 **In the months to come:** See, e.g., "Prodigy Is Sued for Libel," *New York Times* (from Bloomberg), November 12, 1994; "Stratton Oakmont Calls Independent Consultant Report Impractical and Irresponsible" press release, PR Newswire, December 15, 1994; "Stratton Oakmont Smacked with Lawsuit from SEC," by Alan J. Wax, *Newsday,* December 16, 1994; "A New Twist in an On-Line Libel Case," by Peter H. Lewis, *New York Times,* December 19, 1994.

214 **In July 1995:** "The Hard Sell/Money Machine: As penny-stock brokerage Stratton Oakmont tries to shake a sullied reputation, many questions still remain," by David M. Halbfinger, *Newsday,* July 16, 1995.

215 **A joint press release:** The release ran on the Business Wire, October 24, 1994; "$200M Online Libel Case Settled/Prodigy apologizes to LI firm," by Alan J. Wax, *Newsday,* October 25, 1995.

215 **In 1999, Porush:** *USA v. Belfort, et al.,* U.S. District Court for the Eastern District of New York, Docket No. 98cr859; "Stratton Oakmont Executives Admit Stock Manipulation," by Edward Wyatt, *New York Times,* September 24, 1999.

216 **(footnote) This deliciously ironic:** "Jail Time for Stratton Broker, Madden," by Susan Harrigan, *Newsday,* May 4, 2002.

216 **Only one reporter:** Susan Antilla's two *Times* stories on Solomon-Page were "Look Who's Selling Solomon-Page," November 13, 1994, and "Looking beyond the flash in the meteoric rise of Solomon-Page," May 26, 1995.

216 **In fact, the only legal:** *Stratton Oakmont Inc. and Daniel Porush v. Prodigy Services Co.,* order by Justice Stuart L. Ain, dated May 24, 1995.

216 **In 1996, with the enactment:** "How to protect your organization from online defamation," by Nicole B. Casarez, *Public Relations Quarterly,* July 1, 2002.

217 **One of the people:** *Scott Bowen et al. v. ZiaSun Technologies,* California

Superior Court, San Diego County, Docket Nos. GIC762921, GIC772344, February 2001.

219 **The chatter on the popular:** Postings on Silicon Investor, 1998 to 2005.

Chapter Twenty: The Gunfight at ZiaSun Corral

223 **The prime mover:** Interviews with Floyd Schneider, 2002 through 2005.

224 **He is not publicity-shy:** "Revenge of the Investor," by Gary Weiss, *Business Week,* December 16, 2002; *Scam Dogs & Mo-Mo Mamas,* by John R. Emshwiller (New York: Harper Business, 2000).

225 **In June 1999:** *ZiaSun Technologies, Inc., and Anthony L. Tobin v. Floyd D. Schneider et al.,* U.S. District Court, Northern District of California, Case No. C 00-1612 PJH; "Beyond the SEC's Reach, Firms Sell Obscure Issues to Foreign Investors," by John R. Emshwiller and Christopher Cooper, *Wall Street Journal,* August 16, 2000.

225 **"Through this settlement":** "ZiaSun Technologies Settles Groundbreaking Lawsuit over Internet Stock Manipulation," press release, PR Newswire, October 25, 2000.

227 **When Telescan merged:** "ZiaSun Technologies, Inc., and Telescan, Inc., Sign Two-Year Agreement to Provide BusinessWeek Investor Workshops," press release, November 8, 2001; ZiaSun filings with the SEC.

228 **On December 21, 1999:** "The Investor Relations Group Files Libel Suit Against TheTruthseeker.com in Supreme Court," press release, Business Wire, December 21, 1999.

Chapter Twenty-One: Turning On the Lights at Yale

230 **That distasteful chore:** "Steyer Power," by Loch Adamson, *Institutional Investor,* February 14, 2005.

232 **When the *Times*:** "No, You Can't Invest Like Yale. Sorry!" by Joseph Nocera, *New York Times,* August 13, 2005.

232 **In fact, these supposedly:** "In Pursuit of Learning Investments' Whereabouts," by Jonathan Peterson, *Los Angeles Times,* December 19, 2004.

233 **College and university endowments:** *2004 NACUBO Endowment Study,* National Association of College and University Business Officers, January 2005.

234 **One of the principal student:** Interview with Andrea Johnson, 2005.

234 **In the 1990s:** "Yale Unions Attack Ties to Hedge Fund," by Roderick Boyd, *New York Sun,* March 9, 2004; "Lawsuit over Pueblo, Colo.-Area Ranch Still Alive in Federal Court," by Robert Boczkiewicz, *Pueblo Chieftain,* February 1, 2002.

235 **So in early 2004:** "Seeking Investment Disclosure, Coalition Targets Farallon Capital," by Chris Clair, *HedgeWorld News,* March 4, 2004; "Protesters Will Hit Yale Investments," by Kim Martineau, *Hartford Courant,* March 3, 2004.

236 **Swensen's superstar status:** IRS Form 990 filed by Yale University, for fiscal year ending June 30, 2003, May 17, 2004.

236 **Yale does not disclose:** *The Yale Endowment, 2004* (annual report).

237 **In March 2004:** "Protestors question Baca Ranch investments," by Sarah Marberg, *Yale Daily News,* March 4, 2004.

Epilogue: The Second Battle of Trenton

240 **His losses in 2000:** Interviews with Rand Groves, 2004 and 2005.

241 **Trade associations:** Occasionally the truth would sneak past the spin. "Mercer Bullard, a former SEC attorney and founder of Fund Democracy, a leading advocate for mutual fund shareholders and outspoken critic of high fees, says the industry is simply laying low. 'It would be foolish not to want these accounts and position yourself to get them, but it would be more foolish for firms to show how much they wanted them,' he says." "Small Change," by John Churchill, *Registered Representative,* March 1, 2005. As its name implies, *Registered Representative* is read almost exclusively by securities industry professionals.

241 **Neither Groves nor Meyers:** Interviews with Rand Groves and G. Martin Meyers at hearing, 2005.

241 **She was an obscure jurist:** "Judges Ranked Statewide by Overall Score," *New Jersey Law Journal,* January 31, 2005.

245 **Let's just say:** *In the Matter of Eagletech Communications, Inc.,* Administrative Proceeding File No. 3-11832, Securities and Exchange Commission, Initial Decision, June 7, 2005; *SEC v. Labella et al.,* U.S. District Court for District of New Jersey, Docket No. 05-civ-852, February 15, 2005; indictment in *USA v. Labella,* U.S. District Court for District of New Jersey, February 15, 2005.

248 **Gayle Essary was upset:** Interview with Gayle Essary, August 2005.

INDEX